BLACK REASON, WHITE FEELING

JEFFERSONIAN AMERICA
Charlene M. Boyer Lewis, Annette Gordon-Reed, Peter S. Onuf,
Andrew J. O'Shaughnessy, and Robert G. Parkinson, Editors

Black Reason, White Feeling

The Jeffersonian Enlightenment in the African American Tradition

HANNAH SPAHN

UNIVERSITY OF VIRGINIA PRESS
Charlottesville and London

The University of Virginia Press is situated on the traditional lands of the Monacan Nation, and the Commonwealth of Virginia was and is home to many other Indigenous people. We pay our respect to all of them, past and present. We also honor the enslaved African and African American people who built the University of Virginia, and we recognize their descendants. We commit to fostering voices from these communities through our publications and to deepening our collective understanding of their histories and contributions.

University of Virginia Press
© 2024 by the Rector and Visitors of the University of Virginia
All rights reserved
Printed in the United States of America on acid-free paper

First published 2024

9 8 7 6 5 4 3 2 1

Library of Congress Cataloging-in-Publication Data
Names: Spahn, Hannah, author.
Title: Black reason, white feeling : the Jeffersonian enlightenment in the
    African American tradition / Hannah Spahn.
Other titles: Jeffersonian enlightenment in the African American tradition
Description: Charlottesville : University of Virginia Press, 2024 | Series:
    Jeffersonian America | Includes bibliographical references and index.
Identifiers: LCCN 2023055288 (print) | LCCN 2023055289 (ebook) |
    ISBN 9780813951188 (hardcover) | ISBN 9780813951195 (paperback) |
    ISBN 9780813951201 (ebook)
Subjects: LCSH: African Americans—Intellectual life. | African American
    intellectuals. | Jefferson, Thomas, 1743–1826—Influence. | Jefferson,
    Thomas, 1743–1826—Philosophy. | Enlightenment—United States. |
    BISAC: HISTORY / United States / Revolutionary Period (1775–1800)
Classification: LCC E185.89.I56 S63 2024 (print) | LCC E185.89.I56
    (ebook) | DDC 973.4/600496073—dc23/eng/20231229
LC record available at https://lccn.loc.gov/2023055288
LC ebook record available at https://lccn.loc.gov/2023055289

Cover art: Portrait of Thomas Jefferson, Mather Brown, 1786 (National Portrait Gallery, Smithsonian Institution; bequest of Charles Francis Adams; frame conserved with funds from the Smithsonian Women's Committee); detail from frontispiece of *Poems on Various Subjects, Religious and Moral* by Phillis Wheatley, 1773 (Houghton Library, Harvard University); petekarici/istock.com
Cover design: Cecilia Sorochin

Meiner Familie

❖ CONTENTS ❖

Acknowledgments	ix
Introduction	1

Part I. Jefferson's Enlightenment of Feeling — 13

1. I Feel: Therefore I Exist	19
2. Uncritical Reason	37
3. Opinion Is Power	45
4. Deep-Rooted Prejudices	61

Part II. Wheatley's Enlightenment of Principle — 81

5. The Lessons of Reason	91
6. Malignant Prejudice	113
7. Pedagogies of Character	146
8. Above Jefferson's Veil	180
Conclusion: A Jeffersonian Double Consciousness	197
Notes	203
Works Cited	271
Index	295

❖ ACKNOWLEDGMENTS ❖

Considering how much time one seems to be spending alone when writing a book, it is amazing how many people one is obliged to thank after finishing it. I would like to begin by expressing gratitude to my students at the Universities of Berlin and Potsdam, whose interests over many years have been a major source inspiring my own research questions. At the same time, writing this book also required the break from teaching made possible by a three-year grant from the German Research Foundation. In this context I would especially like to thank Peter Schneck, Thomas Wiemer, and the foundation's anonymous reviewers for their helpful advice and support. Work on this book has also profited greatly from invitations to the Robert H. Smith International Center for Jefferson Studies in Charlottesville, Virginia, which has been a beacon for scholars of Jeffersonian America and the transatlantic Enlightenment under its long-time director, Andrew O'Shaughnessy. Many thanks to Andrew and the center's expert staff, including Gaye Wilson, John Ragosta, Anna Berkes, and Whitney Pippin. The book has benefited very much as well from two international manuscript workshops organized at the University of Virginia. Warm thanks to the organizers, Peter Onuf (of whom more below) and Christa Dierksheide, as well as to Robert Parkinson, Charlene Boyer Lewis, Max Edelson, Billy Wayson, Frank Cogliano, Benjamin Carp, Melissa Adler, Tyson Reeder, Armin Mattes, and Adam Jortner. Special thanks to Michael Drexler, Brian Steele, and Sean Harvey for their thoughtful comments on various ideas and chapter drafts during the writing of the book.

For embedding the book in additional contexts through invitations, conversations, and personal inspiration, I would like to thank Marie-Jeanne Rossignol; Heike Paul; Ștefan Brandt; Andrew Gross; Babette Tischleder; Frank Mehring; Kirsten Twelbeck; Catrin Gersdorf; Markus Heide;

Gabriele Pisarz-Ramirez; Carla Peterson; Maurizio Valsania; MaryAnn Snyder-Körber; James McClure; Bland Whitley; Oliver O'Donnell; Edda Luckas; Kristian Döbrich; Michelle Kundmueller; Irene Etzkorn; Tobias Kunzmann; Eran Shalev; Christina Ayazi; Douglas Mooney; Josipa Roksa; Shen Titus; Stephanie Overbeck; Stefanie Leufer; Katrin Erne; Corinna Klessmann; Friederike Müller-Leiendecker; Joanne, Sophia, Alex, and Ethan Fishbane; Paula Viterbo; Andreas Broscheid; Jörn Erdmann; Bettina Blanckmeister; Dirk Praga; Phung Luong; Isabel Mohn; Caitlin Lawrence; and Steffi Dippold.

At the University of Potsdam, I would like to thank Annette Vowinckel at the Leibniz-Center for Contemporary History; Nicole Waller, Simone Heinze, and Verena Adamik at the Department of English and American Studies; Sina Rauschenbach, Matthias Asche, and Stephanie Stockhorst at the Center for Early Modern Studies; and Ulrike Ziler at the university library. At the John F. Kennedy Institute for North American Studies, Freie Universität Berlin, many thanks to the institute's library staff and the members of the research colloquium of the Departments of Culture and Literature. In particular, I am grateful to Alexander Starre, Regina Götz, Winfried and Brigitte Fluck, Martin Lüthe, Simon Schleusener, and Christina Meyer for their company and support on a great variety of occasions.

At the Department of Philosophy and Humanities of Freie Universität Berlin, the book manuscript has been part of the time-honored German custom of the habilitation. I would like to thank the members of the department council as well as the department deans, Ulrike Schneider and Jan Lazardzig, and the members of the habilitation committee, including Andrew Johnston, Irene Pieper, Birte Wege, and Samira Spatzek, for making this a very productive and pleasant experience. In particular, I am deeply grateful to Frank Kelleter, Anita Traninger, Annette Gordon-Reed, and Michelle Ossewaarde for taking the time out of their busy schedules to write extensive habilitation reviews whose insights and advice will continue to inform my work. Together with Peter Onuf (not least in his famed Skype conversations), Frank Kelleter and Annette Gordon-Reed are the scholars who have most decisively encouraged and shaped my research for this book. I thank the three of them for believing in this project and helping me connect it with the wider world, for never tiring of discussing its various drafts, and, of course, for inspiring it by their own brilliant examples.

I have also been fortunate to work again with the University of Virginia Press. My sincere thanks to the four anonymous reviewers who have generously read the manuscript and improved it greatly by their comments, and to the excellent staff and associates of the Press, including Wren Morgan Myers and Susan Murray. Special thanks to my fabulous history editor, Nadine Zimmerli, from whose unique way of mediating between the worlds of writing and publishing I continue to learn in every conversation.

I owe the largest debt of gratitude to my family. I would like to pay tribute to the memory of my late mother-in-law, Lena Susanne Marianne Unger, née Reinhardt, whose kindness and love we greatly miss. Deep thanks to my parents, Peter and Renate Spahn; my aunt, Maria Spahn; and my sister, Barbara Spahn, for being such a spirited, individualist, and warm-hearted family of origin. Special mention should be made of our philosopher cat, James, who has found an admirable way of sharing his Platonic wisdom in some realm beyond language. My husband, Nicolo Unger, and our son, Niklas Spahn, are the center of my universe. The book is dedicated to them with love.

BLACK REASON, WHITE FEELING

Introduction

What and whom do we mean when we talk about the Enlightenment? In this case, the best-known definition of the *what* may entail the least recognized definition of the *who*. In 1784, Immanuel Kant famously summarized his answer to the question "What is Enlightenment?" by the motto *sapere aude* (dare to know) that he borrowed from Horace's *Epistles*. His formula—"Enlightenment is man's release from his self-incurred tutelage"—implied a broader understanding of *self-incurred* than may seem natural today. Kant did not contrast the term with a dependence that was socially imposed, for instance. Instead, he considered all forms of intellectual immaturity that could not be attributed to any fundamental cognitive impairment to be, at bottom, self-incurred, resulting from a "lack of resolution and courage to use it [the understanding] without direction from another."[1]

If *Enlightenment* can thus be understood as a project of emancipation premised on individual mental and moral strength,[2] Frederick Douglass made an intriguing suggestion as to *who* may best have exemplified such a project. In his second autobiography, *My Bondage and My Freedom* (1855), he evoked a world in which the self-reliant use of one's understanding required more "resolution and courage" than even the stern philosopher from Königsberg might have had in mind. Recalling the Maryland of his childhood, Douglass wrote:

> I learned, after my mother's death, that she could read, and that she was the only one of all the slaves and colored people in Tuckahoe who enjoyed that advantage. How she acquired this knowledge, I know

not, for Tuckahoe is the last place in the world where she would be apt to find facilities for learning. I can, therefore, fondly and proudly ascribe to her an earnest love of knowledge. That a "field hand" should learn to read, in any slave state, is remarkable; but the achievement of my mother, considering the place, was very extraordinary; and, in view of that fact, I am quite willing, and even happy, to attribute any love of letters I possess, and for which I have got—despite of prejudices—only too much credit, not to my admitted Anglo-Saxon paternity, but to the native genius of my sable, unprotected, and uncultivated mother—a woman, who belonged to a race whose mental endowments it is, at present, fashionable to hold in disparagement and contempt.[3]

Thus, Douglass placed his mother, the enslaved Harriet Bailey, at the beginning of his own narrative of Enlightenment. He depicted her as the origin of both his "love of knowledge"—or his *philosophy*, in the original sense of the term—and the audacity to pursue it.[4] Today, this genealogy of Enlightenment remains in many ways compelling. However, the individualist and, in terms of personal endowments, elitist dimension of the passage may not gratify every reader. If Douglass's extraordinarily intelligent and courageous mother, who made the impossible possible by learning to read, all by herself, under such adverse conditions, represented the Enlightenment, where would this leave all the other inhabitants of Tuckahoe—or, indeed, the vast majority of us, then and now?

In the context of antebellum America, Douglass had good reasons to develop his philosophy in terms that made such high demands on the individual. It is hardly surprising that he did not try to attribute his intellectual courage to his completely irresponsible father, whom he had to suspect of having been his owner as well: this man had been such a coward as to deprive him even of the knowledge of their relationship. Amply compensating for his obscurantist progenitor, Douglass found Enlightenment and "even" happiness in publicly pursuing his "love of letters" in his mother's imagined company. Against the backdrop of nineteenth-century theories of *race*, this point had important political ramifications. In the original introduction to *My Bondage and My Freedom*, the renowned New York physician and intellectual[5] James McCune Smith seconded his friend's defense against the association of Enlightenment with *whiteness*. "These facts show that for his energy, perseverance, eloquence, invective, sagacity, and wide sympathy, he is indebted to his negro blood," McCune Smith emphasized. "The very marvel of his style would seem to be a development of that other marvel,— how his mother learned to read."[6]

Douglass's own "love of knowledge" also made him aware, of course, that he was actively "attributing" and "ascribing" this trait to his mother and could not actually know its true source; all he knew was the outcome. He must have realized that he and James McCune Smith, for example, were outclassing most of their contemporaries intellectually, but he could not know whether, or in what degree and combination, the cause had to be found in their biological inheritance or their environment, in themselves or in God, in the weather or in the stars. Through the disciplines of intellectual and literary history, it may be easier than in our family histories to disentangle the roots of the Enlightenment, by closely tracing the process of who wrote what when, how, and (ideally) why. And this is what *Black Reason, White Feeling: The Jeffersonian Enlightenment in the African American Tradition* will seek to do. But the more its narrative unfolds, the more it will become apparent that, like a complicated family saga, the history of the Enlightenment is a history of multiple projections, appropriations, and ironies, in which ideas and ideals crisscrossed between individuals and groups in various and often surprising directions.

Black Reason, White Feeling does not attempt to provide an exhaustive overview of the Enlightenment in general, or the American Enlightenment in particular.[7] Instead, it will focus on two intellectual traditions in the American Enlightenment that were in close conversation with one another. One will be labeled "Wheatley's Enlightenment of Principle," the other, "Jefferson's Enlightenment of Feeling." Conventionally, both Phillis Wheatley and Thomas Jefferson have been treated as historical individuals who were "influenced" by a generically construed eighteenth-century philosophy—"the" Enlightenment. In other words, they have been seen less as original Enlightenment thinkers than as a poet and a politician, respectively, who made certain borrowings from Enlightenment philosophy. By contrast, this book will break open the monolith of "the" Enlightenment and treat Wheatley and Jefferson as points of departure for two distinct versions of late Enlightenment thought. These versions interacted on various levels, sometimes undermining and sometimes consolidating one another. Eventually, they moved beyond their own confines to create a new, modernized Enlightenment philosophy that can no longer be identified in terms of either whiteness or blackness, masculinity or femininity, but that now constitutes the core of American universalist ideals.

As has long been pointed out, no other eighteenth-century figure, no other member of the group conventionally known as American "Founding Fathers," and no other American president before Abraham Lincoln loomed as large in African American literature as did Thomas Jefferson.[8] *Black Reason, White Feeling* approaches this constellation as a mutually influential relationship. Not only was Jefferson's Enlightenment of Feeling an important factor in nineteenth-century African American intellectual and literary life, the following chapters will show, but the intellectuals of Wheatley's Enlightenment of Principle also contributed decisively to shaping Jefferson or, more precisely, the Jefferson, and the "Jeffersonian" Enlightenment, we know today. Jefferson is one of very few Americans whose name is convertible into an adjective and an "ism" to denote a worldview emerging with but going beyond the scope of his own ideas. This book argues that it was African American intellectuals, in the main, who made the difference between the historical idiosyncrasies of Jefferson's own philosophy and the enduring universalist appeal of the Jeffersonian Enlightenment.

In retrospect, the authors of Wheatley's Enlightenment of Principle—including Lemuel Haynes, Benjamin Banneker, Daniel Coker, William Hamilton, James Forten, David Walker, Hosea Easton, Maria W. Stewart, James W. C. Pennington, William Wells Brown, Martin Delany, Frederick Douglass, William G. Allen, William J. Wilson, and James McCune Smith—were strikingly prescient, anticipating later developments in Jeffersonianism and the oft-discussed "Jefferson image"[9] in major respects. Although they differed widely in approach, genre, and emphasis, these writers can be understood to have formed a coherent intellectual and literary tradition in that they referenced one another to develop a transgenerational repertory of shared Enlightenment arguments and themes.[10] For instance, from 1776 onward, they consistently offered what has become today's dominant interpretation of what they (unlike the historical Jefferson) identified as the "principles" of the Declaration of Independence. From early on, moreover, writers in this tradition recognized the great historical and symbolic significance of the transracial Hemings-Jefferson family for conceptions of American nationhood.[11] And, perhaps most consequentially, they were undeterred in consolidating a universalist theory of knowledge that took issue, not only with the content of Jefferson's infamous "suspicion only" of "black" intellectual inferiority in *Notes on the State of Virginia* but also with his fateful efforts to conjure up alternative "white" and "black" epistemologies.[12] When the writers of Wheatley's Enlightenment of Principle highlighted Jefferson's shortcomings, they were not simply inverting his racist allegations in binary terms by the tautology of their own intellectual achievements. Instead, they were "co-fabricating"[13] something new: a Jeffersonian Enlightenment capable of consolidating the strengths, and overcoming the weaknesses, of Jefferson's original Enlightenment of Feeling.

And weaknesses there were, as part and parcel of Jefferson's important conceptual innovations. The approach to rationality in his Enlightenment of Feeling, part 1 will show, was far less ambitious than tends to be assumed today. What was historically most characteristic of Jefferson's philosophy was not its focus on universal reason, but its emphasis on concepts of subjective—communal, embodied, and particular—feeling, opinion, and secular faith. Developed as a postcolonial form of opposition to what Jefferson called the "wretched philosophy" of Europe,[14] his Enlightenment of Feeling had the primary aim of making the new American nation subjectively plausible to equal republican citizens. At its best, Jefferson's subjectivist epistemology innovatively "diffused" and democratized knowledge to emphasize the freedom of opinion and conscience, in ways that continue to be crucial today.[15] At its worst, however, it opened the door for a new concept of "racial" identity self-consciously grounded in embodied experience, false opinion, and prejudice. Beginning with the arguments of the American Colonization Society, Jefferson's self-serving form of self-criticism—his combination of subjectively experienced *race*, feelings of guilt, and group prejudice—proved to have a long and disturbing afterlife from the nineteenth century until today.

As I argue in part 2, Wheatley's Enlightenment of Principle developed the tools to deal with many of the problems of Jefferson's Enlightenment of Feeling. Following Phillis Wheatley, who had publicly argued for the "principle" of a universal "love of freedom" more than two years prior to the Declaration of Independence,[16] African American intellectuals had the insight and motivation to place rational constraints on Jefferson's postcolonial experiments. They sought to rein in and stabilize his uncertain departures from the "wretched philosophy" of Europe by such means as their rationalist hermeneutics of the Declaration of Independence, their transformation of *prejudice* from an epistemological to a moral term critiquing what would today be called *racism*,[17] and their pedagogical concepts of *black uplift* as well as *white uplift,* privileging Jefferson's characterological language under Query XVIII over his identitarian language under Query XIV of *Notes on the State of Virginia.* Playing off Query XVIII against Query XIV in ways that would be emulated by countless scholarly approaches later on, they created the African American artifact of "Jefferson," a literary trope that served as the embodiment of the contradictions of a modern slaveholding democracy. By measuring aspects of the historical Jefferson against their own transformations of his philosophy, the writers of Wheatley's Enlightenment of Principle became the inventors of the "Jeffersonian" *double consciousness* that has become the dominant interpretation of Jefferson's life and writings today.

It is ultimately due to the African American artifact of "Jefferson" and the invention of his *double consciousness* that the historical Jefferson seems to modern eyes so incapable of "living up" to the rational standards of the Jeffersonian Enlightenment: as the following chapters will show, this modernized version of Enlightenment philosophy emerged, in fact, only after his thought had been filtered through Wheatley's Enlightenment of Principle. The result of this filtering process was the abstract, rationalized, and universalized version of Jefferson's conceptual world—in other words, Jeffersonianism as an *"ism"*—that became the source of the universalist ideals of American political culture and civil religion in later years. Ironically, these ideals have been so successful in retroactively shaping Jefferson's academic and popular image that today he is often regarded, and indeed often criticized, precisely as the American representative of a supposedly "white" concept of Enlightenment rationality.

To underline the historical irony of a "white" Enlightenment, the book's title, *Black Reason, White Feeling,* has a polemical intent. This book will certainly not try to argue that the distribution of human reason and human feeling is inherently dependent on "race." Nor will it continue Jefferson's postcolonial experiments and evoke alternative "black" or "white" versions of knowledge and reason. Instead, the book seeks to trace the dialectical interaction of two distinct late Enlightenment philosophies, both of which included discussions of human rationality and human emotions, while differing significantly on the question of how to understand the relationship between them. The title's polemical opposition between *Black Reason* and *White Feeling* illustrates the basic readjustment this book seeks to make. In recent years, a monolithic concept of Enlightenment has begun to run the danger of being associated with an equally monolithic concept of *whiteness.*

Indeed, terms such as *Enlightenment, reason, rationality, rationalization, rationalism, universalism, scientific knowledge, mind-body dualism, Cartesianism,* or *Eurocentrism* often risk being conflated, both with a supposedly all-pervasive *whiteness* and with one another, although they obviously refer to different concepts. For instance, while Jefferson's Enlightenment of Feeling was heavily invested in the creation of modern American concepts of "white" and "black" nationalism, it was also an anti-Eurocentric philosophy that emerged in postcolonial opposition to the intellectual hierarchies of European metaphysics; and while it reflected on questions involving human rationality, these reflections did not make Jefferson a rationalist. To the contrary, his thought was a particularly radical example of the larger tendency of the British-American Enlightenment to define itself *against* the abstractions of European rationalism.[18]

In a significant body of writing in the humanities, nevertheless, a mysterious entity called "occidental rationalism" or "Enlightenment rationalism" has come to be regarded as the privileged domain of "dead white males" such as Jefferson.[19] This distorted view may go back to the roots of today's cultural and postcolonial theory, much of whose critical vocabulary was originally formed in opposition to the Continental European, not the American, Enlightenment.[20] Ironically, therefore, even today's most "critical" and purportedly anti-Eurocentric theories of the Enlightenment often persist in treating the Enlightenment, at bottom, as an exclusively European (even, perhaps, central European) phenomenon. Through this narrow lens, they typically fail to take seriously eighteenth- and nineteenth-century African American intellectuals,[21] just as they show themselves, for the most part, unaware of the historical specifics of the "creole" perspectives of Jefferson and other white American revolutionaries.[22]

Today's radicalized "white Enlightenment trope"[23] may seem justified by the fact that, from the eighteenth century onward, there has been a significant number of racist writers on both sides of the Atlantic who tried to exclude people of non-European descent, whether on the basis of their color or their culture, from their own narratives of Enlightenment.[24] However, unless one accepts the allegations made by these writers, this fact does not make the Enlightenment a "white" cultural phenomenon. Nor can it plausibly reveal Enlightenment accounts of universal rationality to have been mere tools of "white supremacy," serving the sinister purpose of hiding the particular interests of an oppressive "white" identity behind the smokescreen of a seemingly universalist language of free discussion, liberty, equality, and natural rights. To be sure, contemporary questions are an inevitable part of any study of the past, and it is both legitimate and instructive today to examine the terms of Western universalism in their dynamic relations to emergent American notions of *whiteness*. But understanding these relations becomes impossible when eighteenth- and nineteenth-century thinkers are forced to carry the entire historical baggage of a twenty-first-century comfort zone. Reduced to this function, their arguments threaten to be crushed beneath the combined weight of two centuries of European Enlightenment critique, the overdetermined certainties of hindsight, and the complacencies that can be involved even in constructions of a guilty historical conscience.

To lighten today's historical baggage as effectively as possible, this book has bracketed default associations of Enlightenment rationality with violence and oppression. The purchase from this heuristic has been the recovery of two specifically American modes of thinking that had been lost from view. The first is Jefferson's Enlightenment of Feeling discussed in part 1, notably the decisive roles its antirationalist opposition to Old World metaphysics and its emphasis on opinion and assent played for its innovation of a modern American concept of *race* as subjective experience. In the nineteenth century, this concept rose to prominence among white American colonizationists, who opposed slavery but sought to exclude African Americans from the polity. Their arguments for exclusion were based, not primarily on pretensions to reason and knowledge, but on what they bluntly admitted was their own subjective "feeling" and "prejudice." In the long run, the oppressive dimension of Jefferson's Enlightenment of Feeling thus turned out to be rooted precisely in its *weak* identification with universal rationality, a weakness that ushered in peculiarly lazy and self-indulgent forms of self-criticism. The result was a concept of *race* that began with self-critical concessions of affect-driven prejudice but that among nineteenth-century writers soon ossified into assertions that their antiblack prejudice was the natural, inevitable, and irredeemable attribute defining the boundaries of their ahistorical "white" American identity. Over the years, what had been an epistemologically modest stance thus morphed into a generalized apology for group-specific false opinions that supposedly eluded white Americans' individual responsibility.[25]

The self-serving weakness at the heart of Jefferson's Enlightenment of Feeling was not lost on the protagonists of part 2, whose original arguments are the second rediscovery made in this book. When reading the sophisticated, self-confident authors of Wheatley's Enlightenment of Principle closely, it becomes very difficult to accept retrospective claims that they must have been collectively duped by the deception maneuvers of a "white" Enlightenment discourse somehow powerful enough to conceal, over decades and even centuries, the full reality of slavery and racist oppression. Why precisely should it be assumed that the writers of Wheatley's Enlightenment were not at least as capable as were their white counterparts of understanding the world around them? From the point of view of early African American authors, there was more than enough evidence of problems that were not caused by too much Enlightenment rationality in American society, but by too little of it. In a world where legal slavery and slave trading were grave threats, the protagonists of Wheatley's Enlightenment did not have to be told that the promises of a universalist rhetoric could not be taken for granted. They knew all too well that, far from residing in lofty places of power and hegemony, the Enlightenment they cherished was a highly precarious, fragile construct, under attack at any moment, and greatly in need of being recognized and strengthened wherever it could be found.

Their tendency to approach Enlightened universalism from the perspective of its dramatic precariousness rather than its supposed power may be the decisive factor explaining the interest the writers of Wheatley's Enlightenment of Principle took in Jefferson's Enlightenment of Feeling. When they responded to this philosophy, they did not blindly attack it or try to suppress its legacy. Instead, they had the "resolution and courage" to critically engage with its arguments and separate the useful from the destructive, highlighting its pathologies while salvaging that which they considered to be its overlap with their own. In the process, they were doing considerably more than applying a "white" Enlightenment to their political goals, or beating its ideas at their own game, trying to use the master's tools to dismantle the master's house, in Audre Lorde's famous words.[26] For these authors, what may today look like the master's tools did not belong to the master, not only because this assumption would weirdly have accepted the property relations of slavery—in the Aristotelian definition of which tools were understood to be analogous to slaves[27]—but also because, in Jefferson's case, the master did not even *claim* these intellectual tools as his own. If African American intellectuals did not blame Jefferson's Enlightenment of Feeling for its "false universalism," accordingly, it was not because they did not realize that the assumption of its universalism would have been false or simplistic, but because they knew that this particular philosophy did not even pretend to be so very universalist to begin with. If they appealed to universal reason, they were not trying to meet "white" standards; they were trying to correct them. And if they were reluctant to emphasize their own subjective feelings, they had other reasons than the goal to please white readers. It should not be assumed too easily that the relationship of early African American thinkers to Enlightenment philosophy was exhausted by the three possibilities of either "complicity" and opportunistic approval, radical resistance, or subtle subversion.[28] A fourth option may be more relevant in this case: a great variety of well-founded philosophical departures from the strong roles granted to embodied experience, subjective opinion, and collective prejudice in Jefferson's postcolonial Enlightenment of Feeling.

Thus, the following chapters will argue against the implication of a kind of Enlightenment deficit on the part of African American thinkers—against the view, held by old-school racists but strangely echoed in some of today's discussions, that they were at best forced to react to a powerful "white" Enlightenment that was not only miraculously coherent and unified, but already fully in place the moment their arguments began. *Black Reason, White Feeling* reframes the conventional narrative, according to which Jefferson and his white peers set the terms—"all men are created equal"—while writers such as Phillis Wheatley, David Walker, or Frederick Douglass assumed the subordinate roles of merely talking back, of being "ambivalent" toward the Enlightenment, or of acquiring a preexistent lingua franca for the limited purpose of entering the American public sphere. Instead, this book shows how the interventions of African American intellectuals contributed decisively to shaping the American Enlightenment and the lingua franca of the American public sphere. It does not leave the totalizing view of a "white" Enlightenment intact but moves back in time to clarify what Jefferson's Enlightenment of Feeling would have been on its own, without the transformations that have turned it into a milestone of Enlightened universalism. It then analyzes the writings of the intellectuals who were on the forefront of making these transformations. It is thus not a book about Jefferson the "man of the Enlightenment" and reactions to him, but a book that seeks to provide a new, historically dynamic interpretation of what is meant by "universalist Enlightenment values" today, of how these values emerged, and who shaped them.

From the perspective of the two intellectual traditions discussed in *Black Reason, White Feeling*, the answer to the classical question of the epigonism of the American Enlightenment is twofold. Not only was Jefferson's Enlightenment of Feeling much more idiosyncratic and original than a practical implementation of ideas from "the" European Enlightenment on American soil. But likewise was Wheatley's Enlightenment of Principle a complex philosophy in its own right that exceeded the contingent needs of a struggle against oppression. The self-serving softness and malleability of Jefferson's postcolonial laissez-faire of opinion and prejudice provided what turned out to be, in retrospect, a productive philosophical challenge, confirming the protagonists of Wheatley's Enlightenment in their perception that it was necessary to go beyond a negatively construed freedom and pursue the more ambitious goal of defining and consolidating rational norms of free and open debate on the common ground of a shared reality. It was thus in their unique combination that both American Enlightenment philosophies "co-fabricated" the Jeffersonian Enlightenment that has helped shape today's ideal of a democracy founded on universally communicable principles.

❖ Part I ❖

Jefferson's Enlightenment of Feeling

"'I feel: therefore I exist.'" Explaining his philosophical outlook to his friend John Adams in the twilight years of their lives, Thomas Jefferson continued: "I feel bodies which are not myself: there are other existencies then. I call them *matter*. I feel them changing place. This gives me *motion*. Where there is an absence of matter, I call it *void*, or *nothing*, or *immaterial space*. On the basis of sensation, of matter and motion, we may erect the fabric of all the certainties we can have or need." Jefferson had been disturbed by Adams's discussion in the previous letter of the "immaterialist" philosophy of George Berkeley. Its "croud of skepticisms," Jefferson complained, had kept him from sleep. "I read it, and laid it down: read it, and laid it down, again and again: and to give rest to my mind, I was obliged to recur ultimately to my habitual anodyne, 'I feel: therefore I exist.'"[1]

This emphasis on *feeling*, imagined as the last source of stability in a world dispossessed of spirit and consisting solely of matter and void, condenses central traits of Jefferson's late empiricist Enlightenment. This Enlightenment will be the subject of the following four chapters. In rephrasing René Descartes's famous remedy to existential uncertainty, "I think, therefore I am," Jefferson programmatically departed from a stance that is today often treated as a shorthand for "the" Enlightenment.[2] In many of the more theory-minded parts of the academic world over the past decades, it has become customary to criticize a concept of the Enlightenment modeled on one-sided interpretations of Descartes's *cogito* as a hierarchical Western "project" that employed a powerful concept of universal reason to

Portrait of Thomas Jefferson by Mather Brown, 1786. The peculiar softness of the paper Jefferson is delicately holding in his hand, reminiscent of the fabrics of his clothing and the draperies in the background, seems to capture the importance of textile metaphors in his Enlightenment of Feeling. Brown's corresponding portrait of John Adams, who had commissioned both paintings, depicts him with Jefferson's *Notes on the State of Virginia*. (National Portrait Gallery)

achieve domination over a universe it relegated to the status of passive objectivity.[3] This project is often associated today with the "Eurocentrism" of an elite group of white men who falsely treated their own positions as neutral and universal while marking as "merely" particular everyone else's.[4] At a moment in his life when he was able to give an overview of his mature philosophy, however, Jefferson deliberately substituted the Cartesian *cogito* with a concretely embodied, ostentatiously nonrational "I feel." Rather than knowledge and thinking, he placed secular belief and feeling at the heart of his vision of Enlightenment. His egalitarian epistemology did not privilege reason but emphasized what was often regarded as the most intimate and immediate, the least detached and domineering, of the senses: the sense of touch. Jefferson did not see himself engaged in an ambitious project of rationally comprehending and classifying the world in its entirety. Instead, he was content to make the far more modest attempt to attain limited certainty about what was merely one material existence among "other existencies."

The following chapters closely reconstruct Jefferson's Enlightenment of Feeling in order to answer the question any reception history has to answer, but particularly the history of a reception that was as deeply transformative as the one of Jefferson's Enlightenment in the African American tradition: What precisely *was* the philosophical raw material its protagonists found at the outset, before their own interventions changed it into the version that has become familiar today? The "ur"-Jefferson emerging from this reconstruction will be radically counterintuitive. For instance, the man who wrote "I feel: therefore I exist" was neither the "apostle of reason" defending universal human rights that his admirers have imagined, nor can he be understood to exemplify the pathologies of "the" Western *cogito* deplored by twentieth-century theorists. He was not simply the Federalist caricature of the eclectic pseudo-philosopher that has been popular since Washington Irving. And, most importantly, he was not yet the man of contradictions, the "ambidexter" personification of both America's original sin and America's greatest promise that he would become in the African American tradition.[5]

In its self-defined state of nature, before being processed through the complex modernizations of the intellectuals studied in this book, Jefferson's "felt" Enlightenment was not particularly contradictory. On its own terms, it was philosophically quite consistent and, over his lifetime, fairly coherent. The following chapters seek to abstain from today's widespread "pick-and-choose" approach to Enlightenment figures such as Jefferson, which tends to pit what appear to be their outstanding intellectual achievements against their racism, celebrating the former while relegating the latter to the realm of psychology. Separating the wheat from the chaff in this manner often has the paradoxical effect, not of explaining the phenomenon of racism in its historical contingency, but of granting it the unmerited status of an ahistorical, ultimately unaccountable force of nature. Avoiding the tendency of thus naturalizing *race* and racism, the chapters take an integrative approach to Jefferson's thought. They argue that his racism was part and parcel of his self-consciously postcolonial Enlightenment of Feeling, motivated by the founding of what he thought was a "white" American nation, and designed against the foil of what he criticized as the hairsplitting hierarchies and "useless" metaphysics of the "wretched philosophy" of Europe.[6]

Due to its deliberate anti-Eurocentrism, Jefferson's worldview departed from characteristics typically associated with "the" Enlightenment today. For example, it appreciated the comforts of ignorance and rested content in the assumption that, before knowledge could be attained, "opinion is power."[7] It tended to distrust the supposedly "enlightened" sense of sight—Monticello was no panopticon—and privileged the sense of touch instead. In its most exclusionary moments, notably in the passages on what was becoming *race* under Query XIV of *Notes on the State of Virginia*, it did not recur to rational quantification and classification, to scientific lists and charts, but relied on nothing but radically subjectivist, disorganized, willfully impressionistic prose. In Jefferson's Enlightenment, it bears repeating, rational thinking tended to be displaced by organic *feeling*—a term that for him was not synonymous with rationally restrained *sentiment* but came closer to the raw emotion of concretely embodied *experience*.[8]

Because of its antirationalist orientation,[9] Jefferson's Enlightenment gave extraordinary weight to secular belief, to (public) opinion, and, in at least one influential case, to prejudice. The following chapters proceed in this order. The first chapter explains Jefferson's qualified concept of knowledge, or what he liked to describe instead as his (materialist, moral, religious, and political) "creeds." Chapter 2 analyzes his comparatively weak concept of human rationality. Caught midway between God's reason and a fully secular human reason, Jefferson's subjective rationality was unable to stand on its own or function according to its own specific rules. It still depended on a traditional metaphysical backup (a dependence complicated by the fact that Jefferson's antirationalist stance made him unwilling, or unable, to acknowledge it). The resulting semi-secularized account of reason was key to both the greatest potential and the greatest problem of Jefferson's "felt" Enlightenment: its inability to draw clear lines between knowledge and opinion in the short- and midterm (as opposed to the long term of his "republican millennium").[10] As will be shown in chapters 3 and 4, this inability proved useful for Jefferson's egalitarian discussions of (public) opinion and the genesis of a national American "creed," but could become a severe liability for his discussions of prejudice.

Prejudice often appears today the antithesis of Enlightenment, including Jefferson's Enlightenment.[11] However, as argued in chapter 4, in the context of his emphasis on feeling and secular "creed," prejudice and even ignorance have to be seen as integral parts of his philosophy, his occasional disclaimers notwithstanding. Under Query XIV of *Notes on the State of Virginia*, Jefferson prominently discussed the prejudice of white Virginians against the people he referred to as "blacks." In the nineteenth century, this text became one of the main foci of the African American reception of his thought, while it also served as a key inspiration for white American colonizationists, who used the ostensibly self-critical concession of their own collective antiblack prejudice to make the case for African Americans having to leave the country. In this unique constellation, Query XIV became instrumental in the evolution of *prejudice*, whether of "color" or "condition,"[12] into the term coming closest in a nineteenth-century vocabulary to what today would be called *racism*.

In retrospect, Query XIV has come to be seen as a radical departure from that which is understood to be the larger universalist thrust of Jefferson's thought expressed, for instance, in the Declaration of Independence. From the perspective of his organically "felt" Enlightenment, however, the problem of prejudice under XIV is better understood as an extreme potentiality of Jefferson's subjectivism than as a contradiction to it. Examining XIV against the backdrop of his experiments with the subjective limitations of sensory experience (especially of the supposedly "enlightened" sense of sight) throughout *Notes on the State of Virginia*, part 1 ultimately aims at illuminating the influential role Jefferson's Enlightenment played in the genesis of a specifically American concept of *race* as subjective experience. As will become clear in the following chapters, Jefferson's contribution to the invention of "racial" identity was not the product of an Enlightenment premised on an arrogant Western *cogito* condescending to quantify and classify a world of passive objects. Instead, it was part of a specific late Enlightenment culture quite content to rely on the contingencies of subjective experience or, in Jefferson's words, *feeling*.

❖ 1 ❖

I Feel: Therefore I Exist

Since Jefferson's "felt" Enlightenment, before its rationalist transformation in the African American tradition, is so unfamiliar today, this chapter will go to some length to systematically reconstruct its premises. To contextualize its counterintuitive grounding in *feeling*, it is worth taking a closer look at the exchange with Adams. In a moment of philosophical crisis Jefferson claimed to reassure himself by retreating from the abstract world of thought to his concrete sensory experience of the material world around him. By his own account, this retreat had become a habit, a "habitual anodyne" against the anxieties that could result from delving too deeply into abstract intellectual problems of existence and causality. Jefferson found his mantra in a programmatic departure from the famous "Je pense, donc je suis," in Descartes's work published in the vernacular French, *Discours de la méthode pour bien conduire sa raison, & chercher la verité dans les sciences* (*Discourse on the Method for Rightly Conducting One's Reason and Seeking the Truth in the Sciences*) (1637). In this shift of priorities from methodical Cartesian rationality to "feeling," Jefferson knew that he was hardly alone. More than a century after the publication of John Locke's *Essay Concerning Human Understanding* (1690), he was placing himself squarely in the tradition of the major work opposing Cartesian concepts of knowledge. Jefferson agreed with Locke that human reason could not be the spontaneous source of knowledge, and that knowledge could be acquired, not through a method of rational doubt geared toward the recovery of innate ideas, but only based on the sensory experience the mind more or less accidentally gained from the material world. Jefferson used *feeling*, roughly, as a synonym for the Lockean term *sensation*. However, near the end of the long eighteenth century that had followed the *Essay*, Jefferson's use also revealed considerable differences between his own and Locke's philosophy. These differences are rarely explored but are necessary for an understanding of Jefferson's more strongly antirationalist Enlightenment.

Locke had contested Descartes's assumption of innate ideas by arguing that human knowledge could only be the product of human *experience*, consisting first of *sensation* and second of *reflection*. He had distinguished further between (outward) *sense* and (inward) *perception* as "the first and simplest *idea* we have from reflection."[1] *Feeling* for Locke referred more specifically to the sense of touch and to experiences of pleasure and pain, hunger and thirst. The concept moved to the fore in the eighteenth-century reception of Locke's *Essay*. In a French tradition of radicalizing Locke's legacy that extended to Jefferson's correspondents among the Idéologues (including Pierre Jean George Cabanis and Antoine Louis Claude Destutt de Tracy), Etienne Bonnot de Condillac's *Traité des sensations* (1754) singled out the sense of touch as providing the model for his theory of immediate sensation. Due to its emotional connotation, which Locke already had related to the ideas of good and evil,[2] this emphasis on *feeling* raised complex moral questions that became especially important in the Scottish Enlightenment. In the opening of his early work, *A Treatise of Human Nature* (1739), David Hume used the contrast between *thinking* and *feeling* to illustrate his division between *ideas* and (more vivid) *impressions* received by the mind.[3] In *Elements of Criticism* (1761), Henry Home, Lord Kames, defined *feeling* as both "one of the external senses" and "a general term, signifying that internal act by which we are made conscious of our pleasures and our pains."[4] The term gained prominence, to take a famous example, in discussions of sympathy and *fellow-feeling* in Adam Smith's *Theory of Moral Sentiments* (1759). *Feeling* became a key word in a new culture of sensibility, as referenced in the title of Henry Mackenzie's *The Man of Feeling* (1771). The genre of the sentimental novel, which Jefferson admired, most of all, in Laurence Sterne's *A Sentimental Journey* (1768), paradoxically gestured toward a realm "beyond words," thus ultimately liberating *feeling* from the need for conceptual discussion.[5]

For his antirationalist mission statement 130 years after Locke's groundbreaking critique of Descartes, then, Jefferson had a number of reasons for privileging *feeling* over *thinking* or related terms such as *perceiving*. His "I feel" evoked at once a concrete corporeality and a form of interiority endowed with an emotional and a moral dimension. In its inability to bridge physical distances, the sense of touch stood in strong contrast to the sense most often associated with "the" Enlightenment: the sense of sight. Whereas, for instance, today's Foucauldian approaches to Enlightenment philosophy focus on the hierarchical detachment of (panoptical) vision, Jefferson's Enlightenment stressed the closeness and intimacy of touching surfaces. In his reliance on *feeling*, he may have been inspired, in particular, by the comparative discussion of the senses in Kames's *Elements of Criticism*. (Jefferson had recommended this book as early as 1771 in a reading list accompanying a letter that discussed the role of "feeling and sentiment" in the reading process of Sterne's *Sentimental Journey* and even of historical works.)[6] In the introduction to *Elements,* Kames had clarified the double nature of *feeling* as both the emotional qualification he supposed to accompany all sense impressions and the specific "organic pleasure" of touch. As Kames saw it, in contrast to the more "elevated" sensory experiences of sight or hearing, the immediate, "organic" sense of touch or *feeling* was influential in shaping the "first attachments" of the unripe mind during infancy.[7] In the transatlantic family drama Jefferson sketched in his draft of the Declaration of Independence, this rudimentary childhood psychology helped shape his lamentation about the loss of his "unfeeling brethren" in the old mother country: to Jefferson's mind, *feeling* became an important criterion distinguishing Americans from their former European compatriots.

Against this backdrop, Jefferson decisively modified Locke's answer to the question of existential certainty. Locke had argued that intuitive knowledge of our own existence was possible on the grounds not only of feeling, but of "every act of sensation, reasoning, or thinking," including even a version of Descartes's methodical doubt ("If I doubt of all other things, that very doubt makes me perceive my own existence, and will not suffer me to doubt that," as Locke put it).[8] By contrast, Jefferson claimed not to recur to any form of rational reflection to reassure himself of his ontological status. Maintaining that he acquired existential certainty exclusively from "organic," primitive, almost childlike *feeling,* Jefferson highlighted what was, compared to the "idea of ourselves, as understanding, rational Beings" in Locke's *Essay,*[9] a radicalized antirationalist stance. As the following chapters will show, Jefferson's ostentatiously simplistic concept of the workings of the mind—the paradox, as it were, of a sophisticated "simple-mindedness"—was characteristic of his Enlightenment of Feeling in many other contexts as well.[10]

Jefferson's organically embodied "I feel" in the place, not only of Descartes's "I think" but also of Locke's "I think, I reason, I feel pleasure and pain,"[11] drew attention to a central problem of this Enlightenment: the problem of perspective and the subjective limitations conditioning all sensory experience. Jefferson was far from oblivious to the problem. For example, in the letter to Adams summarizing his philosophical outlook he not only voiced his expectation that *feeling* conveyed information about the material world that was accurate, or at least accurate enough. The letter also made it plain that this obstinate realism came only as the result of philosophical desperation, habitually administered as an "anodyne" to help him through recurrent moments of existential crisis. In this respect like Descartes's "Je pense," Jefferson's "I feel" came only *after* his confrontation with skepticism. Thus, if Jefferson liked to pose as an epistemological ostrich burying his head in the sand of *feeling*, he knew what he was doing. Far from being naïve, he grappled with his insight into the subjective limitations of sensory experience, including experiential evidence, throughout his life. Unlike rationalist thinkers, however, he saw the slipperiness of experience not mainly as a danger but tried his best to treat it as an asset, most notably in his draft of the Declaration of Independence and in his only published book, *Notes on the State of Virginia*.

Like many of his contemporaries at the end of the long eighteenth century, Jefferson was still trying to cope with the ambiguities of Locke's philosophy and the skeptical conclusions that could be drawn from them. If human knowledge was largely the mind's internal business ("nothing but *the perception of the connexion and agreement, or disagreement and repugnancy, of any of our ideas*," as Locke had defined it),[12] and if the mind was indeed mostly a blank slate at birth, reliant for its ideas on the contingent information it received from the senses and unable to recur to divinely ordained innate ideas, how precisely was it supposed to know that it received accurate information of the world, and how was a morally commendable life possible? Rejecting Berkeley's response of subjective idealism as well as the skepticism in David Hume's philosophy, far removed from Immanuel Kant's transcendental turn while seeking some (but by no means consistent) support from the French materialists and the Scottish Common Sense philosophers, Jefferson sought to carve out his own answers to these questions. These answers retained many Lockean notions but often downplayed the strong role Locke had still granted to rational reflection. The result was a worldview that radicalized

Locke's bottom-up epistemology in a theory of knowledge grounded, first and foremost, in *feeling*.[13]

"My Creed of Materialism"

For Jefferson writing in 1820, the world had no place for spirit, but was composed solely of matter and void. What he one-sidedly tried to interpret as Locke's "materialism" had more recently been confirmed, as Jefferson saw it, by "other materialists," such as Pierre Jean George Cabanis and Antoine Louis Claude Destutt de Tracy.[14] Jefferson showed himself much in favor of the eighteenth-century French tradition of radicalizing Locke's legacy.[15] For instance, he professed to concur with Tracy's answer to "an interesting question, to wit, that on the certainty of human knoledge [sic]." As Jefferson appreciatively told his grandson Francis Eppes, Tracy countered "Malebranche, Barclay and other sceptics, by resting the question on the single basis of 'we feel.'"[16] Yet, while Jefferson promoted the materialism of the Idéologues and their aim to find a physiological basis of thought and morality, he admitted that he was neither equipped nor willing to concern himself much with the intricacies of their arguments. As he put it in the case of Tracy's *Elements d'idéologie*: "His three 8vo. volumes on Ideology [. . .] I have not entirely read; because I am not fond of reading what is merely abstract, and unapplied immediately to some useful science."[17]

Today Jefferson is best known for his love of books and reading, and it cannot be denied that he invested considerable time and money in his famous libraries. Much as he enjoyed reading, however, he also argued against reading (and thinking) too much, whether in the case of his nighttime reading of Adams's letter on Berkeley's philosophy or in his somewhat superficial engagement with Cabanis's and Tracy's works of "ideology." If the subject matter was too abstract for his avowedly practical interests, Jefferson was given to promoting feeling instead of rational reflection. As a result, there was more seriousness than playfulness in the choice of describing his own materialist Enlightenment in terms, not of universally valid knowledge, but of subjective belief. "I believe I am supported in my creed of materialism by Locke, Tracy, and Stewart," he informed Adams. In keeping with referring to his materialism as a "creed," he opposed to it "the heresy of *immaterialism*, this masked atheism."[18]

Jefferson was aware that his belief in a world of matter and void was the position more likely to disturb his contemporaries as heretical than was

Adams's spiritualism. Especially when it led him to question the afterlife ("When once we quit the basis of sensation, all is in the wind. To talk of immaterial existences is to talk of *nothings*"),[19] or when he used it to differentiate himself from Jesus ("I am a Materialist; he takes the side of spiritualism"),[20] Jefferson had good reasons to try to turn the tables on possible charges of atheism. To Adams, who had shown himself annoyingly open to the "heresies" of immaterialism, he therefore made much of a controversial passage on the limitations of human knowledge in book 4 of Locke's *Essay*, implying a simplistically affirmative answer to Locke's much-debated question of whether God might not have employed his omnipotence to endow matter with thought.[21] As his extensive commonplace entries from the philosophical essays of Henry St. John, Viscount Bolingbroke suggest, Jefferson had been pondering this problem since the 1760s. What he appears to have admired the most in the English Tory was Bolingbroke's materialism and his claim that, whether in the case of "a sensitive plant, a reasoning elephant, or a refining metaphysician [. . .], it is nonsense, and something worse than nonsense [. . .] that god cannot give a faculty of thinking [. . .] to systems of matter whose essential properties are solidity, extension &c. not incogitativity."[22] Nevertheless, Jefferson failed to convince Adams, who had used Berkeley's idealist conclusions from Locke specifically to cast doubts on Jefferson's materialist "creed." To end a debate that had been fought with somewhat greater religious fervor by Jefferson than by Adams, both men agreed diplomatically on what for Jefferson had become a default solution in other contexts as well: Michel de Montaigne's "pillow of ignorance" as the "softest pillow" on which to put their argument to rest.[23]

While Adams initially found it "humiliating" to concede ignorance,[24] it was typical of Jefferson not to be bothered by any such qualms. To the contrary, on many occasions he almost seemed to enjoy admitting his ignorance, which he found, in any case, "preferable to error."[25] Jefferson did not regard his celebrations of ignorance as expressions of skepticism, however. Instead, he trusted that his reliance on feeling enabled him to be skeptical without becoming skepticist. This mindset has been plausibly described as "an intellect almost unhealthily appreciative of uncertainty even as it sought and expressed conviction."[26] In the exchange with Adams on the difficulties of conceiving thinking matter, what may today seem a paradoxical combination of accepting high degrees of uncertainty while expressing strong convictions took the form of an uncompromising attack on the "heresy" of immaterialism, juxtaposed with confessions of personal ignorance meandering somewhere between modesty and complacency. The reasons for this seeming contradiction in Jefferson's thought can be found in his particular brand of a bottom-up Enlightenment that drew much of its strength from depicting itself as a *creed* with limited claims to the status of authoritative knowledge. As Jefferson told Adams, he expected his replacement of feeling for rational thinking to provide the foundation, not of knowledge as such, but only of "the fabric of all the certainties we can have or need." But how precisely was such a weak concept of knowledge defensible in Jefferson's Enlightenment?

"All the Certainties We Can Have or Need"

At first glance, Jefferson's contentment with "the fabric of all the certainties we can have or need" recalls Locke's view that God had given to men, not "an universal or perfect comprehension of whatsoever is," but only "that portion and degree of knowledge" that He considered to be "necessary for the conveniences of life and information of virtue." As Locke had memorably summed up his optimistic assessment of human limitations, "[t]he candle that is set up in us shines bright enough for all our purposes."[27] Jefferson found himself in agreement, not only with Locke's oft-quoted modesty in regarding himself as a mere "under-labourer" clearing the ground for the "commonwealth of learning" by removing the Scholastic "rubbish,"[28] but also with Locke's warnings of skepticism and the temptation to "disbelieve everything, because we cannot certainly know all things."[29] However, Jefferson's epistemology went further than had Locke's in upgrading the criterion of subjective confidence at the expense of the other criteria defining knowledge (that is, not only truth itself but also the difficult question of reliable means of accessing truth). The letter to Adams contained only one example of something of which Jefferson not only claimed to be subjectively "sure," but that he actually professed to "know." In keeping with his emphasis on feeling, this lone example of objective knowledge was, and one may suspect Jefferson of some self-ironic overstatement here, highly emotional and subjective (and perhaps not so certain after all): that he loved Adams "with all [his] heart." In the remainder of the letter, Jefferson's emphasis was on subjective confidence rather than actual knowledge. In contrast to his heartfelt love for Adams, he understood his secular "creeds" to be just such cases of (mere) subjective confidence. Locke's *Essay* had patiently distinguished, not only between knowledge and belief or opinion but also between different degrees of certainty in knowledge and assent in opinion. By contrast, Jefferson felt comfortable with passing over the problem of opinion altogether and jauntily conflating "all the certainties we can have or need." The sophisticated vagueness of this phrase glossed over a number of substantive problems. For instance, did the auxiliary "can" refer only to "have" or also to "need"? What happened to knowledge that could be attained but that did not seem immediately useful? And if he expected human knowledge to be a man-made "fabric" based on subjective feeling, where precisely did he draw the line between facts and fabrications?[30]

Jefferson was clearly aware of the ambiguities of "the fabric of all the certainties we can have or need"—not to say he certainly knew of them—but he made a point of not showing himself troubled by this awareness. He found a convenient solution in actively recommending the qualified concepts of knowledge that were available in his culture. Most importantly, knowledge could be qualified by the attribute of utility: "all the certainties we (can) need" can be read as a paraphrase for contemporaneous concepts of *useful* knowledge. In the last year of his life, for example, Jefferson somewhat rudely fended off an unwelcome correspondent who had sent him his book by lecturing him on the utility of knowledge: "I revolt against all metaphysical reading, in which class your 'New pamphlet' must at least be placed. Some acquaintance with the operations of the mind is worth acquiring. But any *one* of the writers suffices for that. Locke, Kaims, Hartley, Reid, Stewart, Brown, Tracy Etc. Those dreams of the day, like those of the night, vanish in vapour, leaving not a wreck behind. The business of life is with matter. That gives us tangible results. Handling that, we arrive at the knolege [sic] of the axe, the plough, the steam-boat, and every thing useful in life. But, from metaphysical speculations, I have never seen one useful result."[31]

Jefferson's antimetaphysical "revolt"—a term that evoked political rebellion as much as something like instinctive physical disgust—was a complicated stance.[32] As will be discussed below, despite his habitual revolt against metaphysics, Jefferson's providential arguments about American progress in fact depended heavily on an extensive metaphysical scaffolding.[33] However, he felt that *useful knowledge*, his counterideal to supposedly "useless" metaphysical "dreams," had sufficient cultural capital to carry him through this contradiction. Not only had he been personally responsible, during his eighteen-year-long stint as president of the American Philosophical Society in Philadelphia (1797–1814), for the Society's goal of "promoting useful knowledge" (a goal emulated by institutions such as the Virginia Philosophical Society for the Advancement of Useful Knowledge, for which Jefferson recorded paying a fee in 1773, the year of its founding).[34] Jefferson also subscribed to Francis Bacon's ideal of useful and collaborative knowledge in his own approach to what were becoming the natural sciences.[35] "A patient pursuit of facts, and cautious combination and comparison of them," he pontificated in semi-secularized cadences, "is the drudgery to which man is subjected by his Maker, if he wishes to attain sure knowledge."[36] Jefferson saw Bacon's method at the root of scientific progress, praising it for "having laid the foundation of those superstructures which have been raised in the Physical & Moral Sciences." He even gave specific instructions to the artist John Trumbull for commissioning an oval group portrait of Bacon along with Locke and Isaac Newton, whom he declared "the three greatest men that have ever lived, without any exception."[37]

Jefferson was not very original in this assessment, of course. A similar adulation of the secular "trinity" of Bacon, Locke, and Newton can be found in one of the intellectual projects of his own time that he admired the most, Denis Diderot and Jean le Rond d'Alembert's *Encyclopédie ou dictionnaire raisonné des sciences, des arts et des métiers, par une société des gens de lettres* (1751–80). Having first borrowed the work from the Virginia Assembly and then taken a notoriously long time to return it, it may also have been the *Encyclopédie* that convinced Jefferson to pay homage to Bacon's method in another context. Beginning in 1783, Jefferson used Bacon's tree of knowledge to structure his libraries and later the library of the University of Virginia by the simplistic assumption of a correspondence between the mental faculties of memory, reason, and imagination and the fields of history, philosophy, and the fine arts, respectively.[38] As Jefferson's case illustrates, the *Encyclopédie* played an important role in reviving and popularizing elements of Bacon's "new" science in the late Enlightenment. Filtered through the *Encyclopédie*, Jefferson and other revolutionary Americans distilled from the Baconian legacy their own concept of useful knowledge. This concept stressed an antimetaphysical emphasis on practical utility, opposition to received (clerical and political) authorities, and the progressive expectation that the pursuit of knowledge was a collective, cumulative, and egalitarian enterprise. As the Encyclopedists emphasized, this enterprise extended to traditionally less prestigious forms of mechanic and artisanal knowledge as well—or, in Jefferson's words, to the "knolege of the axe, the plough, the steam-boat, and every thing useful in life."[39]

With the American Revolution, the encyclopedic Enlightenment gained a new political appeal. In opposition to what Jefferson criticized as the hierarchies of Old World metaphysics, the full egalitarian potential of useful knowledge moved to the fore.[40] Arguably, the concept of useful knowledge had long been in the process of being politicized in the decades leading up to the Revolution.[41] The American Philosophical Society had been languishing for two decades after Benjamin Franklin had proclaimed its foundation in 1743, flowering only when the conflict with Britain appeared on the horizon. Colonial scholars were becoming discontent with their subordinate roles in the imperial "economy of knowledge" after, for example, colonial naturalists such as John Bartram had gone to great pains to send collections of new American seeds to London, only to find they were not getting the appropriate scholarly credit for their research.[42] While there was nothing wrong with Locke's metaphor of serving as an "under-labourer" in the "commonwealth of knowledge," the real-life experience of being regarded as flesh-and-blood under-labourers by the Royal Society was turning out to be considerably less edifying.

During the Revolutionary War, Jefferson found a mode of mitigating the potentially humiliating division of labor in the old imperial economy of knowledge by proactively turning a perceived weakness—the collective, cumulative, necessarily unsystematic empiricism of useful knowledge—into a national asset.[43] His "felt" Enlightenment stressed the horizontal utility of knowledge acquired through collective empirical research, as opposed to the hierarchies and abstractions involved in ordering and categorizing other scholars' findings. Even, for instance, in Lord Kames, for whom he usually had nothing but praise, Jefferson associated problems he considered to be "too metaphysical"[44] with the intellectual distinctions of a "wretched philosophy" in Europe that were becoming useless with the American Revolution. Radicalizing the antimetaphysical tendencies in Bacon's and Locke's arguments, he began to imagine the Atlantic not only as a geopolitical but also as an epistemological border: whatever their "unfeeling brethren" in Europe were thinking, as he tried to see it, Americans were in close physical contact with the New World and could physically *feel* American nature. Parallel to a cult of sensibility that, unlike in Britain, persisted in America in the 1780s and 1790s,[45] Jefferson's national pride in useful knowledge acquired through a self-consciously pedestrian empiricism was to become a key characteristic of

Sarah Presenting Hagar to Abraham, Adriaen Van der Werff, 1699. (Staatsgalerie im Neuen Schloss Schleißheim)

his "postcolonial" Enlightenment—an anti-Eurocentric Enlightenment of subjective experience (or "lived experience")[46] that defined itself against the foil of European metaphysics.[47]

"The Diffusion of Knowledge"

At about the time when his long-term relationship with Sally Hemings is likely to have begun in Paris, Jefferson explicitly styled himself as an American "son of nature" who was so "affected" by a "delicious" depiction of the biblical Hagar that he stubbornly refused to reason: "Above all things those [paintings] of Van der Werff affected me the most. His picture of Sarah delivering Agar to Abraham is delicious. I would have agreed to have been Abraham though the consequence would have been that I should have been dead five or six thousand years," he told the Anglo-Italian painter Maria Cosway in one of his Shandyan epistles to her. "I am but a son of nature, loving what I see and feel, without being able to give a reason, nor caring much whether there be one."[48]

This confession of being unable, and unwilling to reason illustrates Jefferson's signature blend of humility and arrogance. Identifying with the biblical ur-patriarch who is forgiven his transgressions by the people most immediately concerned by them, he performed the passive-aggressive stance of an American provincial-turned-nationalist who no longer found it necessary to subject his feelings to the standards of a transatlantic audience, whether concerning his artistic tastes or his approaches to slavery, sexuality, and *race*. The same deliberately "careless" approach to universal rationality also shaped the concept of useful knowledge in his postcolonial Enlightenment of Feeling. When provided by a member of the French legation, François de Marbois, with the set of questions about his native state that became the occasion for composing *Notes on the State of Virginia,* Jefferson chose to answer the broad philosophical question "A notice of all what can increase the progress of human knowledge?," with little more than his own meteorological measurements. "Under the latitude of this query," he wrote under Query VII, "Climate," "I will presume it not improper nor unacceptable to furnish some data for estimating the climate of Virginia."[49] As the double negation "not improper nor unacceptable" suggests, he knew it could indeed be considered far from proper or acceptable to provide nothing but "some data" in answer to a philosophical question about "all what can increase the progress of human knowledge" (a progress that could be identified, at least in retrospect, with nothing less than "the" Enlightenment itself). But offering "some data" on the local weather to enlighten his readers on the nature of universal progress epitomized Jefferson's concept of *useful* knowledge. The ability not exactly to know, but to gain an "estimate" of meteorological conditions was eminently useful, even indispensable, in the agricultural society of a geographically expanding republic. Attaining this estimate was a collective project (Jefferson never tired of proselytizing new amateur meteorologists). And since weather implied change over time (or even came close to illustrating such change, as suggested by the Latin words *tempus* and *tempora*), getting better at estimating the climate was by necessity a cumulative and open-ended process. Such estimates could even seem particularly close to subjective feeling. "Judging from my feelings only," Jefferson conjectured about the phenomenon of certain mysterious bodies of warm air that seemed to pass too quickly for his thermometer to seize their temperatures, "I think they approach the ordinary heat of the human body."

His "felt" Enlightenment thus presented what was an ostentatiously flat conception of *climate* in a century devoted to sweeping climate theories. Instead of discussing complex interactions between climate, geography, and society—as exemplified by Montesquieu's *De l'esprit des lois* (1748), from which Jefferson had commonplaced extensively in the late 1770s[50]—Query VII deliberately confined itself to listing meteorological data that were necessarily local, contingent, and provisional. In keeping with its modest aims, VII concluded by highlighting the phenomenon of *looming* that was still lacking any definite explanation. As will be discussed below, what mattered most to Jefferson was less to display his knowledge of Virginia than to reflect on his subjective *experience* of Virginia and convey a specifically Virginian worldview or "civic subjectivity."[51] Here as elsewhere, his focus was on creating what were, from this subjective viewpoint, the best social and political conditions for the cumulative progress of the postcolonial Enlightenment in the new American republic.

Jefferson placed himself on the forefront of spelling out a personally embodied, geographically situated, and politically specified postcolonial epistemology. With the American Revolution, the emphasis on utility came to be intertwined with a second qualification he imposed on knowledge: In order to be useful, he thought that knowledge had to be "diffused" within the American republic, socially as well as conceptually ("all the certainties we can have"). Jefferson consistently used the term *diffusion*, from the time of the Bill for the More General Diffusion of Knowledge (1779) to the founding of the University of Virginia.[52] He intended *diffusion* to refer to the broad dissemination of knowledge in white American society, whether through public education, institutions such as the American Philosophical Society, or the power of print. Jefferson never ceased to express faith in the progressive potential of print, concurring with Samuel Johnson that the "mass of every people must be barbarous where there is no printing and consequently knowledge is not generally diffused."[53] In the late eighteenth century, however, to many of his contemporaries it seemed less and less clear whether the opposite were also true, and people really were becoming more civilized where there *was* printing. Faith in the power of print to effectively "diffuse" knowledge was waning: at a time when printed material in books, magazines, and newspapers was proliferating to a previously unknown extent, it appeared more and more likely that what was being diffused consisted, more often than not, in contingent opinion rather than knowledge. Chad Wellmon has plausibly discussed the parallel between the "cultural anxieties" caused by the democratization of knowledge through the wider dissemination of printed materials in the late Enlightenment and a comparable tendency due to the new medium of the internet in the early twenty-first century. In each case, the more broadly knowledge seemed to be diffused geographically and socially, the more contested it became on a conceptual level.⁵⁴

As Jefferson insinuated when leveling knowledge down to "all the certainties we can have or need," the progressive diffusion of knowledge in the new republic was bought at the price of potentially also diffusing the standards of what counted as knowledge. As suggested by his active interest in public education, especially in the founding of the University of Virginia, his postcolonial Enlightenment was not content with a Sophistic reliance on opinion or *doxa* and rhetoric, but ultimately still saw itself engaged in a Platonic pursuit of knowledge.⁵⁵ However, it has to be appreciated that Jefferson was keenly aware of the potential political dilemma emerging from this pursuit. In practice as well as theory, the elite knowledge of an order of Platonic philosopher kings was impossible to align with the idea of the equality of republican citizens, whether in Virginia, the United States, or a future world of "separate & equal" republics. Even as he saw knowledge gradually "diffusing" and science "spreading,"⁵⁶ his efforts at politically and epistemologically "leveling up"⁵⁷ ordinary citizens meant that lesser forms of certainty had to be expected to play important, and likely even decisive, roles in republican politics for some time to come. With these political priorities, Jefferson's egalitarian mode of binding "the fabric" of knowledge to the combined goals of utility and accessibility courted the danger of blurring the lines between facts and fabrications. In a democratically broadened circle of potential knowers, the methodological flexibility of useful knowledge could deteriorate into arbitrariness, resulting in approaches to knowledge that were radically limited in scope and ambition. Such approaches could facilitate decisions to settle for superficial judgments, tempting scholars to refrain from further inquiry when things were becoming too complicated to appear immediately useful.

While the conceptual problems of Jefferson's postcolonial *diffusion* of knowledge are rarely discussed today, they played an important role in the partisan conflicts of his own time. As Linda Kerber has shown in her classic study of the culturally most "articulate" part of the Federalist opposition, these Federalists found much to condemn in Jefferson's project of diffusing knowledge, criticizing him for his "flighty and irresponsible" methods almost more harshly in his office as president of the American Philosophical Society than in his office as president of the United States.⁵⁸ In their eyes, she suggests, Jefferson's diffusion of knowledge may have made him almost an easier target than his democratic politics. Federalist satirists were delighted to stress the contrast between the open-ended observational methods of natural history practiced in the Republican-leaning American Philosophy Society and the rationalist emphasis on natural philosophy and mathematics in the Federalist-leaning American Academy of Arts and Sciences. While they would deride Society members in general for lacking "a particular and accurate knowledge of anything" and having only "a *general acquaintance* with philosophy,"[59] Jefferson in particular would be caricatured as a mad scientist and infidel, who placed, for example, a random trust in myths and rumors from the American frontier, or who showed a perverted interest in bones and skulls to discover the seat of the soul.

Federalist caricatures of Jefferson's democratically diffused epistemology had a long afterlife in the nineteenth century. In his *History of the United States during the Administrations of Thomas Jefferson and James Madison* (1884–91), the self-described "eighteenth-century boy," John Adams's great-grandson Henry Adams, would still criticize Jefferson for his superficiality and "intellectual sensuousness."[60] This assessment was tame by comparison to the caricatures of Jefferson's day. In the first half of the century, Washington Irving's *History of New York* (1809, revised edition 1848) had gone much further in depicting Jefferson as a pretentious pseudo-philosopher of "diffuse" learning. Thinly disguised as the faux-historical Dutch governor of New York, Wilhelmus Kieft or "William the Testy," Irving's Jefferson was not only a hilariously self-important "learned little man" but also a particularly "ingenious" governor. In keeping with being both Dutch and a Federalist caricature, he owed this ingenuity to his childhood habit of "making very curious investigations into the nature and operations" of windmills. As an adult, Jefferson/William stayed true to his Quixotic education and "skirmished very smartly on the frontiers of many of the sciences," showing himself "exceedingly fond of trying philosophical and political experiments," entirely, of course, without making useful discoveries. "It is in knowledge as in swimming," Irving generalized on his caricature of Jefferson's diffusion of useful knowledge, "he who ostentatiously sports and flounders on the surface, makes more noise and splashing, and attracts more attention, than the industrious pearl diver, who plunges in search of treasures at the bottom."[61]

"Without Plunging [. . .] into Dreams and Phantasms"

In the nineteenth century, as will be discussed in part 2, the Federalist critique of Jefferson as a "diffuse" thinker would remain especially popular in New York's African American community of intellectuals surrounding James McCune Smith, who would add further layers to Irving's caricature.[62] As should come as no surprise, however, Jefferson himself had seen things differently. To be sure, if it had been directed at other people than himself, he would have found much that was congenial in Irving's ridicule of William the Testy's "abstruse bewildering science" and "abstract speculations," his "artificial distinctions" and "metaphysical jargon," and especially his Scholastic habits of puzzling "himself considerably with logic and [. . .] the whole family of syllogisms and dilemmas."[63] However, it is less certain that Jefferson would also have agreed with Irving's counterideal of the intellectual "pearl diver" daring to "plunge" to the bottom of knowledge. Jefferson did not regard himself as a Romantic hero on a lonesome quest for precious truths hidden beneath the surface; his horizontal concept of "diffusing" useful knowledge was unsympathetic to "plunging" too deep anywhere. Given what is so often described as his inquisitive nature, it may be asked, what precisely did he think was wrong with intellectual deep-diving?

In his exchange with Adams on matter and spirit, Jefferson explained his personal criterion for distinguishing usefully diffused knowledge ("all the certainties we can have or need") from what he termed "useless" speculation. Ultimately, Jefferson told Adams, knowledge was useful when it produced "anodynes" that led to the Epicurean goal of achieving freedom from pain and tranquility of mind. "Rejecting all organs of information therefore but my senses," Jefferson explained, "I rid myself of the Pyrrhonisms with which an indulgence in speculations hyperphysical and antiphysical so uselessly occupy and disquiet the mind. A single sense may indeed be sometimes decieved [sic], but rarely: and never all our senses together, with their faculty of reasoning. They evidence realities: and there are enough of these for all the purposes of life, without plunging into the fathomless abyss of dreams and phantasms. I am satisfied, and sufficiently occupied with the things which are, without tormenting myself about those which may indeed be, but of which I have no evidence."[64]

This programmatically antimetaphysical conclusion of Jefferson's letter to Adams needs to be understood in the context of both his neo-Epicureanism and his radicalized Lockeanism. Less than a year before detailing to Adams his "anodyne," Jefferson had emphasized his abiding identification with Epicurean ideas, which he had studied both in Lucretius's *De rerum natura* and Pierre Gassendi's *La philosophie d'Epicure*.[65] "As you say of yourself, I too am an Epicurean," he had confessed to his friend and former secretary, William Short, attaching "a syllabus of the doctrines of Epicurus, somewhat in the lapidary style, which I wrote some twenty years ago."[66] To conclude from this "lapidary" compilation, he was attracted to both Epicurean materialism and the Epicurean "*summum bonum*," which he summed up as "in-dolence of body, tranquillity of mind." The concern not to "disquiet the mind" but give "rest" to it did not express any resignation of old age. He had reflected on an "art of life" that was the "art of avoiding pain" at least since the 1780s, when it had been promoted by his *Head* in the famous "dialogue [...] between my *Head* & my *Heart*" addressed to Maria Cosway.[67] In his midlife impersonation of the *Head*, the "art of avoiding pain" had been directly related to "intellectual pleasures" such as "contemplating truth & nature, matter & motion, the laws which bind up their existence, & that eternal being who made & bound them up by those laws."[68] More than thirty years afterward in the letter to Adams, tranquility of mind was still intertwined with his ideal of useful knowledge and the conscious refusal to "indulge" in "useless" supernatural or unnatural "speculations."

In his explanation of why "useless" speculation would eventually lead to "Pyrrhonism" or radical skepticism, Jefferson's use of the loaded term *indulgence* is instructive. Evoking the context of Roman Catholicism, the term served to underline his radicalized Lockean rejection of both Cartesian rationalism and Scholasticism. As has been said, in a world composed of nothing but matter and void, Jefferson tried to attribute to corporeal feeling direct access to material reality. The Scholastic *phantasms* of the "fathomless abyss of dreams and phantasms" of which he warned Adams were immaterial representations of sense impressions that roughly functioned as intermediaries between the world and the mind. Locke had been somewhat ambiguous on this point, allowing his term *idea* "to express whatever is meant by *phantasm, notion, species*."[69] This ambiguity, especially combined with Locke's definition of knowledge as the mind's perception of internal coherence among its own ideas, has led some critics to suppose a "veil of perception" between the mind and reality in Locke's epistemology.[70] By contrast, Jefferson had no patience whatsoever with phantasms. For him, they were extreme intellectual indulgences, threatening to catapult those too eager to inquire into them into the "fathomless abyss" of some kind of epistemological hell. As he explained to Short, Epicurus recommended only "well-regulated indulgences" and taught that "'that indulgence which prevents a greater pleasure, or produces a greater pain, is to be avoided.'"[71] In the letter to Adams, such temperate indulgences implied avoiding the ambition to acquire speculative knowledge through "other organs of information" than the senses. Hence, for Jefferson relying on feeling did not imply any danger of self-indulgent luxury or laziness. To the contrary, trust in one's feelings required what he appears to have considered a difficult effort of restraining the mind from being led astray by too much thinking. In Jefferson's Epicurean simplification of Locke, *feeling* was at once the foundation of useful knowledge and described what it was useful for: the pursuit of happiness, defined here as freedom from bodily pain and security from excessive mental agitation.

Jefferson's version of a feel-good Enlightenment—combining faith in the surface sense of touch with ritualistic reenactments of Locke's blank slate in concessions of personal ignorance—has led some critics, faintly echoing the Federalist satirists of Jefferson's day, to charge him with "naïve empiricism."[72] From today's perspective, it is certainly plausible to characterize as naïve what could turn into a random trust in empirical data sans statistics. When taking into account Jefferson's Epicurean leanings, however, what looks like naiveté appears instead the outcome of a strained effort to find a way out of major philosophical dilemmas of his day. The Epicurean ideals of utility, temperance, tranquility, and prudence helped Jefferson find a workable alternative to both the skepticism that could result from an unfettered empiricism and the determinism that could be fostered by a materialist worldview. As the following chapters will argue, Jefferson did all he could to envision an Enlightenment that enabled him to be skeptical without becoming skepticist, and that left room for man to be a "free agent," as he emphasized in the "Syllabus of the Doctrines of Epicurus," in a pursuit of knowledge that he nevertheless wanted to see existentially dependent on the mechanisms of organic *feeling*.

❖ 2 ❖

Uncritical Reason

From a hindsight perspective, it has become customary to refer to Jefferson as an "apostle of reason."[1] In the context of an age that produced a number of such apostles, however, Jefferson may not be the most likely candidate for this title. On occasions when he needed to sketch a distant horizon for inquiry or political deliberation, he found good enough uses for the term *reason* in his rhetoric. But this rhetorical utility was rarely matched by conceptual depth, and he showed a clear lack of motivation to define what precisely he meant by the term. In his study of Jefferson's religious views, Paul Conkin has therefore gone as far as to ascribe to his use of reason the "demagogic" quality of a "bogus authority" that may even have involved "elements of self-deception."[2] While it may be futile to try to assess whether or not Jefferson sought to deceive himself, it is important to inquire into Conkin's suggestion that he sought to deceive others by demagogic appeals to a false authority. Before it can be squared with his rhetoric, however, the conceptual content of his understanding of reason has to be reconstructed as closely as possible.

On the conceptual level of Jefferson's Enlightenment of Feeling, reason was not absent, but played a decidedly subordinate role. As has been shown, compared to Locke's account of human experience, Jefferson tended to go further in stressing sensation at the expense of rational reflection. If he was reluctant to spend time with conceptual discussions of reason, this reluctance itself may be seen as part of his program of a post-colonial, deliberately "simple-minded" Enlightenment. Nevertheless, on occasion Jefferson also left more explicit hints concerning the place he gave to reason in the workings of the mind. For example, in the letter to Adams discussed in the previous pages, he made it clear that he was speaking of the senses and "*their* faculty of reasoning."[3] One of the "faculties of the mind" in his Baconian classification system, reason for Jefferson belonged to the senses and was unable to function without them. Whereas, for instance, Benjamin Rush assigned to reason the function of actively "correcting" the senses, Jefferson stressed a more egalitarian relationship: reason was not exalted above the senses but served them as an aid or supplement.[4] This secondary role of reason not only set his concept apart from accounts of reason as a spontaneous source of ideas (as influentially in Immanuel Kant's separation of reason not only from the senses, but from the understanding), but also from Locke's discussion. Although Locke is today mostly known for his empiricism, he had in fact emphasized that the "greatest part of our knowledge depends upon deductions and intermediate ideas" and granted reason a decisive function in distinguishing between knowledge and opinion: "the faculty which finds out the means and rightly applies them, to discover certainty in the one and probability in the other, is that which we call reason." Without reason, Locke thought, the mind would be "floating at all adventures, without choice and without direction."[5] By contrast, Jefferson was able to imagine a quasi-sensual reason so embedded in sensory experience as to become almost indistinguishable from it, as when he claimed to reject "all organs of information [. . .] but my senses."[6] As Charles Miller pointed out a while ago, Jefferson's tendency thus to fuse reason with the senses (or his "intellectual sensuousness," as Henry Adams described the same phenomenon), was a potential liability of his Enlightenment insofar as it tended to make him "willing to ignore what he could not sense."[7]

At the end of the long eighteenth century, for Jefferson in contrast to Locke the senses included the moral sense. In a letter that became one of his most elaborate reflections on the topic, he told Thomas Law, who had just sent him his *Second Thoughts on Instinctive Impulses* (1813), that this work "contained exactly my own *creed* on the foundation of morality in man [. . .]. [I]t shews how necessary was the care of the Creator in making the moral principle so much a part of our constitution as that no errors of reasoning or of speculation might lead us astray from it's [sic] observance in practice."[8] Along with his materialist "creed," Jefferson thus also had a secular moral "creed." He had laid out the nonscientific nature of this creed almost three decades earlier in a letter to his nephew Peter Carr. "I think it lost time to attend lectures in this branch," he had told him. "He who made us would have been a pitiful bungler if he had made the rules of our moral conduct a matter of science. [. . .] State a moral case to a ploughman & a professor. The former will decide it as well, & often better than the latter because he has not been led astray by artificial rules."[9]

In form as well as content, Jefferson's moral "creed" thus diminished the leading role Locke had assigned to reason and rational demonstration in moral questions. Whereas for Locke, morality along with mathematics had been the field where reason became most important, Jefferson regarded reason merely as a mental crutch for the morally disabled, whom the Creator had accidentally forgotten to supply with a moral sense. "[W]hen it is wanting we endeavor to supply the defect by education, by appeals to reason and calculation, by presenting to the being so unhappily conformed other motives to do good, and to eschew evil," he told Law.[10] His letter concluded with something that amounted to a confession of faith in instinct: "I sincerely then believe with you in the general existence of a moral instinct. I think it the brightest gem with which the human character is studded; and the want of it as more degrading than the most hideous of the bodily deformities." His only reservation concerned the sources Law had quoted in his book, to which Jefferson thought "might be added Ld Kaims, [. . .] who goes so far as to say, in his Principles of Natural religion, that a man owes no duty to which he is not urged by some impulsive feeling."

"Some Rational Creed"

Jefferson thus tended to downsize the role of reason, and even reasoning, for the sake of his unspecified moral "creed" in something that came closest to Kames's historicized version of the moral sense.[11] At first glance, Jefferson's stance on religion seems an exception to this tendency. Indeed, as the apostolic analogy suggests, his latter-day reputation as an "apostle of reason" likely stems from his religious views and has been transferred from there to other contexts. However, these transfers are often misleading, especially because, upon closer examination, reason had a closely circumscribed function in Jefferson's approach to religion as well. Instead of systematically distinguishing true from false belief, it merely served as one among several tools distinguishing his own subjective (materialist, moral, and, as will be discussed below, religious and political) "creeds" from the official creed of revealed religion, which he feared might be forced on the individual mind by outside authorities. It was thus less as a constructive tool to control questionable operations *within* the mind than as a deconstructive tool to counteract illegitimate forces *outside* the mind that the faculty of reason came into play for Jefferson. Whether inspired by versions of Locke's argument on the distinct domains of reason and faith,[12] or more likely following his early reading of Lord Bolingbroke,[13] Jefferson both preached and practiced a method of rationally interrogating religious revelation as a means to undermine clerical authority in the political world.

For example, when he thought that Peter Carr's reason had grown "mature enough to examine this object," he advised his seventeen-year-old nephew to "[f]ix reason firmly in her seat, and call to her tribunal every fact, every opinion. Question with boldness even the existence of a god; because, if there be one, he must more approve of the homage of reason, than that of blindfolded fear. [. . .] Read the bible then, as you would read Livy or Tacitus." In this historical-critical reading of the Bible, Jefferson announced, Carr would discover that the New Testament "is the history of a personage called Jesus." Carr's approach to this particular personage, in contrast to historical figures such as Henry IV,[14] was not supposed to be based on feeling. Instead, the young man had to rationally weigh "opposite pretensions 1. of those who say he was begotten by god, born of a virgin, suspended & reversed the laws of nature at will, & descended bodily into heaven: and 2. of those who say he was a man of illegitimate birth, of a benevolent heart, enthusiastic mind, who set out without pretensions to divinity, ended in believing them, & was punished capitally for sedition by being gibbeted according to the Roman law." Although the somewhat tendentious terms of this alternative thinly veiled Jefferson's own preferences, his point was less to convince Carr of the humanity of Jesus than to instruct him in a self-reliant use of his own mental faculties when approaching the New Testament. As Jefferson saw it, the question of inspiration was not supposed to be entirely dismissed ("The pretension is entitled to your inquiry, because millions believe it"), but had to be investigated anew by every reader, as part of an open-ended study.

The point of such studies was that they could produce different results; what was crucial for Jefferson was that "everyone must act according to the dictates of his *own* reason."[15] As his penchant for qualifying *reason* by possessive pronouns suggests, he regarded it less as a faculty able to provide universally valid insights than as a faculty that had to be used independently by each individual, with potentially varying outcomes.[16] Thus, he cared not primarily about the details of Carr's religious views but about the young man's methodological ability to divest himself of "all the fears & servile prejudices under which weak minds are servilely crouched." Jefferson's focus was less on religious content than on the political problems caused by "weak minds": the debilitating effects a dogmatically enforced religion could have on the mindset of the American citizenry, undermining its republican virtue by making it susceptible to fearful and servile deference to outside authorities.

Since he thought of revealed religion as the most likely factor to exert such a destructive influence in the new republic, it was in this field that Jefferson sang his most memorable paeans to reason as a weapon against the dogmatic imposition of an artificial creed on the minds of American citizens. A passage that soon became one of the most controversial passages of *Notes on the State of Virginia*, under Query XVII, "Religion," exemplifies this tendency. Lamenting the legal remnants of "religious slavery" in his home state, Jefferson appealed to "reason and free inquiry" to protect what he deemed the "natural rights" of "conscience." In his view, reason and free inquiry would "support true religion, by bringing every false one to their tribunal, to the test of their investigation." For Jefferson, the question of "true" or "false" religion was more a question of personal sincerity or "hypocrisy" than a doctrinal one. As he had argued in the preceding sentences about the case of an apostate, "[c]onstraint may make him worse by making him a hypocrite, but it will never make him a truer man."[17] Reason was supposed to answer the first rather than the second question. To find "true" (as opposed to hypocritical) religion, Jefferson later followed his own advice in what became known as the "Jefferson Bible," the two compilations he made of extracts from the New Testament, entitled "The Philosophy of Jesus" (1804) and "The Life and Morals of Jesus" (1819–20). His dissection of the Gospels—he literally used scissors to cut and paste from the Gospels in different translations and languages—was his analytical method of distinguishing between different degrees of probability, serving the larger goal of undermining the blind faith demanded by religious authorities. Jefferson worked on the premise he had commonplaced from Bolingbroke as a young man, that "[i]t is not true that Christ revealed an entire body of ethics, proved to be the law of nature from principles of reason, and reaching all the duties of life. if mankind wanted such [a] code, [. . .] such a code is still wanting; for the gospel is not such a code[.]"[18] Since the Gospel itself was unable to provide a universal rational standard, Jefferson thought with

Bolingbroke, such a standard could at best emerge if each individual mind was enabled to engage its own faculties in an open-ended reading process.

Despite its freethinking radicalism, Jefferson's rational method led him, in the words of Eugene Sheridan, "ultimately to an affirmation of faith rather than a rejection of religious belief."[19] In keeping with his Epicureanism and his project of diffusing useful knowledge, deciding on doctrinal truth could not be the priority for Jefferson, even as he admitted his personal inclination toward Unitarianism.[20] He was concerned, Sheridan argues, with "the quality of a person's life, not the truth of the doctrines in which he believed or the nature of the church to which he belonged."[21] Jefferson did not put rational reflection in the service of distinguishing systematically between true belief and false opinion. Instead, he pragmatically treated rationality as a function of the occasion: just as he relied on feeling in what he described as his materialist and moral "creeds," he relied on reason in his religious creed—or what he vaguely described as "some rational creed"[22]—because in this particular case he saw reason best equipped to counteract the rival creed threatening to be imposed on the mind by clerical authority. What ultimately mattered for Jefferson was to free all "operations of the mind," as he put it under Query XVII, from the "coercion of the laws."[23] For the survival of the new republic, he thought, it was crucial that American citizens follow the "unrestrained and unperverted operations of their *own* understandings"[24]—operations that possibly included rational reflection but were far from being organized or dominated by it.

"The Freedom of the Human Mind"

Thus, Jefferson's concept of reason was not entirely the "bogus authority" proposed by Paul Conkin,[25] but neither was it systematically separated from, much less exalted above, the other "operations of the mind." It was not particularly privileged in providing access to knowledge but merely served to support Jefferson in the "rational creed" of his personal religion, just as feeling supported him in his materialist and his moral "creeds." Taking a broad view of *reason* in Jefferson's rhetoric, his usage largely reflected this conceptual lack of profile. Strictly speaking, it would therefore be unfair to describe it with Conkin as deceptive and "demagogic," although the impression easily suggests itself. Due to its conceptual flatness, Jefferson was able to evoke *reason* in constellations so similar to his references to other terms, ranging from the ancient intellectual virtue of prudence to the senses, that one is often left to wonder where he drew the lines, or if he drew any. For example, he spoke of the "oracle of reason" and the "oracle of conscience" almost interchangeably;[26] and he could mean similar things when he urged that "reason," "common honesty," "common sense," "the good sense of the nation," and "republican sense" be given "fair play,"[27] or when he demanded that "reason," "thought," "opinion," the "understanding," or the "mind" be left "free."[28] Somehow, he implied, reason and related concepts would ensure fairness and freedom in the future, if only they were treated fairly and left free, themselves. In this circular usage, the unspecific meanings of *reason* tended to diffuse into the meanings of the various abstractions Jefferson liked to use in conjunction with *reason*, such as *liberty, truth, self-government, free inquiry, experiment, persuasion, science,* or *progress*. For instance, he expected "[r]eason and free inquiry" to win the day against error eventually,[29] while he thought that in a republican nation, with principles of "equal right and reason"[30] and a government by "reason and truth,"[31] citizens would be led by "reason and persuasion."[32] In these and many other examples, the terms accompanying *reason* tended to have so much greater weight that, had Jefferson employed one of today's competent copy editors to cut the Germanic length of his syntax down to size, *reason* could often have been eliminated from his sentences without taking away anything important from their content.

Like Jefferson's program of a "diffusion of knowledge," this "diffuse" rhetoric of rationality was useful for a revolutionary statesman who saw his main concern, not in refining or ascertaining his personal "creed" about how the human mind operates, but in effectively creating the social and political institutions that would best "preserve the freedom of the human mind."[33] However, Jefferson's diffuse rhetoric also exposed a central instability of his Enlightenment. This instability consisted in a subjectively "felt" empiricism combined with a strikingly *uncritical* concept of reason.[34] Although Jefferson's statements can easily sound critical in today's sense of critiquing outside authorities, they were far from critical in the contemporaneous Kantian sense of drawing identifiable lines between different mental operations and closely distinguishing between their respective purposes, potentials, and limits. Jefferson was very much aware, even expected, that individual reason, like the mind's other faculties and the senses, could err.[35] But instead of reflecting on the specific causes or characteristics of these errors, he remained content to promote qualified concepts of knowledge or "creeds." In this manner, he left the faculty of reason little room for knowing, and criticizing, itself. If, like Kant, Jefferson used legal metaphors to describe human rationality, these metaphors concerned the side of the "tribunal" or the "umpire" of reason rather than also that of the "plaintiff" and "defendant."[36] Such a one-sided epistemological courtroom made Jefferson's concept of reason sound more authoritative than it actually was: a tribunal able to pass judgments only over irrational culprits could afford to be conceptually quite superficial itself.

The fact that in Jefferson's language *reason* could be replaced so easily and was often in such dire need to be accompanied by related terms further testifies to its shallowness. In the Enlightenment of Feeling, reason was no longer God's reason, but neither was it able to stand by itself as a fully secular human rationality.[37] For his progressive expectations to work—for instance, that "reason and free inquiry" would somehow assign bounds to false opinion in the long run, if left truly "free"—he could rely on nothing inherent in the concept of a specifically human reason, but still needed the metaphysical support of the assumption that a divine rationality had ordered the universe accordingly. Due to his postcolonial "revolt" against Old World metaphysics,[38] however, he had put himself under great pressure not to admit to this need for metaphysical justification or grant human reason an important role in this field. He did his best to distract from this dilemma by moving the focus from his unacknowledged metaphysical premises to questions of political practice. If enlightened revolutionaries such as himself created political institutions able "to preserve the freedom of the human mind," the collective and cumulative diffusion of useful knowledge would vanquish prejudice and false opinion in the long term. Yet, while he thus succeeded rhetorically in hiding his metaphysics behind the screen of a secular future, he remained unable to solve the deeper conceptual problem: his "felt" Enlightenment had no consistent solution for distinguishing between knowledge and opinion in the short- and midterm. In the "mean time"[39] before all minds would eventually see the light in his republican millennium, democratic politics had to replace epistemology when "creeds" were becoming subject to majority decisions. As the next chapters will argue, this uncertainty at the heart of Jefferson's Enlightenment—a "felt" Enlightenment oriented toward subjective belief in the absence of full knowledge—could prove an asset when calling for democratic decisions based on (public) *opinion*. At the same time, however, his Enlightenment of Feeling turned out to be particularly vulnerable to occasions when opinion turned out to be *prejudice*.

❖ 3 ❖

Opinion Is Power

"My country will have my political creed in the form of a 'Declaration &c.' which I was lately directed to draw," Jefferson wrote home to Virginia in a letter to his college friend William Fleming on July 1, 1776. Long before what came to be known as the Declaration of Independence would begin to be associated with his name during the party conflicts of the 1790s,[1] Jefferson thus regarded the document as the expression of his "own sentiments" and his personal "political creed."[2] However, the more famous he became as the Declaration's "author" (a reputation he eventually wished to be carved into his tombstone), the more he made his personal creed retreat behind his concept of a national American creed. In the retrospective discussions of the 1820s surrounding his role in the history of the Declaration, he depicted himself as a man who had not hoped to find out "new principles, or new arguments, never before thought of," but had looked for the most persuasive expression of what he called "the American mind" or the "harmonizing sentiments of the day."[3] According to the retrospective image of himself Jefferson crafted in his final years, his "authorship" of the Declaration was not that of philosopher concerned with refining and ascertaining his provisional beliefs to obtain and convey new knowledge. Instead, he had been the literary medium of something he supposed to have been already in place when he first took up his quill in Philadelphia:[4] a preexisting entity that he would call, beginning in the mid-1780s, the "opinion of the people" or *public opinion*.[5] In keeping with his conceit of being less an individual writer expressing his "own sentiments" than a faithful scribe concerned with endowing public opinion with "the proper tone and spirit called for by the occasion,"[6] he claimed that he had deliberately refrained from defending his draft to Congress. Had the issue been either about deciding on the draft's closeness to universal truth or about expressing the personal "political creed" mentioned to Fleming, an active defense in Congress might have been in order. In retrospect, however, the issue for Jefferson had come to be about something in between the universal and the particular: the expression of a collective creed that supposedly made "it a duty to be, on that occasion, a passive auditor of the opinions of others, more impartial judges than I could be, of it's [the draft's] merits or demerits."[7]

Jefferson's claim that passively submitting to "the opinions of others" had been his "duty" was more than a retrospective effort to find an ingenious excuse for his shyness in Congress or console himself with congressional alterations to his draft that had in fact made him quite unhappy. The claim also harmonized with the epistemology of the Declaration of Independence itself. Especially in Jefferson's draft versions, the document was concerned much less with problems of *reason, knowledge,* and *certainty* than with problems of *feeling, opinion,* and *assent*. This holds true even of the passages usually deemed the most "scientific," such as the "facts" submitted to a "candid world" as proofs of the king's tyranny. In a passage eliminated by Congress, Jefferson had specified that these "facts" were, like his concept of "true" religion discussed in the previous chapter, a matter of subjective faith and personal sincerity rather than objective knowledge and impersonal truth ("To prove this let facts be submitted to a candid world *for the truth of which we pledge a faith yet unsullied by falsehood*").[8] In another deleted passage, Jefferson had spoken of "facts" that had "given the last stab to agonizing affection," causing Americans to "renounce forever these unfeeling brethren" and "forget our former love for them." *Facts* for Jefferson could be matters of feeling and love, tied to identitarian questions of "blood" relations, of "unfeeling brethren" in England who had been "permitting their chief magistrate to send over not only soldiers of our common blood, but Scotch & foreign mercenaries to invade & destroy us." According to the subjective, highly emotional facts of Jefferson's "felt" Enlightenment, the problem seemed not only being invaded and destroyed as such, but also by whom: being destroyed by someone of "common blood" was apparently preferable to receiving the last stab from a Hessian or a Scotsman.

The communal subjectivity of Jefferson's Enlightenment of Feeling also helps explain the Declaration's most prominent feature: the oft-discussed replacement of the third item in the Lockean triad of "life, liberty and estate" with "the pursuit of happiness."⁹ This replacement deliberately left open the question of whether or not *happiness* included (slave) property: by focusing on the subjective realm of emotional experience, Jefferson enabled both interpretations but committed to neither. In keeping with his overall focus on feeling rather than reason, the long second sentence of the Declaration even mentions *happiness* twice, concluding with the goal to build a new government "on such principles, & organizing it's [*sic*] powers in such form, as to them [the people] shall seem most likely to effect their safety & happiness." The subjectively enjoyed right of pursuing happiness thus becomes even more subjective, limiting itself to the communal standpoint of the people's accidental perceptions of appearances ("as to them shall seem") and probabilities ("most likely"). Jefferson's second version of *happiness* further relativizes the universalism of the first, reducing what initially appears to be a universal principle to merely "*such* principles" as are deemed most useful by the people at a given moment in their history. Whether "*such* principles" happened to suggest abolishing or maintaining slavery, they were allowed to dominate the meaning of the sentence in its entirety. Thus, the decisive moral problem of Jefferson's Declaration was not what is often discussed as the question of whether the "men" in "all men are created equal" included African Americans or women, for instance. (Among the few words that were capitalized in Jefferson's "original rough draught" of the document, after all, "MEN" explicitly referred to the men, women, and children who were the victims of the Atlantic slave trade, described as "cruel war against human nature itself.")¹⁰ Rather than in its definition of humanity, the decisive moral problem of the Declaration of Independence—and the one that the protagonists of part 2 of this book sought to remedy—has to be found in the self-conscious weakness of its truth claims, that is, in its insistence on expressing nothing but the contingent standpoint of a national community of feeling on its own historically variable collective affects.

This communally constrained perspective not only shaped the lesser-known ending of the Declaration's second sentence; it also defined its famous beginning, "We hold these truths to be self-evident." What Hannah Arendt has described as an "incongruous phrase"¹¹ is sometimes interpreted today as having made truth a key factor in American history.¹² Understood as part of Jefferson's subjectively "felt" Enlightenment, however, the phrase was less concerned with conveying universal knowledge of "the" truth than with expressing a nationally shared opinion on the nature of an array of particular truths. Ironically one of the least self-evident terms in the enlightened vocabulary, as Frank Kelleter has remarked, *self-evidence* was supposed to characterize truths that were compelling on their own terms rather than being established by assent, consent, or a majority decision.[13] It was precisely this distinction that was elided by the subjectivist emphasis of Jefferson's "We hold." As Michael Zuckert has argued, by emphasizing the process of *holding* truths *to be* self-evident rather than unequivocally stating that they *were* self-evident, "an element of subjectivity and an element of hesitation [we]re introduced into a judgment which should be the most epistemologically solid possible."[14] The ambiguous "We" of the Declaration[15] could not actually know what it claimed as the most certain form of knowledge. While the phrases to follow (starting with "all men are created equal") were characterized as true, they were not, in themselves, *self-evidently* true in any strict sense. The reason was not so much that they might not have had to be declared otherwise. By many eighteenth-century accounts, self-evident ideas had to be "underived and underivable" from other ideas, criteria impossible to fulfill in the syllogistic structure of this part of the Declaration.[16] By replacing the original "sacred and undeniable" by *self-evident*, the draft committee went further in suggesting that the collective subject holding "these truths to be self-evident" was not only holding an opinion (or expressing a belief) rather than imparting knowledge: strictly speaking, it was even holding a false opinion. And not only was it holding a false opinion on its own access to "these truths," but by stubbornly holding them "as if" self-evident, it effectively closed the door to indicating a more reliable method of ascertaining their truthfulness. As a result, the incongruous combination of the highly subjective "We hold" with the overstated claim that what was being held was "self-evident" paradoxically risked dragging the whole array of the Declaration's truth claims into the realm of uncertainty.

In the reception history of the Declaration of Independence, Jefferson's flirtation with uncertainty (also due to his postcolonial refusal, discussed earlier, to grant human reason a role in legitimizing his metaphysical premises) became its major weakness. For instance, nineteenth-century proslavery thinkers would go all the way to doubt, not only the self-evidence but also the truth of its principles.[17] However, Jefferson's willingness to forgo full certainty in the Declaration had strong roots in the general inclination of his Enlightenment to privilege feeling and opinion over reason and knowledge. His drafting of the Declaration of Independence was the moment bringing to light, along with its greatest problem, the greatest advantage of his reliance on opinion in the context of republican founding: unlike knowledge of the truth, which, as he liked to point out, could "stand by itself,"[18] opinion required assent.

Paralleling the political concept of *consent* of the governed among the Declaration's truths, the epistemological concept of *assent* to its propositions[19] became the basis of the nationally shared set of beliefs, the dynamic American "creed" that had supposedly employed Jefferson as its faithful scribe. As has plausibly been argued following Hannah Arendt, the Declaration's "truths would never manifest themselves in the political realm [. . .] unless they were validated by the judgment of others. [. . .] So the people were never mere spectators in Jefferson's account of the Revolution, which was never simply the work of a handful of great men."[20] The great egalitarian potential of inviting the people "into the process of judging"[21] was, despite all its problems, foundational to Jefferson's democratic idea of American citizens who "*became* truly equal" by virtue of their own active "participation in the 'common cause.'"[22] Whereas, for instance, the French Declaration of the Rights of Man and of the Citizen of 1789 would form its argument according to the aristocratic, trickle-down structure of universal knowledge ("considering ignorance, forgetfulness, or contempt of the rights of man to be the only causes of public misfortunes and the corruption of Governments"),[23] the Declaration of Independence, especially in Jefferson's draft version, derived its legitimacy from the bottom-up, democratic structure of opinion (or, at most, a collaborative concept of cumulatively diffusing *useful* knowledge). Its egalitarian epistemology also concerned the world beyond the United States. In the Declaration's first paragraph, "the opinions of mankind" mirror the collective opinion held by the American "We" of the second paragraph. In this sense, opinion, not knowledge, was the first among the historical "causes which impel[led]" American colonials to independence. The Declaration's opening evoked a nation that emerged out of the "decent respect" a dynamic American public opinion offered to, and asked from, the "opinions of mankind," no matter what each opinion's relationship to truth. In the decades to follow, this historical causality continued to inform Jefferson's practical and theoretical engagement with a concept of *public opinion* as "the basis of our governments."[24]

"The Basis of Our Governments"

What has often been discussed, especially following Abraham Lincoln's rhetoric, as the "promise" of the Declaration of Independence for a more inclusive American future[25] had not likely been intended as a promise by Jefferson, the Committee of Five, or the Continental Congress. Instead, what became the Declaration's powerful historical dynamic that can make it look like a (fulfilled or unfulfilled) promise in retrospect, was rooted in the epistemological flexibility of Jefferson's Enlightenment of subjective feeling and assent, with its peculiar blend of conviction and uncertainty.[26] Jefferson most clearly revealed his insight into the benefits of uncertainty in politics—the precariously "illusive" and morally ambiguous origins of the power of opinion—in the context of European, not American history. "Belgium, Prussia, Poland, Lombardy Etc. are now offered a representative organization: illusive probably at first, but it will grow into power in the end," he told John Adams in 1816. "Opinion is power, and that opinion will come."[27]

Deceiving benighted post-Vienna Europeans on the nature of their governments was a good thing, Jefferson suggested, because the "illusion" of being politically represented would at least teach them the right public opinion in the end. In his reply, Adams claimed to agree. Yet between the lines, he remained skeptical of what he may have seen, at best, as Jefferson's wishful thinking, but at worst, as his somewhat cynical, manipulative neglect of the question of truthfulness. Instead of opinion, Adams stressed the importance of knowledge: "Your Speculations into Futurity in Europe are so probable that I can suggest no doubts to their disadvantage. All will depend on the Progress of Knowledge. But how shall Knowledge Advance? Independent of Temporal and Spiritual Power, the Course of Science and Litterature is obstructed by so many Causes that it is to be feared, their motions will be slow."[28]

As discussed above, Jefferson was no stranger to stressing the importance of the progress of (useful) knowledge. Especially when promoting his idea of the University of Virginia, he could be moved to elaborate on the maxim attributed to Francis Bacon[29] "that knoledge [sic] is power" by adding "that knoledge is safety, and that knoledge is happiness."[30] Arguably, however, Jefferson was more deeply interested in the power of opinion, a power that he took to be of such crucial political import that toward the end of his life he described it as "lord of the Universe."[31] His fascination with opinion's universal reign went back to his student days. As a young man he had freely expressed his impatience with the need for attaining knowledge ("But the old-fellows say we must read to gain knowledge; and gain knowledge to make us happy and be admired. Mere jargon!" he had exclaimed to his friend John Page in 1762).[32] In about the same period, long before he would encounter the fashionable term *public opinion* in France in the 1780s, he had voluntarily begun to commonplace difficult philosophical reflections on collective opinion. For example, his first entry from Lord Bolingbroke in his *Literary Commonplace Book* suggests his attraction to the idea that even the Bible may have been written with an eye to an early form, if not of public opinion, at least of popular opinion ("the gross conceptions of the people").[33] While this idea may have helped shape his historical approach to religious revelation in particular, another argument he recorded at length in his *Legal Commonplace Book* may have been foundational to his political thought at large: Montesquieu's "psychologization" of philosophical and political liberty in book 12 of *The Spirit of the Laws*.[34] As part of his mitigating attitude to political universals that was arguably more moral than prudential,[35] Montesquieu had defined these two forms of liberty as "mere" opinions[36] of free will and security, respectively. As he argued in a passage Jefferson commonplaced in its entirety, "[p]hilosophic liberty consists in the exercise of one's will, or at least in the opinion that one exercises one's will. Political liberty consists in security, or at least in the opinion that one has security."[37]

From early on Jefferson showed a deeper philosophical interest in opinion. His favorite novel may have affirmed him in this interest: the first volume (1759) of Laurence Sterne's *The Life and Opinions of Tristram Shandy, Gentleman*, which he owned in various editions to fit the sizes of his different pockets, was headed by a motto from the Stoic philosopher Epictetus, "Men are tormented not by things themselves, but by opinions about them."[38] Against the backdrop of Whiggish celebrations of *opinion* as the civilized alternative to physical force,[39] Montesquieu's psychologization of liberty—suggesting that liberty was as much a matter of subjective opinion as of objective knowledge—may have appealed to Jefferson also because it helped defuse important problems in his various "creeds." In his materialist, moral, and religious creeds, in which the question of free will always ran a certain risk of being negated by the necessity of "organic" instinct and feeling, the idea that the subjective opinion of free will was a sufficient criterion for philosophical liberty mitigated the danger of determinism. And in his political creed, Montesquieu's emphasis on opinion lent a new respectability to its "illusive" origins, helping Jefferson develop *public opinion* as a semi-secularized concept that was legitimately mediating between the universal and the particular, and between truth and untruth. A famous passage under Query XVIII, "Manners," of *Notes on the State of Virginia* seems especially indebted to Montesquieu's subjectivist account of liberty. Characteristically, Jefferson located the "only firm basis" of Virginian liberties neither in God nor in the Virginian people, but in the collective opinion mediating between the two: "a conviction *in the minds of the people* that these liberties are the gift of God."[40]

During his years as American envoy and ambassador in Paris from 1784 until 1789, Jefferson entered more concretely into the French discussions on *public opinion* among the generations succeeding Montesquieu.[41] For example, he used the term when, around 1788, he began translating into English the *Réflexions sur l'esclavage des nègres* (1781) by Jean-Antoine-Nicolas Caritat, Marquis de Condorcet. Jefferson's translation never reached the point where the marquis developed his plan for gradual abolition but stalled early in Condorcet's introductory remarks on the natural equality of "colour" and the opening chapter on the injustice of slavery. To judge from the changes in the manuscript, Jefferson went to great pains to translate a complicated sentence in which Condorcet refused to condone slavery on the grounds of what he merely called *l'opinion* and what Jefferson translated more specifically as *public* opinion.[42] This change in emphasis may not have been accidental. In the preceding year, Jefferson had spent some time reflecting on *public opinion* in a letter to his fellow Virginian Edward Carrington. Although a term very much *à la mode* in Paris on the eve of the Revolution, public opinion was not associated in Jefferson's thought with civilization or a modern public sphere. In the letter, he first used the term when referring to "those societies (as the Indians) which live without government," but among whom "public opinion is in the place of law, and restrains morals as powerfully as laws ever did anywhere." As a result, Jefferson claimed, Indian societies "enjoy[ed] in their general mass an infinitely greater degree of happiness than those who live under European governments."[43]

This use of *public opinion* as a key transhistorical element of a "conjectural" approach to American history[44] had important implications for Jefferson's political thought. When composing *Notes on the State of Virginia* a few years earlier on the other side of the Atlantic, Jefferson had still used the term *manners* to describe the same phenomenon in Native societies ("Their only controuls are their manners").⁴⁵ In the late 1770s, he had commonplaced a similar argument by Montesquieu claiming that with the early Romans *mœurs* sufficed to control their slaves; it was only when Rome became so powerful as to lose its mores that laws had to be introduced to protect cruel slave masters "who lived in the midst of their slaves as among their enemies."⁴⁶ With his conjectural history of primitive governments based on opinion or manners historically preceding modern governments based on laws, Jefferson roughly followed what may be termed the ancient etymological narrative of *nomos*, that is, a historical narrative that paralleled the semantic history of a term whose meanings had evolved in ancient Greek from Pindar and Herodotus's sense of "manners" or "custom" to its later reference of (conventional) "law" among the Sophists, who opposed it to *physis* and natural law.⁴⁷ For Jefferson, both *public opinion* and its intellectual precursor, *manners*,⁴⁸ mediated between particular convention and universal nature (including nature's God). While their specific forms and contents were subject to historical change in time and space (or, as he put it three decades later, "manners and opinions change with the change of circumstances"),⁴⁹ they had the same psychological function in every human society of morally "restraining" and "controlling" its members.⁵⁰ The letter to Carrington was not mainly concerned with the "Indian" stage of American conjectural history, but with the recent "tumults" in western Massachusetts that would become known as Shays's Rebellion. Parallel to his argument under Query XVIII, "Manners," that "the only firm basis" of Virginian liberties had to be found "in the minds of the people,"⁵¹ Jefferson told Carrington that in the American republic, "the opinions of the people" formed "the basis of our governments." With this idea he was superimposing a dialectical element on the temporal dimension of the etymological narrative of *nomos*. Not only had the rule of law *followed* the rule of manners and opinion in the transition from Native to Anglo-American societies; since public opinion formed "the basis of our governments," the rule of law also *followed from* American manners and opinion. This double layer in conjectural history produced an overdetermined concept of public opinion, which was never for Jefferson a flatly descriptive category approaching today's use of the term (assessed by polling, for example) but had to be capable of designating at once the contingent historical and the necessary moral origin of American government.

This conceptual overdetermination was at the root of Jefferson's difficulty with achieving a nuanced understanding of historical developments in which American public opinion was *not* on what he considered to be the right side of history. His arguments were most consistent in situations when public opinion seemed to go in a direction that he welcomed politically. As long as he could assume, as after the landslide victory of his second presidential election in 1805, that there was a national "union of sentiment" promising an "entire union of opinion,"[52] the concept appeared an uncomplicated part of what is often described as his "faith" in the common people. He had experimented with such a concept in Europe in the years leading up to the French Revolution, when he had been telling his correspondents at home and abroad that the "revolution," the "force," or the "weight" of French public opinion was peacefully reducing the absolute power of the monarchy.[53] In Jefferson's retrospective vision of the American Revolution, there supposedly had been "but one opinion on this side of the water,"[54] and opinion seemed to coincide with both moral progress and geography. The same seemed to hold true for the opinion tsunami that he identified with the "Revolution of 1800," the peaceful transition of power following his election to the presidency in 1801. In a famous letter to Joseph Priestley, he celebrated the "mighty wave of public opinion" that had not only washed him into the presidency of an extensive republic but also succeeded in "quickly subsiding over such an extent of surface to it's [sic] true level again."[55] To Jefferson in such situations, American public opinion seemed not only an extraordinarily powerful force of nature but also an extraordinarily well-behaved one. His main point in discussing public opinion was not to depict its need of being "refined" or "enlarged," as James Madison emphasized.[56] To put this in simplified terms, compared to David Hume's understanding of public opinion as "veneration" of government and Madison's stress on public opinion's "vigilance" over both government and itself, Jefferson's homogenizing approach went further in emphasizing something like "self-veneration" *as* government: its articulation "enabled the people to be an ongoing force in government as well as its original source."[57]

As will be shown in part 2 of this book, the soft power of Jefferson's concept of public opinion was to develop its own historical dynamic in the following centuries. Contrary to Martin Luther King's famous interpretation in 1963, the Declaration of Independence had not actually been intended as a "promissory note" for a more diverse American republic.[58] The Declaration's progressive potential consisted instead in the peculiar blend of modesty and arrogance in the Enlightenment of Feeling, its tendency to forgo full knowledge for the sake of creed and opinion. Ironically, it turned out to be precisely the flexibility of Jefferson's semi-secularized faith in public opinion that would eventually mobilize Americans to keep a promise where none had been made.

"But Is Uniformity of Opinion Desireable?"

Despite his faith in public opinion, Jefferson remained aware of its latent instabilities. As discussed from John Locke to John Stuart Mill, opinions had a strong tendency to *appear* self-evident, since they were typically "held" and declared rather than rationally interrogated.[59] For Locke, who had in mind the confessional wars of the seventeenth century, the problem with opinion was that it could rely not only on judgments that were false but on judgments that were no judgments at all: "May we not find a great number (not to say the greatest part) of men that [. . .] imagine themselves to have judged right only because they never questioned, never examined their own opinions? Which is indeed to think they judged right because they never judged at all; and yet these of all men hold their opinions with the greatest stiffness, those being generally the most fierce and firm in their tenets who have least examined them."[60] In other words, the most tenacious opinions could in reality be mere "shortcuts" to judgment[61] that seemed to be self-evident precisely because they were so unfounded. The problem of such "shortcut" judgments, at the point on a spectrum where opinions turned out to be prejudices, was complicated by seventeenth- and eighteenth-century theories of the mind that downplayed the will in the formation of opinion.[62] Jefferson's Enlightenment of moral instinct and organic feeling, in which, as discussed above, the subjective "opinion" of free will sufficed for philosophical liberty,[63] was a natural ally to such theories. Rather than grounding the freedom of opinion in property rights, as did his friend James Madison,[64] he embraced a theory of involuntary opinion in both his 1777 draft of the Virginia Bill for Establishing Religious Freedom and under Queries XVII and XVIII of *Notes on the State of Virginia*. Since "opinions and belief of men depend not on their own will, but follow involuntarily the evidence proposed to their minds," he argued in the opening passage that failed to make it into the act that was eventually passed in 1786, "religious opinion" should not be "object to civil government, nor under its jurisdiction [. . .] any more than our opinions in physics or geometry." Lurking behind Jefferson's theory of involuntary opinion was still Locke's seventeenth-century fear of the dangers of a "conversion economy of belief":[65] When the state began to meddle in (religious) opinions, political chaos was near because opinions and beliefs could not be changed at will.

Since the formation of opinion was an involuntary, quasi-physiological process for Jefferson, legal coercion of opinion not only risked civil war, it would also fail to seriously convince anyone. As he argued under Query XVII, "Religion," if the coercion of opinion did not result in "millions of innocent men, women, and children [. . .] burnt, tortured, fined, imprisoned," it would at best succeed in making "half of the world fools, and the other half hypocrites."[66] Jefferson followed Locke's arguments for tolerating a "*diversity of opinions,* since we cannot reasonably expect that anyone should readily and obsequiously quit his own opinion, and embrace ours with a blind resignation to authority, which the understanding of man acknowledges not."[67] For Locke as for Jefferson, the achievement of uniform opinions was a questionable end in itself. "And why subject it [religious opinion] to coercion?" Jefferson asked under XVII. "To produce uniformity. But is uniformity of opinion desireable? No more than of face and stature. Introduce the bed of Procrustes then, and as there is danger that the large men may beat the small, make us all of a size, by lopping the former and stretching the latter."[68] Just a few years earlier, in the period when he was engaged with the revisal of Virginia laws,[69] Jefferson had excerpted from book 29 of Montesquieu's *Spirit of the Laws* a controversial passage on uniformity that may have inspired his warning of a Procrustean bed in religious opinion. "There are certain ideas of uniformity that sometimes take hold in great spirits, but that unfailingly strike small ones," Jefferson had commonplaced Montesquieu. "They find there a perfection that they recognize because it is impossible not to discover it; the same weights in the police, the same measures in commerce, the same laws in a state, the same religion in all its parts. But is this always appropriate, without exception? Is the harm of changing always less great than the harm of suffering? And the greatness of genius, does it not consist in better knowing in which case uniformity is necessary and in which case there must be differences?"[70]

Montesquieu's antipathy to Procrustean one-size-fits-all solutions was harshly criticized by three thinkers whom Jefferson admired. Destutt de Tracy's *Commentary and Review of Montesquieu's Spirit of Laws* (1811), which Jefferson helped translate into English and anonymously publish with William Duane in Philadelphia, included a chapter of remarks posthumously attributed to the Marquis de Condorcet as well as two letters attributed to Claude-Adrien Helvétius.[71] While Helvétius (or Pseudo-Helvétius)[72] went on record in the *Commentary and Review* chiding his friend Montesquieu for his general "compromise with prejudice," Condorcet's remarks on book 29 of the *Spirit* specifically ridiculed the passage Jefferson had commonplaced on uniformity as "one of the most curious chapters of the book," which "obtained for Montesquieu the indulgence of all the prejudiced people." The *philosophe* and mathematician retrospectively rebuked Montesquieu for his relativism: "As truth, reason, justice, the rights of man, the interests of property, of liberty, of security, are in all places the same; we cannot discover why all the provinces of the state, or even all states, should not have the same [. . .] laws [. . .]. A good law should be good for all men. A true proposition is true every where. Those laws which appear as if it should be necessary they should be different in different countries [. . .] are founded on prejudices and customs which should be extinguished." For Condorcet as published in Tracy's *Commentary and Review*, Montesquieu's "spirit of moderation" was in truth a "spirit of uncertainty which alters by a hundred little irrelative motives, the principles of justice, which are in themselves invariable."[73]

In its emphasis on subjective feeling and opinion, as has been shown, Jefferson's Enlightenment was often more akin to what Condorcet decried as Montesquieu's "spirit of uncertainty" than to the rational certainty of universal mathematical knowledge that Condorcet saw as the basis of his own "spirit of justice."[74] That Jefferson was so keen on seeing Tracy's critical *Commentary and Review* published in America did not mean that he uniformly agreed with all of its claims. As he admitted to Duane when first recommending its publication, "I will not venture to say that every sentiment in the book will be approved: because [. . .] I have not read the whole but so much only as might enable me to estimate the soundness of the author's way of viewing his subject."[75] Jefferson's position has to be located in the middle between that of Montesquieu, whom he commonplaced extensively, but whom he never forgave what he saw as his "predilection" for the British monarchy,[76] and the universalist critique, by Tracy, Condorcet, and Helvétius, of Montesquieu's "spirit of uncertainty," that is, of his focus on manners, opinions, and prejudices instead of certain knowledge.

This middle position between Montesquieu and the more radically universalist *philosophes* shaped Jefferson's argument on the role of manners and public opinion in the slavery question, in the chapter immediately following his discussion of uniformity under Query XVII. For Jefferson under Query XVIII, "Manners," slavery was the most difficult test case for the question of uniform opinions.⁷⁷ In a nation increasingly divided in its opinions on this subject, he regarded Virginia slavery as the most dangerous example of opinions and manners that were quite uniform, but uniformly wrong. At the same time, he did not think that the problem could be solved by imposing on Virginia citizens laws that were uniformly right. At least from *Notes on the State of Virginia* onward, he typically tried to moderate between the extremes of uniformity, arguing that public opinion on slavery had to gradually evolve and "ripen" rather than undergo a sudden transformation. As he put it under Query VIII, "Population," it was important to pass laws ending the Atlantic slave trade to "stop the increase of this great political and moral evil," but the evil itself could only be stopped after "the minds of our citizens" had been "ripening for a complete emancipation of human nature."⁷⁸ Following the etymological narrative of *nomos*, Jefferson depicted it as essential that the organic "ripening" process of manners and public opinion precede laws ending slavery rather than the other way around. In his *Legal Commonplace Book,* he had noted various instances of a gradual refinement of manners slowly "preparing" the introduction of morally progressive laws. "Moral duties, originally weak and feeble," he had excerpted from Lord Kames's *Historical Law-Tracts,* "acquire great strength by refinement of manners."⁷⁹ Or as he had commonplaced Kames's contemporary and fellow Scotsman, the lawyer and historian John Dalrymple, on the history of feudal England, women's "rights were attended to" when the moment had arrived "when the manners of men were softened" and the military "barbarity of the feudal times" had disappeared.⁸⁰ Likewise, English villainage had been abolished at the historical moment when "peaceable manners made the minds of men be shocked with the bondage of their fellow creatures."⁸¹

Similarly to his approach to the individual mind, Jefferson expected the "public mind"⁸² to be liable to error—certainly during the far from peaceful times when he composed *Notes on the State of Virginia*—but he thought that actively correcting these errors could not have the priority; it was more important to ensure that American citizens follow the "unrestrained and unperverted operations of their *own* understandings."⁸³ False opinions in the individual mind should not be "coerced" or "restrained" by laws: as Jefferson argued in the first inaugural address, even citizens aiming "to dissolve this Union or to change its republican form" should be allowed to "stand undisturbed as monuments to the safety with which error of opinion may be tolerated where reason is left free to combat it."⁸⁴ Analogously, what he criticized as corrupt manners or errors of public opinion on slavery—most of all, Virginians' heresy against the quasi-religious belief that their "liberties" were "the gift of God" and thus extended to all human beings[85]—should not be forced to take a different direction. Jefferson's critique of slavery under Query XVIII, "Manners," in *Notes on Virginia* thus attacked the institution first as an epistemological and only secondly as a legal or constitutional problem. Instead of legal coercion, his theory of involuntary opinion inclined him to rely on epistemological coercion: as he expressed it under Query XVIII, "[w]e must be contented to hope that they [antislavery ideas] will *force* their way into every one's mind."[86]

The paradox of liberty and necessity in minds that were left "free" only to be "forced" by empirical evidence helped Jefferson conceive of slavery primarily as a problem of white Virginians' manners and beliefs. The implications of this relegation of slavery to the realm of public opinion were profound. As has been shown, Jefferson's morally overdetermined concept of public opinion could be temporarily, but never fundamentally wrong. In the letter to Carrington discussed above, for instance, he spoke of "keeping" public opinion "right." Keeping it right (rather than actively rectifying it) could only be effected by two indirect factors. One was a free press ("newspapers without a government" rather than "government without newspapers," as he polemically told Carrington). The other was a "sound education," which, as he put it three decades later concerning the University of Virginia, could be expected to give a "wholesome direction to *Public opinion*, the safest guide and guardian of the public morals & welfare, the Arbitress, in every nation, of it's [sic] destinies to happiness or wretchedness, & the source to which, as either pure or corrupted, the changes of condition in every country on earth may be traced and ascribed."[87]

The obvious problem with Jefferson's involuntary, overdetermined concept of *public opinion*—"arbitress" and potentially arbitrary, at once the source and the recipient of (indirect) direction—was that the notion of its ripening process was by necessity "conjectural."[88] That is, the conviction of its morally progressive character was built on the sand of the greatest instability of Jefferson's Enlightenment: it had to rely on metaphysical premises that his antimetaphysical philosophy could only acknowledge by displacing them into the remote secular past or the remote secular future of conjectural history. In Jefferson's account of American public opinion, therefore, its wholesome "ripening" process could hardly fail to take a long time. Jefferson's intellectual modesty in outsourcing the attainment of full knowledge into a better future, concerning both individual and collective opinions, remains important today in its support of the freedom of opinion, of scientific inquiry, religion, and the press. In dealing with slavery, however, the "spirit of uncertainty" of an Enlightenment privileging subjective opinion over objective knowledge ran the danger of morphing into what Condorcet and Helvétius in Tracy's *Commentary and Review* had criticized as a "compromise with prejudice."

❖ 4 ❖

Deep-Rooted Prejudices

Under Query XIV of *Notes on the State of Virginia*, "Laws," Jefferson made it plain that his respect for the opinions of Virginia citizens could extend to their prejudices. In the context of slavery, he thought that the opinions held by white Virginians relied on judgments that were manifestly false; even, as discussed above, on "shortcuts" to judgment[1] that were in truth no judgments at all, but prejudgments or prejudices. Nevertheless, his plans for a revisal of the laws in his home state treated these prejudices as a major political factor to be respected, rather than reformed, by republican lawmakers. Explaining to the American and European audiences of *Notes*[2] why he burdened his plans for an end of slavery by a costly and complicated colonization scheme that would require the formerly enslaved population to leave the state, he argued: "Deep rooted prejudices entertained by the whites; ten thousand recollections, by the blacks, of the injuries they have sustained; new provocations; the real distinctions which nature has made; and many other circumstances, will divide us into parties, and produce convulsions which will probably never end but in the extermination of one or the other race."[3]

What Jefferson classified here as "political" objections to the "incorporation" of "blacks"[4] into the republic—the reasons for party conflicts he expected to produce an existential threat to the body politic—is followed by a much longer discussion of "physical and moral" objections.[5] This discussion has received a great deal of attention over the past half century as the main source of Jefferson's ideas about *race*.[6] A problem that has remained underexplored is its relation to the concession of white Virginians' "deep rooted prejudices" that introduces it. *Prejudice* was a central concept in eighteenth-century discussions about the nature and goals of Enlightenment, and, whether in regard to "color" or "condition," it became one of the major terms in nineteenth-century debates about what today would be called *racism*.[7] Emerging from its original legal and rhetorical contexts in the late seventeenth century, prejudice could range with concepts such as superstition or enthusiasm as possible antitheses of Enlightenment, or as modes of perceiving, thinking, or judging that the Enlightenment was supposed to overcome. However, the self-reflective "epistemological liberalizations" of the late Enlightenment's anthropological turn and the Science of Man complicated the rationalist critique of prejudice.[8] Material definitions oriented toward the criterion of truth and error were increasingly complemented by formal or "modal" definitions that tended to understand prejudice as preliminary judgment rather than falsity. These definitions saw in prejudice "a condition of truth-seeking rather than its other," moving the focus "from the *products* of knowledge-production to the *process* itself."[9] Although this processual focus received a new emphasis in the late eighteenth century, it had been discussed from the outset of the Scientific Revolution. At least since Francis Bacon's conception of *idols* as "deep rooted" mental dispositions that distorted human experience,[10] the attempt to overcome prejudices had been understood as a necessary part of every scientific endeavor.

Contrary to twentieth-century clichés of a supposedly one-dimensional "prejudice against prejudice" in the Enlightenment,[11] at least a lukewarm acceptance of prejudice thus always lurked on the horizon. Degrees of acceptance ranged from pragmatic emphases on its ubiquity and inevitability (for example, in Locke's advice that "every man should let alone others' prejudices and examine his own. No body is convinced of his by the accusation of another")[12] to "positive good" contestations of the personal or group-specific, temporary or even permanent benefits of prejudice (most famously in Edmund Burke's praise for the "latent wisdom" of "just prejudice" in *Reflections on the Revolution in France*).[13] Partial rehabilitations of prejudice could appear in different forms in the late eighteenth century. They often built on earlier discussions, such as Michel de Montaigne's acknowledgment of the therapeutic functions of prejudice for the achievement of inner peace and tranquility[14] or Pierre Bayle's occasional insight, as Benjamin Rush paraphrased him, that in order to do good to mankind it could be necessary to conform "in some measure" to its prejudices rather than "principles."[15] A similar pragmatism concerning prejudice characterized, for instance, James Madison's claim in *The Federalist* No. 49 that "in any other nation [than a nation of philosophers], the most rational government will not find it a superfluous advantage to have the prejudices of the community on its side."[16]

Among late Enlightenment thinkers, such attenuated views of prejudice tended to coexist with the emphatic expressions of disdain for prejudice that are more commonly associated with the period today, for instance, in the *Essai sur les préjugés* by the Baron d'Holbach.[17] This essay, which d'Holbach at the time of its publication in 1770 tried to attribute to the late Encyclopedist César Chesneau Du Marsais, became famous as the starting point of a debate with Frederick II of Prussia on the necessity of reforming prejudice among "the people"—a debate that included the prize question of the Prussian Academy of Sciences in 1780 of whether it was useful for the people to be left in, or even led into, error ("Est-il utile au peuple d'être trompé, soit qu'on l'induise dans les nouvelles erreurs, ou qu'on l'entretienne dans celles où il est?").[18] Jefferson is not likely to have subscribed to the paternalistic cynicism of the Prussian monarch, who condescendingly considered prejudice to be "the reason of the people" ("Les préjugés sont la raison du peuple"). In the context of slavery, nevertheless, he was able to understand the "deep rooted prejudices" he assigned to the collectivity of Virginia "whites" as a major political factor ruling out African American citizenship, without suggesting an immediate remedy. Jefferson certainly did not understand prejudice as "the reason of the people" in Virginia, to be manipulated by the superior rational insights of enlightened rulers and self-identified philosopher kings. His claims about a generic "white" prejudice had another goal in view: not, as in enlightened absolutism, to facilitate the reign of monarchical reason but to exemplify a new American culture of knowledge in which republican leaders could not be expected to be categorically less prejudiced than the mass of the people. Against the backdrop of Old World debates on a hierarchy between monarchical reason and popular prejudice, Jefferson "leveled up" the racist prejudices of white Virginians by granting them the status of a legitimate factor in republican lawmaking, while performatively "leveling down" his own perspective to that of his less enlightened countrymen:[19] "Aware of the bias of self love & prejudice in myself," as he put it in 1784,[20] he admitted to sharing the "deep rooted prejudices" he diagnosed among his fellow citizens. While he condemned prejudice in the abstract, it may have been especially his opposition to European-style intellectual hierarchies that inclined him to offer, as will be discussed further below, an impressive specimen also of his *own* prejudice under Query XIV.

However, the prejudices Jefferson paraded under XIV not only served to illustrate the egalitarianism of his approach to knowledge, setting his postcolonial Enlightenment off against the elitist rationalism of the Old World's "wretched philosophy" (and wretched philosopher kings);[21] they also defined the boundaries of his worldview in another direction. In an imperfectly parallel construction, Jefferson's opening phrase opposed "deep rooted prejudices entertained by the whites" to "ten thousand recollections, by the blacks, of the injuries they have sustained." The term *recollections* is instructive here. The fact that Jefferson emphasized *recollections* suggests that he imagined African Americans not "just" as *men*[22] but, following the distinction of Locke's influential discussion of personal identity, as (legal) *persons* as well, "whose consciousness can extend backwards to any past action or thought."[23] Thus, although Jefferson unlike Locke did not use the term *identity* in this context, what he arguably did under Query XIV was nothing less than extend Locke's discussion of *personal identity* to the collective level of national and "racial" identity.

Query XIV illustrates this far-reaching conceptual innovation by drawing a sharp dividing line between what Jefferson thought were two collective forms of consciousness forming two separate identities. For instance, whereas it qualifies the prejudices of "whites," it merely quantifies the recollections of "blacks." And instead of more plausibly pairing "numberless afflictions"[24] with "numberless" recollections, Jefferson chose to introduce the random mathematical figure of "ten thousand" into a domain as difficult to quantify as that of memory. While the casual quantification of "ten thousand recollections, by the blacks, of the injuries they have sustained" may have reflected the intention to use a large figure, it also conveys a haughty disinterest in the exact dimensions of "black" memory.[25] Oddly appreciative and negligent at the same time, "ten thousand" begged the question of whether Jefferson was calculating per capita or per state, at least potentially leaving most African Americans in Virginia unburdened by any recollection whatsoever.[26] This performative carelessness toward rational quantification—a carelessness, as shown in the preceding chapters, that pervaded the Enlightenment of Feeling—served here to convey the self-conscious limits of Jefferson's perspective. As he made clear, he knew what he was talking about when he described "white" prejudices as "deep rooted," but he imagined himself quite unable to say much about "black" memories (for instance, their qualification by feelings of pain or sadness), other than that they must exist in a certain (or uncertain) number.

As a result, the contrast between "deep rooted prejudices entertained by the whites" and "ten thousand recollections, by the blacks, of the injuries they have sustained" suggested the existence of two separate filters on reality. These filters, two separate sets of feelings, opinions, and creeds, seemed to belong to two opposed collective identities. One had its origins in the past and was oriented toward the future (in one sense of *prejudice:* forming a premature judgment that was possibly mistaken); the other was bent on looking in the opposite direction, from the present toward the past (starting from a legitimate sense of manifestly violated rights). Starkly oppositional in temporal and moral terms, the two opposed ways of experiencing the world seemed to make communication and mutual understanding unlikely, producing instead the political "convulsions" that Jefferson warned against in the same sentence. In this sense, the long introductory phrase under Query XIV that began with his concession of "deep rooted prejudices" performed what it claimed: Jefferson's estimation that open war and even "extermination" would be the inevitable consequence if the formerly enslaved remained in the country—quite an extreme idea, after all—was explicitly based on assumptions already in place *before* he could have presented any evidence of such a likelihood. Beginning with an insight into the tenaciousness of white Virginians' prejudice, when it ended the entire phrase had become an expression of that prejudice, a "shortcut" to judgment[27] made before facts could be established.

"Written in Virginia"

Jefferson's "wall of separation" under Query XIV between African American recollections and Anglo-American prejudices—such as his own to follow, and more generally those that Robert Parkinson has analyzed as belonging to the "darker side" of the revolutionary "common cause"[28]—illustrated his concept of two modern collective identities, two different communities of feeling and "amor patriae,"[29] that were not subject to change in the foreseeable future. As will be argued in the remainder of this chapter, it was the imagination of a deep rift between these communities of feeling, more than any particular "suspicion" (or self-conscious prejudice) of intellectual or physical difference,[30] that constituted Jefferson's rationale against "incorporating" the formerly enslaved into the new republic. In the midterm at least, the democratically "diffused" lines between knowledge, opinion, and prejudice in Jefferson's postcolonial Enlightenment thus went some way to conjure up alternative epistemologies that could no longer be communicated or corrected in rational debate but had to be relocated in space. Like the different "opinions" on American independence, what he depicted in Notes on Virginia as two radically separate modes of experiencing the world seemed best placed each on a different "side of the water."[31]

Arguably, Jefferson's epistemological nationalism was the central project of *Notes on the State of Virginia*. His concept of African Americans as a potentially hostile "captive nation" in need of their own nation-state outside the United States[32] had a pronounced epistemological dimension. The evocation of opposed "white" and "black" subjectivities, each equipped with a radically distinct experience of reality, may have been one of the most enduring as well as most ominous legacies of Jefferson's Enlightenment of Feeling. Following Susan Manning and Robert Pierce Forbes, *Notes* can be read as a "war book."[33] In part at least, it emerged as a coping mechanism at a traumatic moment in his personal life, following his wife's illness and premature death, that coincided with the ill-fated end of his governorship of Virginia at a moment of intense revolutionary crisis and war. When enslaved Virginians followed Lord Dunmore's promise of freedom and joined the British forces, the ancient concept of slavery as a latent state of war was becoming personal for Jefferson. In 1781 when he began composing *Notes*, he was not only forced to leave his main plantation Monticello to escape from Lord Cornwallis's troops, but about nineteen enslaved people from his Elk Hill plantation "fled to the enemy" or "joined enemy," as he put it at the time (an expression he changed into the passive "carried off" after the war had ended).[34] Writing *Notes on Virginia* in a situation of revolutionary turmoil and personal tragedy, Jefferson sought to paint a truthful image of white Virginians' emergent national subjectivity, including their wounded feelings, personal disappointments, and provincial limitations, such as their "deep rooted prejudices" against the potentially hostile nation of "blacks." The goal to delineate, and draw lines around, a particular "white" Virginian worldview informed both the content and form of the book, especially, as will be shown in the following sections, in his wide-ranging experiments with literary perspective.

As Jefferson proudly announced in the first phrase of the "Advertisement" to the Stockdale edition from 1787, the first to carry his name as author, *Notes on Virginia* was "written in Virginia."[35] Describing Virginia from within Virginia, the book that Annette Gordon-Reed and Peter Onuf recently characterized as "an extraordinarily personal text"[36] had a dual focus: the exterior subject matter of Virginia nature and society as well as the interior subject matter of Jefferson's perspective on it; Virginia "from the inside," as it were, in a double sense. Characteristically, he did not heed the advice of his friend Charles Thomson to choose a "more dignified" title for his book, such as a "Natural history" of Virginia.[37] The seemingly unassuming "Notes" of his title succeeded better at illustrating what was at stake for him: less Virginia as the object of his study than the subjective processes in his mind when he took note, or notes, of his home state. An important, if often neglected, theme of Notes thus consisted in its metalevel reflection on perspective and the limitations of its own subjective access to knowledge about Virginia. Again and again the book displayed what has been described as a "sophisticated awareness of an investigator's real problems,"[38] probing the limits of what could be known, how, when, by the author, or by his various informants. In keeping with his qualified concepts of knowledge, Jefferson tended to raise modest epistemological expectations. At the same time, however, he emphasized that it was not only legitimate but even indispensable that his subjective opinions be published "precisely as they are," in exactly the form he chose for them.[39]

Contrary to what is often assumed today of elite white male protagonists of "the" Enlightenment, then, the Jefferson of Notes was quite far from seeking to construct the disembodied perspective of a universalist "view from nowhere" by claiming an unprejudiced viewpoint, or at least identifying the conquest of personal prejudice as an authorial aspiration.[40] With a persona firmly placed at the center of the state[41] or speaking from specific locations within Virginia's landscape,[42] occasionally even in such concretely embodied form that he complained that his observations were giving him "a violent head ach,"[43] Jefferson insisted on emphasizing what today might be discussed as his "situatedness."[44] While the Advertisement stresses the "imperfections" and "want" of his knowledge, it proudly promises to present the work in its "original form and language."[45] Such an insistence on limited, but authentic, personally embodied, locally situated, communal knowledge ("our own knowledge," as Jefferson liked to specify it)[46] clearly went beyond conventional expressions of authorial humility. Placed on the following page as the result of a careful reorganization of Marbois's queries,[47] the first Query, "An exact description of the limits and boundaries of the state of Virginia," lays claims to precision[48] while immediately transferring the Advertisement's theme of epistemological limitations to the question of territorial borders. The state of Virginia, in the form of Jefferson's only book, was at once a state of subjective experience and a geographical and political entity.

In this manner, Jefferson sought to present his views on Virginia through an authorial performance, not of abstract universalism, but of a subjectivist particularism that emerged in the act of exposing its intellectual limitations to the audience of a wider world. As he saw it, his situated, limited, and self-consciously prejudiced performance did not at all go at the expense of his ability to describe what he thought was "real,"[49] because *Notes* was not simply a book "about" a certain landscape, population, or political system. As was the case in Jefferson's favorite travel narrative, Laurence Sterne's *Sentimental Journey through France and Italy*,[50] a crucial part of its subject matter consisted in the presentation less of what was seen than of how it was seen, and by whom: *Notes on the State of Virginia* sought to give a truthful description not only of the Virginian republic but also of Jefferson's closely circumscribed worldview—his subjective feelings, opinions, and prejudices—as a "white" republican citizen of Virginia.

"In Opposition to the General Law of Vision"

Much has been said about the visual emphasis of eighteenth-century accounts of knowledge production. The metaphor of *Enlightenment* itself, of course, is a classical expression of this emphasis. Today's Foucauldian interpretations of "the" Enlightenment tend to stress power-related aspects of vision and light, interpreting them primarily as means of social control and oppression. However, Jefferson's Enlightenment of Feeling does not quite fit the bill for such theorems as the panopticon, the state of surveillance, or the white gaze. The Palladian architecture of his own Monticello, for instance, was concerned at least as much with what remained invisible: just as the building's second floor, containing the residence of the women and children of Jefferson's (white) family, was barely visible from the outside of the house, the residences and workplaces of the enslaved people in the basement and in Mulberry Row remained invisible from the perspective of Jefferson's rooms inside the main building. The dome room on the top of the structure was far from being used as a point of observation to gain full visual control of the plantation. Monticello's architecture and even furniture (such as its dumbwaiters) to the contrary served to make Jefferson and his visitors as blind as possible to the system of slavery at its (literal) foundation. If there was a universalist "view from nowhere" on Jefferson's plantation, ironically, it was reserved to the enslaved, who had to work all over the house and farm, but ideally without being seen themselves. Instead of placing Jefferson in the position of the omniscient observer who remained inscrutable to the observed, Monticello was thus an anti-panopticon that aimed at nothing so much as ensuring the invisibility of the enslaved and putting the master himself on display "for the observation of the curious."[51]

Analogously, while the sense of vision played a role for the personally qualified concepts of communal knowledge Jefferson presented in *Notes on the State of Virginia* (for instance, in his reference to "our own knowledge, derived from daily sight"),[52] the book most often emphasized, not the success, but the subjective limits, of "enlightened" vision. Jefferson's Enlightenment of Feeling was naturally inclined to problematize the sense of sight, relishing situations when the visual focus of its observations was obstructed, redirected, refracted, blurred, or obscured. Instead of a commonly "enlightened" orientation toward visual perception as a term of success, it would therefore be more accurate to say that *Notes* had a self-consciously *optical* orientation. Jefferson was far from imagining himself in full control of the objects of his vision but went to great pains to reflect on his subjective limitations in gaining visual information, reflecting extensively on the means he employed to enhance his vision, and their uncertain success. Instead of constructing a falsely universalist view from nowhere, it was the point of his epistemological nationalism to expose the material conditions and physical limitations of the subjective lens on reality through which he as a representative "white" Virginia republican attained his particular view of the world.

Perhaps a legacy from his father, Peter Jefferson, the surveyor and cartographer known for the Fry-Jefferson map of Virginia (1753), Jefferson had a penchant for using such optical instruments as a camera obscura and a theodolite, telescopes, microscopes, concave mirrors, and perspective glasses.[53] In *Notes*, he transferred his father's scientific and geographic methods to the literary realm, a realm that allowed him to focus not so much on the objects as on the subjective conditions of his vision. Jefferson self-consciously experimented with literary point of view technique to convey the subjective basis of a republican worldview that was, like the shifting perspective through a moveable telescope, at once spatially limited and evolving in time. To understand Jefferson's literary optics—a technique culturally so productive that it inspired the *reverse ekphrasis* of nineteenth-century paintings depicting scenes in the book rather than the actual landscape[54]—the following paragraphs will briefly examine his experiments with literary perspective. These experiments began in earnest under Queries IV, "Mountains," and V, "Cascades," achieved their greatest degree of flexibility under Query VII, "Climate," and came to an abrupt stop under Query XIV, "Laws," as the optical illustration of white Virginians' "deep rooted prejudices."[55]

The landscape descriptions under Query IV of what is now Harpers Ferry, and under Query V of the Natural Bridge, are arranged as two companion pieces that mirror one another. Equally alternating between a first- and a second-person singular, both start "on a very high point of land," from which the viewers look down "into the abyss." At "first glance," the observers of both scenes are overwhelmed by the sublime view downward, which "hurries" their senses into "opinions" on a catastrophic geological history, "a war between rivers and mountains, which must have shaken the earth itself to its center."[56] The scientific opinions on this "war" are only provisional, however. By a narrowing of perspective, "pleasing" views of the horizon are made possible in both scenes when "the eye" looks through a "cleft" in one case as well as up and down a "fissure" in the other.[57] Through instruments that constrict visual range (comparable to blinders for a horse or the optical illusion of a theater stage), Jefferson's point of view technique straitens perspective in the attempt to solve the epistemological crisis of a world in turmoil. Only by limiting visual perception can his observers recover from the painful experience of looking down at a catastrophic world history, eventually achieving the stable, long-distance vision of a calm horizon and a peaceful continental future.

Nowhere is Jefferson's Enlightenment put into perspective as creatively as at his main residence Monticello in the piedmont of Virginia, placed by his "sentimental geography" at the center of both his home state and personal life.[58] As shown under Query VII, at Monticello the glimpse "into the abyss" has already been replaced by the horizontal vision that ended his previous experiments. However, the long-distance view into the continental future turns out to be at least as confusing as the glimpse into a chaotic past, obliging Jefferson continually to adjust the literary equivalent of his various lenses by zooming in and out of Virginia's landscape. The query culminates in a discussion of the philosophically "nameless," as yet scientifically unaccountable phenomenon of *looming*. "Philosophy is as yet in the rear of the seamen, for so far from having accounted for it, she has not given it a name," Jefferson claimed. "Its principal effect is to make distant objects appear larger, *in opposition to the general law of vision*, by which they are diminished."[59] Running counter to universal laws of nature, objects that seemed close as they "loomed" large could turn out to be far away. "[R]are at land, though frequent at sea," looming blurred the boundaries between the Virginia countryside and the Atlantic, just as it destabilized the sense of proportion that seemed so important in the contribution *Notes* sought to make to the transatlantic "dispute of the new world."[60] It even caused a complete "metamorphosis" of Jefferson's vision, quickly transforming familiar outlines into "the most whimsical shapes, and all these perhaps successively in the same morning." Thus, potentially liberating as it was, the "opposition to the general law of vision" of Jefferson's Enlightenment of Feeling could also have the effect of obstructing a shared communal outlook.[61] Making "a circle appear a square, or a cone a sphere," it fundamentally threatened the possibility of achieving a consensus on how to envision the state of Virginia.

To gain control over the dizzying range of possibilities in his subjective vision and establish a firm common ground for Virginia citizens, Query XIV of *Notes* resorts to a radicalized version of the experiment tried out under Queries IV and V. After vision has been partially constricted in the landscape descriptions of Harpers Ferry and the Natural Bridge, under Query XIV it is blocked altogether. Jefferson shows himself confronted with an "immoveable veil of black," almost as if his wide-ranging experiments in literary optics were suddenly interrupted by a group of people standing too closely in front of his telescope. The "immoveable veil" marks the limits of his subjective sensory experience. Unlike in rationalist Enlightenment traditions, in Jefferson's Enlightenment of Feeling the limits of sensory experience defined the limits of his access to knowledge about the world. The "immoveable veil of black" thus marked the limits of Jefferson's own knowledge—much more than, as has been the most frequent assumption among commentators of XIV, the supposed intellectual limits of those whom he dimly assumed to be on the other side of the veil. Far from attempting to discipline or oppress through the achievement of a universal vision, Jefferson's Enlightenment sought to regain a measure of control over a chaotic world of war and revolution by dwelling on its own blindness.

"That Immoveable Veil of Black"

Although Jefferson's impressionistic racism against African Americans under Query XIV has often been discussed at length, it is still necessary to spell out the implications of his discussion of blackness as an optical rather than visual problem. Jefferson was serious when he claimed that his perception of blackness was "real."[62] Needless to say, he was quite far from describing a realistic perception of the many shades of color that make up human skin tone. In a weirdly selective perception that can at best be explained in terms of his optical framework, he depicted himself as physically disabled to "see" African Americans as people with "greater or less suffusions of colour." For him, they were simply "blacks" or, strictly speaking, people of *no* color. Due to his occluded lens on reality, all he could perceive when he tried to decipher their inner lives (including their "ten thousand recollections," as discussed earlier) was the "eternal monotony" of "that immoveable veil of black." At issue was an optical blackness associated with a total absence of light, and thus the technical possibility of enlightenment—and not for "blacks," Jefferson vaguely realized, but for himself. As will be discussed in chapter 8, Jefferson helped initiate here what would become a potent metaphor in African American literature of a "veil" that could be "drawn aside" to reveal "a view of the inner life of the Negro in America," as for instance James Weldon Johnson would ironically put it more than a century later.[63] The significance of the "immoveable veil of black" for Jefferson's thoughts under Query XIV can hardly be overestimated. From the perspective of one side of a screen that he described as impenetrable by light as well as completely static in both temporal ("eternal") and spatial ("immoveable") terms, by necessity Jefferson could come up with nothing but "a suspicion only"[64] of what was happening on the other side.

This optical blackness was Jefferson's metonymy and metaphor for prejudice, the "shortcut" to judgment that precludes actual judgment. Immediately following his concession of "[d]eep rooted prejudices entertained by the whites" (as discussed above, a concession of prejudice that also appears in the form of a prejudice), the "black of the negro" opens his discussion of the supposed characteristics of people of African descent. It does so, however, not as universal knowledge, but as the subjective experience of an imagined "white" community of feeling: "The first difference *which strikes us* is that of colour."[65] After long-winded digressions on a variety of topics, the passage concludes with a return to blackness as the one aspect that seems indisputable to this community. "This unfortunate difference of colour, and *perhaps* of faculty, is a powerful obstacle to the emancipation of these people."⁶⁶ All things considered under Query XIV, Jefferson is eventually left with nothing but his first impression. From the limited perspective of a first-person plural, the "reality" of blackness—"the difference is fixed in nature, and is as real as if its seat and cause were better known *to us*"—is revealed as a subjective feeling that can lay no claim to full knowledge. In a completely circular manner, without any significant development in his argument, the self-conscious prejudice against "black" citizenship at the beginning of the section is simply repeated and reaffirmed by Jefferson's concluding remark that it is ultimately blackness alone that is the "powerful obstacle" blocking his vision of emancipation. The wild assemblage of doubts, suspicions, conjectures, opinions, comparisons, and descriptions of appearances he offers under Query XIV on African Americans' bodies and minds may well have been part of a tortured stream of consciousness. At bottom, however, its precise combination of claims did not matter all that much, from Jefferson's point of view. It was the mere surplus of an argument that ended where it had begun, restating the first impression of "blackness" and the "white" experience of a vision that had been blocked altogether.

Seen in this light (or its absence), Jefferson's racism under Query XIV takes on an aspect that is at once less, and more, sinister than is commonly assumed. It is less sinister, in a sense, because Jefferson does not appear to have taken the details of his musings on African American characteristics very seriously himself—less seriously, certainly, than would most of his commentators. He clearly did not try to claim the intellectual high ground for his observations. His musings under XIV on *race* contain none of the charts and lists that have come to be seen as so characteristic of Jefferson's "scientific" style in *Notes*. They are written in a willfully disorganized prose that follows its own contingent associations and digressions rather than presenting any semblance of a logical argument. As James McCune Smith would complain in 1859, they were "so mixed and so confused" that he first had to order them before his Glasgow-trained scientific criticism could even begin.⁶⁷ And Jefferson's contemporaries and correspondents were not necessarily more impressed.⁶⁸ Despite having to deal with considerable criticism, however, Jefferson never retreated, for instance, from his outrageous reference to Edward Tyson's 1699 account of "orang-utans" lusting after African women, even though it was already antiquated when

Jefferson referred to it in *Notes*.[69] Since he was aware that he was presenting local prejudices rather than scientific knowledge under Query XIV, this anachronism is not likely to have been an accident. Especially for a man who playfully identified with orangutans in his personal correspondence,[70] it would not have been out of character if he had been deliberately flirting with an exoticist performance of what he realized was his provincial Virginia racism. Performing the intellectual backwardness of his narrow local prejudices may have been part of an attitude that included his reported shows of "mock" whippings of his slaves for the amusement of foreign visitors,[71] and more generally the ironic retro-styles and the *hameau*-style mimicking of rural life that were fashionable in Europe during the early 1780s. This possibility would make some of the more outlandish statements under Query XIV the closest Jefferson would ever approach to putting on display of a "white" Virginia folklore, a mode of "leveling down" his perspective to that of the more provincial, less intellectually inclined white Virginians around him. No matter how exactly to imagine the relations between Africans and Tyson's chimpanzees or South Asian orangutans, Jefferson remained aware that any such theory could have nothing directly to do with rational considerations of natural rights and republican citizenship.[72]

It is precisely Jefferson's insouciance about the reception of Query XIV that is a reason why his racism may have to be assessed as even more pernicious than without a consideration of the literary optics of *Notes on Virginia*, or at least as pernicious in a different sense. For the most part, he chose to remain blissfully unaware that his folksy gossip about orangutans and related ideas, ennobled by his authorship, could take on a life of their own.[73] In racist stereotypes of hypersexuality or in "dehumanization" arguments by abolitionists such as David Walker,[74] they would be used on both sides of an increasingly polarized debate about slavery. From Jefferson's side of the "immoveable veil of black," however, such dialectical developments in an interracial American history could not be seen or foreseen. He was trying to evoke two sharply separate experiences of the world that did not have enough common ground to be in conversation with one another and that he did not expect to become the basis of a shared learning process. In his estimation, "blacks" could not be suffering greatly from his dismissive opinions about them because, within what he assumed was their own nationally and racially different experience of reality, they could not be all too interested in what he had to say about them.

Race for Jefferson was a matter of concretely embodied feeling rather than rational argument or exchange. The worst example of the anti-intellectual, almost visceral dimension of his Enlightenment of Feeling was his ridiculous claim, in the absence of any reliable information through the sense of sight, to be sensing "a very strong and disagreeable odour" from people of African descent as a group. Much of the scholarly criticism of Query XIV has focused on the question of intellectual equality and the relative weight Jefferson might have given to African Americans' rational and moral faculties. But how seriously can such abstract considerations be taken in the effusions of a man who made a point of not being ashamed of following his own least rational, most primitive impressions? The olfactory details of Query XIV served as the crudest imaginable illustration of his political goal to keep the foreign nation of "blacks" as physically distant from his own body, and the "white" American body politic, as possible. It is quite impossible for participants in a dialogue, after all, to provide rational proof of smelling as good as their interlocutors.

Experienced through Jefferson's all too concretely embodied feeling in *Notes*, "blacks" and "whites" were members of radically separate epistemological communities that were not supposed to engage in rational debate and exchange. And this may in the end be his most damaging contribution to the development of modern American conceptions of *race*. His invention of an epistemological nationalism conjured into existence sharply separate "white" and "black" cultures of feeling, sensing, perceiving, memorizing, thinking, writing, and knowing. This invention not only left little common ground for Enlightened discussion; in the final analysis, Jefferson even implied that "whites" and "blacks" could not, or at any rate should not, interact very much at all.

"Religion Indeed Has Produced a Phyllis Whately"

Jefferson's epistemological nationalism was the conceptual innovation dominating the passages on *race* under Query XIV, in which he stressed separation with much greater rigor than he did his "suspicion only" of intellectual inferiority.[75] For instance, he went to great logical pains to claim that the inner lives of "blacks" remained isolated from their American environment, and not only due to their mysterious "ten thousand recollections." He even claimed that their inner clocks ran differently, making them "sit up till midnight, or later" and fall asleep during the day.[76] Their bodies seemed to follow separate circadian rhythms, responsible for different lifestyles that would in any case, however exactly they were to be evaluated, make it organizationally difficult for "blacks" and "whites" to interact socially and intellectually. As Jefferson saw it, the relatively few "blacks" who left "their own homes" did not profit from being "liberally educated." Although he insinuated that what seemed to him their lack of impressionability resulted from a difference of intellectual powers, he also left open the possibility that, unlike the enslaved in ancient Rome, the enslaved in modern America were simply not interested in a civilization Jefferson depicted as categorically distinct from what he called "their own society."[77]

In the same spirit, Jefferson's expression of contempt for the literature by Phillis Wheatley and Ignatius Sancho under Query XIV went far deeper than the disparagement of style, talent, or general intellectual endowments for which it has most often been criticized. For him, these writers were not even subject to negative judgment. As he put it in the case of Sancho's *Letters*, they supposedly were "as incoherent and eccentric, as is the course of a meteor through the sky."[78] If Sancho was to be regarded as a fellow man of the Enlightenment, his work offered nothing but a sudden eruption of light in darkness that was, as it were, too brief and unpredictable for Jefferson even to get his optical instruments ready. When Jefferson claimed to exclude the work of Phillis Wheatley from the possibility of his judgment, the artificiality of his rhetorical stance intensified. Although he in fact owned a copy of the original London edition of her *Poems on Various Subjects, Religious and Moral* (1773) and had access to the correct spelling of her name, he introduced as many as four different spelling mistakes into the two words of her name, referring to her under Query XIV as "a Phyllis Whately," as if quoting from the foreign language of a foreign nation that presumably included not one, but several "Phyllis Whatelys."[79] Jefferson's "Phyllis Whately" was no American; she was no poet, no author, no person, no individual, not even a regular part of God's creation: she was mere discourse, mass-"produced" by "religion" rather than created by nature's God Himself.

Jefferson's radical exclusion of Wheatley from American culture would cast a long shadow over the following centuries, extending to denigrations of her psychological, artistic, and political autonomy even today.[80] His elaborate performance of ignoring and dismissing Wheatley's name, reputation, and individuality was only surpassed by the moment when he questioned her authorship directly, referring to her poetry as "compositions" that were "published under" her (badly misspelled) name. From his intentionally limited perspective as a provincial challenged by spelling issues, he claimed that Wheatley's cosmopolitan poetry, published and celebrated in the center of the British Empire and counting both George Washington and George III among its admirers, was "below the dignity of criticism." Having been prejudged from the other side of "that immoveable veil of black," Wheatley for Jefferson exemplified the foreign nation of "blacks" he tried to write into existence in *Notes on Virginia,* who could not be impartially judged by "whites" at all. The inglorious epitome of his epistemological nationalism, his construct of "a Phyllis Whately" was not the product of evangelical "religion," as he had claimed (and as which Wheatley would long continue to be seen) but rather of the democratic culture of knowledge in his own Enlightenment of Feeling, which in its worst moments found expression in a racist American creed.

Following the passages on *race* under Query XIV, Jefferson presented his plans for a law "to diffuse knowledge more generally through the mass of the people."[81] As shown in the preceding chapters, his concept of a *diffusion* of knowledge not only referred to the Enlightenment project of spreading knowledge more broadly in social and geographical space; it also implied a diffusion of what counted as knowledge, potentially leading from Jefferson's political respect for the opinions of Virginia citizens to a toleration of their false opinions and even their prejudices. During the Missouri Crisis, Jefferson used the term *diffusion* as a solution to the slavery problem, suggesting that the institution would be weakened if the enslaved were "diffused" over a larger extent of territory.[82] It has plausibly been argued that his various efforts to democratize property, including slaves, by distributing it more evenly in social and geographical space unexpectedly made slavery more, rather than less, entrenched in Virginia society and politics.[83] Jefferson's conception of the *diffusion* and democratization of knowledge may be seen at the root of a similar dialectic in that it helped establish racist prejudice as an integral part of a specifically "white" American worldview. While Jefferson vaguely hoped that white Americans would eventually overcome their prejudices, he was convinced that this process would take too long for two opposed communities of feeling—two separate "races" and "nations"—to live together peacefully. At bottom, he thus knew, but fatalistically accepted, that prejudice and darkness, not reason and light, were at the root of his exclusion of "blacks" from the polity.

"The Elevation of the Whites"

As part 2 will show, it was Wheatley's Enlightenment of Principle, not Jefferson's Enlightenment of Feeling, that kept the avenues of free Enlightened conversation open. To theorize and consolidate a truly democratic American public sphere, writers in this tradition projected on Jefferson the new concept of a "Jeffersonian" *double consciousness*, depicting him as a man torn between contradictory impulses that were representative of the contradictions in American history at large. Following the African American invention of a Jeffersonian *double consciousness*, even today readers of *Notes on Virginia* typically see a logical contradiction between Jefferson's radical critique of slavery under Query XVIII ("Indeed I tremble for my country when I reflect that God is just")[84] and his outrageous racism under Query XIV.[85] Yet, just as there is no "Adam Smith problem" in the relationship between *The Theory of Moral Sentiments* and *The Wealth of Nations*, there is no "Thomas Jefferson problem" in the relationship between Queries XVIII and XIV. In the terms of Jefferson's own thought, both chapters were complementary parts of the same argument for binding the end of slavery to the necessity of "expatriating" the formerly enslaved. If under Query XIV Jefferson describes himself as empirically blind when confronted with an "immoveable veil of black," under XVIII he explains the causal roots of this limited vision: his blindness is the result of a misguided education process that begins with the harmful visual impressions the children of Virginia planters involuntarily receive when watching their parents' physical abuse of the enslaved. "From [the] cradle to [the] grave," these sense impressions literally blind "white" Virginians such as himself[86] to the intellectual and emotional lives of the people they enslave, disabling them to "see" and experience African Americans as anything other than the victims of oppression.[87]

Situating himself within the imagined boundaries of his community of feeling, Jefferson was to remain unable to envision a transracial American future. Since *race* in his postcolonial Enlightenment was primarily a matter of subjective feeling and opinion, not reason and knowledge, he was adamant in claiming that there were no intellectual means that "blacks" as a group, enslaved or free, could use to change their position in the American republic. And the problem in his eyes had less to do with "blacks" as a separate nation, with its own recollections and feelings of *amor patriae*. In the first place, it was the result of his concept of involuntary opinion combined with what he admitted were the perceptive and intellectual limitations of "whites." Whether or not African Americans proved his "suspicion" of intellectual inferiority wrong and, following the argument of national genius production under Query VI, came up with "ten thousand" Newtons,[88] would not matter: due to its "deep rooted prejudices," Jefferson's community of feeling would be in no position to perceive and rationally acknowledge such intellectual achievements in the foreseeable future.

While the "blacks" under Query XIV thus already seemed "invisible men" to him, as will be discussed in the following chapters in the context of Ralph Ellison's novel, Jefferson was still too much of a surveyor's son not to realize, at least, that it was ultimately the limited focus of his own worldview that was leaving him in the dark. Since he considered slavery to be, first and foremost, a problem of the manners, opinions, and character of Virginia "whites," he thought that any change in the slavery question and in what was becoming, not least through his own "race making,"[89] the peculiar problem of modern American race relations, could only come from long-term developments within his own community of feeling. Beginning in the 1770s and especially in the years of his final retirement, he consistently pointed out the centrality of communal education for the survival of the republic. Retreating from direct antislavery action in the nineteenth century, he tried to see the great project of his retirement years—the University of Virginia—as his personal contribution to this goal. As laid out in his "Rockfish Gap Report" for the university, in his Enlightenment of Feeling the diffusion of knowledge and the gradual improvement of national manners, opinions, and character were intertwined.[90] The institutionalization of his Enlightenment in the University of Virginia was supposed to combine the diffusion of knowledge with the refinement of manners, thus indirectly laying the most realistic groundwork, or so he hoped, for the long-term end of slavery in the state, including the "expatriation" of the formerly enslaved.

As will be detailed in part 2, therefore, the writers of Wheatley's Enlightenment of Principle first had to depart from the original meanings of Jefferson's major writings—most notably, the Declaration of Independence and *Notes on the State of Virginia*—to transform them into calls for an immediate, state-enforced end of slavery combined with equal African American citizenship and education. On its own terms, Jefferson's Enlightenment of Feeling did not offer the degree of universalism with which it has later become associated. Although such arguments have been tied to his worldview in retrospect, his concepts of universal reason and knowledge were simply not strong enough to make him interested in a project of *black uplift* in an interracial American republic.[91] However, Jefferson's Enlightenment of Feeling did provide an important educational impetus in another direction. As will be argued in the following chapters, it initiated a discourse that can be summed up as leveling up "white" Americans, or *white uplift*: a "weaning" from "narrow prejudices," as the African American astronomer Benjamin Banneker put it in 1791, or, as Charles Chesnutt would have it a century later, a pedagogical project effecting "not so much the elevation of the colored people as the elevation of the whites."[92]

❖ Part II ❖

Wheatley's Enlightenment of Principle

"[I]n every human Breast, God has implanted a Principle, which we call Love of Freedom; it is impatient of Oppression, and pants for Deliverance; and by the Leave of our Modern Egyptians I will assert, that the same Principle lives in us."[1] When Phillis Wheatley wrote these now-famous lines in her early twenties, she had already become a transatlantic celebrity. She had recently returned from London, where her *Poems on Various Subjects, Religious and Moral* (1773) had been published. In London, she had met and mingled with such political figures as Benjamin Franklin, Granville Sharp, and Lord Dartmouth, eventually turning down an invitation by the Countess of Huntingdon and an audience with King George III, in order to nurse her dying mistress in Boston.[2] The occasion for her letter, which was reprinted almost immediately in nearly a dozen New England newspapers,[3] was a reply to the Mohegan minister Samson Occom on the question of natural rights. For the newly emancipated Wheatley the question was so important that it required an immediate response. "I have this Day received your obliging kind Epistle," she told Occom, "and am greatly satisfied with your Reasons respecting the Negroes, and think highly reasonable what you offer in Vindication of their natural rights: Those that invade them cannot be insensible that the divine Light is chasing away the thick Darkness which broods over the Land of Africa; and the Chaos which has reign'd so long, is converting into beautiful Order, and reveals more and

Portrait of Phillis Wheatley attributed to Scipio Moorhead, unidentified engraver. Frontispiece of *Poems on Various Subjects, Religious and Moral* by Phillis Wheatley (London, 1773). (Houghton Library, Harvard University, AC85.A£245. Zy773w)

more clearly, the glorious Dispensation of civil and religious Liberty, which are so inseparably united, that there is little or no Enjoyment of one without the other."[4]

Wheatley's "Principle" of civil and religious liberty—a phrase also used by enslaved Bostonians at the time[5]—reflected not simply her Christian universalism; it was part of a worldview that was secular as well. A classical performance of the secularization inherent in the term *Enlightenment*, her narrative of light and order replacing darkness and chaos transferred the *fiat lux* from the book of Genesis to the context of civil history. For Wheatley, the "Principle" of liberty was not mainly a matter of faith or belief. In her letter to Occom, it emerged as the result of a rational conversation, in which her correspondent had proposed "Reasons" for his argument on natural rights that she accepted as "highly reasonable."

Wheatley had given her own reasons for the "Principle" in a 1772 poem addressing the Earl of Dartmouth, who had just then become the secretary of state for the colonies. Hailing him into the position of an opponent of "wanton *Tyranny*" in New England by heaping advance praise on him, Wheatley tied her support of the American colonists to her origins in Africa:

> Should you, my lord, while you peruse my song,
> Wonder from whence my love of *Freedom* sprung,
> Whence flow these wishes for the common good,
> By feeling hearts alone best understood,
> I, young in life, by seeming cruel fate
> Was snatch'd from *Afric's* fancy'd happy seat:
> What pangs excruciating must molest,
> What sorrows labour in my parent's breast?
> Steel'd was that soul and by no misery mov'd
> That from a father seiz'd his babe belov'd:
> Such, such my case. And can I then but pray
> Others may never feel tyrannic sway?[6]

From Wheatley's perspective, her Enlightened "Principle"—her love of freedom and her idea of universal equality as well as her republican orientation toward the "common good"—did not stand in any sort of tension to what her life in America had transformed into her "African" origins.[7] To the contrary, as she saw it, her dedication to these values stemmed from her personal experiences with its radical opposite in the Middle Passage and slavery. Like others forced to undergo these experiences, she knew all too well what the denial of her "Principle" meant. In the aquatic language of Wheatley's poem, the source from which her "love of *Freedom*" had "sprung" and "flowed" was not the Classical and Christian education she had received from the Wheatley family in Boston. Instead, the "Principle" (in the Latin reference of *principium* as beginning or origin as well as rule) went back to the memory of the traumatic moment in her African childhood when she had been "snatch'd" and "seiz'd" into slavery. Remarkably, she did not describe this memory in terms of her own feelings, but as the "pangs" and "sorrows" the grown-up Wheatley imagined her father must have felt after their forced separation.[8] The poem thus depicted her rational "Principle" as the rationalized hindsight perspective on her father's emotional legacy, anticipating Frederick Douglass's retrospective attribution, as discussed in this work's introduction, of his philosophy to his mother's intellectual legacy. Wheatley's concept of liberty translated the neoclassical terms of the westward course of empire of *translatio imperii* into a narrative that might be described as *translatio principii:* from its African source in her father's "breast," where God had "implanted" the "Principle," her love of freedom had flowed west as it accompanied the *Phillis* that carried her across the Atlantic into American slavery. In America, in turn, her poetry was designed to strengthen the "Principle" in the breasts of the American colonists, and of Lord Dartmouth, in what she described as the universal project of opposing "wanton *Tyranny*."

For Wheatley, what would become known as the principles of the American Revolution were by no means "white" or even, originally, American. Superficial readings might condemn her seeming condescension toward Africa (for instance, "the Darkness which broods over the Land of Africa," and the "*seeming* cruel fate" that separated her from it, in the above quotation) as attempts to cater to the preferences of her American enslavers. The opposite was more likely.[9] As illustrated by the moving image of her father in the poem praising Lord Dartmouth, Wheatley's Christian outlook on the "Land of Africa" was a moral topos of paganism that was not mainly concerned with the geographical location and its population; obviously, it did not mean that she considered her contemporaries of African descent to be in any way inferior to the people with "steel'd" souls who had kidnapped her into slavery. In her analogy to Exodus in the letter to Occom, it was not the enslaved, but the American enslavers whom she described as "Modern Egyptians" and thus as the true inhabitants of her topos of moral deprivation.

As Wheatley's possessive pronoun in the letter to Occom suggests—"*our* Modern Egyptians"—what Ralph Ellison would describe as the goal of taking "the responsibility for all of it, for the men as well as the principle"[10] was not a novelty in the twentieth century. Even before American independence, a young woman who had personally suffered in the Middle Passage and American enslavement was so secure in her intellectual possession of the "Principle" that she succeeded in casually combining the dire warning implied in her Egyptian analogy with the friendly irony of an almost paternalizing tone, as if she were merely talking about some of the more difficult teenagers in the family. That American slaveholders needed to change their ways was "not for their Hurt," Wheatley's letter to Occom specified. They simply had to gain what was intellectually an absolutely unchallenging insight, learning to accept "the strange Absurdity of their Conduct whose Words and Actions are so diametrically opposite. How well the Cry for Liberty, and the reverse Disposition for the Exercise of oppressive Power over others agree,—I humbly think it does not require the Penetration of a Philosopher to determine."[11]

Wheatley's paralipsis would become a prominent ironic device among the writers of the African American tradition to be discussed in the following chapters. Explaining her universal "Principle" by claiming not to have to explain it, precisely because it was so universal, she demonstrated her intellectual control over her argument at the same time that she illustrated her universalist ethics and epistemology. In the twentieth century, Ralph Ellison would acknowledge a similar philosophical self-possession in the Invisible Man's grandfather, who despite being born into slavery had always inhabited the "principle" of a universalist Enlightenment: "Hell, he never had any doubts about his humanity—that was left to his 'free' offspring. He accepted his humanity just as he accepted the principle. It was his."[12] In a similar vein, Ellison's friend Albert Murray would emphasize "that which the folk wisdom of the fugitive slave and the Reconstruction freedman took for granted long ago: The Declaration of Independence and the Constitution are the social, economic, and political heritage of all Americans."[13] Du Bois before him had stressed the notion of spiritual property, claiming that "there are to-day no truer exponents of the pure human spirit of the Declaration of Independence than the American Negroes."[14]

For all these thinkers, the principles of a universalist Enlightenment, including the documents and historical figures involved in expressing them in the American Revolution, were far from "white" property. Instead, they belonged to a "folk wisdom" that differed in the United States from the folk wisdom in other parts of the world in that it also found highly intellectual modes of expression in an African American literary tradition. Arguably, for example, the eighteenth-century freedom struggles of Black Forest bondspeople in what is now Germany did not leave behind an influential intellectual heritage of their own.[15] By contrast, in a New World culture defined by the jarring juxtaposition of democracy, slavery, *race,* and Protestant literacy, Wheatley's "Principle" was able to create the rich repertory of a unique literary and philosophical tradition.[16] As the following chapters will argue, this tradition shaped decisively what is today understood as the "Jeffersonian" Enlightenment.

Ironically, as shown in part 1, Thomas Jefferson himself had gone out of his way to disparage Wheatley's work. This irony tends to be understood simply in terms of Jefferson's racism. While certainly racist, however,

Jefferson's statements under Query XIV may also suggest something else: that he recognized the fundamental philosophical challenge Wheatley's thought posed to his Enlightenment of Feeling. This challenge was not only due to Wheatley's growing international reputation as a poet who would eventually count Voltaire, George Washington, Benjamin Rush, Ignatius Sancho, Thomas Clarkson, John Gabriel Stedman, Gilbert Imlay, Johann Friedrich Blumenbach, the Abbé Grégoire, and Samuel Taylor Coleridge among her many admirers.[17] It was also posed by the radical universalism of her "Principle," publicly declared more than two years prior to the Declaration of Independence. As has been shown in part 1, Jefferson's own more limited universalism prioritized the creation of a national community of feeling and opinion. This community was held together by an epistemological nationalism that excluded others—"blacks," Europeans, and, on occasion, Federalists—on the grounds of what he admitted was his subjectively colored vision as a "white" Virginia republican. Jefferson's disparagement of Wheatley went deeper than literary criticism; as he well knew, it was less a negative judgment than an effective exclusion from his judgment, that is, a prejudgment or prejudice. Whereas his Enlightenment of Feeling deliberately left room for such prejudices, Wheatley's Enlightenment of Principle did not. As illustrated by her paralipsis in the letter to Occom, in her universalist epistemology her "Principle" was not merely held to be self-evident by a particular national community; it was logically accessible to everyone. Long after Wheatley's death, her analysis of the contradiction between "the Cry for Liberty, and the reverse Disposition for the Exercise of oppressive Power over others" would become established as America's greatest national (and Jefferson's greatest personal) contradiction. Even before Samuel Johnson made a similar point in his pamphlet *Taxation no Tyranny* (1775), she had already made it clear that the contradiction was plain to see and did "not require the Penetration of a Philosopher to determine."

Wheatley could never complete her second volume of poetry nor elaborate on her "Principle" very often. Tragically, in a postwar depression that hit the African American population particularly hard, she shared the fate of countless other women in the eighteenth century, including (almost contemporaneously) that of Jefferson's wife and one of his daughters. Weakened by childbirth and the loss of children under primitive medical conditions, Wheatley died together with her last infant daughter on Sunday, December 5, 1784, at the age of only about thirty-one[18] (younger than Jefferson was when he drafted the Declaration of Independence). By the time Jefferson was preparing the two editions of *Notes on the State of Virginia* in 1785 and 1787, she therefore no longer had to deal with Jefferson. However, Jefferson still found that he had to deal with Wheatley. Apparently feeling cornered by her universalism, he saw in the exclusion of her poetry from his subjective judgment under Query XIV the only possibility to meet the challenge posed by her work: there simply was no rational argument available for the purpose. Ironically, although designed to trivialize Wheatley's reputation, what his antirationalist "cancelling" of her work eventually effected was nothing so much as a serious detraction from his *own* reputation as a man of the Enlightenment.

There are further ironies in the relationship between Jefferson's Enlightenment of Feeling and Wheatley's Enlightenment of Principle. In the following two centuries, Wheatley's and Jefferson's posthumous reputations came to resemble one another in sharing an equally bipolar structure. Like that of Jefferson, Wheatley's historical image has oscillated between being greatly admired and greatly reviled. Beginning in the late nineteenth century, and especially during the Black Arts Movement in the 1960s, critics have berated Wheatley's poetry for what seemed to them its inauthenticity, mediocrity, and epigonism. And instead of being taken seriously as a political thinker, she has been disdained for her supposed weakness, self-hatred, and ambition to be "white."[19] Henry Louis Gates has pointed out the irony that this form of criticism, far from being aesthetically innovative or politically progressive, actually perpetuated the racist epistemology first laid out by Jefferson's Query XIV: "it's striking that Jefferson and Amiri Baraka, two figures in American letters who would agree on little else, could agree on the terms of their indictment of Phillis Wheatley."[20]

Aspects of the Jefferson-Baraka heritage still linger today in occasional portrayals that demean Wheatley as a mute victim of "white supremacy" or a mere "black exhibit."[21] However, the sophisticated body of Wheatley scholarship that has emerged since the 1960s has recognized her outstanding significance as a poet, intellectual, and founding mother of African American literature. This view of Wheatley has its roots in the late eighteenth and nineteenth centuries. Relatively soon after her death, she came to be seen as an intellectual ancestress and an important literary and political precursor by a broad range of very different writers including, for example, an anonymous contributor to *Freedom's Journal*, Martin Delany, Charlotte Forten, William Cooper Nell, William G. Allen, William Wells Brown,

William Wilson, Anna Julia Cooper, Mary Church Terrell, and W. E. B. Du Bois.[22] In other words, Wheatley's poetry and her principled call for equality became a shared point of origin for a transhistorical collectivity of writers who conceived of themselves as a heterogeneous but nevertheless coherent literary and intellectual tradition.

For the inner coherence of this tradition, Jefferson played a crucial, if often ironic, role.[23] Arguably, Jefferson's exclusion of writers of African origin on the grounds of his subjective experience of *race* intensified African American calls for the creation of a unified literary tradition open to being judged by objective, universally accessible standards. The collective effort to demonstrate the limitations of Jefferson's Enlightenment of Feeling by measuring it against the universal standards of Wheatley's Enlightenment of Principle had effects in two directions. "Jefferson" became a frequent rhetorical trope in an intertextual web of African American writings, through which authors could refer not only to Jefferson as a historical figure but also to one another, conveying the sense of a collective literary and political endeavor. Conversely, the intertextual use of "Jefferson" as a recognizable trope for America's logical contradictions had long-term effects on the evolution of his historical image. By being processed through the universalist tradition of Wheatley's Enlightenment of Principle, the following chapters will argue, Jefferson's Enlightenment of Feeling gradually acquired the more universalist meanings that have become associated with the Jeffersonian Enlightenment today.

Thus, chapter 5 will discuss how as early as 1776, Lemuel Haynes abridged the second phrase of the Declaration Independence and gave it the form that has become familiar today, fundamentally changing its philosophical implications in the direction of Wheatley's contemporaneous "Principle." From 1776 onward, African American writers used what will be called in this book the "Haynes abridgment"—"We hold these truths to be self-Evident, that all men are created Equal, that they are Endowed By their Creator with Certain unalienable rights, that among these are Life, Liberty, and the pursuit of happiness"[24]—to rationalize Jefferson's original meaning into that which Frederick Douglass would eventually identify as the Declaration's "saving principles."[25] Chapter 6 will move on to the African American reception history of Query XIV of *Notes on Virginia*. Evoking a dystopian vision of Jefferson's community of feeling, nineteenth-century writers gradually transformed his "deep rooted prejudices" from an epistemological, involuntary, and collectivist to a moral, voluntarist, and individualist concept. Especially in arguments directed against the American Colonization Society, it became crucial to show that racist prejudice was no transhistorical attribute that God had "implanted," to use Wheatley's and Douglass's term,[26] in white Americans collectively, but that it was a grave moral problem—even, potentially, a sin—from which individuals had to rid themselves if the republic was to survive. Chapter 7 analyzes the transformation of Jefferson's language of *character* under Query XVIII, especially his metaphor of being "stamped" by slavery and his performance of guilt-ridden "trembling" at the thought of God's justice. The chapter describes how various "trembling" Jefferson likenesses began to wander through nineteenth-century literature, often glad to receive rational instruction from interlocutors who corrected the errors of his Enlightenment of Feeling by following the tenets of Wheatley's Enlightenment of Principle. Chapter 8, finally, follows these dialogues into twentieth-century literature. In classical modernist texts, Wheatley and Jefferson's metaphor of the "veil" came to illustrate the alternative epistemology of Jefferson's Enlightenment of Feeling, waiting to be rendered obsolete by the more rigorous universalism of "principles" that continued to be invoked from Wheatley's letter to Occom in 1774 to Ralph Ellison's novel *Invisible Man* in 1952.

❖ 5 ❖

The Lessons of Reason

In the tradition of Wheatley's Enlightenment, African American intellectuals immediately took responsibility for what they called the *principles* of the Declaration of Independence. From 1776 onward, they continued Wheatley's use of the contested term[1]—in the sense of both beginning and foundational rule—to radically transform the Declaration's meaning. Late in life, Jefferson himself had still been able to depict 1776 as a revolution merely in governmental *form*—reserving the term *principle* for his own election to the presidency, which he retrospectively claimed was "as real a revolution in the principles of our government as that of 76 was in it's [sic] form."[2] By contrast, *principle*—as defined, for instance, by Martin Delany, who from early on showed himself "determined never to be governed by the frivolous rules of *formality* but by PRINCIPLE, suggested by *conscience,* and guided by the light of REASON"[3]—became the dominant term in the African American hermeneutics of the Declaration of Independence. Whereas Jefferson's Declaration near the end of its long second phrase had restricted itself merely to "*such* principles" as were subject to the changing feelings and contingent opinions of American citizens, African American writers moved beyond such historical limitations.[4] Their interventions transferred the term *principle* back, as it were, from its original place at the end of the Declaration's second phrase to its beginning, where it became associated with the words from "We hold these truths" until "the pursuit of happiness." Against the backdrop of a revolutionary culture in which antislavery authors borrowed from one another from both sides of what was becoming the "color-line,"[5] African American authors thus wrote into existence radically universalist (if not, as Martin Luther King would later have it, "extremist")[6] principles that departed significantly from many of the original ideas of those who had drafted and signed the Declaration.

As will be discussed in this chapter, these universalist interpretations of the Founding document may be summed up by a term that the Philadelphia merchant James Forten used in 1813, *rational liberty,* and that has recently made it, for instance, into the title of Jürgen Habermas's history of philosophy, *Vernünftige Freiheit* (2019).[7] In the early African American context, *rational liberty* denoted a concept that had a solid religious as well as secular foundation, relying on a Protestant God in combination with strong concepts of divine as well as human reason. If, in retrospect, this concept no longer looks particularly innovative, the innovation may in part have become the victim of its own success: even if they did not get the proper credit for it, it may have been early African American readers who first dramatized what is today regarded as the Declaration's full normative potential.[8] From the late eighteenth and early nineteenth centuries onward they offered what have turned out to be the most lasting interpretations of the "immortal document,"[9] long anticipating the ideal that later become famous in Abraham Lincoln's reading of what he by then also called the Declaration's "*principle*" of universal liberty, as an "apple of gold" framed by the "picture of silver" of the federal Constitution.[10]

As shown in part 1, the Declaration of Independence had not originally promoted a concept of *rational* liberty. Neither its draft nor Congress versions had insisted on the criterion of reason, divine or otherwise, whether in the characterization of its own position or in the indictment of George III. Although a universal rationality had been implied in "the laws of nature and of nature's God," the weight of the Declaration's rhetoric, especially in Jefferson's draft version, had been on feeling rather than reason, privileging subjective opinion and faith over authoritative knowledge. Thus, the Declaration's most famous phrase, "We hold these truths to be self-evident," had originally foregrounded the agency of the communal subject that was "holding" an opinion on a particular array of plural "truths" rather than highlighting the universal authority—whether God and divine reason or a secular human reason—that made knowledge of "the" truth possible. Ostentatiously bracketing the question of whether the truths it proclaimed were self-evident by a universal standard or not, Jefferson's civic subjectivity had made a point of nevertheless treating them as if they were, thus also refusing to indicate any other, more reliable source of its knowledge of them. Writers in the African American tradition did not tend to go along with this approach. Unimpressed by the characteristic blend of humility and arrogance of Jefferson's semi-secularized stance, they privileged the authority of full knowledge over the bounds of communal opinion. For instance, in 1779 petitioners in New Hampshire made it clear that they did not merely think, feel, or opine: they professed to "*know* that the God of nature made us free."[11] A few months later, Dartmouth petitioners likewise emphasized their own active knowledge rather than Jefferson's concept of involuntary opinion, claiming to have "apprehended," that is, understood as well as willfully grasped or seized, the meaning of the Declaration's second phrase.[12]

In order to underline their intellectual possession, the writers of Wheatley's Enlightenment of Principle deliberately changed the Declaration's wording and syntax. While it could often be rhetorically useful to pretend that they were merely taking Jefferson by his word, relying for their truth claims on the civic subjectivity of his community of feeling hardly seemed sufficient. The authors discussed below realized that Jefferson's postcolonial democratization of knowledge had come at a price: his goal to do justice to the subjectively "felt" equality of white American citizens had been achieved at the expense of watering down the universalism of his Enlightenment. Writers in the African American tradition actively sought to remedy this problem by developing more ambitious concepts of *rational* liberty. Their uses of the Declaration were not merely motivated by the goal to show their proficiency in a preexisting lingua franca of an American community of feeling.[13] Rather than making subservient attempts to inscribe themselves into a hegemonic American discourse—the discourse could not possibly have become hegemonic when their interventions began in 1776—African American thinkers fundamentally challenged and transformed Jefferson's terms and premises. And, on an intellectual level at least, their revisions turned out to be hugely successful.

Truncating Jefferson, Extending Liberty

Lemuel Haynes's early manuscript essay *Liberty Further Extended: Or Free Thoughts on the Illegality of Slave-keeping* (1776) inaugurated this transformative tradition.[14] It opened with an abridgment of the Declaration's second sentence, placed in the position that would have been occupied by a verse from the Bible in a Puritan sermon. That the reference to a political document formally took precedence over a reference to Scripture can only be described as a groundbreaking secularization. If Haynes's secularization of what was thus becoming "*American Scripture*"[15] no longer looks revolutionary today, it is also because his alteration of the Declaration's second sentence has anticipated later uses so precisely that it is now taken for granted: arguably, most people all over the world still know the phrase best in the truncated version of Haynes's epigraph from 1776, quoted only from "We hold these truths" until "life, liberty, and the pursuit of happiness." Although not published until 1983, *Liberty* was likely written in the year of the Declaration of Independence, a time when the former minuteman briefly served in the Continental Army. During his exceptional career as minister to white congregations in Vermont, Haynes would later employ his New Divinity teachings in the service of antislavery, but he would rarely address the situation of African Americans as directly as he did in this early essay.[16] The text that he described as a "Small *Treatise*" and may have intended to publish under his name[17] opened by quoting the Declaration's second sentence verbatim. But what may today look like a conventional borrowing from a hegemonic discourse may be most remarkable for the parts of the original it radically *silenced*: in one bold move, Haynes chose to quote Jefferson's long phrase only until the first mention of "happiness," thus eliminating the entire argument before the sentence's second and final mention of "happiness," including the "consent of the governed" and the right of the people to "institute a new government, laying it's [*sic*] foundation on such principles & organizing it's powers in such form, as to them shall seem most likely to effect their safety & happiness" (a phrase that had already appeared in similar terms in 1774 in Jefferson's *Summary View of the Rights of British America*).[18]

Haynes's abridgment had several decisive philosophical consequences. To begin with, it shattered the syllogistic structure of the original phrase, thus taking away an argument in favor of the view that Jefferson's community of feeling had indeed been justified in its opinion that the truths it was holding were "self-evident."[19] Moreover, the abridgment radically downplayed the Declaration's original stress, as discussed in the previous chapters, on collective *assent* and *consent* as its primary means to establish the authority of "these truths." In a similar vein, it reduced the communal aspect of the Declaration's rights claims as well as Jefferson's historical relativization of the terms *principle* and *form*. The original sentence had specified the people's right to self-government by "*such* principles" and in "*such* form" as they collectively deemed best, according to the contingent factor of their own subjectively limited impressions of a changing historical reality, in such ways as "*to them* shall *seem* most *likely* to effect their safety & happiness." Haynes's truncated version froze the phrase's enumeration of separate truths, from equal creation to the inalienable rights of "life, liberty, and the pursuit of happiness," into the status of ahistorical universals. What for Jefferson had been a "safety" (including life and liberty) and "happiness" that were historically relative problems of subjective opinion and assent, in Haynes's influential abridgment became a matter of timeless truth and absolute knowledge.

In Haynes's interpretation of the Declaration, self-evidence, truth, and natural right had to come from other sources than the subjective mental operations of Jefferson's historicized community of feeling. For the "Black Puritan," the primary source was not difficult to identify: an Edwardsean God who overruled the providential sins of fallen man.[20] Since for Haynes every "privilege that mankind Enjoy have their Origen from god," and liberty was "a Jewel which was handed Down to man from the cabinet of heaven," he concluded "as it proceed from the Supreme Legislature of the univers, so it is he which hath a sole right to take away." The "[u]nreasonable, and tyrannic power" of slavery "had its Origin from the infernal regions," it being "a Lamentable consequence of the fall, that mankind, have an insatiable thurst after Superorety one over another."[21] With an increase of epistemological ambition that would be continued by later writers in the tradition (most notably by David Walker), Haynes described his own position as "reasonable" as well as "candid" rather than merely expecting these attributes from the audience of a "candid world," as had Jefferson's Declaration. Meanwhile, Haynes understood his treatise as an "appeal to the conscience of any rational and honest man," as opposed to "such Short-Sited persons whose Contracted Eyes never penitrate thro' the narrow confines of Self."[22]

Since God, reason, and the sense of sight were thus aligned on the side of republicanism as well as antislavery,[23] Jefferson's optical "veil of black" and the people suffering from Ellison's "peculiar disposition of the eyes" would have been unmistakably placed on the wrong side of salvation history. Nevertheless, there was also a decidedly secular, "freethinking" dimension to the historical narrative of *Liberty Further Extended*. In what Haynes described as his "free thoughts" in both his title and the text

Tray depicting Lemuel Haynes, ca. 1835–40. Oil paint on papier-mâché. (RISD Museum, Providence, Rhode Island; gift of Miss Lucy T. Aldrich)

itself,[24] he achieved a synthesis of Jefferson's emotional language and his own rational argument that "an *African*, or, in other terms, *that a Negro may Justly Chalenge, and has an undeniable right to his* [. . .] *Liberty: Consequently, the practice of Slave-keeping, which so much abounds in this Land is illicit.*"[25] Haynes supplemented the Declaration's concept of English "consanguinity" by complex reflections on "Affrican-Blood,"[26] adding to the "agonizing affection" of Jefferson's inner–Anglo-Saxon family feud "the Sorrows, the Greif the Distress, and anguish"[27] of the enslaved during the Middle Passage. In contrast to Jefferson, however, he used this language, not to evoke two separate communities of feeling, but to expose the "narrow confines of Self" in a "Short-sited" society of unregenerate American enslavers. For him, the abstraction of natural rights did not have to be mediated by communal emotion and opinion. Instead, it was a "principle" that was universally accessible to both reason and the sense of sight: "Liberty & freedom, is an innate principle, which is unmovebly placed in the human Species; and to see a man aspire after it, is not Enigmatical, seeing he acts no ways incompatible with his own Nature; consequently, he that would infring upon a mans Liberty must reasonably Expect to meet with opposition, seeing the Defendant cannot Comply to Non-resistance, unless he Counter-acts the very Laws of Nature."[28]

For Benjamin Banneker less than two decades later, Haynes's rationalist transformation of the Declaration's second sentence had already become a "true and invaluable doctrine, which is worthy to be recorded and remember'd in all Succeeding ages."[29] In 1791, and thus even at a time when Jefferson had not yet become widely known as the Declaration's author,[30] the Maryland astronomer wrote a personal letter to the then secretary of state that can be seen, in the words of Annette Gordon-Reed, "as the beginning of blacks' formal political and personal engagement with Thomas Jefferson, save for his own slaves who always engaged him personally."[31] Together with Jefferson's politely evasive reply, Banneker's letter was published as a pamphlet in 1792, launching what was to become its prolific career in antebellum antislavery publications.[32] While the letter engaged specifically with Jefferson's restricted vision in regard to "blacks" under Query XIV of *Notes on the State of Virginia* (of which more in the next chapter), it also plays an important role in the rationalist reception history of the Declaration of Independence. Like Haynes, Banneker quoted the Declaration's second sentence verbatim until "happyness." And like Haynes, he took great care to insist on a universalist epistemology, even resorting to similar rhetorical devices: following Wheatley, both men showed a predilection for paralipsis to claim the common ground of a single theory of knowledge, as when Haynes spoke of "a truth which has Been so clearly Evinced [. . .] that to spend time in illustrating this, would be But Superfluous tautology,"[33] or when Banneker lamented "a truth too well attested to you, to need proof here, that we are a race of Beings who have long laboured under the abuse and censure of the world, that we have long been looked upon with an eye of contempt, and that we have long been considered rather brutish than human, and Scarcely capable of mental endowments." (Banneker's use of the device can even be described as an ironic meta-paralipsis, drawing attention to the fact that Jefferson had more than one means of accessing this particular truth.)

Although Banneker's "universal Father" appears closer to his Quaker environment than to Haynes's New Divinity theology, he served a similar function in his argument as the main foundation of its universalist truth claims. Banneker specified an array of such claims in elaboration of Haynes's abridgment, such as that "one universal Father" had given to all men "the Same Sensations" as well as "the same faculties" and that the "rights of human nature" included "every part of the human race" and "every Individual of whatsoever rank or distinction." In support of these claims, Banneker did not vaguely "pledge a faith yet unsullied by falsehood," as Jefferson had in his draft of the Declaration, but sharply distinguished his knowledge from "absurd and false ideas and oppinions" as well as "narrow prejudices."

Like Haynes, Banneker thus drew a sharp line between knowledge and opinion. Again and again in his letter, he emphasized that knowledge of the truth in regard to the "principles" of the American Revolution led to inescapable logical conclusions as well as universally binding moral duties, as when he expressed his hope that Jefferson could not "*but* acknowledge, that it is the indispensable duty of those who maintain for themselves the rights of human nature, and who profess the obligations of Christianity, to extend their power and influence to the relief of every part of the human race, from whatever burthen or oppression they may unjustly labour under, and this I apprehend a full conviction of the truth and obligation of these principles should lead all to."

As an astronomer whose African ancestors may already have been engaged in astronomical observations,[34] Banneker had philosophical as well as political reasons to privilege authoritative, mathematical knowledge over subjective opinion. In both sacred and secular terms, he discerned the instabilities of Jefferson's Enlightenment of Feeling in the Declaration of Independence: "Here Sir, was a time in which your tender *feelings* for your selves had engaged you thus to declare, you were then impressed with proper ideas of the great valuation of liberty," Banneker told Jefferson, "but Sir how pitiable is it to reflect, that although you were so fully convinced of the benevolence of the Father of mankind, and of his equal and impartial distribution of those rights and privileges which he had conferred upon them, that you should at the Same time counteract his mercies, in detaining by fraud and violence so numerous a part of my brethren under groaning captivity and cruel oppression, that you should at the Same time be found guilty of the most criminal act, which you professedly detested in others, with respect to yourselves." If ideas of liberty stemmed from "tender feelings" rather than reason, Banneker implied, they were so unstable as to collapse into their opposite at any moment, leading to captivity and oppression, fraud and violence, "pitiable" guilt and crime.

"Rational Liberty"

By the time of James Forten's argument for the concept that he identified as "rational liberty" in his *Series of Letters by a Man of Color* (1813), what Haynes had abridged and Banneker already understood as a "doctrine" had metamorphosed into truth in the singular as well as God in the active voice: "We hold this truth to be self-evident, that GOD created all men equal."[35] The successful Philadelphia businessman and Patriot veteran of the Revolutionary War, who would begin to oppose the colonization movement in the following years, still remembered having listened to the first public reading of the Declaration of Independence in Philadelphia as a boy.[36] In his first letter of the *Series*, he went on to explain his alteration of what had been passive voice in both the Declaration of Independence and the Pennsylvania constitution. As he saw it, the self-evident truth that God created all men equal was "one of the most prominent features in the Declaration of Independence, and in that glorious fabric of collective wisdom, our noble Constitution. This idea embraces the Indian and the European, the Savage and the Saint, the Peruvian and the Laplander, the white Man and the African, and whatsoever measures are adopted subversive of this inestimable privilege, are in direct violation of the letter and spirit of our Constitution."[37] Forten used this universalist reading of the Declaration's and the state constitution's meaning as the normative foundation of his (eventually successful) campaign against what he called an "unrighteous bill"[38] that had recently been proposed in Pennsylvania, which would have restricted African American immigration into the state by draconian measures. Appealing to Pennsylvanians' pride in their own rationality, he asked rhetorically (and somewhat hyperbolically): "This is almost the only state in the Union wherein the African have justly boasted of rational liberty, and protection of the laws, and shall it now be said they have been deprived of that liberty, and publicly exposed for sale to the highest bidder?"[39]

In New York on January 1 of the same year, George Lawrence had given an anniversary speech on the abolition of the slave trade that similarly spoke with "the voice of reason and justice."[40] Like Forten, Lawrence stressed God's active role in relation to the "principles" of the Declaration of Independence but voiced the implications of this role even more forcefully: "the land in which we live gives us the opportunity rapidly to advance the prosperity of liberty. This government founded on the principles of liberty and equality, and declaring them to be the free gift of God, if not ignorant of their declaration, must enforce it."[41] For Lawrence as for many other African American thinkers before and after him, the Declaration's "principles" were straightforward matters of knowledge and "ignorance," not subjective belief and assent. They were more than a "creed" comfortably binding Americans together in a national community of feeling. Once known, the Declaration's universalist principles had to be immediately acted upon and "enforced," especially within American national boundaries.

With this interpretation, the weight of the Declaration's second sentence shifted further away from its original meanings, along the trajectory first outlined by the Haynes abridgment. For Jefferson, government had been founded, not directly on universal principles of liberty and equality dispensed by universal reason, but on the consent of the people; government assumed only "*such* principles" as suited the people, according to what "to them shall seem most likely" to ensure their rights. For Lawrence, there was no room for subjectively changing appearances and probabilities. Government was unequivocally under the obligation to follow the timeless rational principles he declared (or declared that the Declaration had declared) were at its foundation, and which he claimed Americans had received immediately from God. Once the *logos* of the Declaration had become known, in Lawrence's argument, there was only one solution, and "rational man" had to "walk undauntedly in the very jaws of death to retain his liberty."[42]

Echoes of Lawrence's stress on both divine and secular reason could be found in the later nineteenth century as well, including among critics of the Declaration of Independence. As, for instance, the influential intellectual and Episcopal pastor Alexander Crummell argued in 1881:

> [T]here are two factors in all civil government, and in the exercise of all civil authority; and it is one of the gravest of all mistakes that it was not laid down thus, in the infancy of the nation, in the great charter of freedom, the "Declaration of Independence." When Thomas Jefferson declared that "governments derive their just powers from the consent of the governed," and left his dogma crudely, at that point, he shut out a limitation which the pride and self-assertion of degenerate humanity is always too reluctant to yield, and too tardy to supply. The theory of the Declaration is incomplete and misleading. Governments [. . .] derive their just authority, *first* of all, from the will of God; and then *next*, from the consent of the governed.[43]

What Crummell's biographer Wilson Jeremiah Moses has identified as "a strenuous black 'protestant' ethic"[44] found the remedy to "this cheap idea of government," that is, the "notion of government [. . .] that it is mostly a subjective thing," in authoritative knowledge and rational principle. "One grand corrective to this error lies in the region of thought and principle. 'People who have been entrapped by false opinions must be liberated by convincing truths.'"[45]

In the decade following Lawrence's "Oration on the Abolition of the Slave Trade," William Hamilton's Fourth of July oration celebrating the abolition of slavery in New York couched the rationalist interpretation of the Declaration in more fully secular terms.[46] The prominent New York antislavery activist and reputed son of Alexander Hamilton was likely Jefferson's most outspoken African American critic before David Walker.[47] He used the occasion in 1827 to include a philosophical reflection that made explicit previous and later thinkers' efforts to endow the Declaration's language with a single, rational, universally valid meaning. On a historically overdetermined day of celebration that happened to coincide with the first anniversary of Jefferson's death and that was heavily debated, for instance, in *Freedom's Journal*,[48] Hamilton combined his own philosophical exegesis of the Declaration with sharp personal criticism of its principal author. He had been developing this criticism at least since 1809, the year when not only Washington Irving's Federalist caricature of Jefferson as a Quixotic pseudo-philosopher was published in *A History of New York*, as discussed earlier, but when Hamilton himself, in "An Address to the New York African Society for Mutual Relief," had incisively ridiculed Jefferson's postcolonial Enlightenment as that of a "willful novice" in logic who was "blind intentionally."[49]

Hamilton's 1827 oration opened diplomatically with a celebration of universalist "principles." He began by felicitating New Yorkers "on the victory obtained by the principles of liberty, such as are broadly and indelibly laid down by the glorious sons of '76." Quoting the Declaration's second sentence verbatim (almost needless to say, in Haynes's truncated form), he proclaimed victory "by these principles over prejudice, injustice, and foul oppression" and expressed amazement "at the quiet, yet rapid progress the principles of liberty have made."[50] The oration gradually built up an angrier tone, however. "The names of Washington and Jefferson should not be pronounced in the hearing of your children," Hamilton advised, "until they could clearly and distinctly pronounce the names I am about to give," including those of John Jay as president of the Manumission Society, and "general Alexander Hamilton, that excellent soldier, and most able civilian and financier, and first of his profession at the bar."[51] In the oration's second half, William Hamilton became more and more explicit in denouncing the other Hamilton's nemesis. He first alluded to Jefferson as an example of "our enemies," who were (as Banneker had suggested earlier) "more the objects of pity and commiseration, than of anger and hate." Eventually, however, he offered a full indictment of Jefferson as a philosopher. "Man is a moral being, and ought to be governed by his reason. The lessons of reason are the lessons of morality," he began his critique. By contrast, Jefferson was "an ambidexter philosopher, who can reason contrarywise, first tells you 'that all men are created equal, and that they are endowed with the unalienable rights of life liberty, and the pursuit of happiness,' next proves that one class of men are not equal to another, which by the bye, does not agree with axioms in geometry, that deny that things can be equal, and at the same time unequal, to one another."[52]

In a series of rhetorical questions, Hamilton summed up the weaknesses of Jefferson's philosophy: "Would not such a reasoner only show a heterogeneous mind? Although he should be called an abstruse reasoner, what kind of superiority does he discover? Does he not reason, and act, like one that battles with the elements? Does he reason like a man of true moral principles? Does he set a good example? Does he act in conformity to true philosophy?" What Hamilton regarded as Jefferson's frivolously overrefined, irrational, and immoral thinking clearly did not qualify as a true love of knowledge. As he saw it, the main point of the Declaration of Independence might have been expressed with greater precision as well: "True philosophy teaches, that a man should act in conformity to his reason, and *reason, and the law of God and nature, declare* that all men *are* equal, and that life, liberty, and the pursuit of happiness are their inalienable rights."[53] What in Jefferson's Declaration had been declared by American colonists-becoming-citizens as an emotional, communally shared opinion on the epistemological status of equal creation, in Hamilton's rationalist ethics had been transformed into full and universal equality declared by reason itself.

"Wretchedness in Consequence of Ignorance"

With their strong concepts of divine as well as human reason, writers in the African American tradition thus caused the primary meaning of the Declaration of Independence to shift from the partial relativism of a "decent respect" for contingent subjective opinions in a world of "separate and equal" nations to a sharp contrast between ignorance, on the one hand, and authoritative, universally valid and communicable knowledge, on the other. This development culminated two years after Hamilton's 1827 oration in *Walker's Appeal, in Four Articles, together with a Preamble, to the Coloured Citizens of the World, but in Particular, and Very Expressly to Those of the United States of America*, whose "third and final edition" appeared shortly before David Walker's mysterious death in 1830. Often placed at a watershed moment in the transition to the more radical forms of abolitionism of the last three decades before the Civil War, the discussion of slavery, *race*, and colonization in *Walker's Appeal* referred to various historical figures from Hannibal to Las Casas, including Americans as different as Richard Allen, on the one hand, and Henry Clay, on the other. However, the central historical figure of *Walker's Appeal*, after Walker himself, was no doubt Jefferson,[54] in extensive quotations and discussions of both Queries XIV and XVIII of *Notes on the State of Virginia* (as will be discussed in the next chapter) and the Declaration of Independence. Moreover, like Hamilton before him, Walker showed a great interest in redefining terms that had been prominent in these texts, such as *candid*, *wretched*, and especially *ignorance*, which Jefferson had used in ways almost diametrically opposed to Walker.

Walker's Appeal developed the theme of knowledge and ignorance on various levels throughout its four articles, culminating in long quotations from the Declaration of Independence. In its preamble, the pamphlet addressed those readers "who are not blinded" but "who are able to lay aside prejudice long enough to view candidly and impartially, things as they were, are, and probably will be."[55] *Walker's Appeal* thus went beyond the Declaration's characterization of its audience as a "candid world." Walker's speaker voiced high expectations not only in regard to his various overlapping audiences,[56] but also in regard to himself, more than once explicitly characterizing himself as "candid" and unprejudiced. In his claim to knowledge of "things as they exist" not only in American but also world history, this speaker assumed a near-omniscient, prophetic perspective, putting himself in the position of having the overview of all continents and all periods "since the world began."[57] As one means to make this universal perspective plausible, he prominently resorted to paralipsis, as had Wheatley, Haynes, and Banneker before him.[58] In the secular spirit of a universalist Enlightenment, he further strengthened his claims to full and universal knowledge by attacking *ignorance* as one of the four major terms coupled with the term *wretchedness* in the four articles of *Walker's Appeal* (entitled "Our Wretchedness in Consequence of Slavery," "Our Wretchedness in Consequence of Ignorance," "Our Wretchedness in Consequence of the Preachers of the Religion of Jesus Christ," and "Our Wretchedness in Consequence of the Colonization Plan").

Compared to Jefferson, who had defined his postcolonial stance in *Notes on the State of Virginia* in opposition to the elitism of the Old World's "wretched philosophy,"[59] on several occasions Walker thus almost appears closer to European concepts of *Ecrasez l'infâme*. Instead of the elitist love of knowledge that Jefferson's term *wretched philosophy* had attacked, Walker's targets include more traditional objects of Enlightenment scorn, such as corrupt clerics, ignorance, and prejudice. Where Jefferson had coupled wretchedness and European intellectualism, Walker saw wretchedness in American ignorance. Especially in the second article, written in opposition to white Americans who "keep us in abject ignorance and wretchedness" while holding him "up to the public as an ignorant, impudent and restless disturber of the public peace,"[60] his speaker emphasized full knowledge rather than opinion, seeing fewer problems than had Jefferson in addressing himself to an intellectual elite. His Enlightenment project of awakening "in the breasts of my afflicted, degraded and slumbering brethren a spirit of inquiry and investigation"[61] tended to require a certain amount of intellectual hierarchization: "Men of colour who are also of sense for you particularly is my APPEAL designed," Walker specified. "Our more ignorant brethren are not able to penetrate its value. I call upon you therefore to cast your eyes on the wretchedness of your brethren, and to do your utmost to enlighten them—*go to work and enlighten your brethren!*"[62]

In Walker's hierarchical conception of the "work" of Enlightenment as spreading authoritative knowledge, ignorance had not only an epistemological but also a pronounced moral dimension. In the context of slavery, he repeatedly tied ignorance to "treachery" and (servile) "deceit," including among the "wretched" and the enslaved themselves.[63] By contrast, as shown in the preceding chapters, Jefferson had made a point of showing himself comfortable with ignorance, especially his own. And not only had he often abstained from morally condemning ignorance; he had gone as far as to find moral justifications for it. For instance, he had habitually praised the appeal of ignorance as that of Montaigne's "pillow," which "a benevolent creator has made so soft for us, knowing how much we should be forced to use it."[64] Moreover, he had blithely claimed in *Notes on the State of Virginia* that "[i]gnorance is preferable to error; and he is less remote from the truth who believes nothing, than he who believes what is wrong."[65] This facile acceptance of ignorance—whether illustrated by the soft fabric of a "pillow" or that of a "veil"—was supposed to demonstrate his openness to the progress of his postcolonial Enlightenment but was willfully shallow even on its own terms.[66] It might have been persuasive on the premise that "believing nothing" was a realistic possibility—for a human mind that somehow managed to remain a lifelong version of Locke's tabula rasa, for example—but Jefferson's own theory of involuntary opinion rendered such a premise highly implausible.

Walker's Appeal thus had strong epistemological as well as moral reasons to distinguish itself sharply from Jefferson's vaguely ironic, deliberately superficial appreciation of ignorance. These reasons throw new light on what might be identified as Walker's forays into early *black uplift* ideology: for example, his admonitions to African Americans to overcome ignorance and strive for "higher attainments than *wielding the razor* and *cleaning boots and shoes*," his exhortations addressed specifically to African American students not only to write "a neat hand" but also "to correct the false grammar of their language" and learn to "write a neat piece of composition in prose or in verse," and in sum to "seek after the substance of learning" instead of making mere "pretensions to knowledge."[67] Against the backdrop of Jefferson's egalitarian laissez-faire epistemology, Walker's insistence on strong concepts of knowledge and ignorance was far from an appeal to a generic "white" standard. To the contrary, Walker's argument on the "wretchedness in consequence of ignorance" implied a harsh criticism of Jefferson's lax intellectual standards from the perspective of an epistemologically much more ambitious Enlightenment tradition.

This Enlightenment tradition also shaped Walker's use of the Declaration of Independence. The critique of colonization in the fourth and final article of *Walker's Appeal* culminates in repeated exhortations to Americans to "let us reason"[68] and in the quotation of the Declaration's first four long sentences in full. Rather than departing from the African American tradition, however, Walker immediately added his version of the Haynes abridgment, with idiosyncratic alterations in punctuation and typography[69] that served to underline his conception of authoritative knowledge and immoral ignorance:

> See your Declaration Americans!!! Do you understand your own language? Hear your language, proclaimed to the world, July 4th, 1776—☞ "We hold these truths to be self evident—that ALL MEN ARE CREATED EQUAL!! That they are *endowed by their Creator with certain unalienable rights;* that among these are life, *liberty,* and the pursuit of happiness!!" Compare your own language above, extracted from your Declaration of Independence, with your cruelties and murders inflicted by your cruel and unmerciful fathers and yourselves on our fathers and on us—men who have never given your fathers or you the least provocation!!!!!![70]

With this robustly didactic use of the Declaration as the culmination of his anticolonization jeremiad, Walker radicalized the tradition of associating the document with authoritative truth. Illustrating the main political direction of his hierarchical conception of knowledge, he left little doubt that the problem of ignorance concerned, not only the "wretched" among the "coloured citizens of the world" but the great mass of white Americans, whose perceptive and cognitive weaknesses extended even to understanding "their *own* language," and who were "ignorant enough to tell us, that we ought to be submissive to them, that they may keep their feet on our throats."[71] In a complex paralipsis in the second Article, Walker's speaker ironically acknowledged Jefferson's admission of whites' ignorance in regard to African Americans: "as Mr. Jefferson wisely said, they have *never found us out*—they do not know, indeed, that there is an unconquerable disposition in the breasts of the blacks, which, when it is fully awakened and put in motion, will be subdued, only with the destruction of the animal existence."[72] Blending Wheatley's "Principle" of universal liberty ("in every human breast, God has implanted a Principle, which we call Love of Freedom") and Lawrence's "rational man" walking "undauntedly in the very jaws of death to retain his liberty," Walker thus asserted that his own version of rational liberty (the only term he italicized in Jefferson's triad of inalienable rights) was a problem of knowledge and ignorance, not opinion and assent. In the fourth Article, he added manicules, capital letters, and italics to the Haynes abridgment, in order to remedy what he depicted as white Americans' deprivations of enlightened thinking, following the conceit developed in the African American tradition that it was ultimately a deplorable Enlightenment deficit, an immoral ignorance resulting from an insufficient intellectual apprehension of the Declaration's true meaning, that stood in the way of the end of slavery. Rather than following Jefferson in placing each community of feeling and opinion on a different "side of the water,"[73] Walker thus powerfully consolidated the common ground of a universalist Enlightenment as the most important precondition for an effective fight against slavery, racism, and colonization. At bottom, it was this radical departure from Jefferson's postcolonial thought that allowed him to envision at least the possibility of a "united and happy people" in the United States.[74]

"Every Avenue to Knowledge"

Almost immediately, the "most noble, fearless, and undaunted David Walker," as the Boston teacher and public speaker Maria W. Stewart praised him in the year following his death,[75] came to be depicted as a major figure in an emergent intellectual tradition, including by Henry Highland Garnet, Frederick Douglass, and later W. E. B. Du Bois, among others.[76] In her speeches, Stewart took up Walker's concern with strong concepts of knowledge and ignorance, tying it to Wheatley's language of liberty in the "breasts" of the "sable race."[77] "[K]nowledge is power," Stewart stated in even clearer terms than had Walker, "AND WE CLAIM OUR RIGHTS."[78] *Walker's Appeal* was republished in the revolutionary spring of 1848 together with Garnet's controversial *Address to the Slaves of the United States of America* and a short hagiographic narrative, Garnet's "Brief Sketch of the Life and Character of David Walker."[79] In the *Address to the Slaves*, whose encouragement of violent resistance among the enslaved had prevented its earlier publication at the national convention in Buffalo in 1843, Garnet continued to explore Walker's theme of knowledge and ignorance. Praising the Declaration of Independence as "a glorious document" admired by "Sages" all over the world for its "God-like sentiments," he lamented the contrarian force of American "public opinion (which in this country is stronger than law)" and which threatened to completely destroy the "intellect" of the enslaved as well as the enslavers.[80]

After the Compromise of 1850, during his extended exile as a fugitive slave in England, William Wells Brown drafted *An Appeal to the People of*

Great Britain and the World (1851). It was recited by a fellow fugitive, Alexander Duval, at a meeting Brown had organized at the Hall of Commerce in London to celebrate Emancipation Day, the anniversary of the abolition of slavery in most of the British Empire on August 1, 1834.[81] While the title recalled *Walker's Appeal to the Coloured Citizens of the World*, the text of Brown's *Appeal* rephrased the language of the Declaration of Independence. "We consider it just, both to the people of the United States and to ourselves," the *Appeal* inverted the perspective of the Declaration's opening paragraph, "in making an appeal to the inhabitants of other countries against the laws which have exiled us from our native land, to state the ground upon which we make our appeal, and the causes which impel us to do so." Brown's *Appeal* positioned itself as a text that went beyond the Declaration, both in the question of who was included in its claims and in the content of these claims themselves. For Brown, the enslaved in America were "not only" deprived of natural laws. Like his predecessors in the African American hermeneutical tradition of the Declaration, Brown was concerned with the problem of knowledge and divine wisdom: "These people are not only deprived of the rights to which the laws of Nature and of Nature's God entitle them, but every avenue to knowledge is closed against them, and the blessed teachings of the Savior denied them." For Brown, white America was assuming the role Jefferson had assigned to George III in the Declaration's list of grievances. "The history of the negroes in America is but a history of repeated injuries and acts of oppression committed upon them by the whites." Therefore, Jefferson's association of American independence with the Haynes abridgment of the Declaration's second phrase was a lie: "In their Declaration of Independence, the Americans declare that 'all men are created equal; that they are endowed by their Creator with certain inalienable rights; that among these are life, liberty, and the pursuit of happiness.' Yet, one-sixth of the inhabitants of the great Republic are slaves. Thus they give the lie to their own professions."

Two years after Brown's *Appeal*, the first edition of his novel *Clotel; or, The President's Daughter: A Narrative of Slave Life in the United States* was published in London. As will be discussed in chapter 7, its plot about Jefferson's enslaved family transformed the argument of the *Appeal* into fiction. This transformation was illustrated by the title page, which directly juxtaposed the fictional fate of Jefferson's enslaved daughter with the Haynes abridgment of the Declaration of Independence. A similar rhetoric of contrast between slavery and the Declaration was employed throughout the novel's narrative as well as, for instance, in the preface of William and Ellen Craft's *Running a Thousand Miles for Freedom* (1860) and, in the year of *Clotel's* publication, in Solomon Northup's *Twelve Years a Slave* and James M. Whitfield's poem "America."[82] In an ironic twist that had been preceded by the Anglophilia of the later editions of *Walker's Appeal*,[83] Brown thus moved the moral center of both his *Appeal* and the London edition of *Clotel* from the American Declaration of Independence "back" to Britain. Especially since the new version of the American Fugitive Slave Law from 1850 had "converted the entire country, North and South, into one vast hunting-ground," as Brown put it in the *Appeal*, the "People of Great Britain" were now the guardians of "every principle of human brotherhood." By the early 1850s, the "spirit of liberty and equality" appeared to have returned to the old mother country.

Douglass's "Thin Veil"

Brown's powerful revision of the Declaration of Independence is comparatively little-known today, as his editor has recently remarked.[84] One possible explanation may be that its international argument was quickly overshadowed by the national focus of Frederick Douglass's "What to the Slave Is the Fourth of July?" address in 1852, which appears today as the most prominent heir to the revisions of Jefferson's postcolonial Enlightenment in *Walker's Appeal*. Invited by the Rochester Ladies' Anti-Slavery Society for July 4 and delivering his speech on July 5, Douglass reflected on the day that had, even before he began to speak, become the most contested anniversary in American history. In 1826 and 1831, three of the first five American presidents had already used it to great "stage effect,"[85] turning it into a patriotic anniversary of both liberty *and* death. In 1831, Nat Turner had at first contemplated the Fourth as the date for his revolt, perhaps inspired directly by the interpretation of the Declaration in *Walker's Appeal*.[86] And even prior to Walker's decision to include the date in his quotation of the Declaration of Independence in his pamphlet, contributors to *Freedom's Journal* had discussed not only the date's symbolism but also its material dangers. A serious problem many African Americans then saw in celebrating the Fourth of July, for instance, on the day of the abolition of slavery in New York, was not so much the risk of being regarded as complicit with "white" values, but the very real danger of being attacked by white mobs.[87]

Douglass crafted a rhetorical masterpiece on the historical significance of this contested date that can be read as a summary reflection, not only on the Declaration of Independence itself, but especially on the transformations of its meaning in the African American tradition. Even as he famously distanced himself from celebrating the anniversary of the Declaration, he made a point of taking for granted the document's rationalist interpretation. Following, for instance, Haynes, Banneker, and Walker, Douglass prominently resorted to paralipsis to explain the Declaration's universal meaning, but he went a step further: unlike his predecessors, he no longer quoted the Haynes abridgment of the Declaration's second sentence verbatim. In fact, although he quoted many other authorities, from the Bible to Shakespeare and even Garrison, he no longer quoted Jefferson's language directly at all. Instead, he insisted that the Declaration's meaning had been so clearly "settled by the rules of logic and argumentation" that any further discussion or "speaking of it relatively and positively, negatively, and affirmatively" would "offer an insult" to his audience's intellect. "Would you have me argue that man is entitled to liberty? That he is the rightful owner of his own body?" he asked, adding drily, "You have already declared it." Since for Douglass the rational case against slavery had already been made, he considered further "light" or "convincing argument" to be completely unnecessary and claimed that it was only left to him to resort to irony, sarcasm, and ridicule.

Douglass also went further than his predecessors in meditating on the Declaration's key position in American history—"the RINGBOLT to the chain of your nation's destiny," in his oft-quoted phrase—and distinguishing closely between its historically contingent and its universal aspects. While he historicized "the great controversy of 1776" by sketching the specific political and technological environment of the late eighteenth century, he implicitly placed himself in a new "ringbolt" position by emphasizing that he was making his speech at a point in time that came exactly "76 years" after the first 1776. The Founders of the United States had been "great in their day and generation," he argued, and though their bravery and patriotism were "not the highest form of human excellence," these virtues had to be respected as part of the emotional factor—the "passionate feats of revolutionary will," as Ellison would later put it—that made the American Founding possible.[88] In contrast to this historical account of revolutionary *feeling*, what Douglass identified as the Declaration's rational "saving principles" were timeless. When he exhorted white Americans to "stand by those principles, be true to them on all occasions, in all places, against all foes, and at whatever cost,"[89] he described what had become, in the African American tradition before him as well as in his own rhetoric, the Declaration's absolute, transhistorical, "eternal"[90] truth. Toward the end of the speech, he placed "the Declaration of Independence" in quotation marks.[91] Especially in their inclusion of the definite article, these scare quotes would be somewhat counterintuitive, unless understood as a means to distinguish the original document in its historical contingency from Douglass's universalist interpretation of it in the "ever-living now"[92] of a new "76."

In his "Fifth of July" speech, "the all-pervading light"[93] of Douglass's universalist Enlightenment powerfully overwrote what has today become the lost vision of Jefferson's postcolonial Enlightenment of Feeling. Following his historical exposition on the original 1776, in a section entitled "THE PRESENT," Douglass made explicit the normative foundation of his universalism, in contradistinction to the qualified universalism of Jefferson's generation. Quoting Henry Wadsworth Longfellow, he explained: "My business, if I have any here today, is with the present. The accepted time with God and his cause is the ever-living now. *Trust no future, however pleasant, Let the dead past bury its dead; Act, act in the living present, Heart within, and God overhead.*'" Whereas Jefferson's semi-secularized philosophy had been able to postpone the abolition of slavery into a potentially far-off future, the compromise of a similarly "conjectural" approach was no longer possible after Douglass's transformation of the Declaration. As described earlier, Jefferson's antirationalism had enabled him to "trust" the pleasant future of a secularized afterlife by relying on a progressively evolving public opinion, without detailing the metaphysical premises on which this trust was based. By contrast, Douglass fully committed to the religious premise of "God and his cause," on the one hand, and the secular political action of an "ever-living now," on the other.

In the conclusion of his speech, Douglass distinguished his nineteenth-century vision from more limited eighteenth-century concepts of the progress of Enlightenment. According to Jefferson's postcolonial "diffusion" of knowledge, as has been shown, the democratization of knowledge had been part of an anti-Eurocentric stance that led to a valorization of communal feeling and national "creed" rather than knowledge. Building on the sharper division between knowledge and ignorance in the African American tradition, by contrast, Douglass asserted a universalist epistemology by evoking a secular modernity in which universal knowledge was democratized on a global rather than a national scale. "Knowledge was then confined and enjoyed by the privileged few, and the multitude walked on in mental darkness," he described the bygone world of Jefferson's postcolonial Enlightenment. "But a change has now come over the affairs of mankind. Walled cities and empires have become unfashionable. The arm of commerce has borne away the gates of the strong city. Intelligence is penetrating the darkest corners of the globe. It makes its pathway over and under the sea, as well as on the earth. Oceans no longer divide, but link nations together. From Boston to London is now a holiday excursion. Space is comparatively annihilated.—Thoughts expressed on one side of the Atlantic, are distinctly heard on the other."[94]

According to Douglass's universalist Enlightenment, ignorance, darkness, and a loss of vision—"that blindness which seems to be the unvarying characteristic of tyrants"[95]—were at the opposite pole from this modern worldview. As he exalted the "saving principles"[96] of his own rationalist hermeneutics of the Declaration of Independence, he opposed them to an irrational practice of slavery that revealed the celebration of the Declaration's anniversary to be "mere bombast, fraud, deception, impiety, and hypocrisy—a thin veil to cover up crimes which would disgrace a nation of savages."[97] Douglass's use of the metaphor of the "thin veil" is instructive. After Jefferson had evoked "that immoveable veil of black" in *Notes on the State of Virginia* to write into existence two separate national communities of feeling, Douglass spoke of a "thin veil" that to him, in contrast to blind and ignorant "tyrants," was entirely transparent. As his metaphor suggests, the "thin veil" of white Americans' "prayers and hymns" celebrating the Fourth of July resembled Jefferson's soft "veil" of *race* in that both were communal belief systems that sought to hide from view the national crime and savagery of slavery. However, following the stronger concepts of knowledge and ignorance in the African American tradition, neither communal belief system could be effective in concealing the truth. Harking back to Wheatley's hopes for epistemological transcendence of the "sable veil," and anticipating W. E. B. Du Bois's expectation that "America shall rend the Veil,"[98] Douglass's abolitionist rhetoric of deception and revelation thus asserted that the "all-pervading light" of a universalist American Enlightenment illuminated the destinies of enslaved and enslavers alike.

❖ 6 ❖

Malignant Prejudice

"What Shall We Do with the White People?" Writing under a pen name reminiscent of one of Phillis Wheatley's literary personae—"Ethiop"—the Brooklyn teacher and journalist William J. Wilson asked this "grave question" in the title of an article he contributed to the *Anglo-African Magazine* in February 1860.¹ Wilson's *gravitas* was at once sincere and ironic.² On the eve of the Civil War, the question of what the "we" of an imagined Anglo-African community was supposed to do with white Americans could be understood as a serious expression of exasperation. At the same time, Wilson's "grave question" was a parody. It signified on a question that by the mid-nineteenth century had already had some history. For instance, more than four decades previously, the phrase "What shall we do with the free people of color?" had opened the pamphlet *Thoughts on the Colonization of Free Blacks* (1816) by one of the organizers of the American Colonization Society, Robert Finley.³ The original version of the question had appeared even earlier. Under Query XIV of *Notes on the State of Virginia*, it had concluded Jefferson's discussion of "white" Virginians' "deep rooted prejudices" against the people he was identifying as "black." The association with prejudice proved to be long-lived, reemerging in both Finley's and Wilson's discussions of the question. To underline his notion of the collective nature of prejudice, Jefferson had refrained from asking the question himself. Instead, he had pretended to quote an anonymous group of his contemporaries who were, supposedly, in the habit of asking about emancipated African Americans, "What further is to be done with them?"⁴

By framing the topic as a question in a discussion of prejudice, Query XIV initiated a flexible, epistemologically ambiguous discourse that turned out to provide a fertile ground for nineteenth-century appropriations and criticism. In its original context of Jefferson's circular discussion of "deep rooted prejudices," however, the question had served only to express a conviction that had already been formed. Beginning in the 1780s, Jefferson rarely departed from his idea that American "blacks" had to be "expatriated"—a term that he also used for American colonists in relation to England—so they could found their own nation-state.[5] In this sense, the question "What further is to be done with them?" had originally been far from flexible or ambiguous. Instead, it had crudely turned the people he called "blacks" into a problem to be solved by "white" Virginians' agency.

It is thus hardly surprising that Wilson was provoked to invert the question's relation between subject and object, with white rather than black Americans emerging as "problem-people."[6] Yet, his revision was no zero-sum game of *blackness* replacing *whiteness*. Challenging the evasiveness of Jefferson's method, Wilson took issue with Query XIV on a conceptual level that comprised politics as well as epistemology. Politically, as he put it, the expatriation of white people "would be wrong in conception, and prove abortive in attempt; nor ought it be desirable on our part were it even possible to forcibly remove them."[7] And epistemologically, Wilson claimed, there was something deeply wrong with grounding such an existential political decision solely in communal opinion and prejudice.

As had been characteristic of Jefferson's Enlightenment of Feeling, his question under Query XIV had not actually derived its claim to the objectification of "blacks" from any pretensions to scientific knowledge. Rather, its assumed authority had rested on what he imagined to be the shared feelings and prejudices of "white" Virginians, who did not yet know how to conceive of their new nation. Jefferson had stressed that he and his peers were as yet quite in the dark about how exactly to draw the "color-line," even by the lax standards of what was arguably, at the time of his writing, an already-antiquated natural history.[8] "To our reproach it must be said," Jefferson had admitted, "that though for a century and a half we have had under our eyes the races of black and of red men, they have never yet been viewed by us as subjects of natural history."[9] Wilson took his cue from there. Echoing Jefferson's language but replacing the object of his concern, he sarcastically worried about white Americans: "For many centuries now have they been on this continent; and for many years have they had entire rule and sway; yet they are to-day no nearer the solution of the problem, '*are they fit for self-government*'—than they were at the commencement of their career."

In Wilson's dystopian vision of Jefferson's Enlightenment of Feeling, what had seemed promising national beginnings, the "truthful language" of the Haynes abridgment of the Declaration of Independence, had soon become neglected as "glittering generalities"[10] by a people who had no control over their "prejudice and bitter hate against the oppressed, the outcast, and the lowly." Jefferson's democratization of knowledge, his upgrading of opinion, and his laissez-faire approach to prejudice had left behind a polarized political climate. Instead of "those honest and frank differences of opinion that beget and strengthen sound opinion," American public opinion had become defined by the "low petty captiousness and cowardly vindictiveness" of a people who were "grappling each other by the throat for opinion sake." As a result, America was now a country where section was "divided against section, and clan against clan, and each cheered on by fierce leaders and noisy demagogues on the one side; while compromise and harmony and quiet are sued for on the other by men who are denounced as fogies and fossils by the general voice of the whole people." Despite its auspicious beginnings, Jefferson's Enlightenment of Feeling had left behind "a tower of Babel, [. . .] a confusion of ideas infinitely more disintegrating than a confusion of tongues." White Americans could "feel" that something was "wrong, that a screw [wa]s somewhere loose in the general machinery of society," but were afraid to "bind what they find loosed, and [. . .] loosen what they find bound. They stand a powerless, self-condemned body, and call up all our pity, and we can scarcely mingle with it any tincture of bitterness."[11]

Wilson's "pity" for white Americans may seem counterintuitive today. At the time of his writing in 1860, however, it was a long-standing feature of the African American discussions of Query XIV that will be discussed in this chapter. For Wilson, it was white Americans who had yet to solve "the problem, '*are they fit for self-government.*'" Today, W. E. B. Du Bois's identification of the "problem" with African Americans is much better-known. As discussed in the famous first chapter of *The Souls of Black Folk* (1903), Du Bois sensed in the white world around him the "ever [. . .] unasked question [. . .] How does it feel to be a problem?"[12] However, nineteenth-century African American intellectuals such as Wilson or Frederick Douglass[13] did not see the world in these terms. There definitely was a problem with "feeling" in American society. But, for Wilson, the problem had to be found among American whites.

This chapter examines how Query XIV of *Notes on Virginia* could be used to identify the "problem" with white Americans such as Jefferson who made no secret of grounding their views on racial separation in subjective feeling and prejudice. Over the course of the eight decades between its publication and the Civil War, Query XIV evolved into a representative example of a failed subjectivity—of the collective misperceptions, false judgments, prejudgments, and prejudices that had been left insufficiently controlled by Jefferson's Enlightenment of Feeling. Jefferson's discussion, and performance, of the "deep rooted prejudices" he saw at work in Virginia society, both among his peers and in his own thought, became the reference point for a broad nineteenth-century discussion of prejudice that was closely intertwined with evolving modern notions of *race* and racism. African American readers of Query XIV including Wilson, Benjamin Banneker, William Hamilton, David Walker, Maria Stewart, Hosea Easton, James W. C. Pennington, and James McCune Smith developed their critiques of prejudice under XIV by further sharpening the contrast between Enlightened knowledge and prejudice. Their Enlightenment of Principle was unique in negotiating between two different periods of Enlightenment philosophy: it not only recurred to early eighteenth-century notions of Enlightenment as an uncompromising struggle against prejudice and superstition; at the same time, it already had to address the problem of less ambitious late eighteenth-century notions of Enlightenment inclined, like Jefferson's Enlightenment of Feeling, to accommodate prejudice by integrating a certain amount of what may be called, in anticipation of the sections below, self-serving self-criticism. As will be shown, especially in arguments directed against white colonizationists who were confessing to their antiblack prejudice as an irredeemable attribute of their *whiteness*, African American intellectuals developed a modernized discourse able to show how destructive prejudice was while also demonstrating that prejudice could, nevertheless, be overcome.

After briefly clarifying Jefferson's position in antebellum debates, the following sections will trace the conceptual transformation of his "deep rooted prejudices" in the African American tradition. They will not greatly concern themselves with the ethnographic *content* of Query XIV, which, even by the standards of Jefferson's own time, offered little that could be taken seriously.[14] For the writers discussed below, Query XIV mainly became useful as a repertoire of recurring rhetorical figures. For instance, Jefferson's orangutan analogy came to be used as a stand-in for *Notes on Virginia* or for Jefferson himself; his Roman comparison, as an illustration of self-serving historical ignorance; the question taken up by Wilson, as a figure of ironic inversion, etc. Instead of the content of Jefferson's prejudice, the sections below will thus focus on the *concept* of prejudice, in its development from an epistemological to a predominantly moral, from an involuntary to a voluntary, and from a collective to an individual problem. As Wheatley's Enlightenment of Principle gradually overwrote Jefferson's Enlightenment of Feeling, what many contemporaries regarded as a joint "system" of slavery and prejudice came under attack, as will be suggested in the conclusion, by the new, dialectical concept of the Jeffersonian Enlightenment.

"Some View Our Sable Race with Scornful Eye"

In what may be her best-known, and most controversial, poem today, "On Being Brought from AFRICA to AMERICA," Phillis Wheatley introduced the problem of American prejudice that will be discussed in this chapter. She warned against a form of racist prejudice that she depicted as a problem of the subjective limits imposed on the sense of sight, resulting in the contingent views of "some," but not all, Americans: "Some view our sable race with scornful eye / 'Their colour is a diabolic die.'"[15] From the late eighteenth century onward, American discussions of prejudice typically revolved around the question, not of whether racist prejudices were widespread in white America, but of whether these prejudices were occasioned by African Americans' *condition* or their *color*.[16] Especially if prejudice was understood to involve the visual perception of skin pigmentation, discussions of the term could usher in calls for racial segregation and national separation. Although this train of thought seems far from self-evident in retrospect, white proponents of colonization used their ostensibly self-critical awareness of their own racist prejudice—"prejudice, too deep rooted to be eradicated," in the words of Robert Finley[17]—as an argument in favor of African Americans having to leave the country.

Today we may be inclined to regard the cultivation of self-criticism, as concerning the moral and epistemological limitations of a collective *whiteness*, as a necessary step toward antiracism. As the arguments of white American colonizationists show, however, the assumption of a limited, group-specific epistemology could also go some way in the opposite direction. For example, in his 1796 *Dissertation on Slavery* the Bermuda native and Virginia law professor St. George Tucker, referring to the authority of Jefferson's *Notes on Virginia*, asked rhetorically about the incorporation of free African Americans into the polity: "who is there so free from prejudices among us, as candidly to declare that he has none against such a measure?" It was only a small step from confessions of the supposed ubiquity of white Virginians' prejudice to the justification of prejudice as a majority opinion, as when Tucker asked, almost in the same breath: "And if prejudices have taken such deep root in our minds, as to render it impossible to eradicate this opinion, ought not so general an error, if it be one, to be respected?"[18] In the rhetoric of the American Colonization Society in the following decades, such views ossified into claims that antiblack prejudices were a natural and permanent part of whites' group-specific perception of difference, claims that became increasingly difficult to differentiate from assertions that it was not the perception, but the difference itself, that was natural and permanent.[19] To argue against colonization and for equal American citizenship, accordingly, African American intellectuals had to break apart the dogma that antiblack prejudice was the eternal attribute of an ahistorical *whiteness*. They had to accomplish the rare feat of depicting prejudice as an existential danger to the American polity, while also making a case *against* its supposed ubiquity and invincibility in white America. As Frederick Douglass summed up the challenge in 1849, "the Colonization Society says this prejudice can never be overcome—that it is natural—God has implanted it. Some say so; others declare that it can only be removed by removing us to Liberia. I know this is false, from my own experience in this country. [. . .] Prejudice has given way and must give way. The fact that it is giving way proves that this prejudice is not invincible."[20]

To his credit, unlike later proponents of colonization, Jefferson had not gone as far in *Notes on Virginia* as to describe antiblack prejudice as "natural" or even God-sent.[21] While his concept of involuntary opinion combined with his Baconian metaphor of the "deep roots" of prejudice is easily apparent, in retrospect, as a precursor to this idea, he had made it clear under Query XVIII that the manners and attitudes of his slave society were due to tyrannical habits that were necessarily corrupt, pathological, and against God's will, and that Virginians' opinions had to change in the future if the republic was to survive. As the nineteenth century progressed, however, this part of his argument became submerged when *Notes on Virginia* was instrumentalized by white colonizationists. In 1852, the abolitionist college professor William G. Allen, who in the following year would have to flee from a racist mob to England after marrying a white woman (publishing his account of the experience as *The American Prejudice Against Color* in 1853)[22] emphasized the difference between the two positions by criticizing Jefferson's exhumation by the colonizationists. "Colonizationists have recently dug up Thomas Jefferson for the twofold purpose of helping them berate African intellect, and thus make out that the race is not fit to live among 'white folks;' and to aid Colonization," he wrote. "Those who desire to make capital of the 'notes' [*Notes on Virginia*], will do well, also, to remember that Jefferson advanced his views of African intellect, in the language of conjecture, merely, and not in the language of one settled as to the point at issue."[23]

When nineteenth-century critics such as Douglass or Allen expressed the conviction that, like slavery, prejudice could and should be overturned, they were opposing a spectrum of at least three different positions on prejudice: that of proponents of slavery who were not likely to consider color prejudice to be prejudice at all; of later white colonizationists, who tended to admit to their color prejudice but depicted it as "natural" and irredeemable; and of Jefferson under Query XIV, who thought a pathological but "deep rooted" prejudice redeemable in the long run but, as has been shown, refused to actively interfere with the redemption process. Since on this spectrum, Jefferson's Enlightenment of Feeling occupied the position that was still, comparatively, most akin to their own, it rhetorically made sense for the African American writers discussed in the following pages to focus their critique of prejudice on Jefferson. By demonstrating the intellectual weakness of Query XIV, they did not have to bother with refuting all the other positions on the spectrum that were even further removed from theirs. In their exhortations to eradicate racist prejudice and make a racially diverse nation possible, disqualifying Jefferson's flexible middle position promised to convey a sense of how far white America still needed to go to reach the egalitarian goals of Wheatley's Enlightenment of Principle.

When African American thinkers reflected on Query XIV, they challenged its logic (or rather, the willful lack of one) by following two different, but often interconnected, lines of argument. The first can be summed up, roughly, as *black uplift*, the second, as *white uplift*.[24] *Black uplift* deliberately passed over Jefferson's categorical exclusion of African Americans from the polity on the grounds of his subjective perception of their "black" color. Abstracting from the emotionality of Jefferson's approach, arguments in this vein showed themselves expectant that rationally communicable evidence of African American intellectual achievement would have to convince people like Jefferson of the irrationality of slavery and colonization. Meanwhile, *white uplift* rhetoric made a point of recognizing that, by Jefferson's own account, the true cause of African Americans' exclusion consisted, not in anything they could ever do or achieve, but in the color prejudices of white Americans who had been blinded by their irrational education in a slave society. From today's perspective, the rhetoric of racial uplift and elevation is sometimes suspected of having been insufficiently emancipated from supposedly "white" ideals of education, morality, and progress. As will be argued in the following sections, however, neither the *black uplift* nor the *white uplift* rhetoric in the African American reception history of *Notes on Virginia* bears out such suspicions.[25]

"Wean Yourselves from These Narrow Prejudices"

The beginning of African Americans' public engagement with *Notes on the State of Virginia* was Benjamin Banneker's correspondence with Jefferson in 1791.[26] The personal exchange between the astronomer from Maryland and the first US secretary of state was widely published at the time (including in Banneker's own almanac of 1793), and Banneker's sophisticated combination of *black uplift* and *white uplift* discourses would be quoted and retold throughout the nineteenth century.[27] For example, in the abovementioned letter to *Frederick Douglass' Paper* in 1852, William Allen quoted Jefferson's polite response to Banneker in full. In 1849, he had already published the letter together with Wheatley's and Samuel Moses Horton's poetry, with Jefferson's comment to Banneker, "No one wishes more than I do to see such proofs as you exhibit, that nature has given to our black brethren talents equal to those of the other colors of men," serving as the book's epigraph.[28]

As described in the previous chapter, Banneker contrasted his full knowledge of the universal truths in the Haynes abridgment of the second phrase of the Declaration of Independence with white Americans' "tender feelings" for their own limited interests. Unlike reason, these subjective feelings were so inconstant as to be able to pass from effecting liberty to effecting "cruel oppression" at any moment. A second line of argument addressed Jefferson as the author of the *Notes on Virginia*. Through most of his letter, Banneker focused on the conceptual frame of Query XIV—"the almost general prejudice and prepossession with is so prevailent [sic] in the world against those of my complexion," and "the abuse and censure of the world"—while he apparently found most of its racist content, to quote Jefferson against his intentions, "below the dignity of criticism."[29] Banneker only became somewhat more explicit when he lamented the "eye of contempt" (his version of Wheatley's "scournful eye"), which according to Banneker saw in African Americans "a race of Beings [. . .] considered rather as brutish than human, and Scarcely capable of mental endowments." These prejudices bore a striking resemblance to those Jefferson had voiced under Query XIV. Banneker's allusion to a separate "race" that was more "brutish than human" recalled Jefferson's polygenetic insinuations and his analogy between the supposed sexual preferences of "the Oran-ootan" for "black women" and those of "black" men "in favour of the whites."[30] Following this analogy, Jefferson's prejudices had comprised an array of epistemologically unstable claims about the people he identified as a transatlantic collectivity of "blacks." These unstable claims had included the "conjecture, that nature has been less bountiful to them in the endowments of the head," the "opinion, that they are inferior in the faculties of reason and imagination," and the "suspicion only, that the blacks, whether originally a distinct race, or made distinct by time and circumstances, are inferior to the whites in the endowments both of body and mind." Jefferson had combined these conjectures, opinions, and suspicions with an empirical "observation" that seemed to imply a greater amount of certainty. At least within the boundaries of his imagined community of "white" Virginians, it was supposedly shared by everyone: "The improvement of the blacks in body and mind, in the first instance of their mixture with the whites," he had claimed, "has been observed by everyone, and proves that their inferiority is not the effect merely of their condition of life."[31]

To counter this blend of prejudices and subjectively colored observations, Banneker employed a dual method. First, he authoritatively referred to the divine wisdom of "one universal Father" who had given all men the "same faculties." And secondly, he turned his own letter into rationally as well as empirically comprehensible evidence of the absurdity of Query XIV. To exemplify the falseness of the observations about racial "mixture" that according to Jefferson had been made "by everyone," Banneker made a point of having inherited the dark skin of his father, who had been "a Slave from Africa." Anticipating the expressions of race pride, for instance, by William Wilson's "Ethiop" or Martin Delany in the nineteenth century—Delany would in fact conclude from Query VI of *Notes on Virginia* that "we [colored people] are actually superior to the rest of mankind"[32]—Banneker "freely and Chearfully [sic]" acknowledged that he was "of the African race, and in that colour which is natural to them of the deepest dye." To reveal how white Americans' prejudice resulted in distorted observations and "absurd and false ideas and opinions," he combined the expression of pride in his skin color with the evidence of his expertise in mathematics and astronomy, fields understood to be among the most challenging to the faculty of reason.

As evidence of his intellectual "curiosity" and the "correctness and accuracy" of his mathematical and astronomical achievements, the letter contained a significant gift to Jefferson: the manuscript of the first of Banneker's six almanacs, which had already led him to a work of national significance, his "calculation for the Federal Territory" begun in early 1791 with Jefferson's approval. Banneker's series of almanacs would be published in twenty-eight editions between 1792 and 1797. The series can be read as a multilayered rebuttal of Query XIV. Not only did it display Banneker's mathematical skills, but it included republications of Phillis Wheatley's poetry, thus helping solidify the literary reputation that Jefferson had so desperately sought to bring into disrepute under XIV. Moreover, it published and disseminated Jefferson's own antislavery views, as expressed both in his polite response to Banneker in 1791 and under Query XVIII of *Notes on Virginia*. In this sense, Banneker's almanacs contributed to the founding of a long intellectual tradition, lasting from the late eighteenth century until today, of playing off the antislavery stance of Query XVIII against the racism of Query XIV, thus even within the interpretation of a single book pitting Jefferson against Jefferson himself.[33]

But Banneker went further than showcasing his own intellectual powers in his rhetoric and almanac. He also contrasted his rationality and intellectual maturity—"my arduous Study in this my advanced Stage of life," a phrase that would much later become part, for instance, of William Still's uplift rhetoric[34]—with a childlike image of white Americans, including Jefferson. "[W]ean yourselves from these narrow prejudices which you have imbibed in regard to them ['my brethren']," he told Jefferson, "and as Job proposed to his friends 'Put your Souls in their Souls stead,' thus shall your hearts be enlarged with kindness and benevolence toward them, and thus shall you need neither the direction of myself or others in what manner to proceed herein."[35] In the context of personal growth and development, Banneker's metaphor of "weaning" evoked a provocative analogy between white Americans and small infants just learning to do without their mothers' breasts. This analogy signified on key elements of Jefferson's Enlightenment of Feeling. In keeping with his Kamesian idea of feeling as the earliest and most primitive of the senses, Jefferson had granted a key role to childhood experiences in deforming the manners and morals of American slaveholders. As he had admitted under Query XVIII, the blindness he was associating with white Virginians' "deep rooted prejudices" under Query XIV had psychologically resulted from young children's exposition to watching their parents' physical abuse of the enslaved.[36] Moreover, Jefferson had followed the Baconian view that prejudices (or idols) had to be eradicated before the cumulative acquisition of knowledge could be successful. Banneker thus took direct aim at what he knew were the soft spots of Jefferson's Enlightenment of Feeling. White Americans would be unable to progress morally and intellectually, he implied, until they moved beyond their infantile attachments and ceased to passively "imbibe" the poisoned mother's milk of their "narrow prejudices."

Through the identification with young children, Banneker not only preempted racist allegations of supposed childlike qualities in African Americans, which Jefferson would come to voice in an 1814 letter that would occasionally be discussed in the nineteenth century.[37] He also painted a devastating picture of the moral and intellectual state of a slaveholding nation. His advice of putting "your Souls in their Souls stead" was both a biblical precept and a classical procedure in rhetoric, enabling a speaker to persuade an audience by assuming its perspective. For Banneker and the writers following in his footsteps, it was an integral part of their moral and literary education. It enabled them to do something that Jefferson, blinded by his "immoveable veil of black" under Query XIV, had declared himself, for the most part, unable to do: empathize with "the other race," enter into its thoughts, and understand its motivations.[38] If white Americans learned to follow the precept and "enlarged" their hearts, Banneker hoped, they would become independent of his "direction" in the future. By expressing this hope in the future tense, however, what he was really suggesting here was a statement about the present: as yet, white Americans were far from independent of his guidance. As Jefferson's "deep rooted prejudices" under Query XIV had demonstrated, they were in dire need of Banneker's didactic letter to reach even the first elementary stages of a long, emotionally and intellectually challenging process of learning to act according to universal rational standards.

In this manner, Banneker suggested that the American Revolution had largely been an educational failure. Although the American revolutionaries had at first been passively "impressed" with the right ideas strengthened by their "tender feelings," in the years following the birth of the nation they had not only failed to progress; they had morally regressed to the status of "criminals." In just a few words, Banneker thus described the Revolution as the history of a downfall, almost directly from the breast to the bottom of society, a process he described as "pitiable." The theme of pity in this inverted bildungsroman narrative would become a prominent feature in the African American reception history of Query XIV, voiced by commentators including Hamilton, Pennington, McCune Smith, Wilson, and even the anonymous writer identifying as "A Slave," who wrote an angry personal letter to Jefferson in 1808.[39] Failing to "wean" themselves from their "narrow prejudices" and to "enlarge" their hearts (or "[e]nlarge the close contracted mind," as Wheatley had put it in the context of salvation history),[40] narrow-minded white Americans appeared to be doomed.

Banneker's *white uplift* rhetoric already contained the keys to the conceptual transformation of *prejudice* from a predominantly epistemological to a moral concept. Unlike in Wheatley's Enlightenment of Principle, in Jefferson's Enlightenment of Feeling "deep rooted prejudices" had not been directly subjected to the human will. Following his ideas on the involuntary workings of the human mind, Jefferson had argued that republican citizens could and should not be compelled to give up their opinions, even if these were leading them to regrettable conclusions. As he had memorably put it under Query XVII, "Religion," of *Notes on Virginia*, the coercion of opinions and beliefs would only succeed in making "one half the world fools, and the other half hypocrites."[41] Even by the individuals who were holding them, false opinions could not be willed away; rather, he believed, they had to be allowed to evolve in harmony with macrolevel changes in historical circumstances. If things went well, as he hoped, a general diffusion of knowledge and refinement of manners would gradually shape (white) public opinion in a progressive direction. For him, it was thus only as the long-term side effect of progressive institutions such as the University of Virginia that racist prejudice could be expected to release its grip on American society.

By contrast, from the beginning of the African American reception history of Query XIV, *prejudice* appeared as something that was so destructive that it had to be actively and immediately eliminated. It soon came to be understood as a sin, appearing in conjunction with blasphemy and cardinal sins such as pride and avarice. In opposition to Jefferson's notion of involuntary opinion, African American intellectuals from early on understood prejudice as a problem of the will, even a "disease of the will," as the *Colored American* had it in 1841.[42] Banneker's metaphor of a "weaning" from prejudice gave a first glimpse into this voluntarist understanding of prejudice. In a reflexive form framed as an advice ("recommending to you and all others, to wean yourselves from these narrow prejudices"), Banneker's phrase turned prejudice into the potential object of both his and Jefferson's will. At the same time, the verb's origins in the context of early infancy suggested doubts whether Jefferson and other white Americans actually had the capacity of weaning *themselves*.[43]

As it turned out in subsequent decades, whether or not such self-willed weaning projects had been undertaken, they could not have been overly successful in transforming the collective mindset. Racist prejudices such as those voiced under Query XIV were not going away but appeared to grow ever-deeper roots. Accordingly, as the following sections will show, prejudice began to assume more demonic aspects, leaving behind Banneker's infantilizing image of "imbibing" and being "weaned" from familial prejudices. The antebellum imagery illustrating prejudice evolved from mother's milk to "deadly poison" and "pestilential breath"; prejudice could morph into a "demon," a "sore-eyed vixen," a "dreadful monster," and "a compound of all evil." Eventually, prejudice appeared the moral equivalent to the institution that could be seen to have produced it, identified as slavery's "auxiliary" or "slavery in disguise."

"Objects of Pity and Commiseration"

Among early nineteenth-century readers of Query XIV, the prominent New York antislavery activist William Hamilton was particularly concerned with critiquing Jefferson's vocabulary on slavery and *race*. As public abolitionist intellectuals, Hamilton's sons Thomas and Robert would follow in his footsteps: for instance, Thomas Hamilton would publish the *Anglo-African Magazine*, which in 1859 and 1860 carried James McCune Smith's and William Wilson's articles on Query XIV. And in an editorial in the *Weekly Anglo-African* in 1861, Robert Hamilton again took up Jefferson's question ("What shall be done with the Slaves?"), insinuating that Jefferson had been in favor of giving the rights of "citizens of the United States" to freedmen.[44] William Hamilton's own public statements on Jefferson spanned the first three decades of the nineteenth century. On January 2, 1809, he gave the first anniversary address celebrating the abolition of the Atlantic slave trade to the New York African Society for Mutual Relief, of which he was president. Focusing on the limitations of the American Revolution, slave trade orations on January 1 were beginning to form a cultural counterpoint to Fourth of July celebrations and a "distinct black tradition of protest," as Manisha Sinha has explained.[45] Within this emerging protest tradition, a considerable part of Hamilton's slave trade oration addressed Jefferson—not, however, as the American president who had recently signed the law prohibiting the Atlantic slave trade, but as the author of *Notes on Virginia*. Without doing him the honor of naming him other than by ironically alluding to "men who claim a preeminence in the learned world," Hamilton focused recognizably on Query XIV. In particular, he attacked Jefferson's self-serving comparison between the enslaved in modern America, who were supposedly lacking in cultural achievements, and "white" slaves in ancient Rome, who had been, in Hamilton's words, "their greatest artists and most excellent scientific characters."[46] Jefferson's claim that "Epictetus (Diogenes, Phaedon), Terence, and Phaedrus" had been "of the race of whites," and that, therefore, ancient unlike modern slaves must have been so intelligent as "to be usually employed as tutors to their master's children" could easily be demolished on two accounts. First, as writers from Phillis Wheatley to Samuel Ringgold Ward and James McCune Smith were pointing out before and after Hamilton, Roman writers such as Terence had come from North Africa and were, if anything, more African than European.[47] And secondly, as ridiculed by Hamilton in his 1809 address, Jefferson was obviously confusing cause and effect when he attributed differences of profession between the enslaved in antiquity and modernity to different degrees of intellectual and cultural achievement. "My brethren, it does not require a complete master to solve this problem," Hamilton scoffed, "he must be a willful novice and blind intentionally, who cannot unfold this enigma."[48]

In their reinterpretations of the Declaration of Independence, as seen in the last chapter, the intellectuals of Wheatley's Enlightenment of Principle frequently resorted to paralipsis to illustrate their universalist epistemology. Claiming not to have to explain the obvious, Hamilton also used this device in his reading of Query XIV. His emphasis on Jefferson's ignorance of well-known facts about ancient Roman history left a taste of the Federalist caricature of the pretentious pseudo-philosopher William the Testy, whose faux erudition would begin to amuse Americans, including many African American writers, later that year when Irving's *History of New York* was published.⁴⁹ However, Hamilton also made it clear that Jefferson could not have been that dim by nature; rather, he depicted him as "a willful novice and blind intentionally." Hamilton was not betrayed by the naïve and "simple-minded" appearance of Jefferson's Enlightenment of Feeling. Like Banneker, he was able to see through Jefferson's facade and knew that he was dealing with an artful, self-conscious construction.⁵⁰ Whether or not Jefferson's prejudices were "deep rooted," it was simply not true that nothing could be done about them: for Hamilton, they had to be understood as something that had been deliberately cultivated by a man who was "blind *intentionally*."

Hamilton's universalist paralipsis led the way to projecting a voluntarist meaning on Jefferson's original construction of prejudice. In the remainder of his speech, his rhetoric signified on a second major problem of Query XIV. Hamilton defended Phillis Wheatley's poetry against Jefferson's haughtily ignorant disparagement, not only explicitly (recognizing her for "some original ideas that would not disgrace the pen of the best poets"), but also implicitly, by redefining key terms of Jefferson's vocabulary in *Notes on Virginia*, the *prodigy* and the *blush*. After Jefferson had lamented the effects of slavery on the slaveholders under Query XVIII, claiming that the "man must be a prodigy who can retain his manners and morals undepraved by such circumstances," Hamilton inverted the perspective and lamented the depressing effects of a racist society on African Americans: "must not he who makes any considerable advances under present circumstances be almost a prodigy."⁵¹ African Americans were beginning to vindicate themselves through their literary achievements, Hamilton announced, and "we shall soon put our enemies to the blush; abashed and confounded they shall quit the field, and no longer urge their superiority of souls." To Jefferson's attempt to see in their supposedly greater ability to blush ("the fine mixtures of red and white, the expression of every passion by greater or less suffusions of colour") a unique potential for beauty and civilization among "whites," Hamilton retorted that, if they blushed, it could only be out of shame for the willful ignorance and prejudice exemplified by Query XIV.⁵²

Hamilton's image of driving "enemies" from the field was also used in another slave trade oration on that same January 2, 1809, in New York City. Addressing the Wilberforce Philanthropic Society, the African American Federalist Joseph Sidney asked about Jefferson: "Besides, is the great idol of democracy our friend? That he is not, is evident; else he would respect the rights of our African brethren; several hundreds of whom he keeps as slaves on his plantations [. . .]. Can you then, my countrymen, for a moment hesitate in choosing between your enemies and your friends? Between slavery and freedom? Will you run into the camp of your enemies? Will you flock to the Slavery-hole of democracy?—Or will you patriotically rally round the standard of liberty?—a standard which was erected by the immortal Washington; and which has been consecrated by the blood of the martyred Hamilton."[53]

Sidney's partisan approach throws into relief the ingenuity of William Hamilton's reading of Jefferson. As William Hamilton knew, Federalism alone was hardly a sufficient remedy against slavery and racist prejudice.[54] In his later speeches, he would occasionally resort to the contrast between "friends" and "enemies," but he would do so in a more nuanced manner than had Sidney. For instance, in his oration celebrating the abolition of slavery in New York on the Fourth of July, 1827, Hamilton not only criticized Washington along with Jefferson, but he used the term *enemies* outside of party politics in relation to an array of racist arguments he vaguely associated with Query XIV. "My brethren, our enemies have assumed various attitudes," he told his audience at the African Zion Church, "sometimes they have worn a daring front, and blasphemously have said, the Negroes have no souls, they are not men, they are a species of ourang outang. Sometimes, in more mild form, they say, they are a species inferior to white men. Then again they turn to blasphemy, and say, God hath made them to be slaves."[55] In the vein of Banneker's *white uplift* rhetoric and anticipating Wilson's stance in 1860, Hamilton tied the problem of racist prejudice to the theme of pity. Immediately following this passage on blasphemy, he invited his audience to commiserate with their enemies: "Let us look at them, and we shall see, with all their pomp, and pride, and hauteur, they are more the objects of pity and commiseration, than of anger and hate."

This appeal to pity was by no means a meek submission to "white" standards. To the contrary, it implied a self-confident condescension to people such as Jefferson, who undermined their own credibility by heretical analogies to orangutans and endless changes in artificial "attitudes" and "fronts," which made them so confused about their own ideas that they were inconsistent even in their blasphemy.[56] In this speech, as discussed in the previous chapter, Hamilton's rationalist elaborations on the intellectual shortcomings of the "ambidexter philosopher" could allow room for moments when the "glorious sons of '76" had done the right thing, and the "principles" of the Declaration of Independence had obtained a victory "over prejudice, injustice, and foul oppression." In the context of the abolition of New York slavery on the Fourth of July, 1827, nevertheless, Hamilton could not resist correcting another of Jefferson's key terms on slavery. Whereas Jefferson had worried under Query XIV that "the" slave would be "staining the blood of his master" if allowed to remain in the country after emancipation, Hamilton changed the meaning of *stain* from blood to slavery: "This day has the state of New York regenerated herself—this day has she been cleansed of a most foul, poisonous, and damnable stain."[57]

When, two years before his death, Hamilton gave the introductory address to the National Convention of 1834, he admonished the convention's delegates to put "the best possible construction on each other's language, rather than charging each other with improper motives." In the universalist spirit of Wheatley's Enlightenment of Principle, he applied this mode of optimistic critique also to his enemies, hoping for the best and envisioning the eventual disappearance of "deep rooted prejudices" such as those Jefferson had voiced under Query XIV. After he had condemned the "demon of prejudice and persecution" and the "evil minded" influence of the American Colonization Society that was trying to turn American public opinion against African Americans, he claimed that, nevertheless, intellectual and moral progress was already taking place. "That hitherto strong-footed, but sore-eyed vixen, prejudice, is limping off, seeking the shade. [. . .] Man is capable of high advances in his reasoning and moral faculties. Man is the pursuit of happiness."[58]

Pride and Prejudice

Hamilton's paralipsis on Query XIV would reappear in other slave trade orations. As, for instance, George Lawrence put it in 1813: "There could be many reasons given, to prove that the mind of an African is not inferior to that of an European; yet to do so would be superfluous. It would be like adding hardness to the diamond, or lustre to the sun. [. . .] [T]heir most prominent arguments are lighter than vanity, for vacuous must the reasons of that man have been, who dared to assert that genius is confined to complexion, or that nature knows difference in the immortal soul of man: No! the noble mind of a Newton could find room, and to spare, within the tenement of many an injured African."[59] For Lawrence, antiblack prejudice could only be the product of utter ignorance or ill will, and both were destined to disappear as part of the general progress of Enlightenment:

"radiant beams" were already "dispersing the dark clouds of ignorance and superstition," and it was clear that "malice shall not be gratified."[60]

Not every reference to Query XIV shared Lawrence's equanimity, however. The most famous example of an engagement with "the very learned and penetrating Mr. Jefferson,"[61] written in a tone that presented itself as severely angered, if not enraged, was certainly David Walker's abolitionist jeremiad from 1829/30. As discussed in the previous chapter, in Article IV *Walker's Appeal* concluded with a long reinterpretation of the Declaration of Independence, but its opening Articles I and II, "Our Wretchedness in Consequence of Slavery" and "Our Wretchedness in Consequence of Ignorance," concerned themselves at great length with Query XIV. "Mr. Jefferson's very severe remarks on us have been so extensively argued upon by men whose attainments in literature, I shall never be able to reach, that I would not have meddled with it," Walker claimed, "were it not to solicit each of my brethren, who has the spirit of a man, to buy a copy of Mr. Jefferson's 'Notes on Virginia,' and put it in the hand of his son. For let no one of us suppose that the refutations which have been written by our white friends are enough—they are *whites*—we are *blacks*. We, and the world, wish to see the charges of Mr. Jefferson refuted by the blacks *themselves*."[62]

Walker thus recommended *Notes on Virginia* as a textbook, as it were, on what *not* to think about American history. This recommendation fused *black uplift* and *white uplift* rhetoric. From today's perspective, Walker's argument in the *black uplift* mode can be difficult to understand. Lawrence's or Hamilton's paralipsis appears much closer to modern sensibilities than does Walker's insistence that it was existentially necessary that African Americans "refute Mr. Jefferson's arguments respecting us"[63] by their own good moral and intellectual examples. Since Walker made so much of Query XIV as an "insupportable insult" to African Americans,[64] one might think today, the refutation of obvious absurdities may not have been the best strategy, as it threatened to drag the insulted down to the level of the insult. And indeed, Walker showed himself outraged, not only by white Americans' injustice and cruelty but also by enslaved African Americans' ignorance, cowardice, and deceit[65] as well as the indolence, superficiality, and "pretensions to knowledge" of free African Americans in northern cities.[66] However, his jeremiad-style exhortation to disprove Jefferson's racist suspicions by way of uplifting examples of reason, virtue, and literacy significantly transformed the hermeneutics of Query XIV. In the *white uplift* mode, it radically redirected Jefferson's argument toward a voluntarist concept of prejudice that no longer stood in the way of national unity.

As noted above, Jefferson had listed white Virginians' "deep rooted prejudices," independently from the question of their truthfulness, as the primary reason for racial and national segregation. If he had occasionally shown himself "delighted" by the possibility of being proven wrong, as he put it in his letter on Banneker's achievements to the Marquis de Condorcet,[67] this openness did not mean that he was ready to include the people he identified as "blacks" into the nation. Jefferson did not see any direct connection between degrees of intellectual excellence and American citizenship. His notion of involuntary opinion in combination with his ideal of republican liberty inclined him toward accepting subjective states of mind such as "prejudices" and "recollections," no matter what their degree of truth, as political factors to be respected in a republic. To some extent, he may even have welcomed them as factors that made national belonging subjectively plausible to republican citizens and that could be mobilized in times of war and crisis.[68] From the vantage point of his Enlightenment of Feeling, Jefferson could therefore be relaxed about efforts such as Banneker's to prove his racist prejudices wrong. Such proofs, when they came, might be somewhat unpleasant for his reputation as an amateur natural historian but could never compel him to change his mind on who was included in the American nation.

By projecting on Jefferson's thought a close association between American citizenship and the proof of moral and intellectual equality—that is, between citizenship and objective knowledge rather than subjective prejudice—Wheatley's Enlightenment of Principle decisively turned things around. Today, we are the heirs of this turn, but we need to be clear that Jefferson himself had never made it in this form. Instead, it was the result of African American revisions of Query XIV, which transformed Jefferson's language into a point of attack for their own claims for equal citizenship. As had Banneker, Hamilton, and Lawrence before him, Walker realized the dramatic possibilities of proving Jefferson wrong. He knew what the demonstration of Jefferson's intellectual weaknesses could do for him: the obvious historical blunders of Jefferson's Roman comparison, his dance along the borders of blasphemy in the orangutan analogy and musings on "unfortunate" color differences, and the crudeness of his question, "What further is to be done with them?" could be used to great effect to make plausible his own rational counterargument for national inclusion.[69] To this end, Walker vastly exaggerated the historical influence of Query XIV, claiming that its assertions of natural black inferiority had been "swallowed by millions of the whites" and that Jefferson's ideas had "injured us more, and ha[d] been as great a barrier to our emancipation as any thing that has ever been advanced against us."[70] Following this monocausal argument, liberty and citizenship would become possible by "refuting" Jefferson, removing the "barrier to our emancipation" by demonstrating the absurdity of his claims about natural inferiority, and persuading white Americans to cure themselves of the poisonous prejudices that they had, supposedly, "swallowed"[71] by uncritically reading *Notes on Virginia*.

Walker thus continued to promote Banneker's and Hamilton's individualist and voluntarist concept of prejudice against an amoral, fatalistic understanding of prejudice as a quasi-natural group phenomenon. He realized that it was the latter notion of prejudice that threatened to dominate American debates, both as a concept in colonizationist rhetoric, and as a psychological effect of that rhetoric (in the sense that a persuasive emphasis on the inevitability of prejudice had the power of a self-fulfilling prophecy to shape actual prejudices). To undermine the notion of irredeemable collective prejudice, Walker consistently legitimized his own position as "unprejudiced."[72] And he urged his readers, if they thought they were unable to renounce their prejudices altogether, to at least "lay aside" or "dispense with" them "long enough" to form an impartial judgment.[73] Especially in his Preamble and the conclusion, he appealed to "the candid and unprejudiced of the whole world,"[74] emphasizing that for him, unlike for Jefferson or the activists of the American Colonization Society, color prejudice was not a "deep rooted," "natural," or, as Walker quoted Henry Clay, "unconquerable"[75] attribute of *whiteness*. For Walker, it was individuals, not collectivities, who had to be held accountable for prejudice. Mentioned in the same breath as pride and avarice, prejudice for him came close to a cardinal sin. "I am awfully afraid that pride, prejudice, avarice and blood, will, before long prove the final ruin of this happy republic, or land of *liberty!!!!*," Walker exclaimed in the *white uplift* passages of his jeremiad, urging white Americans to "REPENT" and deliberately "throw away your fears and prejudices."[76]

In his reckoning with the colonization movement in Article IV, he directly attacked the colonizationists for using their concept of "unconquerable" group prejudice as a rationale for dispossessing African Americans of their country. "This country is as much ours as it is the whites, whether they will admit it now or not, they will see and believe it by and by," he argued. "They tell us about prejudice—what have we to do with it? Their prejudices will be obliged to fall like lightning to the ground, in succeeding generations; not, however, with the will and consent of *all* the whites."⁷⁷ For Walker, prejudice was a problem to be solved by American individuals. Some would voluntarily get rid of it, whereas others would try to resist. However, prejudice would doubtless disappear eventually because, in his millennial vision, its disappearance was part of God's plan. "And there is not a doubt in my mind, but that the whole of the past will be sunk into oblivion, and we yet, under God will become a united and happy people," he told his audience of enslaved and free, white and black readers and listeners. "The whites may say it is impossible, but remember that nothing is impossible with God."⁷⁸

Walker's Appeal proved to be a milestone in the reception history of Query XIV. If Walker's claim that *Notes on the State of Virginia* had a lasting impact on "millions" of Americans was a projection of what he was really hoping for *Walker's Appeal*, these hopes would not have turned out to be unjustified. In retrospect, his pamphlet has come to be seen in close connection with the dramatic polarization of American attitudes to slavery and *race* around the end of the third decade of the nineteenth century: as a possible influence on both the turn to immediatist abolitionism in the North and the various measures by southern states to prevent the circulation of this and similar texts, such as in laws to restrict African American education and mobility. Likely, *Walker's Appeal* may also have contributed to the mobilization for southern slave resistance, perhaps even, in some measure, to the origins of Nat Turner's insurrection in Virginia, which had originally been planned to take place on the Fourth of July, 1831.⁷⁹ Walker's reading of Query XIV would then have to be seen at the heart of the possibility that had made Jefferson "tremble" under Query XVIII—the state of race war that William Hamilton in 1815 had called "Mr. Jefferson's doomsday."⁸⁰

"Slavery in Disguise"

Ironically, *Walker's Appeal*, and Walker's own growing posthumous reputation, was an important factor ensuring Jefferson a lasting role in the increasingly polarized debates on slavery and race prejudice in the nineteenth century. After Walker had urged every African American "to buy a copy of Mr. Jefferson's 'Notes on Virginia' and put it in the hand of his son,"

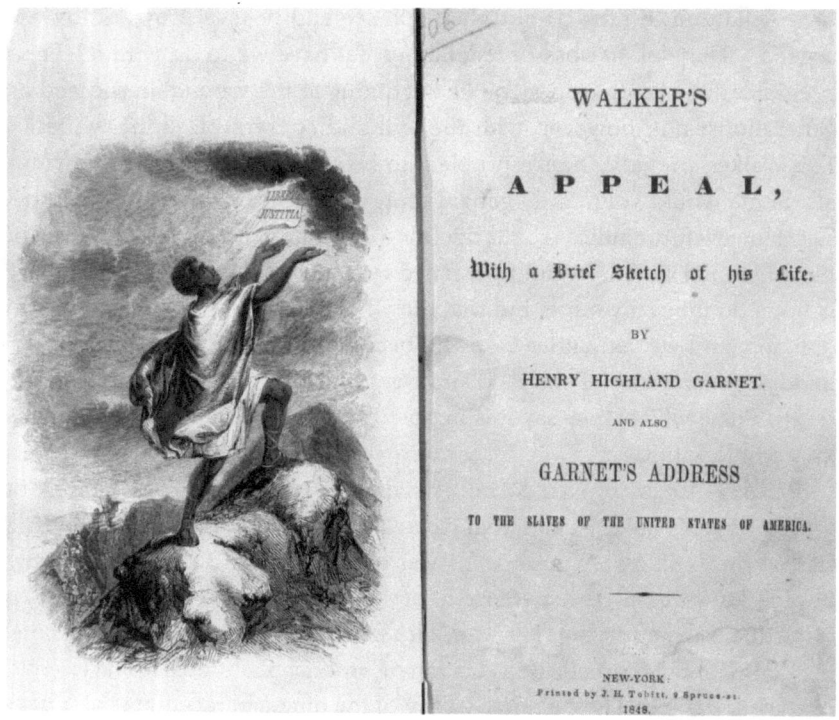

Frontispiece from *Walker's Appeal, with a Brief Sketch of His Life*, by Henry Highland Garnet, and Also *Garnet's Address to the Slaves of the United States of America* (New York, 1848). (Library of Congress, Prints and Photographs Division, Washington, DC)

the Connecticut abolitionist Amos Beman, for instance, recommended in 1863 that *Walker's Appeal* "should be in the hands of all, especially of all our soldiers."[81] A book in a book passed from hand to hand, *Notes on Virginia* thus began to travel through time in the form of Walker's interpretation. In her eulogy on Walker in the year following his death in 1830 ("Though Walker sleeps, yet he lives, and his name shall be had in everlasting remembrance"), Maria Stewart accepted Walker's mode of tying *black uplift* to the refutation of Query XIV when appealing to her audience to prove "to the world that you are neither orang-outangs, nor a species of animals, but that you possess the same powers of intellect as those of the proud-boasting American."[82] In 1848, the prominent political abolitionist Henry Highland Garnet wrote in the vein of Walker's *white uplift* rhetoric when he blamed "the old doctrine of the natural inferiority of the colored race" on "Mr. Thomas Jefferson" personally.[83] In the same year, Garnet published his influential new edition of *Walker's Appeal*, which joined Walker's ad hominem criticism of Jefferson with a hagiographic sketch of Walker's life and his own (and likely Julia Ward Williams Garnet's)[84] "Address to the Slaves of the United States," which had been rejected as too radical by the black national convention in Buffalo in 1843. With its appeal to the enslaved, "Let your motto be resistance! *resistance!* RESISTANCE!,"[85] the 1848 edition was likely sponsored by the, as yet, relatively obscure John Brown.[86] In this manner, Walker's use of Jefferson's "deep rooted prejudices" under Query XIV would eventually become connected to yet another iteration of "Mr. Jefferson's doomsday."

A Treatise on the Intellectual Character, and Civil and Political Condition of the Colored People of the U. States; and the Prejudice Exercised toward Them (1837) by the Hartford minister Hosea Easton evoked Jefferson's "trembling" under Query XVIII in its concluding poem. Easton came from a family of free African Americans who had been remarkable for their educational activism in his parents' generation. When Easton wrote the *Treatise*, however, he had already had to witness his family's uplift activity being thwarted by local racists, which may account for a work that shows little of Walker's millennialist optimism.[87] Yet, there are several parallels between Walker and Easton, including a shared interest in contrasting the language of the Declaration of Independence to that of *Notes on Virginia*. Like Walker, Easton died young, shortly after publishing a work that, like Walker's, sought to redefine prejudice by giving it an individualist and voluntarist meaning. Although the *Treatise* never received the attention garnered by *Walker's Appeal*, it is remarkable for its conceptual precision. Perhaps in an effort to systematize discourses on prejudice that he found discussed during meetings of the Convention Movement in which he participated during the early 1830s, Easton distinguished closely between "harmless" epistemological prejudice caused by a mere "error of judgment" and what he called "malignant prejudice," a term taken up in the same year, for instance, by James Forten Jr. in his address at the American Moral Reform Society.[88] Easton defined "malignant prejudice" as "a principle calling into action the worst passions of the human heart."[89] Malignant prejudice was "destructive to life," "more fatal than the pestilence," "a compound of all evil," a "dreadful monster," a "dreadful sin," and "the very essence of hell."[90] To differentiate this concept from its harmless variant, human volition was key. In his analysis of the difference between epistemological or involuntary and moral or voluntary prejudice, Easton argued that it was the "peculiar" nature of prejudice to become malignant in proportion to the act or intention of injury associated with it. Easton regarded the "system" of slavery (rather than "color" as such) as the "true cause" of malignant prejudice.[91] In this "system," malignant prejudice was at once cause and effect: In the South, "prejudicial" slave laws had been the result of "public sentiments" corrupted by prejudice; recalling the early modern legal context of *prejudice*, they were prejudices in the form of laws. In the North, malignant prejudice had survived in extralegal form. As Easton explained in an argument akin to Jefferson's overdetermined concept of public opinion, slave laws alone could not survive without the support of the prejudiced public sentiments that had been at their moral and historical root. Malignant prejudice was thus a necessary "auxiliary" of slavery; while in the North, it became "slavery in disguise."[92]

Although Easton only once referred to *Notes on Virginia* explicitly, Jefferson's terms and ideas resonate throughout the *Treatise*. For instance, to illustrate "the language used by moderns to philosophize, upon the negro character," Easton ironically spoke of "nature's God" and framed his critique of polygenesis in the terms of Jefferson's insinuations ("that they sustain the same relation to the orang outang, that the whites do to them").[93] However, in his use of what had by then almost become a canonical reference to Jefferson's orangutan analogy, Easton differed from his predecessors. He did not employ it, as had Hamilton, Walker, or Stewart before him, to exemplify white Americans' moral and intellectual weakness—blasphemy and provincialism—in order to persuade his audience of a *black* or *white uplift* project. Rather, Easton was interested in the question of what was morally wrong with Jefferson's prejudices at a deeper conceptual level. For him, Jefferson's claims to ignorance under Query XIV would not do: his habitual emphasis on doubts, opinions, and conjectures did not absolve him since leaving things open to scientific progress was no valid excuse for prejudice. "For if the prejudiced person has the means of knowing, or if he has any doubt with regard to the justness of his opinions of his neighbors, and still neglects to use the means of informing himself, and to solve his doubts on the subject, but persists in the exercise of his prejudice, he is equally guilty of all the mischief produced thereby, as he would be if he knew ever so well, and persisted in his wrong course in the light of that knowledge."[94]

As Easton saw it, Jefferson could and should have known better; therefore, Jefferson was no less guilty of malignant prejudice than were outspoken racists who did not bother with the fine distinctions of his Enlightenment of Feeling. Claiming that color prejudice presented an "insurmountable barrier" to interracial "social and political relation" was nothing but "folly."[95] Aware of how widespread this folly was, however, Easton was much less optimistic than Walker, Hamilton, or Banneker had been. Dwelling on the omnipresent psychological mechanisms of prejudice, he showed himself, at times, deeply doubtful about the eventual success of abolitionism. He took up Jefferson's argument under Query XVIII that racist prejudice was rooted in childhood experiences, but he offered a much broader panorama of both causes and effects of prejudice. As had, for instance, the Boston educator Susan Paul in her *Memoir of James Jackson* (1833),[96] he focused both on the mental corruption of white children and on the psychological injuries potentially inflicted on young African Americans. Malignant prejudice was transmitted from generation to generation, not only by the visual information children received from watching their parents act, but also, for instance, by what he called the "oral" information of a racist language.[97] What counted for Easton in the use of language was, again, evil intent: outside of the slavery "system" (for instance, in England), the same "opprobrious term" would not be as malignant as it was in America because it did not flow "from the fountain of purpose to injure."[98] Since Easton thought that slavery and prejudice were shaped by the same "deep design,"[99] he believed that focusing on either prejudice or slavery would not be enough. In his radical, and radically bleak, vision of the American future, the entire "system" would have to be overthrown before things could get any better.

"Supreme Selfishness"

Easton saw himself as an "individual" who acted "in direct opposition to the public sentiment, and the tide of popular prejudice."[100] In 1841, four years after the publication of the *Treatise,* James W. C. Pennington published *A Text Book of the Origin and History, etc. etc. of the Colored People,* which added new, more optimistic layers to the redefinition of Jefferson's "deep rooted prejudices."[101] A likely acquaintance of Easton's in Hartford and like him a minister originally trained as a blacksmith, Pennington had escaped from slavery in Maryland when he was nineteen. Although as the first African

American to attend classes at Yale University he had been compelled to stay outside the lecture rooms, he would become an internationally renowned abolitionist and intellectual who was awarded an honorary doctorate at the University of Heidelberg in 1849,[102] the year in which he published his autobiography, *The Fugitive Blacksmith*.

Under the unassuming title of his *Text Book*, Pennington promised a simple statement of "facts" for the practical purpose of providing "families, [. . .] students and lecturers in history" with historical arguments.[103] His historical overview was premised on an Enlightenment project of eradicating prejudice: "Prejudices are to be uprooted, false views are to be corrected, and truth must be unveiled."[104] Taking up where Easton had left off, Pennington dedicated a whole chapter to the redefinition of prejudice as a moral problem involving human volition. Alluding to Easton's argument for prejudice as "slavery in disguise," he even lifted a conspicuous metaphor from the work of his Hartford predecessor when he emphasized "the fact that slavery is the fountain of this bitter stream. The prejudice of which I have been speaking would not exist but for this corrupt fountain."[105] Pennington's argument was designed to corroborate the voluntarist concept of prejudice that he found in the African American tradition before him, while expressing it in starker and simpler terms. To "avoid saying what has already been said by many," Pennington claimed, "I shall not be making an argument of the fact that it [prejudice] is hating the image of God, nor of that, it is founded in a will to tread down the weak and poor."[106] Following this paralipsis, he nevertheless went on to argue that prejudice was a moral problem before it became an epistemological one. In the first place, prejudice was *"supreme selfishness,"* and it was "emphatically *ill will.*"[107] It was only in a second step that it became *"blindness of mind."*[108] And this blindness, a necessary "opposition to the truth," was itself more moral than epistemological: following Pennington's list, it produced in white Americans *"injustice," "dishonesty," "[h]ypocrisy," "brutish and uncivil manners," "sacraligion:* abuse of sacred things," and *"blasphemy,"* threatening to carry *"the total nation down to a state of refined heathenism."*[109]

Unlike Easton, Pennington promised what he called, in the early modern tradition of *medicina mentis*, a "cure" for prejudice. Essentially, the antidote to the "poison" of prejudice consisted in teaching the truths of the Bible to make them act on the "consciences" of the prejudiced.[110] And it consisted in African Americans' superior Christian virtue: *"forebearance," "good will and piety,"* and *"love and pity."*[111] Especially Pennington's point that "[c]olored people must bear and forebear"¹¹² may itself be difficult to bear from today's perspective, but it had its own radical implications in the context of the 1840s. First, it needs to be seen as the outcome of Pennington's unilaterally moral concept of prejudice, developed in radical opposition to the largely amoral concepts of prejudice that had found an early spokesman in Jefferson and that were threatening to dominate antebellum discourse in colonizationist rhetoric. And secondly, especially the emphasis on *pity*, which had already informed Banneker's and Hamilton's *white uplift* rhetoric, implied a radical inversion of contemporary moral and intellectual hierarchies. This inversion also shaped the chapter of the *Text Book* that was more specifically concerned with Jefferson's Query XIV, or what Pennington called the "pitiful" arguments of "my opponents of the Jefferson school." Writing shortly after the appearance of Samuel George Morton's *Crania Americana* in 1839, Pennington suggested that Query XIV had sparked a whole "school" of thought. In this manner, he could use Jefferson to attack the polygenetic arguments of the American school of ethnology that was on the rise in the 1840s.¹¹³ Pitying the intellectual inferiority of Jefferson's literary criticism of Ignatius Sancho and Phillis Wheatley under Query XIV, Pennington thus also took aim at his racist contemporaries. "I have only to regret that Mr. Jefferson has so plainly discovered to the world the adverse influence of slavery on his great mind," he claimed, ironically granting Jefferson the environmentalist explanation of his rational deficiencies that he and the American school of ethnology tried to deny to African Americans. "O that he had reflected for a moment that his opinions were destined to undergo a rigid scrutiny by an improved state of intellect, assisted by the rising power of an unbiased spirit of benevolence. Had he done this, he would, as a wise man, have modified that ill-judged part of his work that relates to the colored people." Whereas Jefferson had complained, to Walker's chagrin,¹¹⁴ that differences of skin pigmentation were "unfortunate,"¹¹⁵ for Pennington what was unfortunate was Jefferson's own inability even "for a moment" to engage in rational reflection. "The most unfortunate thing for the memory of this man is, that he seems to have committed himself against our claims. He makes a labored effort to conclude his proof against us, and reasons throughout as if he intended to make the case, but his conclusion is a budget of confusion."¹¹⁶

The Yoke of Public Opinion

Pennington's historical assessment of Jefferson's thought proved prophetic. That today's "memory of this man" conforms so closely to Pennington's estimate, however, may be the result less of our own "improved state of intellect" and "unbiased spirit of benevolence" than of the emphasis on these values by nineteenth-century African American intellectuals such as Pennington. As shown in the previous pages, it was the tradition of Wheatley's Enlightenment of Principle, rather than a philosophical innovation in the twentieth or twenty-first century, that transformed the hermeneutics of Query XIV. This transformation culminated in two reinterpretations of Query XIV in the *Anglo-African Magazine* in 1859–60, William Wilson's "What Shall We Do with the White People?" that has opened this chapter, and James McCune Smith's "On the Fourteenth Query of Thomas Jefferson's Notes on Virginia." On the eve of the Civil War, "On the Fourteenth Query" presented two major remedies to Jefferson's "deep rooted prejudices": modern scientific knowledge and a new approach to American public opinion, both of which he combined in a new, dialectical version of a more truly progressive Enlightenment.

Born into slavery in New York and rejected by New York medical schools after the Emancipation Act of 1827, McCune Smith arguably became "one of the most highly educated human beings of any nationality or ethnicity," a polymath physician with three degrees from the University of Glasgow, who knew more languages than Jefferson and whose essays displayed not only his erudition but also a unique penchant for protomodernist literary experimentation.[117] Writing under his pseudonym "Communipaw," which had fought a number of philosophical disputes with Wilson's "Ethiop" in the previous decade, McCune Smith introduced his lead article from August 1859 by quoting the concluding question of Query XIV verbatim. As he clarified indignantly, "What further is to be done with them?" was supposed to refer "to the colored population of these United States." Like Wilson, McCune Smith thought that the question had the wrong object. "'What further is to be done with them?' 'What is to be done with them? Can they be elevated to the same rank with the white citizens of this great Republic?' This question involves another: Is the standard occupied by the whites really elevated above that occupied by the black population? It is hard to say who is more elevated: the master, learned, acute, ingenious, [. . .] with a slave-whip in his hand—or the poor Christian slave, his breast heaving, his eyes raining tears, his flesh rooted up, quivering beneath the lash, whilst he prays to God to soften the heart of the accomplished torturer. Who is the more elevated?"[118]

By the time McCune Smith asked these rhetorical questions, the meaning of Jefferson's Query XIV had become intertwined with questions of *elevation*. As described in this chapter, Query XIV had been transformed into a touchstone for African American discourses of *black uplift* as well as *white uplift*. According to McCune Smith, however, it was "better to lay aside [. . .] this word '*elevation*,' because it is uncertain in its meaning. Let us put the same question in another form: Can the black and the white live together in harmony under American institutions, each contributing to the peace and prosperity of the country, and to the development of the problem of self-government involved in American institutions?"[119] Thus rephrasing the question, he recovered some of Jefferson's original meaning. As should come as no surprise, however, in his affirmative answer McCune Smith radically departed from the original, crushing the "deep rooted prejudices" of Query XIV under the combination of his Glasgow-trained science, his sophisticated prose, and the latest philosophy he had found at Baillière's book shop, including John Stuart Mill's *On Liberty* (1859).[120]

Written as a companion piece to an earlier article entitled "Civilization" (1844; 1859), "On the Fourteenth Query" employed the contrast between mid-nineteenth-century science and Jefferson's provincial natural history in the service of McCune Smith's argument for the immediate abolition of slavery and equal American citizenship. Debunking Jefferson's claims by measuring them against the scientific standards of his own time, McCune Smith moved on to a conclusion that focused on the problem of public opinion. He quoted the passage on white Virginians' "deep rooted prejudices" verbatim, before he began to disprove, one by one, assertions by Jefferson and other "impotent voices"[121] that American democracy required racial homogeneity. In the vein of both Irving's caricature of Jefferson as a faux philosopher and Pennington's "budget of confusion," McCune Smith made a point of first having to impose his own scientific structure on Jefferson's impressionistic racism, which he found "so mixed and so confused"[122] as to be an insufficient object even of refutation. Focusing at great length on Jefferson's allegations of physical inferiority while promising to detail his views on mental and moral differences in another article (which is not extant), he combined insights into the latest research on human bone structure, hair, and skin pigmentation with ironic asides on the "the apostle of democracy"[123] that made the article not only informative but also entertaining and politically persuasive.

At times, McCune Smith ridiculed Jefferson by way of shortcut summaries that flatly revealed the latter's lack of intellectual ambition: for instance, in his inference from differences in human hair structure to the idea "that the two races cannot live in the same land."[124] At other times, he resorted to more complex means. After decades of outrage about Jefferson's orangutan analogy, McCune Smith found a refutation below his dignity as a scientist, while he also knew that he could effectively evoke its absurdity by paralipsis. "We regret that a sense of propriety prohibits us from finishing this quotation," he claimed after quoting the phrases immediately preceding Jefferson's views on the love life of the orangutan, "for the argument against the part which must be omitted is full and conclusive."[125] This emphasis on Jefferson's violations of Victorian "decencies and proprieties," which had appeared earlier in the essay as well,[126] was largely a pose, since McCune Smith himself was not a prudish writer. Immediately following the paralipsis on the orangutan, he explored with great relish the theme of Jefferson's interracial family that he had treated several years previously for *Frederick Douglass' Paper*.[127] "Mr. Jefferson himself has left living testimony against his own expressions above quoted—testimony whose close resemblance to himself, and partial inheritance of his talents, should forever close the mouths of men who refer to Jefferson's *Notes on Virginia* as proof of the impossibility of incorporating the colored race into the state. 'That testimony [. . .] is a colored grand-daughter of Thomas Jefferson.'"[128]

After this iteration of the classical African American technique of pitting Jefferson against Jefferson himself—especially since he had left "living testimony" to testify against him—McCune Smith offered further evidence against an imaginary racial purity. He deconstructed Jefferson's idea of *whiteness* also by way of an alternative scientific classification, according to which "white" skin was a "color of *defect*" reserved for albinos and certain animals such as hogs, monkeys, or rats, who likewise had "colorless skin." A second, "xanthous" variety of skin pigmentation supposedly included northern Europeans, Eastern Siberians, and African highlanders whom he described as light-skinned but "not white," and to whom he attributed "a sanguine temperament" and "a certain degree of irritability and delicacy"—a characterization that may directly have alluded to both Jefferson's self-ascribed "sanguine" temperament and Irving's caricature of Jefferson, the "irritable" William the Testy.[129] The entire rest of the world, from southern Germany onward, according to McCune Smith was peopled by the "melanocomous, or dark-haired variety of mankind," who had "generally sounder and more vigorous constitutions, and are less susceptible of morbific impressions from external causes than the sanguine." Following this view of things, African Americans were "part and parcel of the great original stock of humanity—of the rule, and not of the exception." By contrast, people like Jefferson would have to be classified as neither "white" nor "black," but as part of an odd human variety naturally inclined to pestering their countrymen with "morbific impressions," such as those exemplified by Query XIV.[130]

In an earlier essay, McCune Smith had criticized "[l]earned men" who "in their rage for classification and from a reprehensible spirit to bend science to provoke popular prejudices, have brought the human species under the yoke of classification."[131] While as a learned man of his age, McCune Smith was not entirely free of this rage himself,[132] his notion of "popular prejudice" and "popular opinion" gave a scientific grounding to the moral and voluntaristic concept of prejudice in the African American tradition. Unlike Jefferson under Query XIV, who had treated popular prejudices as an unavoidable stage of the long-term progress of science, McCune Smith warned that these prejudices resulted from voluntary actions that dangerously undermined scientific progress. In his view, scientific results were being deliberately manipulated to "provoke" popular prejudices that served extrascientific goals of exploitation and oppression.[133] In the conclusion of his essay, he supplemented this notion of the oppressive "yoke" generated by popular prejudice by a concept of the "yoke" of public opinion by quoting a passage from John Stuart Mill's *On Liberty* fresh from the press:

> The modern *regime* of public opinion is, in an unorganized form, what the Chinese educational and political systems are in an organized; and unless individuality shall be able successfully to assert itself against this yoke, Europe, notwithstanding its noble antecedents and its professed Christianity, will tend to become another China. What is it that has hitherto preserved Europe from this lot? [. . .] Not any superior excellence in them, which, when it exists, exists as an effect, not as a cause; but their remarkable diversity of character and culture. Individuals, classes and nations have been extremely unlike one another, they have struck out a great variety of paths, each leading to something valuable, and although at every period those who traveled

in different paths have been intolerant of one another, each has in time endured to receive the good which the others have offered. Wilhelm von Humboldt points out two things as necessary conditions of human development, because necessary to *render people unlike one another*—namely, freedom and variety of situations."[134]

When reading Mill's *On Liberty* soon after its appearance, McCune Smith was attracted by its analysis of the tension between "individuality" and an oppressive public opinion. Yoking together "popular prejudice" and "public opinion" by the same metaphor in his essay, he was speaking as a critic of Jefferson's Enlightenment of Feeling who had personally experienced what Mill described as "a tyranny of the prevailing opinion and feeling."[135] McCune Smith knew firsthand what happened when people had "been encouraged in the belief by some who aspire to the character of philosophers, that their feelings [. . .] are better than reasons, and render reasons unnecessary."[136] Earlier in his article, McCune Smith had hinted at Alexis de Tocqueville's *Democracy in America* (1835; 1840) by claiming that the only "stain" on its "literary merit" consisted in its uncritical plagiarism of "Mr. Jefferson's views [. . .] in Mr. Jefferson's own words" in its chapter on the "Condition of the Three Races" in America.[137] By implication, McCune Smith thus indicated that he knew, and admired, the remainder of what he called Tocqueville's "great work," including its influential discussion of the conformity of opinion in American democracy.

However, McCune Smith did not need Tocqueville to inform himself about the "tyranny of the majority."[138] And if he treated Mill as a kindred spirit, he could not resist pointing out that he, James McCune Smith, had been making similar arguments long before *On Liberty* had been published. Some fifteen years earlier in the draft of his "Civilization" essay, he had illustrated the importance of diversity rather than identity for Western progress.[139] Since then, his idea that the "mingling" of individual and group differences constituted the foundation of civilization had been a recurrent theme in his writings, implicit in his pseudonym "Communipaw" (referring to the interracial community described in Irving's *History of New York*) and reappearing in a number of his essays, for instance, in the intriguing *Anglo-African Magazine* article from February 1859 entitled "The German Invasion."[140] From this perspective, Jefferson's devotion to an American public opinion shaped by "deep rooted prejudices" in favor of a homogeneous national identity amounted to the opposite of progress. "The question asked by Mr. Jefferson in his fourteenth query, would never have been propounded had he been acquainted with the philosophy of human progress," McCune Smith accordingly argued in the conclusion of his essay. "Instead of asking, How shall we get rid of them?—instead of affirming that they could never be safely incorporated in the State—had he possessed the insight or sagacity for which he is so celebrated, he would have welcomed their presence as one of the positive elements of natural progress."[141]

McCune Smith's philosophy of progress through individuality and diversity managed to do two things at once: it not only critiqued Jefferson's identitarian views but also suggested that Jefferson's Enlightenment of Feeling had paradoxically helped till the ground for the full flowering of Wheatley's Enlightenment of Principle.[142] According to McCune Smith's own arguments and his reading of Mill, even antagonistic difference, however painful at the time, could lead to a "valuable" exchange of ideas producing a new stage of Enlightenment progress in the future. If McCune Smith wished to imply such a dialectical view of a Jeffersonian Enlightenment, based less on a religious idea of redemptive suffering than on a secular notion of "antagonistic cooperation,"[143] he must have known that African American readings of Query XIV in general, and his own "On the Fourteenth Query" in particular, were providing his most compelling examples.

❖ 7 ❖

Pedagogies of Character

In Virginia in November 1818, a forty-eight-year-old enslaved woman named Hannah sent a remarkable letter to Thomas Jefferson. The occasion was his unexpected absence from Poplar Forest, the remote plantation where she was working as a housekeeper. Due to a prolonged illness that would still be mentioned, for instance, in the memoirs of his son Madison Hemings in 1873, Jefferson had been unable to travel there.[1] Reassuring him that his house was "all safe," Hannah expressed regrets that he was "so unwell," adding her hopes and "encouragement" for an improvement of his situation. While these lines may look like nothing but a deferential letter by a social inferior and dependent, it is not likely that Hannah's intention for writing them had consisted mainly in the wish to please her legal owner. Her regrets about her master's illness may well have been sincere, but less because she was attached to him personally than because she must have feared what the death of the seventy-five-year-old, heavily indebted Jefferson could mean for her: the dispersal of her family by sale.[2] Against this backdrop, Hannah's well wishes contained a significant "but" that can be interpreted as an admonition, rather than uncritical encouragement, of Jefferson. "I was sorry to hear that you was so unwell you could not come it greive [sic] me many time," she told him, "but I hope as you have been so blessed in this that you considered it was god that done it and no other one we all ought to be thankful for what he has done for us we ought to serve and obey his commandments that you may set to win the prize and after glory run."[3]

This vision of Jefferson's glory was not what it may seem from today's perspective. Hannah referred to a passage from Paul's First Epistle to the

Letter from Hannah, enslaved at Poplar Forest, to Thomas Jefferson, 15 November 1818. (Collection of the Massachusetts Historical Society)

Corinthians fraught with allusions to liberty, slavery, and the need for self-discipline in the service of God (1 Corinthians 9). Paul was a difficult source in the context of slavery as especially his Epistles to the Ephesians and the Colossians were used to induce the enslaved to obey their masters.[4] However, Hannah referenced Paul differently. In 1 Corinthians 9, Paul spoke about his rights as an apostle and suggested the moral superiority of Christians who were free, but voluntarily gave up their freedom for the sake of others ("Though I am free and belong to no one, I have made myself a slave to everyone, to win as many as possible" [1 Corinthians 9:19]). Paul urged all Christians, not just a privileged few, to discipline themselves for winning the race after glory (1 Corinthians 9:24–27). Although Hannah's use of the first-person plural while singling out Jefferson for running after glory thus seemed to suggest her acceptance of her inferior position in slavery, what it actually stressed was the principle of universal equality in relation to God. And it was Jefferson, not Hannah, who was failing to "consider" this relation and who had to be admonished by her to thank God and "serve and obey" His rules.

It is not recorded whether Jefferson, who was spending the fall of 1818 prostrated on his stomach, having a wholesome cure of mercury and sulphur applied to a painful infection of his buttocks,[5] felt edified enough by Hannah's admonitions to consider that "it was god that done it." Neither is it clear how helpful he found, if he understood it, her implicit suggestion to pull himself together to achieve some self-mastery ("I strike a blow to my body and make it my slave" [1 Corinthians 9:27]). However, it is likely that he recognized the pertinence of her point about God's gifts since he himself had made it, and to great effect, in what became one of the most often-quoted passages in *Notes on the State of Virginia*. "And can the liberties of a nation be thought secure," he had famously asked under Query XVIII,

> when we have removed their only firm basis, a conviction in the minds of the people that these liberties are of the gift of God? That they are not to be violated but with his wrath? Indeed I tremble for my country when I reflect that God is just: that his justice cannot sleep for ever; that considering numbers, nature, and natural means only, a revolution of the wheel of fortune, an exchange of situation, is among possible events: that it may become probable by supernatural interference! The Almighty has no attribute which can take side with us in such a contest.[6]

Born in Monticello in 1770, Hannah may already have been present at Poplar Forest in the early 1780s when Jefferson composed parts of *Notes on Virginia* there. Perhaps she or other members of the plantation's enslaved community had used printed copies of the text for learning to read and write in his absence; in any case, it is possible that she sooner or later had access to a version of the text. By the time she sent the letter, the vision of "Mr. Jefferson's doomsday" under Query XVIII had already become known far beyond the provincial seclusion of Poplar Forest, and was about to gain a wide resonance in nineteenth-century antislavery and abolitionist literature in general, and African American literature in particular.[7] An involuntary movement that seemed to elude Jefferson's control, his "trembling" could be referenced in the justification of abolition. It demonstrated that, even by the subjective standards of Jefferson's Enlightenment of Feeling, slavery was unmistakably wrong. The institution destroyed the moral foundations of the American republic so thoroughly that it made its representatives fear that a vengeful God would become sufficiently enraged to interfere again in his creation.

And this was not the only attractive argument African American readers could find under Query XVIII. Jefferson had used his answer to the query on the "particular customs and manners" in Virginia for a psychological analysis of a slaveholding society that was "daily exercised in tyranny." From the moment when white Virginian children were exposed to seeing their parents' "passionate" and "intemperate" violence toward the enslaved, their education and habit formation was taking a wrong turn: as "imitative animals," they would never be able to keep their "manners and morals undepraved by such circumstances."[8] To illustrate the inevitable moral corruption slavery caused in his countrymen, Jefferson entered an age-old discourse of *character* that would be continued in discussions of slavery and *race* until the twentieth century. Since its origins in ancient Greek, *character* had denoted the stamp, mark, or imprint made on another material, such as the metal used for minting coins, or, in modernity, the paper on which "characters" or letters were written or printed. Alluding to the etymological origins of the term, Jefferson illustrated the damaging imprint of the peculiar institution on the nation by claiming that white Virginians "cannot but be stamped by it [slavery] with odious peculiarities."[9] As will be argued in this chapter, Query XVIII thus not only became an important source for abolitionist arguments but also a particularly rich fund for African American reflections on individual and national character.

"Stamped [...] with Odious Peculiarities"

In its application of the "stamp"-metaphor to the destructive influence of the peculiar institution on the slaveholders, Jefferson's Query XVIII differed radically from the language that would be employed, for example, by the Mississippi senator and future leader of the Confederacy, Jefferson Davis. In a Senate speech in 1860, the "other" Jefferson would maliciously apply the image of the stamp and the mark ("stamped from the beginning, marked in decree and prophecy") to emphasize his views on a providential racial hierarchy. In sharp contrast to Davis's use, which has recently been immortalized in a book title,[10] in one of his most famous writings Thomas Jefferson had employed the metaphor to show that it was white Virginians who were stamped from the beginning, and not by God, but by the "odious peculiarities" of slavery. With this analysis of the corrupt manners and degraded national character of a slaveholding democracy, Query XVIII initiated a rich discourse on white American pathologies in African American literature. In the nineteenth century, this discourse included abolitionist narratives about the dehumanizing effect of slavery on the enslavers, extending to depictions of southern "white trash" and northern white mobs and ushering into the intriguing genre of twentieth-century "white-life" novels.[11] In many of the texts from this archive, the problem of white racism tended to be analyzed as a class issue resulting from the distinctive American manners that Jefferson had been among the first to describe as the problem of the misguided character education in a modern democracy corrupted by slavery. In nineteenth-century celebrations of Anglophilia (for instance, in what may today be the counterintuitive discourse of "black anglo-saxonism"),[12] Canada and Britain served African American writers as positive foils for the deplorable morality of the democratic but racist society in the United States. In traditional European cultures still oriented toward some notion of "blue" blood, the distinction between "white" and "black" could appear beside the point. Hence, African American accounts were able to suggest a rough gradation from the aggressive racism of the white American lower class to the somewhat less blatant but equally destructive racism of the white American middle class and "parvenu" upper class to the actual or supposed racial egalitarianism among the European, especially British, nobility.[13]

From the perspective of a social ideal where aristocratic manners signaled a potential for antiracism, African American writers looking back to *Notes on Virginia* found that they could locate the Jefferson of Query XVIII somewhere between the latter two positions, in a realm where there still seemed hope for the moral reformation of his character. Coming from a social space, as it were, between European and American manners, and expressed at a historical moment when colonial America was just beginning to be transformed into the new American nation, Jefferson's expectation under Query XVIII that "the spirit of the master" was "abating, that of the slave rising from the dust,"[14] evoked a sense of openness about the American future. His fear that he would be on the wrong side of an existential historical conflict was condensed in the image of his "trembling" fear of God, a quasi-physiological movement between two positions that concerned not only himself, but the entire nation ("Indeed I tremble *for my country* when I reflect that God is just"). To nineteenth-century writers, therefore, the Jefferson of Query XVIII could become useful as a representative American character still malleable enough to be reformed.

In a letter from his retirement that would occasionally be quoted in the nineteenth century,[15] Jefferson himself had elaborated on the image of his trembling. When, during the War of 1812, he was approached for public endorsement by his young neighbor Edward Coles, who was planning to liberate his slaves and leave the state with them, Jefferson vaguely sympathized. However, he not only advised Coles against this project but also refused to return to the public sphere to support this cause. To illustrate his reasons, he paraphrased Virgil's *Aeneid*, telling Coles that his request was "like bidding old Priam to buckle the armour of Hector 'trementibus aevo humeris et inutile ferrum cingi' [armor, long unused, on shoulders trembling with age]."[16] In this ambivalent image, what had been Jefferson's trembling fear of God under Query XVIII became the trembling of senility. While the first trembling promised an end of slavery in the approaching future, the second no longer did. Yet, Jefferson's identification with the ancient patriarch suggested hope along with despair. If Virgil's trembling Priam had lost his most heroic son and was envisioning the fall of his kingdom, he was also the patriarch of a dynasty that would not die with him: after Troy had burnt to ashes, a member of its next generation would eventually found a new city and a more powerful empire. Even in his explicit refusal to support Coles's antislavery project, Jefferson was thus able to use his "trembling" as a central metaphor for his Enlightenment of Feeling. It became the perfect embodiment of a flexible philosophy that somehow managed to combine an avowed sense of uncertainty with the promise of a better future.

The following sections analyze how African American intellectuals defied Jefferson's 1814 wish to be kept out of the public sphere by transforming his character into that of a representative American who "trembled" between two positions. This Jefferson lent himself easily to sophisticated metalevel reflections on a key concept of the nineteenth century that, unlike related concepts such as *personality* or *identity*, never entirely lost its ancient relationship to the world of things. As has been said, since its origins in antiquity *character* had not only referred to personal psychology or temperament but also to the stamp or imprint made on something else—in other words, to a person's *likeness*.[17] What became productive for African American literary and intellectual history was not so much Jefferson himself, but his likeness, his character as it trembled between personhood and thinghood, fact and fiction, history and literature, liberty and slavery. The flexibility of this character moved to the fore, for instance, when writers such as Daniel Coker, William Wells Brown, William Wilson, or James McCune Smith portrayed a Jefferson who participated in a personal interaction and a dialogue. It also became productive in discussions of slavery. Arguably, these writers enjoyed projecting back on Jefferson what was called the slave's *double character*: the American legal construction of the slave as both property *and* person.[18] African American intellectuals literally appropriated Query XVIII, in the sense that they not only used its argument for their own purposes but also claimed Jefferson as their philosophical and literary possession. As both person and property, subject and object, Jefferson's character could be put to many different uses. It could emerge as a personality in a memoir, a portrait in an imaginary gallery, or a figure in a novel, as an object of moral uplift or a ghost, as an inept clockmaker or an amputated African American street vendor, as a slaveholding patriarch and a commodity sold to the British. Jefferson's character thus eventually inverted the trajectory from property to personhood suggested by the original subtitle of Harriet Beecher Stowe's seminal novel *Uncle Tom's Cabin* (1852). Unlike "The Man That Was a Thing," the Jefferson of African American literature became, it could be said, the thing that had been a man.

"The Height of Reason"

A year after the end of his second administration, a likeness of Jefferson returned to the public sphere, in the form of both participant and subject matter of Daniel Coker's *A Dialogue between a Virginian and an African Minister* (1810).[19] A rare case of an antislavery pamphlet published in the South, the *Dialogue* appears as an anomaly also when viewed in the context of Coker's later career. Although the Methodist minister from Baltimore had designed the *Dialogue* for the double purpose of persuading white southerners to end slavery and convincing them of African Americans' trustworthiness as fellow citizens, he would become interested in African colonization only two years after its publication. Inspired by his friend Paul Cuffe, in 1820 Coker and his family would be among the passengers of the *Elizabeth*, the first ship sailing for Africa under the auspices of the American Colonization Society. In the private American colony that would become today's Liberia, Coker and his descendants would assume leadership roles.[20]

When Coker composed the *Dialogue* in 1810, however, he was still concerned with national American problems. As Richard Newman suggests, the fictional conversation between an "African Minister" and a "Virginian" transferred the Banneker-Jefferson correspondence into fiction.[21] That Coker was inspired by the well-publicized exchange between the two men is plausible not only because of the genre of the dialogue and the generic characters of an educated African American and a polite but provincial white Virginian. Arguably, Coker gestured toward Banneker's letter also by means of his selections from the Bible. The *Dialogue* opens with an epigraph composed of selections from the book of Job that are themselves put in dialogue (Job 32:17–18 and Job 21:3). Coker arranged these verses as an exchange between Job's critic Elihu and Job on the freedom of opinion, in which both insist on the necessity of voicing their different viewpoints. In his letter to Jefferson, Banneker had likewise referred to Job, transforming Job's statement to his friends, "if your soul were in my soul's stead, I could heap up words against you, and shake mine head at you" (Job 16:4) into a recommendation to Jefferson and his white peers to "wean" themselves from prejudice against African Americans and "Put your Souls in their Souls stead."[22] Following this analogy, Banneker and the minister were on the side of Job, while Jefferson and the Virginian assumed the roles of Job's interlocutors. However, these roles were subject to change. The dialogical practice of putting "your Souls in their Souls stead" aimed at an inversion of perspective that pursued the larger rhetorical and pedagogical goal of conveying universal insights into the injustice of slavery.

Coker's epigraph thus set the terms for an optimistic Enlightenment narrative that promised moral and intellectual progress. While the biblical exchange between Job and Elihu is more disputatious in tone than the polite conversation to follow in the *Dialogue*, the allusion to the Old Testament, where Job is eventually restored to his former state of health and happiness, suggests a hopeful ending for Job's modern analogues. Coker's *Dialogue* implies what may be called a double typology: the character of the minister offers both a Christian version of Job and a fictional version of Banneker as well as, perhaps, Coker himself. Meanwhile, Jefferson is split into two characters, the historical figure and a fictional Virginian who is successfully subjected to a program of *white uplift* supervised, as it were, by Job, Banneker, and Coker. In the moments when he refers to Jefferson as a historical personality, Coker's minister shows himself grateful to Congress and the "late president of the United States" for "their humanity" in passing the law to abolish the Atlantic slave trade, which "will engrave their names on every heart that is warmed with the least drop of African blood."[23] He also expresses his approval of "the president's plan (inserted in his notes on Virginia)" for a gradual abolition of slavery, while passing over Jefferson's necessary condition of African American colonization.[24] Yet, while Coker speaking through the fictional minister honors the historical Jefferson for opposing slavery and helping abolish the Atlantic slave trade, he also makes the fictional version of Jefferson, in the form of the generic Virginian, "weep (and well you may)" by confronting him with the continued existence of the domestic slave trade.[25]

As the dialogue progresses, it becomes apparent that the Virginian seldom reads the Bible. Indeed, he shows so little interest in the topic that he seems ignorant of what the term *concordance* means and, what is worse, still needs to be instructed in the antislavery hermeneutics of Paul's epistles (an existential need that would also be recognized, as we have seen, by the enslaved Hannah of Poplar Forest eight years later).[26] On the upside, Coker's fictional Jefferson is a polite interlocutor who turns out to be open to the force of the better argument—someone who is initially misinformed but shows himself eminently teachable. The minister's rational critique of the "unreasonableness" of slavery is thus eventually perceived as "the height of reason" by his Virginian student, who apparently has to ascend such intellectual altitudes from the abyss of his initial ignorance that he needs the entire dialogue to grasp the full implications of the minister's rational approach.[27] From early on, the minister and the Virginian thus enter into a relationship of teacher and student, and even of minister/father and son. In the vein of Banneker's infantilization of Jefferson as a suckling who still had to be "weaned," and contrary to the relationship Jefferson himself would imagine between a paternalistic slaveholder and childlike slaves in the abovementioned letter to Edward Coles four years later,[28] Coker evokes a paternal relation in which the slaveholding patriarch and "trembling" speaker of Query XVIII assumes the childlike role. "A sinful nation, a people laden with iniquity, a seed of evil doers, children that are corrupters! They have forsaken the Lord, they have provoked the Holy

One of Israel unto anger, they are gone away backward," the minister quotes from Isaiah 1:4. "My son, hand father the bible."[29]

Fifty years later, Jefferson continued to be portrayed as a student eager to learn from Benjamin Banneker. During the Civil War, the dialogical version of his character was put to new uses when, in the first of the fifty-three biographical sketches that were assembled in *The Black Man: His Antecedents, His Genius, and His Achievements* (1863), William Wells Brown rehistoricized Coker's narrative of pedagogical success.[30] As a "trickster narrator" moving back and forth between fact and fiction,[31] Brown reintroduced Banneker and Jefferson as historical personalities, while adding fictional elements to their relationship. For instance, within a long tradition of imagining a dialogical Jefferson as the host of a dinner invitation,[32] he falsely claimed that in 1803 Banneker "was invited by Mr. Jefferson, then President of the United States, to visit him in Monticello," but could not make it.[33] In the historical-documentary mode, meanwhile, Brown included into his own prose excerpts from the published correspondence. As had William G. Allen before him, he offered his readers extensive quotations from Banneker's letter and a full quotation of Jefferson's brief reply.[34] The interpretation of these sources, however, was very much Brown's own. As he saw it, the "letter from Banneker, together with the almanac, created in the heart of Mr. Jefferson a fresh feeling of enthusiasm in behalf of freedom, and especially of the negro, which ceased only with his life."[35] Brown's Civil War version of Jefferson was morally so uplifted that he decided to make Banneker's genius known among his friends in revolutionary France and thus supposedly helped "giving liberty to the people of St. Domingo." This conceit of a Jefferson who had been converted to the right side of history (a rehistoricized version of Coker's uplifted Virginian) was made possible in *The Black Man* by a fusion of the perspectives of Banneker, Jefferson, and Brown himself into one and the same universalist vision. In 1863, Brown chose to see in Jefferson a man of the Enlightenment attuned to the voice of universal reason. Such a man could not possibly have avoided admiring a Banneker who "believed in the divinity of reason, and in the omnipotence of the human understanding with Liberty for its handmaid. The intellect impregnated by science and multiplied by time, it appeared to him, must triumph necessarily over all the resistance of matter."[36]

As we have seen, Jefferson's Enlightenment of Feeling had not actually shared this rationalist confidence in the triumph of intellect and reason over matter.³⁷ Speaking in the year when *The Black Man* was published, Frederick Douglass showed himself conscious of the difference between the two Enlightenment traditions. By then, Douglass's rhetorical repertory contained a largely sympathetic but nonhagiographic vision of Jefferson's "wisdom," expressed, for instance, in an 1850 lecture on slavery he included in his second autobiography, *My Bondage and My Freedom* (1855), that referenced Query XVIII.³⁸ In 1863, Douglass partook in Brown's wartime recuperation of Jefferson while remaining aware of the dangers of a tradition that, he thought, had not been intellectually and morally ambitious enough. According to Douglass's discussion of the freedom of opinion in his Cooper Institute speech "The Proclamation and a Negro Army," Jefferson's philosophy had turned out to have been far too lenient toward prejudice and error in the slavery question. As Douglass put it diplomatically: "Jefferson has left as nothing more worthy of his profound mind than his saying that error may be safely tolerated where truth is left free to combat it. Equally true, though not always equally manifest, is it that error can never be safely tolerated when truth is not left free to combat it. [. . .] A stupendous error, long tolerated, and protected even from discussion, held too sacred to be called in question, has at last become belligerent and snatched the sword of treason for permanent dominion."³⁹

"When You Can't Put the Wheels of a Clock Together"

Many different versions of Jefferson's character could be used to expose the errors that had been left uncorrected by his Enlightenment of Feeling. In October 1848, *Frederick Douglass' Paper* quoted from the *New York Star* a humorous anecdote involving the renowned Massachusetts clockmaker Simon Willard, who had recently passed away. It told the story of a personal visit Willard had supposedly paid to Jefferson. According to the narrative, Jefferson struck up a conversation on Jay's Treaty, exposed Willard's ignorance of it, and afterward "begged" him to take a look at "a beautiful French clock" in his possession. Willard took the clock to pieces, made some further conversation, and rose to leave. On Jefferson's request to Willard to first put the clockwork back together again, Willard allegedly replied: "Why, you expected that I should be familiar with treaties, [. . .] when you can't put the wheels of a clock together."⁴⁰

There is some limited historical grounding to this anecdote. Jefferson's enthusiasm for clocks, including French clocks, is well-known. He personally oversaw the design of various timepieces at Monticello and elsewhere, including the "Great Clock" in the Entrance Hall at Monticello, a curious construction that symbolized the toleration of technological imperfection in his Enlightenment of Feeling by hiding the Saturday of its weekly calendar beneath the ground floor.⁴¹ Moreover, clock symbolism became important in Jefferson's political rhetoric in an oft-quoted letter to Joseph Priestley in 1801, in which he compared the American government after the peaceful "Revolution of 1800" (his own election to the presidency) to a clock "wound [. . .] up again."⁴² Jefferson's acquaintance with Willard is documented as well, although Willard's personal visits to Monticello appear to have been apocryphal. Willard had received several patents for his famous horological improvements during Jefferson's presidency and eventually came to Charlottesville as the designer of the central clock of the University of Virginia. Jefferson had left him detailed instructions on June 4, 1826, a month before his death, and would not live to see either the completion of the clock or, indeed, Willard himself. According to a biography by his great-grandson, Willard showed himself very impressed with the precision of these instructions and was, in general, very proud of what he depicted as his friendship with Jefferson.⁴³ As Willard family lore had it, he had shared an anecdote about discussing politics with Jefferson, but he had done so in the context of recounting that Jefferson afterward presented him with a cane made from a sapling at Monticello that became one of his (Willard's) most treasured possessions.⁴⁴ According to the correspondence about Willard in the Jefferson family papers, by contrast, Jefferson had to be reminded who Willard was, and only commissioned him with the university clock at the recommendation of Benjamin Waterhouse and his great-grandson-in-law Joseph Coolidge.⁴⁵ With such a questionable historical accuracy, and almost half a century after the supposed event, what may have been the motivation to include the vignette on Jefferson, Willard, and the French clock in *Frederick Douglass' Paper*?

The anecdote presents, again, a character engaged in dialogue. It shows Jefferson in a personal, and moderately personable, exchange. He emerges as a somewhat arrogant and ignorant interlocutor who is, however, open to argument. Like the fictionalized Jeffersons in Coker and Brown, he is enabled to follow a steep learning curve through the peaceful means of dialogical irony. The anecdote contrasts Jefferson's ostensible expertise in politics with his technological incompetence and his inability to get the relevant work done. Putting a clockwork together was not just any work, of course:

it represented an important technology fraught with theological and political associations. In a late Newtonian world, the clockwork had become a conventional image of a universe created by a divine clockmaker. Moreover, Jefferson himself had compared republican government to a clock that could be wound up again. Against this backdrop, the anecdote implied a political allegory of Jefferson's hubris. It revealed a character who prided himself on his political wisdom but who was, when left to his own devices, completely unable to repair the clockwork of government and put it back together once it had been taken apart.

Especially in the context of other African American constructions of a dialogical Jefferson likeness, it may have been the illustration of political hubris that made this anecdote attractive for *Frederick Douglass' Paper* in 1848. Coker had alluded, and Brown explicitly referred, to the Banneker-Jefferson correspondence and thus to a historical exchange between Jefferson and a famous clockmaker that was, unlike the Willard anecdote, fully documented. In his almanac for 1797 Banneker had identified his entire character with his horological expertise. In his curious "Epitaph on a Watch-Maker," he had styled himself as

> *Peter Pendulum,* Watch-Maker,
> Whose abilities in that line were an honour
> To his profession.
> Integrity was the main *spring,*
> And prudence the *regulator*
> Of all the actions of his life,
> Humane, generous and liberal,
> [. . . . .]
> So nicely *regulated* were all his *motions,*
> That he never *went wrong*
> Except when set a *going*
> By people
> Who did not know
> *His key:*
> Even then he was easily
> *Set right* again.[46]

Following this conceit, Banneker was such a good watchmaker that his own character could be described in the terms of a fully rational clockwork. As his famous wooden clock had demonstrated, he had been able to take clocks apart and, unlike Jefferson, put them back together again, even in very innovative ways. As part of this discourse, the Willard anecdote in *Frederick Douglass' Paper* presented a Banneker in whiteface, whose joke at Jefferson's expense exposed Banneker's rational superiority over Jefferson's dilettantism. As shown in the "Epitaph," Banneker's rationality had a moral and political dimension as well, regulating such values as integrity, prudence, and humanity. In the print environment of *Frederick Douglass' Paper*, the whiteface Banneker of the Willard anecdote could thus be used as a critical commentary on Jefferson's reification of government as a clockwork in need of tending. If something in American government "went wrong," it suggested, an African American rationalist like Banneker was needed to set it "right again."

"Pictures Are Teachings by Example"

Almanacs such as Banneker's continued to be an important inspiration as the nineteenth century progressed. "I always had a penchant for pictures," the narrator of William Wilson's "Afric-American Picture Gallery" begins his description of an imaginary art collection. "Even when so small as to be almost imperceptible, I used to climb up, by the aid of a stool, to my mother's mantle piece, take down the old family almanac and study its pictures." Serialized in the *Anglo-African Magazine* in seven installments between February and October 1859, the description of a fictional African American art gallery by Wilson's "Ethiop" promised "to the careful observer and the thinker much that is valuable and interesting."[47] Wilson's foray into fictional ekphrasis, the literary description of visual artworks, opens with the picture of a slave ship and moves on to describe portraits, landscapes, genre paintings, and busts. Like Banneker's "Epitaph on a Watchmaker," Wilson's "Picture Gallery" fuses the boundaries between persons and things. Playing with the inherent doubleness of *character* as personality and imprint, and of *double character* as person and property, the text includes descriptions of human characters that seem to move seamlessly in and out of its discussions of art.[48] Among these characters floating between the world of art and the human world are gallery employees and visitors to the museum. Moreover, on an excursion to a mysterious place called the "Black Forest," the narrator enters the narrative as a character, as does Bernice, the idealized African American "*Artist*" in his studio. "Bust, statues statuettes; landscapes, portraits, fancy pieces; paints, pencils, pallets, mallets chisels; half finished sketches, studies in plaster," Ethiop enthuses over this space of African American creativity, "all, all lay in profusion on every hand."⁴⁹

In Ethiop's world of art, Jefferson's character likewise meanders back and forth between history and portraiture. Wilson's engagement with it is motivated by the question of who should be represented in an art form that he understands as a didactic dialogue between the work of art and the mind. In modification of Lord Bolingbroke's early Enlightenment aphorism, "History is teaching by examples," Ethiop finds that "[p]ictures are teachings by example."⁵⁰ It is not the genre of historical writing, much less the historical events themselves, that promise didactic success. Instead, Ethiop is interested in the role of aesthetic mediation. As he sees it, it is from the visual arts that "we often derive our best lessons. A picture of a great man with whose acts we are familiar, calls up the whole history of his times. Our minds thus become reimpressed with the events and we arrive at the philosophy of them." The visual "imprint" of character engenders a "philosophy" or, as Wilson's allusion to Bolingbroke suggests, a *philosophical history* whose aesthetic appeal furthers the goals of a universalist Enlightenment. For this new philosophical history, it matters greatly who are the "great men" that serve as its didactic examples. "A picture of Washington recalls to the mind the American Revolution, and the early history of the Republic," Ethiop explains. "A picture of Thomas Jefferson brings before the mind in all its scope and strength that inimitable document, the Declaration of Independence; and in addition, carries us forward to the times, when its broad and eternal principles, will be fully recognized by, and applied to the entire American people."⁵¹

However, it soon becomes clear that Jefferson's character is, to a certain extent, fungible. Ethiop does not need this particular likeness to be reminded of the "broad and eternal principles" of the Declaration of Independence and their promise for the future. Instead, his mind is "impressed" with its philosophical history by "a most beautiful portrait of one of the greatest men the world ever saw—TOUSSSAINT L'OUVERTURE." The impression by Toussaint's portrait is so overwhelming that it seems to elude Ethiop's descriptive powers. "Far be it from me to venture to a description of either the picture or the man," he claims. "I have no pencil and no pen with which I can do it." Therefore, in a single long sentence, his argument moves from the "great man" of the Haitian Revolution to the Haitians as a people:

To say nothing of him who led the breathing of this people after liberty; the breaking in pieces the yoke that galled them their heroic struggles, the routing finally and utterly from the soil their oppressors; their almost superhuman efforts thereafter, to rise form the low state in which the degradation of slavery and chains had placed them and their final triumph over every obstacle; in fine the whole history from first to last of this Island and this people is so vividly brought before the mind, by merely this likeness of the inimitable Toussaint l'Ouverture, that it is reimpressed with the extraordinary, *useful and touching lesson it teaches.*[52]

Thus, Ethiop's pedagogy of character uses the artistic representation of Toussaint to convey a whole nation's fight for liberty. However, Toussaint's portrait is not the only opportunity to blend personal and national character and teach a "useful and touching lesson."[53] For instance, Ethiop describes a double portrait of "the first and the last colored editor," in which Samuel Cornish of *Freedom's Journal* is looking over the shoulder of a man who could be Thomas Hamilton, editor of the *Anglo-African Magazine* in which "Picture Gallery" is published. This work of art establishes African American journalism as a self-conscious tradition.[54] Another painting depicts the head of Crispus Attucks, "the First Martyr of the American Revolution." Playing with the terms *head* and *likeness,* Ethiop suggests that the "fine likeness" of this man of African and Native American descent who was shot during the Boston Massacre was the portrait of a man "likely to head a revolution to throw off oppression."[55] Further portraits destabilize the *"American prejudice Market"*[56] by celebrating the recent emperor of Haiti, Faustin Soulouque, whose government had just been overthrown in early 1859, and participants in the African American Convention Movement including William Hamilton (Thomas Hamilton's father), James Forten, Richard Allen, and Hosea Easton.[57] The line of character studies culminates in "A HEAD OF PHILLIS WHEATLEY [. . .] decidedly one of the finest in the collection, whether viewed in an artistic light or in point of fact."[58] Like Banneker, Ethiop muses, Wheatley instructively carries his mind back to the Enlightenment beginnings of the literary and intellectual tradition he is celebrating. As he points out, her likeness should have taught lessons to "America's paler daughters contemporary with her," none of whom "ascended so far up the hill of just fame at any age" as she.[59]

The "Gold" of Character

"Picture Gallery" thus partook in a self-referential discourse of African American achievement. For instance, four years before its publication, this rhetoric had shaped William Cooper Nell's *The Colored Patriots of the American Revolution* (1855). And four years afterward, William Wells Brown would deploy it in *The Black Man: His Antecedents, His Genius, and His Achievements*. When this book appeared in 1863, Brown already included biographical sketches of both Nell (praising him for "a book filled with interesting incidents connected with the history of the blacks of this country") and Wilson (recommending him as "a sketch writer of historical scenes and historical characters").[60] Among the three texts, "Picture Gallery" was the one most intensely concerned with metalevel reflections on the role played by artistic mediation. In his column for *Frederick Douglass' Paper* in 1853, Wilson had lamented the relative absence of African American art, and art subjects, in the American public sphere (a problem that was worrying James McCune Smith as well).[61] Recounting an experience at a gallery in Manhattan, where he found "Franklin and Adams, Lafayette and Jefferson, Clay and Webster," but "not the Emperor of Hayti, nor of Dohomey, nor the President of Liberia, nor any other distinguished *black*," Wilson had argued that a "radical change in the process of our development is here demanded. [. . .] [W]e must begin to tell our own story, write our own lecture, paint our own picture, chisel our own bust [. . .], acknowledge and love our own peculiarities if we have any. [. . .] The encouragement and self-reliance it will inspire will do more to push us forward than all the speculations about our 'manifest destiny,' &c., that has emanated from the brains of all the fools, white or black, in Christendom."[62]

Focusing on the world of art, "Picture Gallery" presents not only historical characters but also a fictional character who emerges in positive contrast to Jefferson: the young "gallery Boy" Tom. Entering the gallery "with his own likeness" in hand, Tom moves through the narrative in the form of both a human character and a portrait.[63] He is at once an individual and a type: "This boy *Thomas Onward* (I call him *Tom* for shortness,) though he has seen all of life—yea more, is not an *Old Tom* by any means; nor an *Uncle Tom*, nor a *Saintly Tom*, nor even what is commonly deemed a good Tom; but a shrewd little rogue, a real live *Young Tom*, up to all conceivable mischief and equal to all emergencies. He is a perfect model of a little fellow in his way, and a fair representative of his class. Sound in limb, symmetrical in form and robust in health, jovial, frank, easy mannered and handsome—infinitely so compared with even the likeness I hold, one would scarcely conclude that this boy has come down to us through nearly three hundred years of hard trial."64

In his progressive Enlightenment narrative, Ethiop directly contrasts the "rising fortunes" of the new African American generation personified by his "real life *young Tom*," with older generations of white Americans such as Jefferson. Tom "was toiled into life, he has been toiled through life, toiled out of life. He has been robbed of his toil, robbed of his body, robbed of all but his soul. He has been hated for what he was, hated for what he was not, and hated for what he ought to have been." Nevertheless, "out of all these mountains of dust and ashes," Tom has somehow managed to "come forth fresh, smiling, and free." In sharp contrast, it is the privileged older generation of white politicians who now appear as objects of pity due to their lack of civilized polish.65 "What sorry figures do the hard, grave, iron, half savage and half barbarous faces of Washington and Jefferson, of Clay, Webster and Calhoun, present beside the fine expressive likeness of this rising little fellow," Ethiop continues. "The American Nation, if it can, may try its hardened hand yet a few centuries longer upon our live little Tom; but it will hardly mould him to their liking. Like gold ore he will lose but the alloy and become brighter and brighter in the oft passing through the furnace of their oppression."66

While the contrast between Jefferson's "iron" and Tom's "gold" may have hinted at the myth of the metals in Plato's *Republic*, Wilson's young hero is perhaps best understood as standing between nineteenth- and twentieth-century discussions of heroic character formation. In some measure, the comparison between Tom's "fine expressive likeness" and the artisanal context of refining metal anticipated the dialectical concept of *antagonistic cooperation* in the twentieth century, which Albert Murray would see condensed in "the image of the sword being forged." As Murray defined "heroic action, in fiction or otherwise," what for Wilson had been the "furnace" of oppression became the "fire in the forging process," which is "of its very nature antagonistic, but [. . .] also cooperative at the same time. For all its violence, it does not destroy the metal which becomes the sword. It functions precisely to strengthen and prepare it to hold its battle edge."67 Antebellum conceptions of character tended to be less focused on the violence involved, but likewise stressed the idea that its formation, like the extraction and refinement of metal, required a physical struggle with the material world. In his 1848 lecture "What Are the Colored People Doing for Themselves?," Douglass gave one of the most elaborate accounts of character as a "thing" that had to be actively obtained if African American progress was to take place.[68] "What we, the colored people, want, is *character*, and this nobody can give us. It is a thing we must get for ourselves. We must labor for it. It is gained by toil—hard toil," he had stressed. "'There is gold in the earth, but we must dig it'—so with character. It is attainable; but we must attain it, and attain it each for himself [. . .]. Character is the important thing, and without it we must continue to be marked for degradation and stamped with the brand of inferiority. With character, we shall be powerful. Nothing can harm us long when we get character."[69]

Although *character* is often associated with conservative thought today, evoking a Victorian ethics of keeping a stiff upper lip while pulling oneself up by the bootstraps, from the perspective of the nineteenth century the concept had considerable emancipatory potential. While this potential is also felt, for instance, in the alternative to the "'made' or manufactured man" of John Stuart Mill's contemporaneous science of character or what he called *ethology*,[70] it was particularly pronounced in the African American context. By attaining the "thing" or "gold" of character and taking control of the process of "marking," "stamping" and "branding" the metal themselves, to use Douglass's metaphors, African Americans could actively resist being marked, stamped, and branded by others. This voluntarist character ideal was shared by many, including female educators such as Ann Plato, Susan Paul, or Frances Watkins Harper. For instance, like Douglass, Harper called for teaching "our people how to build up a character for themselves—a character that will challenge respect in spite of opposition and prejudice."[71] However, when Martin Luther King famously evoked the echoes of this discourse in his "I Have a Dream" speech in 1963—"I have a dream that my four little children will one day live in a nation where they will not be judged by the color of their skin but by the content of their character"[72]—his focus on "judgment" (rather than prejudgment or prejudice) may also have been alluding to another aspect of the African American reception of Query XVIII. As texts such as Wilson's "Picture Gallery" had made clear, heroic character building and positive self-branding were only one side of the coin. African American intellectuals also thought about rebranding the former branders and passing judgment on the character of a nation that had been, to come back to Jefferson's words, "stamped" by the "odious peculiarities" of slavery.

"Like the Witches of Macbeth"

In practical terms, "Picture Gallery" illustrated Wilson's pedagogy of character by a theme he had already broached in his 1853 column in *Frederick Douglass' Paper*. A genre painting about urban life showed "a *beautiful colored girl*, with a hideous monster of a white-faced doll in her arms."[73] As Wilson had complained to Douglass, "[e]veryone of your readers knows that a black girl would as soon fondle an imp as a black doll."[74] However, this reference to "imps" and white-faced "monsters" did more than simply reflect on Wilson's real-life experiences as a teacher. In "Picture Gallery," it was connected to an aesthetics of "monstrous" *whiteness* that became increasingly devastating as the narrative progressed. In part, this aesthetics elaborated on the gothic potential of Query XVIII, where Jefferson had given vent to existential fears of an "exchange of situation" between master and slave, going as far as to exclaim that it "may become probable by supernatural interference." He had seen in the observation that "the spirit of the master is abating, that of the slave rising from the dust" the first sign of a "total emancipation" of the enslaved. However, the "trembling" voice of Jefferson's Enlightenment of Feeling had been uncertain as to how to interpret this uncanny movement of "spirits." It could either signify "the consent of the masters" to the abolition of slavery, or be the harbinger of an apocalyptic race war, in which white Americans would be compelled to fight on the wrong side and which would necessarily end in their "extirpation."[75]

Wilson extracted Jefferson's existential fears from Query XVIII, lifting from the text the prophetic tone, the allusions to the supernatural as well as the uncanny discourse about the communicating "spirits" of master and slave, and dropping them into the nineteenth-century environment of a gothic phantasy. The occasion is Ethiop's excursion from the gallery to a location called the *"Black Forest"*—not the future geographical home of Martin Heidegger and Black Forest Cake, but a mystic "dense and pathless forest" he has first encountered in his gallery as a *"Work of Art."*[76] In the *Artist's* studio hidden deep within this Romantic forest that is described in terms of "magic" and the "grotesque,"[77] Ethiop finds a *"Tablet* of stone" that "challenges the attention of the Historian, the Ethnologist, and the Antiquarian." Its relation to reality is uncertain. "Is it fiction, is it history, is it prophecy? Who can tell?" he asks.[78] The pseudo-archaic language on the tablet describes "THE AMECANS, OR MILK WHITE RACE" from the perspective of a universal Enlightenment in the year 4000, an "age of pure light and perfect liberty" long after slavery has been abolished and the Amecans have "perished."[79] According to the tablet, white "Amecans" resembled a maximally unflattering portrait of Jefferson, in the worst possible interpretation of his own guidelines for deciphering *whiteness* under Query XIV of *Notes on Virginia*. "And lo and behold, as one appeared, so appeared all of them," the tablet declared. "They had *milk white skins*, [. . .] and their hair was long and strait and uncomely; and in hue as the yellow or red clay of our fields. [. . .] And their faces were long and narrow, and their noses sharp and angular, and their nostrils thin; so also were the lips of their sunken mouths. [. . .] They had sharp white teeth, like unto the teeth of the shark; and their eyes were blue as the cloudless sky, and sometimes leaden as when it is overcast; and their brows were large even unto the hiding of their eyes; and they were terrible to look upon, yea even fearful."[80]

As it turns out, the proprietor of the tablet, the "*Artist*" Bernice, holds the living incarnation of the evil "Amecan" enslaver captive in a cell beneath his studio. A shocked Ethiop describes the captive as a thing rather than a man: "an object the most appalling my eyes ever beheld stood before us. Was it a man, was it even human?—When we entered he stood crouched in one corner of his cell. His figure was gaunt and tall; his head large and covered with long snow white hair, which hung in disordered masses over his pale and shriveled face."[81] As Bernice explains to Ethiop, the captive is his former owner, whom he is keeping in lifelong bondage as a revenge for killing his (Bernice's) son and selling his wife and other children. The "trembling" captive continues to beg his "*sable master*" for his freedom, but to no avail. In the language of Chief Justice Roger B. Taney's majority opinion in the *Dred Scott v. Sanford* decision of 1857, Bernice tells him that "he had no rights that I was bound to respect."[82]

Thus, the *Artist* adds to Ethiop's art collection a nineteenth-century version of Jefferson's worst fears of an "exchange of situation" between master and slave, a gothic instantiation of the "trembling" slaveholder from Query XVIII. Wilson's language makes it clear that this scene belongs to the imaginary world of art and phantasy. The *Artist* and his captive partake in a tale in a tale, in a location outside historical time and space that the *Artist* can render invisible "with one touch of his hand."[83] For Wilson, African American art had the function of designing alternative worlds, whose agents did not have to be historical or fully human to "impress" themselves on the mind and inspire "encouragement and self-reliance."[84] In its double valence of personhood and thinghood, *character* was an important tool in this approach to art. As Deidre Lynch has emphasized, the history of character and the history of the individual are not the same. In the late eighteenth and nineteenth centuries, *character* was subject to two interrelated developments: The first had the aim to conceal what Lynch calls character's "eerie thingness" behind the illusion of "realist" characters, that is, letters on a page, or colors on a canvas that were supposed to be read or perceived as persons rather than things.[85] The second served the abolitionist goal to reveal as a fiction the American legal construction of the *double character* of the slave as both person and property. A claim to character could thus imply a claim to equality, or, as James Pennington asked in the preface of *The Fugitive Blacksmith*, "has a man no sense of honour because he was born a slave? Has he no need of character?"[86] In their uses of Jefferson's character, African American writers complicated this claim to equality. Reversing the trajectory of humanization in literary illusionism and abolitionism ("The Man That Was a Thing," as Harriet Beecher Stowe had it), they transformed his historical personhood into an object ready to receive the "stamp" of their choice. It was this inverted personification or reification of Jefferson that informed Wilson's gothic rendering of the African American *Artist* holding a white enslaver captive ("Was it a man, was it even human?").

The "eerie thinghood" of Jefferson's character could also take other forms.[87] In 1829, three years after Jefferson's death, David Walker symbolically killed him off as an equal partner in dialogue: "Here let me ask Mr. Jefferson (but he is gone to answer at the bar of God, for the deeds done in his body while living,) I therefore ask the whole American people."[88] When the New York printer and abolitionist David Ruggles, who likely knew *Walker's Appeal*, published *The 'Extinguisher' Extinguished, or David M. Reese, M.D. 'Used Up,'* Walker's dead partner in dialogue seemed to be morphing into an "eerie" entity that was, like character, in between the human and the nonhuman: a ghost. The pamphlet was published in 1834, the year when Ruggles opened a bookstore specializing in antislavery and abolitionist literature (such as, for instance, Maria Stewart's *Productions*).[89] In his attack on David Reese, a white physician and proponent of colonization, Ruggles quoted from, and ventriloquized, Reese's critique of the American Anti-Slavery Society that had recently been founded. "But [. . .] oh! what a *desecration!* Shades of '76! 'The Declaration of Independence was read,' and in proximity to it, 'that insignificant and treasonable production—the *Declaration* of the Anti-Slavery Convention!' Oh! what a political SIN to name these

Declarations *in the same day,* and especially to connect them together in the hallowed services of our country's Sabbath!' Methinks I see the ghosts of Washington, Jefferson, and Madison, start up, like the witches of Macbeth, and dance a jig of horror over the desecrated ruins of their country!'"[90]

In this analogy between the first three US presidents from Virginia and the three witches leading Macbeth to his doom, something remarkable happened. Although Ruggles was the speaker of the hyperbolic exclamations, he used them to ridicule Reese's argument that the Anti-Slavery Society's Declaration of Sentiments was a desecration of America's founding ideals. According to *'Extinguisher' Extinguished,* it was Reese, not Ruggles, who invoked the "shades of '76"; it was Reese who saw the ghosts and was about to be led to his doom by Shakespeare's weird sisters. By implication, Ruggles emphasized that he himself, like so many other African American intellectuals since Lemuel Haynes, saw a direct continuity between the Declaration of Independence and the abolition of slavery. Through the very act of telling the ghost story, Jefferson's ghost was thus made to vanish again. The moment Ruggles conjured up the "jig of horror" danced by Jefferson's shade, he turned him back into a complex historical figure, whose position on slavery could not be legitimately appropriated by the American Colonization Society. As *'Extinguisher' Extinguished* made clear, the historical author of the Declaration of Independence was not the property of white colonizationists. Instead, it was Ruggles and his allies who had the power not only to call up the "spirit of '76" but also, when necessary, immediately put it back into the bottle again.

"Incontestable Descendant of Thomas Jefferson and Black Sal"

Jefferson would long continue to be, as William G. Allen had it, "dug up"[91] by the colonizationists, but his character also haunted Americans in other contexts. In 1859, *Frederick Douglass' Paper* reprinted from the *New York Tribune* a notice alerting the public that, by "some strange process of transmigration," Jefferson had "turned up again in the Old Dominion, though in so obscure a way that those desirous of seeing so celebrated a character, are obliged to offer a pecuniary reward for the discovery of his whereabouts." What followed was a runaway advertisement from a recent number of the *Richmond Enquirer* for "my man THOMAS JEFFERSON," for whom his former owner had offered a hundred Dollar reward.[92]

And this was not the only fugitive Jefferson of the polarized 1850s. Another African American likeness conspicuously made an appearance in New York City. Under the pseudonym "Communipaw," James McCune Smith introduced his series of character sketches for *Frederick Douglass' Paper*, "Heads of the Colored People" (1852–54), with a self-emancipated slave from Virginia who had "lost both his legs by frost and the surgeon's knife" and earned his living as a stationed "news-vender" on West Broadway.[93] Half-human, half–literary character, the "news-vender" seems to merge with the papers he sells. "Behind the papers, and almost part of them, is the figure of a black man, razed to the knees, as if for the convenient handling of his literary peltry."[94] Communipaw's literary portrait conflates him in size and appearance not only with characters on paper but also with a bust-length portrait of Jefferson: "Our colored news vender *kneels* about four feet ten; black transparent skin, broad and swelling chest whose symmetry proclaims Virginia birth, fine long face, clean cut hazel eyes, buried beneath luxuriantly folded lids, and prominent perceptive faculties. I did not ask him to pull off [his] cloth cap [covering] long greasy ears, lest his brow should prove him the incontestable descendant of Thomas Jefferson and Black Sal."[95]

McCune Smith used this portrait of Jefferson[96] to make two major points. The first concerned the theme he would develop further in "On the Fourteenth Query of Jefferson's Notes on Virginia" seven years later: Jefferson's subjectivist account of *race* in *Notes on Virginia*, which had helped write into existence *whiteness* and *blackness* as separate national identities and epistemologies. As the portrait of the "news-vender" demonstrated, Jefferson had not only been deeply mistaken in assuming a sharp dividing line between "white" and "black" ways of feeling and perceiving; he himself could not possibly have believed in it as he had been habitually transgressing the supposed line in his sexual behavior. To make public Jefferson's interracial progeny ("black babies and yellow so far as Tom Jefferson is concerned"), McCune Smith used the portrait as part of a recourse to paralipsis that was prominent, as has been shown, in many other African American engagements with Jefferson as well. "It is well known," Communipaw repeats, "it is well known that Jefferson contradicted his philosophy of negro hate, by seeking the dalliance of black women as often as he could, and by leaving so many descendants of mixed blood, that they are to be found as widely scattered as his own writings throughout the world. One at least, a granddaughter, is a shouting Methodist in Liberia. I have heard from an eyewitness that on more than one occasion, when the sage of Monticello left the retreat for the Presidential abode at Washington, there would be on the top of the same coach, a yellow boy of his own begetting, 'running away.' And when told that one of his slaves was going off without leave, Jefferson said, 'Well! Let him go, his right is as good as his father's! And, somehow, that boy would get a *douceur* [tip] before the "parting of ways."' "[97]

As long as he treats Jefferson as a historical individual, Communipaw evaluates his behavior as something that was depressing and comical at the same time; on a petty level generous, and blending a certain warmth with callousness. When he refers to Jefferson as a representative character, however, he is less forgiving. In a passage that anticipated William Wells Brown's novel *Clotel*, which would be published in the following year, Communipaw explains: "These crocus-colored products of unphilosophical lust are now reared, and penned up, and branded, and sold by slaveholding fathers in Old Dominion, who go to Presbyterian and Methodist churches, and to the altars of Episcopacy [. . .]; and thank God that they are not heathen Circassians who sell their daughters as prostitutes to *Mahommedan*, not *Christian*, lust!"[98]

The character of the "black news-vender" is not merely a piece of evidence in abolitionist rhetoric, however. Apart from furnishing living proof of the "boisterous passions" that Jefferson under Query XVIII had described as the result of slavery,[99] his likeness also serves a second function in the text. Communipaw establishes an analogy between Jefferson's descendants and his writings: the former "are to be found as widely scattered" as the latter "throughout the world."[100] The significance of Jefferson's African American descendant on West Broadway thus at least potentially parallels what is supposed to be the worldwide influence of Jefferson's writings. Portrayed as a hybrid between the human and the literary, whose "black transparent skin" evokes both Jefferson's "veil of black" and the interplay of black characters and white paper, the "news-vender" not only sells news but also adds a new element to the philosophical discourse initiated by *Notes on Virginia*. Leaving behind Jefferson's racial zero-sum game—an uncompromising contrast between *whiteness* and *blackness* under Query XIV that threatens to result in an equally uncompromising race war under Query XVIII—Communipaw explains that this new element is the "news-vender's" ability to bring out the best in his contemporaries, a universal human sympathy and pity that transcends racial divides morally as well as epistemologically. As Jefferson's likeness is "fastened near the ground by his terrific misfortune, the true heart of the American people beats kindly and with warm sympathy towards him! [. . .] and many a dandy, who thinks, in a political sense, the negro almost a dog, snatches up a paper, and with half-averted face, throws down four times its worth, and rushes away from the *human sympathy* that has stolen into his heart, in spite of, and through the chinks of the thrice-ribbed armor with which American Church and American state [. . .] have endeavored to encase his affections. Merciful God! what a living fountain of human sympathy hast thou planted on that stone stoop, linking human creature to human creature, in spite of all the bars which society has placed between them!"[101]

In the remainder of the character sketch, Communipaw enacts his universalist ideal of "linking human creature to human creature" by entering, himself, into a dialogue with Jefferson's fugitive likeness. In the course of the conversation, he is told that the news-vendor's maimed legs are, as a harsh irony of fate, the reason why even after the Compromise of 1850 he no longer worries about being kidnapped back into Virginia slavery ("what would they want with me?").[102] Inquiring further after the origin of the injury, Communipaw learns that the "news-vender" lost them as a sailor in a shipwreck on the very same Christmas eve in 1849 when he, Communipaw, lost his first-born daughter.[103] The character of the "news-vender" thus eventually turns out to be much more than a mere Jefferson likeness: anticipating such twentieth-century literary characters as Claude McKay's Lafala, another sailor who loses both his legs to frostbite after an Atlantic crossing,[104] he exemplifies the fundamental likeness of all humanity in the face of disability and death. "Your story must be printed and sold," Communipaw concludes his own story of this human and humane literary character. "And your first stock in trade shall be purchased from the sum left behind by the little girl who found rest in heaven, while you manfully met and battled with your severest ill on earth."[105]

"Retaliation"

William Wells Brown's *Clotel; or, The President's Daughter: A Narrative of Slave Life in the United States* (1853) is widely known today as the first preserved African American novel. As this chapter has shown, however, in its engagement with Jefferson's character it also needs to be seen as a condensation of more than half a century of previous and contemporaneous African

The Death of Clotel, frontispiece from *Clotel; or, The President's Daughter: A Narrative of Slave Life in the United States*, by William Wells Brown, 1853. (Documenting the American South, Libraries of the University of North Carolina, Chapel Hill)

American reflections on the theme. Published in London and written for a British audience during Brown's extended sojourn in Europe as a "fugitive slave from the American house of bondage,"[106] the 1853 edition differed from the novel's three later versions from the 1860s in focusing explicitly on the fictional lives of Jefferson's daughters and granddaughters. Its complex "tragic mulatta" plot opens with the auction where Currer, Jefferson's fictional housekeeper and concubine, is sold together with her two teenage daughters, Clotel and Althesa. The following twenty-eight chapters paint a broad panorama of the slaveholding South, introducing a host of diverse characters and sensational events, partly historical and fictional, to develop the tragic fates of the three women. To meet sentimental expectations, the narrative ends with the happy reunion of Clotel's daughter Mary with her lover in Europe. The plot's true climax, however, comes in chapters 24 and 25, "The Arrest" and "Death Is Freedom," when, disguised as a man,[107] Clotel returns to Virginia in search of her daughter. In the wake of Nat Turner's insurrection, the state she returns to is engulfed in a race war reminiscent of Jefferson's worst fears under Query XVIII ("carnage was added to carnage, and the blood of the whites flowed to avenge the blood of the blacks").[108]

In an atmosphere of extreme doom and distrust, Clotel's disguise is uncovered, and she reenacts her father's "trembling" when she is arrested with "trembling heart" and returned to slavery.[109] She escapes again, but only to meet her death when, pursued by slave-catchers, she leaps from a bridge into the Potomac, "within plain sight of the President's house and the capitol of the Union." Brown's narrator makes no secret of the political irony of this event. "Thus died Clotel, the daughter of Thomas Jefferson, a president of the United States; a man distinguished as the author of the Declaration of American Independence, and one of the first statesmen of that country."[110]

Exploiting the double valence of *character* as person and thing, the novel cruelly dwells on the process by which it turns its heroine, a thinking and feeling subject, into a mere physical object: "The body of Clotel was picked up from the bank of the river, where it had been washed by the strong current, a hole dug in the sand, and there deposited, without either inquest being held over it, or religious service being performed."[111] Clotel's suicide in her futile attempt to resist objectification is paralleled by Brown's construction of her historical father's character. During his long exile in Europe, Brown decided to sell Jefferson, not exactly down the river, but to the British: Arguably, the novel commodified Jefferson as much as it did his fictional daughter. As an anonymous subtitle character in "The President's Daughter," Jefferson first appears as an object placed, without a name, on the title page, an imprint used to increase the sale and distribution of the book. His character is defined solely by three aspects: his representative function in a slaveholding democracy; his paternal relation to the eponymous heroine; and, in an ironic juxtaposition displayed on the title page and repeated at different moments in the novel, by the written characters of his words, the Haynes abridgment of the Declaration's second phrase.[112]

As the protagonist's nameless father, Jefferson initially resembles the enslaved people on the auction block in the novel's exposition, "The Negro Sale," in that he is mainly advertised by the novel for his "generating qualities."[113] Since it is thus in some sense not only Jefferson's daughters but Jefferson himself who is up for auction, he is first introduced into the plot as nameless physical matter: as part of "the blood of the first American statesmen" coursing "through the veins of the slave of the South" in the novel's first paragraph, about to be sold away in the "bones, muscles, sinews, blood, and nerves" of his daughter a few pages afterward.[114] From physical matter, he is turned first into a social function and only second into an individual, appearing as "a young slaveholder" for whom Clotel's mother kept house, and only afterward mentioned by name as "Thomas Jefferson, by whom she had two daughters."[115] The next stage of personification is his position in American history as "the writer of the Declaration of Independence, and one of the presidents of the great republic,"[116] but this stage is never specified in relation to his identity as a "young slaveholder." In keeping with its uncertain position in historical time, Jefferson's character simply fades away as the plot progresses. Like so many other characters in a chaotic world of slavery and displacement, it ceases to be mentioned as the novel's London edition gradually moves its moral center from the Declaration of Independence and the United States to the Old World, concluding in Europe with the author's hope to "let the voice of the whole British nation be heard across the Atlantic."[117]

In chapter 17, "Retaliation," Brown ties this objectifying use of Jefferson's character specifically to Query XVIII. The chapter describes the physical abuse of Jefferson's granddaughter Mary at the hands of her white mistress and evil stepmother, Mrs. Green. The "white slave-girl" is forced to work in the sun without protection, "until she sank down in the corner of the garden, and was actually broiled to sleep."[118] Due to this sadistic "seasoning," Mary's offensive pallor disappears, but Mrs. Green is determined to continue her abuse because "the child was not only white, but she was the granddaughter of Thomas Jefferson, the man who, when speaking against slavery in the legislature of Virginia, said, 'The whole commerce between master and slave is a perpetual exercise of the most boisterous passions.'"[119] With this insight into Mrs. Green's motivation, Brown's narrator abruptly drops the plotline to quote long extracts from Query XVIII on the depravity of Virginia slaveholders and Jefferson's subsequent "trembling" for his country, followed by an excerpt from observations Jefferson sent Jean-Nicolas Démeunier for his article on the United States in the *Encyclopédie méthodique* making a similar point on God's justice ("doubtless a God of justice will awaken to their distress, and by diffusing light and liberality among their oppressors, or at length by his exterminating thunder, manifest his attention to the things of this world"), which is followed by a second verbatim quotation of Jefferson's "trembling" under Query XVIII.[120] Despite this extreme focus on Jefferson's language—his words under Query XVIII seem powerful enough to bring Brown's own narrative to a halt—the chapter concludes by pointing out the fungibility and ineffectiveness of Jefferson's character. Jefferson is shown unable to fulfill a central promise of his political philosophy, the respect for the rights of future generations.[121] "But, sad to say," Brown's narrator concludes, "Jefferson is not the only American statesman who has spoken high sounding words in favour of freedom, and then left his own children to die slaves."[122]

Thus, for Brown, the problem was not that Jefferson had expressed the wrong attitude under Query XVIII. As Mrs. Green's behavior demonstrated, Jefferson had been entirely justified in condemning the slaveholders' corruption. And as his granddaughter's change of status and skin color showed, he had also been right to fear a providential "exchange of situation" between master and slave. The problem was instead that Jefferson had been unable to rationally abstract from his emotions enough to discern the dialectical relationship between his feelings of guilt or shame and his fears of racial violence. As Brown's extensive quotations from Query XVIII in this chapter on "Retaliation" suggest, in her desire to humiliate Jefferson's enslaved granddaughter, Mrs. Green had been provoked, in part, by Jefferson's moralizing about the slaveholders' depravity. Since the moral qualms of Jefferson's Enlightenment of Feeling had not engendered sufficient rational measures to end slavery, they had inadvertently contributed to a political polarization that turned out to make retaliative racial violence rather more than less likely. Following this reading, Jefferson's navel-gazing regrets about being on the wrong side of history turned out to be not only ineffective for, but even highly detrimental to, the well-being of future American generations, including that of his own family.

Brown's devastating critique of the tragically self-serving dimension of Jefferson's self-criticism may still be holding out a mirror to early twenty-first-century debates. In his subsequent writings, however, Brown soon retreated from this critique. When he rewrote the novel for American audiences in the 1860s, Jefferson's character vanished, like the ghost in Ruggles's *'Extinguisher' Extinguished*. His daughters became his "descendants," and his paternity that of an anonymous American senator.[123] A decade after the London edition of *Clotel*, Jefferson did return in Brown's *Black Man*. As has been shown, however, in the context of the Civil War he reemerged as a wholly sympathetic character, unburdened by the hypocrisy of hiding a second family from public view. In one sense, nevertheless, this version remained true to Brown's earlier interpretation of Query XVIII. It likewise illustrated that indulging in one's feelings of guilt or shame was, at best, irrelevant; as a true man of the Enlightenment, Brown's improved Civil War version of Jefferson had to be open to receiving rational instructions from Benjamin Banneker.

Taking the Life Mask of Jefferson

It would be interesting to know how Jefferson's children and grandchildren with Sally Hemings responded to such fictional representations as in "The Black News-Vender" and *Clotel*. The memoir by Jefferson's son Madison Hemings, published as "Life among the Lowly, No. 1" in the *Pike County (Ohio) Republican* on March 13, 1873, is the most important source here.[124] If this brief autobiographical statement seems to have little in common with Brown's and McCune Smith's characters, it was not only because Hemings knew, of course, that he had neither leaped into the Potomac nor lost his legs, but also because he appears to have been intent on presenting a text that might be described as an anti–Query XVIII. Hemings's memoir was a markedly sober and rational account of the personal relations between the enslavers and the enslaved in Virginia that actively defied Jefferson's emotional laments about "boisterous passions" and "degrading submissions." Even more radically than had McCune Smith and Brown before him, Hemings's narrative decentered Jefferson's subjectivity. Beginning with his only white ancestor known (or rumored) to be named Hemings, Madison Hemings's great-grandfather, the narrative consistently follows the different Hemings generations down to Madison Hemings and his siblings Beverly, Harriet, and Eston, who "all married and have raised families," a phrase Hemings proudly repeats about his own children at the end of the memoir.[125] Jefferson merely enters this elaborate Hemings family tree, as it were, by a side entrance, as "a visitor at the 'great house' of John Wales," Madison Hemings's grandfather.[126] In a similar vein, Hemings's "earliest recollections" are not of Jefferson but "of my grandmother Elizabeth Hemings."[127] Jefferson's character is thus subdued, in a double sense: although likely the main interest of the Ohio audience of S. F. Wetmore, the Republican editor of the *Pike County Republican* (and countless historians to follow), it fails to organize Hemings's narrative. The character is temperamentally subdued as well. Hemings describes his father as "the quietest of men," with a "smooth and even" temperament, who "was very undemonstrative." He could be "irritated" occasionally (a term weirdly reminiscent of Irving's and McCune Smith's Jefferson caricatures) "but even then he hardly ever allowed himself to be made unhappy any great length of time."[128] Hemings emphasizes that the restraint of Jefferson's emotional economy was not universal. While within the community of feeling of his official family he was

The Descendants, Drew Gardner (Thomas Jefferson/ Shannon LaNier). (https://www.drewgardner.com/descendants; courtesy of Drew Gardner)

"affectionate" toward his "white grandchildren," he was "not in the habit of showing partiality or fatherly affection to us children." The relationship with the Hemings family came closer to a reliable business transaction, in which Jefferson, in contrast to other white people such as Dolley Madison, at least kept his promises and respected his "treaty" with Sally Hemings to guarantee her liberty and that of her children.[129]

Could this painstakingly "undemonstrative" character have been the "trembling" speaker of Query XVIII? Madison Hemings apparently found it necessary to rationalize his father's image, not only in the sense of generally coming to terms with it but also of rendering it more rational in the eyes of the American public. To be sure, few people enjoy imagining "boisterous passions" and "degrading submissions" in their parents' relationship. But in post–Civil War Ohio, after Jefferson's apocalyptic prophecy under Query XVIII had been overtaken by American history, and slavery had turned out to be abolished both without the "consent of the masters" *and* without their "extirpation," there is also the possibility that Hemings simply found no use for the uncompromising emotional dichotomies of Jefferson's Enlightenment of Feeling. It almost seems as if Hemings's dispassionate Jefferson of 1873 had successfully been subjected to the pedagogies of character discussed in this chapter—as if this character had, indeed, learned its lessons in rational self-control from writers such as Hannah of Poplar Forest, Benjamin Banneker, Daniel Coker, or William Wells Brown.[130]

Other personal memoirs from the postwar period continued in the style of the rationally balanced portrait painted by Jefferson's son. The recollections of Hemings's "old friend and former companion at Monticello," Israel Jefferson (a member of the Gillette family who took the name Jefferson at the suggestion of the Charlottesville clerk issuing his free papers), were published in the *Pike County Republican* later in 1873.[131] While Israel Jefferson corroborated his friend's case for the paternity of Sally Hemings's children, he was less given to decentering his namesake's character in the narrative. Israel Jefferson's "earliest recollections" dated back to 1804, with the beginning of the elder Jefferson's presidency. Working for him as a waiter, postillion, and personal servant who "made the fire in his bedroom and private chamber, cleaned his office, dusted his books, run of errands and attended him about home," he could plausibly claim that Jefferson's "private life" was "very familiar" to him.[132] However, this familiarity did not translate into anything close to the emotional approach to slavery of Query XVIII. In a detached tone, Israel recalled that his former master "was esteemed by both whites and blacks as a very great man." He therefore considered him to be in the same league, if morally somewhat inferior by comparison, with the "great and good Lafayette." According to Israel's memory of a conversation between the two aged revolutionaries he overheard while taking them out for a drive in 1824, Lafayette pointed out to Jefferson his great disappointment with Americans' failure to abolish slavery after the American Revolution, which he had supported in the belief "that they were fighting for a great and noble principle—the freedom of mankind."[133] Israel Jefferson drily recorded a rather lame response that did not have any of the moral efflorescence of Query XVIII: "Mr. Jefferson replied that he thought the time would come when the slaves would be free, but did not indicate when or in what manner they would get their freedom. He seemed to think that the time had not then arrived."[134] In a similar spirit, when he described Jefferson's death as "an affair of great moment and uncertainty for us slaves," he did so, not because of any deep emotional involvement with Jefferson's character, but because of the harsh reality that the disappearance of Monticello's patriarch meant for him and the vast majority of the plantation community: the dispersal of families and the loss of loved ones who would be "sold from the auction block" to pay off Jefferson's debts.[135]

In 1898 and 1900, the Cincinnati minister Peter Fossett, who had been an eleven-year-old house servant at Monticello when Jefferson died, was interviewed by the *New York Sunday World* and the *Colored American*.[136] A version of Madison Hemings's rational Jefferson still held sway, although Fossett's long-term memory painted the unrealistically positive image of an "ideal master" who had supposedly "made arrangements to free all his slaves at his death."[137] What seems to have endeared the "very learned" Jefferson the most to Fossett was that, unlike other slave owners, Jefferson had allowed his white grandchildren to teach enslaved children such as himself to read (if not always also to write, as pointed out by Israel Jefferson).[138] After he suddenly found himself "put upon an auction block and sold to strangers" following Jefferson's death,[139] Fossett was able to use this legacy to write free passes for his sister and others. However, despite his relative enthusiasm for his first owner, Fossett abruptly ended his 1898 interview with an uncanny impression of Jefferson's character. He recalled the day in the last fall of Jefferson's life when the process of taking his life mask had gone so badly wrong that he had nearly suffocated and, in the words of Annette Gordon-Reed, "the 'life mask' had almost become a death mask."[140] "The report got around that Mr. Jefferson had been killed, and there was the greatest excitement until we all saw Mr. Jefferson again alive and well," Fossett recalled. As might be concluded, taking Jefferson's likeness and preserving his imprint was a dangerous business. If the "stamp" of character went wrong, it could pose a serious threat to the individual as well as the community. In the last year before the enslaved families at Monticello were about to be dispersed by sale, and in the last year of what Fossett described as his carefree childhood, the "stamp" of character was becoming a question of life and death, almost as Jefferson had predicted under Query XVIII. "I see a magazine writer says there was no trouble about taking the life mask, but I know better," Fossett concluded his recollections, "for I was there."[141]

❖ 8 ❖

Above Jefferson's Veil

In the twentieth century, African American writers continued to break the rules of the zero-sum game of *whiteness* and *blackness*—an imaginary conflict between two distinct epistemologies only to be resolved by either national separation or race war—that Jefferson had designed under Queries XIV and XVIII of *Notes on the State of Virginia*. For their project of consolidating the universalist epistemology of Wheatley's Enlightenment of Principle against Jefferson's insistence on separate ways of knowing and feeling, the "veil" became a central metaphor. Jefferson's lament about "that immoveable veil of black which covers all the emotions of the other race" under Query XIV of *Notes on Virginia* had marked the literal and figurative boundaries of his postcolonial vision.[1] As argued in this book, the metaphor has to be historicized as part of his Enlightenment of Feeling ("I feel: therefore I exist"), according to which human reason was unable to function without concretely embodied sensory experience. From this position, Jefferson could claim ignorance of that which he could not sense. The metaphor accordingly shifts focus, illuminating the position directly opposite the one often taken for granted in discussions of his concept of *race*. By its internal logic, the image of an "immoveable veil of black" could throw light only on the subject and the process, not the object, of sensory perception. At issue in the phrase was no serious attempt to detail the supposed characteristics of "the other race." A homogeneously "black" veil was incapable of giving a visual account of the countless shades that make up human skin tone, let alone the "greater or less suffusions of colour" in each individual's appearance.[2] For Jefferson, strictly speaking, the people he referred to as "blacks" were people of *no* color: in the final analysis, his screen of total blackness was only plausible as an optical, not a visual metaphor. He was describing, not the success, but the breakdown of his subjective vision due to the occluded lens of what he called "white" Virginians' "deep rooted prejudices." The "veil of black" referred to the personal and collective blindness that Jefferson knew was limiting his *own* pursuit of light, knowledge, and Enlightenment.

Ironically, the association of a "sable veil" with optics rather than vision, with moral and epistemological darkness and an inhibited sense of sight, was akin to the uses to which Phillis Wheatley, for whose poetry Jefferson expressed so little regard under the same Query, had put the metaphor a decade before him, in her *Poems on Various Subjects, Religious and Moral*.[3] Jefferson might have found another inspiration for "that immoveable veil of black" in Immanuel Kant's contemporaneous axiom in the *Critique of Pure Reason* (1781; 1787) that thoughts without content were "empty," while intuitions without concepts were "blind."[4] By stubbornly characterizing his subjective sense impression of the veil's blackness as "real" and "fixed," "eternal" as well as "immoveable,"[5] Jefferson insisted on what amounted to an insurmountable barrier to knowledge in his radically empiricist Enlightenment. Eventually, the subjectivist concept of *race* he thus developed in *Notes on Virginia* would have portentous implications for many other people as well. First and foremost, however, for Jefferson *race* meant dramatically lowering his expectations in regard to his own perceptive and cognitive abilities.

These reduced expectations were not mainly motivated by personal modesty; they served important political goals. As has been shown, in Jefferson's postcolonial Enlightenment the interrelated concepts of *nation* and *race* could no longer be grounded in hierarchical claims to knowledge following the "wretched philosophy" of European metaphysics. Jefferson went further than did most of his contemporaries in theorizing nationhood as both a political and an epistemological entity, stressing the importance of an anti-Eurocentric "diffusion" or democratization of knowledge for the founding of the new nation. In his view, it was a communally specific set of feelings, beliefs, and opinions, rather than the universal knowledge authorized by an intellectual elite centered in Europe, that made American nationhood subjectively plausible to equal republican citizens and that could be mobilized in war and politics. Along with a republican American "creed," this set of beliefs included "deep rooted prejudices." For Jefferson, the "veil" illustrated the epistemological constraints of his imagined community of feeling, binding "white" Americans together while blinding them to "all the emotions of the other race." Ultimately, his evocation of "that immoveable veil of black" thus has to be understood as the complacent complaint of a postcolonial philosopher willfully placing himself at his wit's end.

As an epistemological rather than chromatic metaphor, based on an optical rather than visual notion of blackness as blindness rather than pigmentation, the "veil" had a long and prestigious career in African American intellectual and literary history. Throughout the African American tradition, authors would elaborate on Jefferson's close association between (racist) prejudice and a failure of the sense of sight.[6] At the beginning of a new century still concerned with overcoming the "color-line" Jefferson's "veil" had helped establish, the metaphor received several famous revisions: an elaborate philosophical theme developed throughout W. E. B. Du Bois's *The Souls of Black Folk* (1903) and what may be an ironic commentary on both Du Bois and Jefferson in the 1912 preface of James Weldon Johnson's *The Autobiography of an Ex-Coloured Man*. A radically different interpretation of the veil metaphor was cast in bronze a few years later in the Booker T. Washington Monument at Tuskegee, a double statue sometimes referred to as *Lifting the Veil of Ignorance* (1921), whose composition recalled the Emancipation Monument that Frederick Douglass had rhetorically unveiled in Washington, DC, at the nation's centennial in 1876. Just as Johnson's narrator transformed Du Bois's version of the veil into fiction, Ralph Ellison's narrator in *Invisible Man* (1952) provided fictional commentary on the Tuskegee variant of the veil. Jefferson's insight that the "odious peculiarities"[7] of the peculiar institution were causing white Virginians' blindness thus eventually resonated in Ellison's analysis of the "peculiar disposition of the eyes"[8] that rendered his protagonist invisible, in the "very peculiar" constellation that James Baldwin described in 1965, in another textile metaphor, as a "curtain of guilt and lies behind which white Americans hide."[9]

This chapter argues that despite their many differences, classical African American revisions of Jefferson's Enlightenment of Feeling shared the goal of Wheatley's Enlightenment of Principle of consolidating a universalist epistemology by illuminating the blind spots of his "veil of black." Jefferson's "immoveable" veil had demarcated the fixed boundary between two epistemological (and, for him, national) communities of feeling that should each be placed on a different "side of the water,"[10] since they were static and "eternal." By contrast, African American conceptions of the veil were historically dynamic. With different emphases, they were united by the unfinished Enlightenment project described, for example, in Frances Harper's *Iola Leroy, or, Shadows Uplifted* (1892) as a "Further Lifting of the Veil," or in Charles Chesnutt's *The Marrow of Tradition* (1901) as enabling moments when even for southern racists "the veil of prejudice" could be "rent in twain."[11] This Enlightenment project consolidated the universalist pursuit of knowledge and reason that had been heavily destabilized by the "postcolonial inversions" of the democratization of knowledge in Jefferson's antirationalist philosophy.[12] Its authors transferred Jefferson's "veil of black" from its original context of darkness and ignorance to the domain of light and knowledge. In the emerging synthesis of Jefferson's Enlightenment of Feeling and Wheatley's Enlightenment of Principle in the Jeffersonian Enlightenment, the "veil" functioned as the key metaphor of a complicated but eventually consolidated universalism.

Wheatley's "Sable Veil"

"Black" or "lifted" veils are no rare occurrences in Anglophone literature, whether in Charles Dickens's "The Black Veil," Nathaniel Hawthorne's "The Minister's Black Veil," or George Eliot's "The Lifted Veil." Unlike such predominantly gothic uses of the veil motif, the best-known veils appearing in African American literature take up the Enlightenment concern with knowledge, perception, and perspective that had informed Wheatley's and Jefferson's uses. In the tradition of Wheatley, they tended to enrich the problem of visual perception by more or less secularized allusions to the biblical theme of the "veil of the temple [. . .] rent in twain" when Jesus died on the cross (Matthew 27:51).[13] Wheatley had set the tone for the salvation-historical dimension of the veil metaphor when reflecting on *Daily Devotion Assisted and Recommended, in Four Sermons* by the dissenting English minister Thomas Amory. In her poem "To the Rev. Dr. Thomas Amory on reading his Sermons on Daily Devotion," she had emphasized the idea that the universal vision of divine wisdom could transcend the "sable veil" of limited human existence:

> When God's eternal ways you set in sight,
> And *Virtue* shines in all her native light,
> In vain would Vice her works conceal,
> For *Wisdom's* eye pervades the sable veil.[14]

In "Thoughts on the Work of Providence," Wheatley continued the theme of the morning devotion in Amory's first sermon that after each night's sleep "we are restored to the use of our *Reason,* and of our *Active Powers.*"[15] Moving the focus from divine to human reason, her speaker exclaimed, "What pow'r, O man! Thy *reason* then restores, / So long suspended in nocturnal hours?"[16] In the opposition between the "sable veil" of night and the power of human reason, the metaphor's moral meanings were overlayered by the epistemological meanings of irrational darkness and silence. In addition, the "sable veil" alluded to the realm of "Chaos" and "sable-vested Night" in Milton's *Paradise Lost:* "The sable veil, that *Night* in silence draws / Conceals effects, but shews th' *Almighty Cause.*"[17] While the metaphor of the "sable veil" may also have played with associations to the "sable race" she mentioned in other poems in the collection,[18] for Wheatley a fundamental moral and epistemological darkness tended to color all human experience alike, regardless of what would become Jefferson's subjective divisions into separate communities of feeling. In Wheatley's universe ordered by the contrast of divine light and earthly gloom, the attempt to attribute moral value to subjective problems of sensory perception (let alone of perceived skin pigmentation) would have been petty at best, sinful at worst. Whereas Jefferson presented the "veil of black" as an insurmountable epistemological barrier separating the American population into different nations, for Wheatley such a separation would have missed the point. For Jefferson the only hope for redemption lay in the founding of separate, subjectively plausible nation-states, whereas Wheatley stressed God's universal transcendence of the "sable veil" and the "chaos" of human existence.

Among the writers following in her footsteps, the evangelical Protestantism enabling her hopes for the veil's transcendence would lose ground. However, it would clearly be mistaken from a more secularized perspective to belittle Wheatley's thinking, as Jefferson did under Query XIV, as the unenlightened expression of "mere" religion.[19] In her letter to Samson Occom discussed in the beginning of the introduction to part 2, Wheatley had explained what she called "the Principle" of universal liberty, making it clear that "civil and religious Liberty [. . .] are so inseparably united, that there is little or no Enjoyment of one without the other."[20] For Wheatley unlike more traditional thinkers, demands for religious liberty and demands for civil liberty were intertwined. Her "Principle" of universal liberty was not the expression of humble devotion to a traditional Christian universalism but had a pronounced secular dimension, thrown into sharp relief by the practice of its radical opposite in the Middle Passage and slavery. Wheatley opposed being sent to Africa as a missionary in terms that were decidedly secular. In a letter to the English merchant and philanthropist John Thornton in 1774, she added a new level to the Enlightenment game of inverting perspective à la Montesquieu's *Persian Letters:* politely declining Thornton's suggestion of missionary return (preceded by a similar suggestion by Samson Occom in 1771), she pictured herself, both ironically and seriously, as an American who would look "like a Barbarian [. . .] to the Natives" at her arrival on African shores.[21]

This sophisticated universalist position, able at the same time to foreground and to transcend difference,[22] posed a formidable intellectual challenge also to the secular ethics of the American revolutionaries—a constellation that may help explain, along with her literary fame, why Jefferson felt under such pressure not only to disparage her work, but to go as far as to "pre-judge" and categorically exclude it from his judgment altogether. As both sacred *and* secular, Wheatley's emphatically universalist theory of knowledge still shines through even in modernist African American revisions of Jefferson's postcolonial "veil." Dressed in imagery involving darkness and light, blindness and vision, chaos and order, her concern with the "Principle" was not only influential in the late eighteenth century but may still be felt, as the following sections will develop, in revisions of Jefferson's "veil" by writers as far removed from her in time and literary form as were W. E. B. Du Bois, James Weldon Johnson, and Ralph Ellison.

"America Shall Rend the Veil"

To begin with what may have been the most famous use of the metaphor in the twentieth century, in *The Souls of Black Folk* Du Bois spoke of a capitalized "Veil" as a synonym for an American concept of *race,* separating those "within" from those "without" the "color-line" Jefferson's "veil of black" had helped draw. Du Bois was not satisfied with Jefferson's figure of "ten thousand recollections," but announced sketching the "spiritual world in which ten thousand *thousand* Americans live and strive." Du Bois substituted Jefferson's "feelings" with "thoughts," having the book's "afterthought" end with an appeal to "infinite reason."[23] Unlike the Jefferson of Query XIV, Du Bois's speaker explicitly promised insights on "the two worlds within and without the Veil."[24] These double insights were possible since he claimed that African Americans "born with a veil" were "gifted with second-sight in this American world." Thus alluding to a specific kind of veil, the whitish membrane named caul or caput galeatum that continues to cover some children after birth, he followed transcultural folk traditions in attributing unique gifts and fortunes to the people "veiled" in this manner. While in this context the Veil was connected to nativity, it was both transparent and transitory and thus emphasized qualities diametrically opposed to Jefferson's "eternal" and "immoveable veil of black."

Du Bois supplemented this allusion to a "moveable veil of white" with his oft-discussed appropriation of the concept of *double consciousness*.[25] For him, *double consciousness* was the ambivalent result of African Americans' fateful but permeable and impermanent Veil. It placed them under increased pressure of "always looking at oneself through the eyes of others," but this difficult double perspective also had the crucial moral and epistemological advantage of opening up two worldviews that were temporarily separate but could eventually be integrated. Unlike Jefferson's veil, Du Bois's Veil was no fundamental obstacle in the pursuit of knowledge. Casting an "awful shadow," it could at worst "imprison" those within and make them "grow choked and deformed."[26] At the very least, it functioned as a "dull gauze of caste" that prevented social and intellectual recognition, hanging "between us and Opportunity."[27] But the Veil did not cause permanent blindness or ignorance for African Americans, as had its precursor for Jefferson under Query XIV. Whereas Jefferson had been immersed in the nation- and race-making project of establishing two separate civic subjectivities, the Du Bois of *Souls* followed the tradition of Wheatley in envisioning himself, someone else, "America," or a supernatural power "raising" or "lifting" the Veil,[28] freeing those born "within" and enlightening those born "without." "If somewhere in this whirl and chaos of things there dwells Eternal Good, pitiful yet masterful, then anon in His good time America shall rend the Veil and the prisoned shall go free," Du Bois wrote, concluding *Souls* with the hope addressed at a secularized "God the Reader" that "*in Thy good time may infinite reason turn the tangle straight.*"[29]

Jefferson had tried to solve the veil's problem of permanently limiting the process of Enlightenment by spatializing and nationalizing knowledge, going some way in the direction of alternative epistemologies. By contrast, in *Souls* Du Bois stressed the crucial importance of a dynamic but universally applicable theory of knowledge, with the complication that, at his historical moment at the "dawn" of a new century concerned with the "color-line," those "within" the Veil could increase the knowledge of those "without" considerably more than vice versa. Whereas Jefferson had seen himself confronted with an "immoveable veil of black" at eye level, Du Bois placed his speaker "above the Veil," in sight of a secularized "Promised Land." At this point in his long and complex career, Du Bois envisioned his speaker as part of a universalist Enlightenment that made it possible for him to be "wed with Truth."[30]

Insofar as residing *above* the Veil made his union with Truth (including "true self-consciousness")[31] possible, the Veil for Du Bois was connected not only to ignorance but also to untruth. James Weldon Johnson complicated the metaphor by transferring it into fictional literature, hiding both the "veil of black" and the "veil of white" behind the veil of fiction. In his faux autobiography of a fictional narrator who had supposedly crossed Du Bois's "color-line" by passing for white and thus exchanging one fictional identity for another that was, if possible, even "more" fictional, the Veil's relationship to truth entered a hall of mirrors. "In these pages it is as though a veil had been drawn aside: the reader is given a view of the inner life of the Negro in America, is initiated into the free-masonry, as it were, of the race," the "PUBLISHERS" of the first, anonymously published version of the *Autobiography of an Ex-Coloured Man* announced in the preface.[32] To Johnson's surprise, first readers of his narrative took the bait and believed what had ostentatiously been marked as fiction ("it is as though") to be reality. These readers naively felt themselves initiated into a true "inner life" from which they had felt excluded since the days when Jefferson had complained about "that immoveable veil which covers all the emotions of the other race." In the ironic words of the preface, they thought they were "given a glimpse behind the scenes of this race drama" as well as a "bird's-eye view of the conflict." In other words, they were under the illusion of fulfilling the impossible task of entering a realm located at once "behind" and "above" Du Bois's Veil.

Claiming to conjure "in a dreamlike way things that seem to have happened ages ago in some other world," Johnson condensed the fictional dimension of his account of lifting the "Veil" by another veil-like image, "a hedge of vari-coloured glass bottles stuck in the ground neck down" in the garden of his childhood home.[33] What may in part have been an allusion to an architectural African survival,[34] this intermittent, polychrome boundary, like Du Bois's analogy to the whitish caul, signified on Jefferson's "immoveable veil of black." When as a child the Ex-Coloured Man tries to dig up the bottle necks to uncover the roots of their apparent similarity to the rest of nature ("whether or not the bottles grew as the flowers did"), he receives a "terrific spanking." In ways his older self distinctly remembers, he is severely punished for the attempt to solve the riddle of a pseudo-natural "color-line" that is oscillating between the "veil of black" and the veil of fiction. As discussed in chapter 4, the "veil of black" had already had a fictional quality for Jefferson. After he had claimed that the "eternal" and "immoveable veil of black" limiting his vision was "real," there were only two possibilities for his subsequent account of what was on the veil's other side: either the details under Query XIV of "black" Virginians' supposed inner lives were part of some imaginary "other world," or the claim about the empirical reality of impermeable blackness was itself a fiction. Both could not be true at the same time, even if one or the other subjectively felt "real" to Jefferson. Echoing Hume's discussion of the necessarily "fictitious" dimension of personal identity and diversity,[35] Jefferson's Shandyan attempt to ground collective "racial" identity in subjective consciousness remained an irresolvable "puzzle."[36]

Johnson's sophisticated metafiction took Hume's, Sterne's, and Jefferson's problems of the fictitious (false) or fictional (imaginary) dimension of identity to a new level by further doubling the Veil's doubleness. *The Autobiography of an Ex-Coloured Man* refuses to clarify how far a fictional transcendence of the "veil of black" could substantially differ from a non-fictional one. If African Americans as a group had collectively been "a sphinx to the whites" in the preface to the novel's first edition, before the "great secret" of both the narrator's and, subsequently, the author's lives had been "divulged,"[37] it cannot be taken for granted that they had collectively become less of a sphinx at the end of the second edition. In the *Autobiography*, the problem of collective identity left behind by the man who was later said to share the character of a "sphinx"[38] remained a puzzle. Thus, while the *Autobiography* may have been somewhat less enthusiastically engaged than was *Souls* with a universalist Enlightenment oriented toward "infinite reason," it continued the project of bringing to light the multiple absurdities resulting from Jefferson's "veil of black." And it did so by superimposing on Du Bois's mode of universalizing the "Veil" the very different universalism of the world of fiction.

At the close of the *Autobiography*, the Ex-Coloured Man recalls attending a Hampton Institute meeting focused on Booker T. Washington. Now an "ordinarily successful white man," he wistfully professes to admire

Washington as a representative of "that small but gallant band of coloured men who are publicly fighting the cause of their race," who "have the eternal principles of right on their side," and "who are making history and a race" while he himself is only making "a little money."[39] The clichéd and purposefully sloppy terms of this profession (for instance, Washington is supposedly "fighting the cause" of a "race" he is simultaneously "making") raise some doubts as to the unreliable narrator's, or Johnson's, sincerity. However, it is significant that the book ends with Washington, whom Du Bois had likewise criticized extensively in *Souls*. Washington presented yet another influential approach to the project of solving the problems of Jefferson's "veil of black." A posthumous interpretation of this approach was depicted by the Booker T. Washington Monument at Tuskegee University (then Tuskegee Institute). Created by the white American sculptor Charles Keck, this monumental version of the veil motif contrasted sharply with the veils of Du Bois, Johnson, and even the postcolonial Jefferson, as it placed the burden of ignorance on African Americans. Yet, even this outlier in the tradition of the Veil, which turned into bronze and concrete what had been spirit and light in Johnson and Du Bois, was unable to rid itself entirely of the metaphor's long-standing immersion in the ambiguities of perception.

The monument displays the likeness of a standing Washington in everyday attire rather than an academic gown, shown in the act of helping withdraw a large veil from a seated younger man. Since the young man is seated on an anvil, surrounded by a plow and other tools, and holding a compass and drafting square in his hand, the large book he is holding on his lap is unlikely to prepare him for the philosophical and literary "Promised Land" in the world "above the Veil" that Du Bois had envisioned. Instead, the bronze youth, whose bare torso may express closeness either to classical conventions or to slavery, seems clearly intended for a Bookerite industrial education, supposed to "improve" himself for a career whose humble beginnings and modest goals are cemented into an inscription praising the institute's founder for having "lifted the veil of ignorance from his people and pointed the way to progress through education and industry."

However, it would be too easy to say that the difficult, racially segregated negotiations about the monument's form and content produced nothing but a whitewashed anti–Du Boisian interpretation of the Veil.[40] As has often been pointed out, the young man's facial features bear a striking resemblance

Lifting the Veil of Ignorance, statue of Booker T. Washington at Tuskegee University. (The George F. Landegger Collection of Alabama Photographs in Carol M. Highsmith's America, Library of Congress, Prints and Photographs Division)

to those of Washington, making him appear a younger version of the same self, allowing for interpretations that at least potentially exceed the narrow goals of industrial education and reflect on universal problems of personal growth. Moreover, the monument's composition draws heavily from, and invites comparisons to, another monument financed by African Americans nearly half a century earlier: the Freedmen's Memorial or Emancipation Monument in Washington, DC, which frontally depicts a standing Lincoln whose outstretched hand hovers over a kneeling freedman presented in profile.[41] In reflecting on "the humble offering we [i.e., not only President Grant] this day unveil to view," Frederick Douglass in his Freedmen's Memorial Address had managed to counterbalance the visual hierarchies of the monument by distinguishing the reception of Lincoln among African

Americans from that among white Americans, speaking from a position he specified as that of Lincoln's "stepchildren."[42] He acknowledged Lincoln's achievement in solving the problem Jefferson had left behind: "while Abraham Lincoln saved for you a country, he delivered us from a bondage, according to Jefferson, one hour of which was worse than ages of the oppression your fathers rose in rebellion to oppose."[43] However, Douglass also made it clear that African Americans took the "comprehensive view of Abraham Lincoln," insofar as their qualified gratitude was far from "a blind and unreasoning superstition."[44] Lincoln's visionary, reasoning, and unsuperstitious "stepchildren" remained aware that the "first martyr president of the United States" had been "preeminently the white man's president."[45] Like Jefferson in his blind loyalty to the "deep rooted prejudices" of white Virginians, "Mr. Lincoln shared the prejudices of his white fellow-countrymen against the Negro."[46]

Insofar as the Tuskegee version of *Lifting the Veil of Ignorance* conspicuously replaced "Mr. Lincoln" with Booker T. Washington as the standing heroic figure, and the kneeling freedman with a seated younger version of Washington, it could be read as a continuation of Douglass's refusal in 1876 to regard Lincoln as "either our man or our model."[47] The position of man and model, the Tuskegee monument suggests, had now been filled by Washington. In his implicit inheritance of Lincoln's monumental position, a shadow of the historical Booker T. Washington's intentions may be felt: it is almost as if his famously accomplished methods of manipulating his (white) audiences had managed to extend beyond his death, posthumously shaping an artifact that remained ambiguous as to *whose* veil of ignorance, precisely, was being lifted. Just as Johnson produced an ironic metafiction of Du Bois's Veil, the Tuskegee Veil may be read as a metamonument that comes close to depicting Washington in the act of unveiling his own role as "our man and our model" to posterity.

The "Principle"

Ralph Ellison's midcentury masterpiece *Invisible Man* offers the most complex meditation on the many "puzzling" aspects of the Tuskegee Veil, and indeed of the long metaphorical tradition that had preceded, and would succeed, this controversial artwork. The Invisible Man follows Johnson's Ex-Coloured Man in removing the Veil to a realm "ages ago in some other world"⁴⁸ in a distant fictional time and place. "It's so long ago and far away that here in my invisibility I wonder if it happened at all," Ellison's protagonist muses.

> Then in my mind's eye I see the bronze statue of the college Founder, the cold Father symbol, his hands outstretched in the breathtaking gesture of lifting a veil that flutters in hard, metallic folds above the face of a kneeling slave; and I am standing puzzled, unable to decide whether the veil is really being lifted, or lowered more firmly in place; whether I am witnessing a revelation or a more efficient blinding. And as I gaze, there is a rustle of wings and I see a flock of starlings flighting before me and, when I look again, the bronze face, whose empty look upon a world I have never seen, runs with liquid chalk—creating another ambiguity to puzzle my groping mind: Why is a bird-soiled statue more commanding than one that is clean?⁴⁹

This mental picture of the "cold Father symbol" subtly fuses different generations of founding fathers and father symbols. Strictly speaking, the Tuskegee monument does not depict a "kneeling slave." The Invisible Man's memory betrays him, and he conflates the seated likeness of Washington as a young man (thus no longer enslaved) with the kneeling freedman of the Freedmen's Memorial. He may even be conflating the two with the emblematic figure of an actual "kneeling slave," as in Josiah Wedgwood's medallion "Am I Not a Man and Brother?" from 1787, the year when Jefferson's "veil of black" reached a wider audience with the publication of *Notes on the State of Virginia*. Simultaneously unveiling a kneeling slave, a kneeling freedman, and a seated future founder, Ellison's "cold Father symbol" may thus refer to either, or all, of the typological line of black and white patriarchal founders that shaped the monument's history, including Washington, Douglass, Grant, Lincoln, and Jefferson.

Besides compressing time and historical personality, the Invisible Man's evolving mental picture follows the Ex-Coloured Man's recollections in explicitly fusing nature and art, fact and fiction. Impossibly "fluttering" in "hard, metallic folds," the bronze Veil is doubled by the rustling wings and the greenish-black and white color of the "flock of starlings flighting before me." In a partly eerie, partly humorous image, the starlings transform the "cold Father symbol" by their very own method of whitening. As if in anticipation of what today might have been a white paint bomb thrown at a Founder's statue in protest, the "liquid chalk" endlessly complicates the interpretation of Ellison's ekphrasis. Like its monumental representation in "fluttering" metal, the Invisible Man's mental vision of the Veil is kept in suspense, caught between motion and stillness, blackness and whiteness, knowledge and ignorance, history and farce, heaven and earth, solidity and fluidity, plenitude and emptiness, purity and soil, power and powerlessness, revelation and blindness. In this manner, the Invisible Man's approach to the Tuskegee Veil continues and amplifies the secret of the "vari-coloured" veil in the *Autobiography of an Ex-Coloured Man*. Not incidentally perhaps, Ellison's description repeats the term that had been applied to the fictional roots of identity at least since *Tristram Shandy*: All that the Veil seemed to reveal or disguise was a "puzzle."[50]

However, skepticism is not the novel's final word on the subject, as *Invisible Man* opens up new possibilities for lifting Jefferson's "veil" and affirming the tenets of a universalist Enlightenment. The Invisible Man leaves behind the philosophical framework of the founding figure who had first theorized the effect of invisibility from a collective "refusal" to see:[51] Ellison's protagonist decides against Jefferson's method of defeating his existential skepticism by "deadening [his] sense of perception"[52] and resigning himself to the twilight of one particular community of feeling. Having experimented with different such communities, he eventually transcends the limits of his subjectivity and approaches what is, arguably, a full secularization of the universalist telos that Phillis Wheatley had envisioned long before him, in her journey from darkness, or what she, Du Bois, and Ellison prominently term "Chaos,"[53] to light. The penultimate step on his secularized journey consists in the technical construction of an "underground" Enlightenment. As if to claim the space beneath the underground roots of Johnson's "hedge of vari-coloured glass bottles stuck in the ground neck down,"[54] the Invisible Man turns a coal cellar "forgotten during the nineteenth century" into a space *"full* of light." Echoing the metaphors of light and shadow that abound, for instance, in Harper's and Du Bois's approaches to the Veil, he claims not only that light "confirms [his] reality" and "gives birth" to his (literary) "form" surrounded by "chaos," but also, somewhat ambiguously, that "[t]he truth is the light and light is the truth."[55]

When he becomes aware of the paradoxical superficiality of his underground Enlightenment, finding that "true darkness lies within [his] own mind,"[56] he decides to synthesize his pursuit of light with the upward movement of Wheatley's nineteenth-century literary legacy. In the novel's conclusion, he plans to reemerge above ground to act on his Enlightened vision and assume a "socially responsible role."[57] This politically active rather than contemplative Enlightenment entails "a process of *rising* to an understanding of his human condition," an "intellectual" process that requires coming to terms with the enigmatic inheritance left behind by his paternal ancestors.[58] As part of his dialectical "boomerang" theory of history,[59] the Invisible Man begins to understand the connections between the different "puzzles" of his life: the "puzzle"[60] of the typological line of "cold Father symbols" he had encountered in the Tuskegee Veil and the "puzzle"[61] of his grandfather's "sphinx-like"[62] deathbed advice to his father, "Agree 'em to death and destruction."[63] The aggressively affirmative stance of his grandfather, he begins to realize, had not just been a tactical form of "treachery" in "the enemy's country" defined by the continued state of "war" that was slavery, nor had "the old man [. . .] gone out of his mind."[64] Instead, his grandfather's belligerent affirmation referred to a consistent method of his own, "a kind of jiujitsu of the spirit, a denial and rejection through agreement."[65] In a series of queries that seems to contain more answers than questions, the Invisible Man begins to understand this rejection through agreement in relation to a national as well as universal entity that he calls "the plan" or "the principle."[66]

This "principle" overlaps with the "sacred principles" that Ellison later described as Americans' source of union as well as contention: "Actuated by passionate feats of revolutionary will which released that dynamic power for moralizing both men and nature, [. . .] these principles—democracy, equality, individual freedom, and universal justice—now move us as articles of faith. Holding them sacred, we act (or *fail* to act) in their names." For Ellison, the common ground for agreement as well as conflict, "[t]he rock, the terrain upon which we struggle, is itself abstract, a terrain of ideas that, although man-made, exerts the compelling force of the ideal, of the sublime: ideas that draw their power from the Declaration of Independence, the Constitution, and the Bill of Rights."[67] Significantly, in this definition Ellison's Enlightened principles *predate* the American Founding documents. Like the Invisible Man draining off his share from "Monopolated Light & Power" to illuminate his underground Enlightenment,[68] the principles "draw their power," but do not originally or causally emerge from America's sacred texts. In a similar spirit, the novel's protagonist at first distinguishes between "the principle" and the white American revolutionaries connected to it, wondering whether his grandfather had meant to affirm "the principle on which the country was built and not the men, or at least not the men who did the violence [...] the principle, which they themselves had dreamed into being out of the chaos and darkness of the feudal past, and which they had violated and compromised to the point of absurdity even in their own corrupt minds?" In a second step, Ellison's protagonist moves on to broaden affirmation of "the principle" to include the men who helped give it expression:

> Or did he [his grandfather] mean that we had to take the responsibility for all of it, for the men as well as the principle, because we were the heirs who must use the principle because no other fitted our needs? Not for the power or for vindication, but because we, with the given circumstance of our origin, could only thus find transcendence? Was it that we of all, we, most of all, had to affirm the principle, the plan in whose name we had been brutalized and sacrificed—not because we would always be weak nor because we were afraid or opportunistic, but because we were older than they, in the sense of what it took to live in the world with others and because they had exhausted in us, some—not much, but some—of the human greed and smallness, yes, and the fear and superstition that had kept them running.[69]

While the Invisible Man's affirmation of "the principle on which the country was built" is not absolute—he had made affirmations earlier in the plot that had made him "ill of affirmation"[70]—it presents an important vanishing point in the African American tradition of transforming Jefferson's postcolonial Enlightenment. The notion of inheriting and taking "responsibility for all of it, the men and the principle" out of a sense of moral and epistemological maturity, a relative lack of "fear and superstition," points back to the tradition's origins in the eighteenth century. For the Invisible Man, the transcendence of "the chaos and darkness of the feudal past" during the American Revolution is an open-ended process. His notion of inheritance and responsibility synthesizes "the men as well as the principle," or the two strands of Enlightenment thought that had been represented, on the one hand, by the soft, emotionally qualified universalism of the African American tradition's "midwife" and, on the other hand, by the more ambitious, intellectually assertive universalism of its "mother."[71] In Ellison's account of the "principle," the latter approach had the historical priority, as if in recognition of Phillis Wheatley's 1774 letter mentioned above. Even before the Declaration of Independence, the former "skinny black girl"[72] had spelled out the universalist content of Ellison's "principle," elegantly setting it off against its weaker definitions: "in every human breast, God has implanted a Principle, which we call Love of Freedom, it is impatient of Oppression, and pants for Deliverance, and by the Leave of our modern Egyptians I will assert, that the same Principle lives in us."[73]

❖ CONCLUSION ❖

A Jeffersonian Double Consciousness

Among the two late Enlightenment philosophies analyzed in this book, Wheatley's Enlightenment of Principle was a high-end approach to the Enlightenment that grounded its universalism in ambitious concepts of reason and knowledge. It differed from earlier Enlightenment traditions in Europe in that it already had to find ways of dealing with the problems of Jefferson's postcolonial Enlightenment of Feeling, a low-key approach that prided itself on offering a democratic alternative to the hierarchies of European rationalism. The peculiar challenges posed by Jefferson's philosophy have long been overlooked. As this book has shown, his priority of creating a new national community of feeling was intertwined with his creation of a modern American concept of *race* as subjective experience, self-consciously based, not on reason and knowledge, but on a laissez-faire attitude to both individual "pillows of ignorance" and "deep rooted prejudices." Jefferson was still hoping that these prejudices would eventually evaporate thanks to a free press and educational institutions such as the University of Virginia. However, his complacent form of self-criticism, combined with his self-serving invention of alternative "white" and "black" epistemologies, was to have a long and troubling afterlife, from the insistence of the American Colonization Society on whites' supposedly "unconquerable" race prejudice to some of today's more self-obsessed concerns with a supposedly irredeemable but all-powerful *whiteness*.

The African American intellectuals discussed in the previous chapters recognized both the potential and the limitations of the traditions emerging from Jefferson's epistemological nationalism. They saw that American democracy required a fundamental respect for feeling and opinion, but they also emphasized that it could not survive without the common ground of a solidly universalist epistemology. (Indeed, as has become apparent again more recently, the vote could not be counted without one.) Beginning with Lemuel Haynes in 1776, the writers of Wheatley's Enlightenment of Principle were on the forefront of crafting the universalist hermeneutical tradition of what came to be known as the "principles" of the Declaration of Independence. And beginning with William Hamilton and David Walker in the first decades of the nineteenth century, they developed *black uplift* as well as *white uplift* discourses on *Notes on the State of Virginia*, connecting claims for equal citizenship to calls for achieving moral and intellectual excellence. In retrospect, all three clusters of ideas have come to be seen to originate with Jefferson himself. As shown in this book, however, they were in fact the result of the transformations of his thought by Wheatley's Enlightenment of Principle.

Their consolidation of a universalist theory of knowledge, often expressed in a rhetoric of paralipsis, led many African American writers to the claim that Jefferson could, and should, have "known better." Beginning with Benjamin Banneker in 1791, the protagonists of Wheatley's Enlightenment developed multiple methods to play off Jefferson against Jefferson himself, pitting the patriarch of a slaveholding family against the author of the Declaration of Independence, the Declaration of Independence against *Notes on the State of Virginia*, and Query XIV of *Notes on the State of Virginia* against Query XVIII of the same book. In contrast to the historical Jefferson, who is not likely to have felt any more torn between two opposite perspectives than most of his contemporaries, the literary version of Jefferson emerging in the African American tradition was not only a man of stark contradictions but could become a character who seemed split into opposites, both prophet and sinner, a quasi-Faustian figure with two souls dwelling in his breast, an "ambidexter philosopher" who could "reason contrarywise,"[1] able at once to see, and not to see, the true and the good. This construction of a "Jeffersonian" *double consciousness*, a mental state that could be depicted as representative of the moral and intellectual polarities of the United States at large, remains the dominant interpretation of Jefferson's legacy to this day.

At the turn of a new century, when eighteenth- and nineteenth-century notions of *character* were beginning to be replaced by *personality* and, eventually, *identity* as leading cultural concepts, the African American artifact of a Jeffersonian *double consciousness* was influentially appropriated. No longer related to the (modern) human condition in general, as it had been in Goethe, Emerson, Thoreau, or William James, or to Jeffersonianism, as suggested by Banneker, Hamilton, Walker, Brown, Douglass, or McCune Smith, *double consciousness* was famously redefined by W. E. B. Du Bois as both an impediment and a unique source of wisdom for "black folk" in particular—a transfer that, arguably, preserved elements from both Wheatley's universalist Enlightenment and Jefferson's identitarian Enlightenment for the following generations. Read through the lens of the African American tradition, Jefferson's "trembling" character under Query XVIII may thus ironically have helped in the birth of Du Bois's oft-discussed *double consciousness*. In its own way, this character—a character "stamped" by the "odious peculiarities" of slavery while being painfully aware of outsiders' views at his nation, and a character that had become, as shown in this book, the explicit object of "pity" for the writers of Wheatley's Enlightenment of Principle—may have understood something of the phenomenon still described as "peculiar" by Du Bois: "a peculiar sensation, this double-consciousness, this sense of always looking at one's self through the eyes of others, of measuring one's soul by the tape of a world that looks on in amused contempt and pity."[2]

Black Reason, White Feeling has approached the American Enlightenment by distinguishing between three different levels of interpretation that have so far been conflated: Jefferson's own philosophy in its original context, an African American intellectual tradition of transforming this philosophy, and today's understanding of this transformed philosophy as the Jeffersonian Enlightenment. It has analyzed Jeffersonianism as a composite American Enlightenment, in whose genesis the writers of Wheatley's Enlightenment of Principle have played the key part of reining in the excesses of Jefferson's postcolonial subjectivism. Their achievement of abstraction and modernization was made possible by strong concepts of rationality and multilayered pedagogies of character that functioned as something like the American equivalent of a categorical imperative, systematizing and universalizing the democratic vision that Jefferson had so eloquently voiced for his own "chosen people."[3] Ironically, African Americans' rational systematization of Jefferson's philosophy has been so successful that for much of the twentieth century until today he has been personally associated both with their rationalism and, increasingly, with his own failure to live up to its Jeffersonian standards.

Of course, one might inquire after the reasons for this irony—for the fact that the rationalist transformations of Jefferson's Enlightenment of

Feeling have tended to nominally efface their multiple authors and are still associated with Jefferson's name, making him more or less the only US president in possession of an "ism." Apart from the obvious factor of nineteenth-century power relations and aggressively racist discourses attempting to deny people of non-European descent rational equality, the irony also results from retrospective Romantic and post-Romantic distortions of "the" Enlightenment. From the nineteenth century until today's body of cultural theory, seemingly critical views of the eighteenth century have tended to fuse highly disparate Enlightenment philosophies into one, with the ironic effect of giving thinkers such as Jefferson much more credit for their supposed rationalism than they themselves would ever have dreamed of. Against these views, this book has focused on the intellectual tradition without which Jefferson's postcolonial Enlightenment would not have gained its universal appeal. The protagonists of this book did not wait for Abraham Lincoln's famous claim about the "future use" of the Declaration of Independence,[4] but from 1776 onward developed critical arguments that, in retrospect, formed a strikingly coherent intellectual and literary tradition, in which the character of Jefferson as author of the Declaration and *Notes on the State of Virginia*, as American president and "patriarch" of an enslaved family, functioned as the central trope for the contradictions of a modern slaveholding democracy.

Today American history often seems divided into two sharply opposed narratives. One narrative is about a nation founded on ideas of liberty and equality, whereas the other is the story of a nation founded on slavery and oppression. It is not a great challenge to see why both the positive exceptionalism of the "great ideas" approach to American history and its mirror image, the negative exceptionalism of the "cruel oppression" approach, have important points to make. All over the world, after all, history has often turned out to include, among other things, both great ideas and cruel oppression. What is much more challenging to understand is why, in the case of the United States, the two narratives should be understood as mutually exclusive. In part at least, the binary nature of today's debates, putting their participants under pressure to choose between two forms of exceptionalism, may be a long-term effect of the semi-secularized communities of feeling, opinion, and assent that Jefferson's Enlightenment helped bring into the world. As this book has shown, his postcolonial defiance toward a powerful transatlantic empire tempted him to prioritize, at least in the short- and midterm, the wounded feelings of a white Virginia republican over universal reason, and the public opinion of a white American republic over full knowledge. In his attempts to create a safe space for the subjective standpoint of his new nation in a world of potentially hostile powers, he did not always know when to stop. At its most extreme, what may have been an otherwise laudable democratization of knowledge in the American republic thus left in its wake a destructive modern concept of *race*. Jefferson was aware, but fatalistically accepted, that this concept could lay no claim to knowledge, but merely to the lived experience and the stubborn prejudice of a particular community of feeling that refused to see itself bound by universal standards.

In the long nineteenth century, the writers of Wheatley's Enlightenment of Principle had the "resolution and courage" to deflate the polarizing influence of this concept, not only because they saw themselves targeted by it but also because they recognized it as a central problem of American democracy. Unlike Jefferson and the white colonizationists who followed him, they discerned the existential dangers that lay in trying to reduce the complexity of a modern world by hiding behind the moral and epistemological "veil" of a self-constrained community of feeling. Demonstrating the absurdity of Jefferson's postcolonial invention of alternative epistemologies, these thinkers fought for keeping the avenues of free Enlightened discussion open. They played crucial roles in the creation of what has come down to us as a universalist Jeffersonian Enlightenment, but they were not Jeffersonians in the sense of passively following Jefferson's philosophy, or of being forced to enter into ambivalent, ultimately debilitating relationships of admiration and repulsion. Rather, they were Jeffersonians in the sense of deliberately using their own readings of Jefferson's character (and characters) for the purpose of redefining and consolidating the idea of a modern democracy founded on rational principles, a democracy expressing itself in universally communicable cultural and literary achievements, and a democracy endowed by its Jeffersonian *double consciousness* with the far from self-evident ability to recognize its shortcomings. The intellectuals of the African American tradition discussed in this book have to be restored to their rightful place as both protagonists of the Jeffersonian Enlightenment and leading exponents of its universalist legacy.

❖ NOTES ❖

INTRODUCTION

1. Immanuel Kant, "What Is Enlightenment?," in *The Portable Enlightenment Reader*, ed. and introd. Isaac Kramnick, 1–7 (New York: Penguin, 1995), 1. This oft-used translation may itself be a long-term product of the Jeffersonian Enlightenment discussed in this book as it uses *reason* and *understanding* interchangeably, as was characteristic of Jefferson's Enlightenment of Feeling (part 1).
2. A famous continuation of Kant's theme of courage is in the preface of Ernst Cassirer's *The Philosophy of the Enlightenment* (1932): "The slogan: *Sapere aude* (dare to know), which Kant called 'the motto of the Enlightenment,' also holds for our own historical relation to that period. Instead of assuming a derogatory air, we must take courage and measure our powers against those of the age of the Enlightenment, and thus find a proper adjustment. The age which venerated reason and science as man's highest faculty cannot and must not be lost even for us" (Cassirer, *The Philosophy of the Enlightenment*, with a new foreword by Peter Gay [Princeton, NJ: Princeton UP, 2009], xvii). On the context of Cassirer's *Enlightenment* on the eve of his exile from Germany, see Johnson Kent Wright, "'A Bright Clear Mirror': Cassirer's *The Philosophy of the Enlightenment*," in *What's Left of Enlightenment?: A Postmodern Question*, ed. Keith Michael Baker and Peter H. Reill, 71–101 (Stanford, CA: Stanford UP, 2001).
3. Frederick Douglass, *My Bondage and My Freedom* (1855; New York: Arno and New York Times, 1968), 57–58.
4. For Douglass's use of the phrase "love of knowledge" in reference to himself, compare ibid., 169.
5. Although the emergence of *intellectual* as a noun is usually associated with the Dreyfus affair at the end of the nineteenth century, the combination of philosophical interests and political activism stressed by this term may

justify its avant la lettre usage in this book in reference to the writers of Wheatley's Enlightenment of Principle (part 2).

6. James McCune Smith, "Introduction," in Douglass, *My Bondage and My Freedom*, xxx. Not inclined to subscribe to the racial essentialism of the 1850s, McCune Smith found a middle position here by combining the emphasis on superior "negro blood" with his usual emphasis on the benefits of what he called racial *mingling*. "The versatility of talent which he wields," he continued, "in common with Dumas, Ira Aldridge, and Miss Greenfield, would seem to be the result of the grafting of the Anglo-Saxon on good, original, negro stock." McCune Smith's concept of "mingling" is discussed in chapter 6.

7. Works on the American Enlightenment include Bernard Bailyn, *The Ideological Origins of the American Revolution* (1967; Cambridge, MA: Harvard UP, 2017), 26–30; Gordon S. Wood, *The Creation of the American Republic* (Chapel Hill: U of North Carolina P, 1969), 1–124; Henry F. May, *The Enlightenment in America* (Oxford: Oxford UP, 1976); Henry S. Commager: *The Empire of Reason: How Europe Imagined and America Realized the Enlightenment* (Garden City, NY: Doubleday, 1977); Gertrude Himmelfarb, *The Roads to Modernity: The British, French and American Enlightenments* (1994; London: Vintage, 2008); Michael Warner, *The Letters of the Republic: Publication and the Public Sphere in Eighteenth-Century America* (Cambridge, MA: Harvard UP, 1992); Wolf Kindermann, *Man Unknown to Himself: Kritische Reflexion der amerikanischen Aufklärung: Crèvecoeur—Benjamin Rush—Charles Brockden Brown* (Tübingen: Narr, 1993); Robert A. Ferguson, *The American Enlightenment* (Cambridge, MA: Harvard UP, 1997); David S. Shields, *Civil Tongues and Polite Letters in British America* (Chapel Hill: U of North Carolina P, 1997); Roy Porter, *Enlightenment: Britain and the Creation of the Modern World* (New York: Allen Layne/Penguin, 2000); Leigh E. Schmidt, *Hearing Things: Religion, Illusion, and the American Enlightenment* (Cambridge, MA: Harvard UP, 2000); Frank Kelleter, *Amerikanische Aufklärung: Sprachen der Rationalität im Zeitalter der Revolution* (Paderborn: Schöningh, 2002); Robert Darnton, *George Washington's False Teeth: An Unconventional Guide to the Eighteenth Century* (New York: Norton, 2003); Susan Manning and Francis D. Cogliano, eds., *The Atlantic Enlightenment* (Aldershot, UK: Ashgate, 2008); Jonathan Israel, *Democratic Enlightenment: Philosophy, Revolution, and Human Rights, 1750–1790* (New York: Oxford UP, 2011), 443–79; Jonathan Israel, *The Expanding Blaze: How the American Revolution Ignited the World* (Princeton, NJ: Princeton UP, 2017); Mark G. Spencer, ed., *The Bloomsbury Encyclopedia of the American Enlightenment* (New York:

Bloomsbury Academic, 2015); Caroline Winterer, *American Enlightenments: Pursuing Happiness in the Age of Reason* (New Haven, CT: Yale UP, 2016); and Frank Kelleter, "A Literature of Civic Indignation: The Empathies and Resentments of American Liberalism, 1767–1826," unpublished manuscript.

8. Henry Louis Gates has read the disparaging remarks on Phillis Wheatley's poetry under Query XIV of Jefferson's *Notes on the State of Virginia* as the paradoxical starting point of an African American literary tradition, providing "the strongest motivation for blacks to create a body of literature that would implicitly prove Jefferson wrong" (see Gates, *The Trials of Phillis Wheatley: America's First Black Poet and Her Encounters with the Founding Fathers* [New York: Basic, 2003], 50–51, 56–57). On Jefferson's unique place in African American culture, see also Benjamin Quarles, "Antebellum Free Blacks and the 'Spirit of '76,' " in *Black Mosaic: Essays in Afro-American History and Historiography*, 92–108 (Amherst: U of Massachusetts P, 1988); Gates, *Figures in Black: Words, Signs, and the "Racial" Self* (Oxford: Oxford UP, 1989), chap. 1; Annette Gordon-Reed, "Engaging Jefferson: Blacks and the Founding Father," *William and Mary Quarterly* 57.1 (January 2000): 171–82; and Gene Jarrett, *Representing the Race: A New Political History of African American Literature* (New York: New York UP, 2011), chap. 1.

9. Merrill D. Peterson, *The Jefferson Image in the American Mind* (New York: Oxford UP, 1960); Peter S. Onuf, "The Scholars' Jefferson," *William and Mary Quarterly* 50.4 (1993): 671–99; Merrill D. Peterson, with Jan E. Lewis, "American Synecdoche: Thomas Jefferson as Image, Icon, Character, and Self," 1998; reprinted in Peter S. Onuf, *The Mind of Thomas Jefferson* (Charlottesville: U of Virginia P, 2007), 50–64; Frank Cogliano, *Thomas Jefferson: Reputation and Legacy* (Edinburgh: Edinburgh UP, 2006); Andrew Burstein, *Democracy's Muse: How Thomas Jefferson Became an FDR Liberal, a Reagan Republican, and a Tea Party Fanatic, All the While Being Dead* (Charlottesville: U of Virginia P, 2015); Robert M. S. McDonald, ed., *Thomas Jefferson's Lives: Biographers and the Battle for History* (Charlottesville: U of Virginia P, 2019).

10. On the concept of a distinctively African American literary tradition, see Henry Louis Gates Jr., *The Signifying Monkey: A Theory of Afro-American Literary Criticism* (New York: Oxford UP, 1988); and Gates and Nellie Y. McKay, "Introduction: Talking Books," in *Norton Anthology of African American Literature*, 2nd ed. (New York: Norton, 2004). For a discussion of what the African American literary tradition is or was, and what periods it included, see also Kenneth W. Warren, *What Was African American*

Literature? (Cambridge, MA: Harvard UP, 2011), and the debates that surrounded it, as in Glenda R. Carpio, Gene Andrew Jarrett, R. Baxter Miller, Sonnet Retman, Marlon B. Ross, Xiomara Santamarina, Rafia Zafar, and Kenneth W. Warren, "What Was African American Literature?," *PMLA* 218.2 (2013): 386–408. The locus classicus for the multidirectional temporality of the concept of *tradition* is in T. S. Eliot's "Tradition and the Individual Talent," reprinted in *The Sacred Wood*, 42–53 (London: Methuen, 1920).

11. Annette Gordon-Reed, *Thomas Jefferson and Sally Hemings: An American Controversy* (Charlottesville: U of Virginia P, 1997); Jan E. Lewis and Peter S. Onuf, eds., *Sally Hemings and Thomas Jefferson: History, Memory, and Civic Culture* (Charlottesville: U of Virginia P, 1999); Shannon Lanier and Jane Feldman, *Jefferson's Children: The Story of One American Family* (New York: Random House, 2000); Annette Gordon-Reed, *The Hemingses of Monticello: An American Family* (New York: Norton, 2008); Annette Gordon-Reed and Peter Onuf, *"Most Blessed of the Patriarchs": Thomas Jefferson and the Empire of the Imagination* (New York: Liveright, 2016); Gayle Jessup White, *Reclamation: Sally Hemings, Thomas Jefferson, and a Descendant's Search for Her Family's Lasting Legacy* (New York: Amistad, 2021).

12. Thomas Jefferson (hereafter cited as TJ), *Notes on the State of Virginia*, ed. William Peden (1954; Chapel Hill: U of North Carolina P, 1982), 138–43. Since this book analyzes the problems of Jefferson's Enlightenment of Feeling, it has to keep a critical distance from his influential use of the terms *black, white,* and *race.* In order to distinguish the book's argument from Jefferson's thought, these terms will often be italicized, placed in quotation marks, or replaced by other terms (such as the less historically overdetermined *African American*). For the historical terminology used by African Americans in the long nineteenth century, see chapter 3 on the "names controversy" in Patrick Rael, *Black Identity and Black Protest in the Antebellum North* (Chapel Hill: U of North Carolina P, 2002), 82–117. For an overview of today's discussion of alternative epistemologies and its origins in Marxism and in feminist standpoint theory, see Charles W. Mills, *Blackness Visible: Essays on Philosophy and Race* (Ithaca, NY: Cornell UP, 1998), chap. 2, 21–39. Although this may be somewhat counterintuitive today, for the origins of an alternative to the "familiar Cartesian figure, the abstract, disembodied, individual knower" (22), Mills could have gone further back in time than Marx and found them in Jefferson. As will be discussed in chapter 4, with his emphasis on the unique potential and limits of "our own knowledge" in *Notes on Virginia,* Jefferson would likely

have subscribed to the view that, from the particular standpoint of white republicans in a revolutionary Virginia struggling against a major imperial power, "one's group membership will determine, at least tendentially, the kinds of experience one is likely to have [. . .] experiences that are outside the hegemonic framework in the sense of involving an external geography" (28).
13. On the interracial "co-fabrication" of key concepts of American intellectual culture, see Rael, *Black Identity*, 5, 150 (term).
14. TJ, *Notes*, 64.
15. Onuf, *Mind of Jefferson*, esp. 139–201; Robert M. S. McDonald, ed., *Light and Liberty: Thomas Jefferson and the Power of Knowledge* (Charlottesville: U of Virginia P, 2012); John Ragosta, *Religious Freedom: Jefferson's Legacy, America's Creed* (Charlottesville: U of Virginia P, 2013); Kevin R. C. Gutzman, *Thomas Jefferson—Revolutionary: A Radical's Struggle to Remake America* (New York: St. Martin's, 2017); Peter S. Onuf, *Jefferson and the Virginians: Democracy, Constitutions, and Empire* (Charlottesville: U of Virginia P, 2018); Andrew O'Shaughnessy, *"The Illimitable Freedom of the Human Mind": Thomas Jefferson's Idea of a University* (Charlottesville: U of Virginia P, 2021).
16. Phillis Wheatley (hereafter PW) to Samson Occom, 11 February 1774, in PW, *Complete Writings*, ed. Vincent Carretta (London: Penguin, 2001), 152–53.
17. In the late eighteenth and nineteenth centuries, the term *prejudice* could also be tied to social "condition" (slavery and its aftermath) rather than physical characteristics (see Joanne P. Melish, "The 'Condition' Debate and Racial Discourse in the Antebellum North," *Journal of the Early Republic* 19.4 [Winter 1999]: 651–72).
18. On enlightened antirationalism, see Peter Gay, *The Enlightenment: An Interpretation*, vol. 2: *The Science of Freedom* (New York: Knopf, 1969), esp. 145–50, 187–207; Panajotis Kondylis, *Die Aufklärung im Rahmen des neuzeitlichen Rationalismus* (Stuttgart: Klett-Cotta, 1981); Kelleter, *Amerikanische Aufklärung*, 32–37; and Kelleter, "A Literature of Civic Indignation."
19. For example, see Paul Gilroy's analysis of the "counterculture" of modernity in *The Black Atlantic: Modernity and Double Consciousness* (Cambridge, MA: Harvard UP, 1993), e.g., at 55–56 ("occidental rationalism") or 38 ("occidental rationality"). According to Gilroy, individual African Americans such as Martin Delany could also be "rationalists," but only in terms of a "politics of fulfilment [. . .] mostly content to play occidental rationality at its own game." For another influential, if less complex, example, see the definition of *critical race theory* in the first paragraph of

Richard Delgado and Jean Stefancic's *Critical Race Theory: An Introduction*, 3rd ed. (2001; New York: New York UP, 2017), 3: "Unlike traditional civil rights discourse, which stresses incrementalism and step-by-step progress, critical race theory questions the very foundations of the liberal order, including equality theory, legal reasoning, Enlightenment rationalism, and neutral principles of constitutional law."

20. For instance, although largely written in the United States, Max Horkheimer and Theodor Adorno's influential work of critical theory, *Dialektik der Aufklärung* (1947; Amsterdam: de Munter, 1968), does not take into account the specific intellectual constellations of the American Enlightenment.

21. Recent examples include Achille Mbembe's *Critique of Black Reason* (Durham, NC: Duke UP, 2017), whose claims of a supposedly pervasive modern equation of blackness with the nonhuman rest not only on ignoring such sources as Jefferson's draft of the Declaration of Independence, which explicitly defined the victims of the Atlantic slave trade as (capitalized) "MEN," but, quite ironically, these claims also rest on muting the rationalist arguments made by Kant's African American contemporaries and their nineteenth-century successors. See also Tyler Stovall's *White Freedom: The Racial History of an Idea* (Princeton, NJ: Princeton UP, 2021), which for its account of *freedom* as a "white" concept has to exclude African American thinkers from its argument. Even scholars who insist on the inevitability of Enlightened universalism today tend to overlook the African American tradition, thus in part perpetuating the cliché of the historical Enlightenment as an exclusively European event. See Gayatri Chakravorty Spivak, *A Critique of Postcolonial Reason: Toward a History of the Vanishing Present* (Cambridge, MA: Harvard UP, 1999); Gayatri Chakravorty Spivak, *An Aesthetic Education in the Era of Globalization* (Cambridge, MA: Harvard UP, 2013); and Emmanuel Chukwudi Eze, *On Reason: Rationality in a World of Cultural Conflict and Racism* (Durham, NC: Duke UP, 2008). As will be discussed in part 2, a similar neglect of African American Enlightenment perspectives has informed the reception history of Phillis Wheatley.

22. A famous exception that inverts the perspective and looks east from the American side of the Atlantic is Benedict Anderson's *Imagined Communities: Reflections on the Origins and Spread of Nationalism* (1983; New York: Verso, 2016).

23. For a compelling critique of what he has called the "white Enlightenment trope," see Matthew Stewart, *An Emancipation of the Mind: Radical Philosophy, the War over Slavery, and the Refounding of America* (New York:

Norton, forthcoming), esp. part 3, chap. 7. As do other recent studies such as Eric Herschthal's *The Science of Abolition: How Slaveholders Became the Enemies of Progress* (New Haven, CT: Yale UP, 2021), Stewart reveals as untenable today's claims that Euro-American abolitionism was not the result of the secular Enlightenment but of religious revival.

24. There has been excellent scholarship on this important issue, from Winthrop D. Jordan, *White over Black: American Attitudes toward the Negro, 1550–1812* (Chapel Hill: U of North Carolina P, 1968) and George M. Fredrickson, *The Black Image in the White Mind: The Debate on Afro-American Character and Destiny, 1817–1914* (New York: Harper & Row, 1971) to, most recently, Henry Louis Gates and Andrew S. Curran, *Who's Black and Why? A Hidden Chapter from the Eighteenth-Century Invention of Race* (Cambridge, MA: Harvard UP, 2022).

25. As is discussed in chapter 6, Frederick Douglass was among the most outspoken critics of the concept of "natural," irredeemable, group-specific prejudice (see Douglass, "The American Colonization Society," 8 June 1849, in *The Life and Writings of Frederick Douglass*, ed. Philip S. Foner, 1:387–99 [New York: International, 1950–52]). On American colonizationism as a major factor helping "remodel American race relations," see John Saillant, *Black Puritan, Black Republican: The Life and Thought of Lemuel Haynes, 1753–1833* (Oxford: Oxford UP, 2003), 5–6; and John Saillant, "The American Enlightenment in Africa: Jefferson's Colonizationism and Black Virginians' Migration to Liberia, 1776–1840," *Eighteenth-Century Studies* 31.3 (Spring 1998): 261–82.

26. Audre Lorde, "The Master's Tools Will Never Dismantle the Master's House," in *Sister Outsider: Essays and Speeches*, 110–14 (1984; Berkeley, CA: Crossing, 2007). For the argument that dismantling the master's house is a "misguided project" also from today's perspective, see Lewis R. Gordon and Jane Anna Gordon, eds., *Not Only the Master's Tools: African-American Studies in Theory and Practice* (London: Routledge, 2006), ix.

27. Aristotle, *The Politics*, trans. Harris Rackham, Loeb Classical Library (Cambridge, MA: Harvard UP; London: Heinemann, 1932), I, 7:1255b 30–35.

28. For succinct discussions of this point see, e.g., Rafia Zafar, *We Wear the Mask: African Americans Write American Literature, 1760–1870* (New York: Columbia UP, 1997) ("Subversion, resistance, and opposition are not the only indicators of an African American literary identity" [13]); and the essays assembled in *Beyond Douglass: New Perspectives on Early African-American Literature*, ed. Michael J. Drexler and Ed White (Lewisburg, PA: Bucknell UP, 2008). For a skeptical view of the frequent characterization

of African American appeals to universal reason as "strategic" in the poststructuralist sense of *strategy* that goes beyond personal intention, see Adolph Reed Jr. and Kenneth W. Warren's introduction to *Renewing Black Intellectual History: The Ideological and Material Foundations of African American Thought*, ed. Reed and Warren (Boulder, CO: Paradigm, 2010), vii–xi.

I. JEFFERSON'S ENLIGHTENMENT OF FEELING

1. TJ to John Adams, 15 August 1820. Jefferson's correspondence will be quoted from Founders Online, based on the authoritative Founding Fathers Papers projects, at https://founders.archives.gov/. For an instance of grounding knowledge in a collective "we feel" rather than only "I feel," see TJ to Francis Wayles Eppes, 27 June 1821.
2. On the problems of critiquing Descartes in more recent postcolonial contexts, see the discussion of Léopold Senghor's "We feel, therefore we are," in Henry Louis Gates Jr., "Editor's Introduction: Writing 'Race' and the Difference It Makes," in "'Race,' Writing, and Difference," special issue, *Critical Inquiry* 12.1 (Autumn 1985): 13.
3. On the influence of one-sided interpretations of the "Cartesian" *cogito* (as originating mainly in Germany between the wars at both ends of the political spectrum, as in the works of Martin Heidegger and Max Horkheimer) on the understanding of a monolithic Western Enlightenment in today's cultural theory, see Hans Sluga, "Heidegger and the Critique of Reason," in *What's Left of Enlightenment?: A Postmodern Question*, ed. Keith M. Baker and Peter H. Reil, 50–70 (Stanford, CA: Stanford UP, 2001); Kelleter, *Amerikanische Aufklärung*, esp. 99–101 ("project"), 145–86, 150–56; and Jerrold Seigel, *The Idea of the Self: Thought and Experience in Western Europe since the Seventeenth Century* (Cambridge: Cambridge UP, 2005), esp. 41–42, 55–74, 568–69. On the influence of "a trivialized—and thus all the more effective—version of Martin Heidegger's counter-enlightenment stand" on academic Afrocentrism, see also Frank Kelleter, *Con/Tradition: Louis Farrakhan's Nation of Islam, the Million Man March, and American Civil Religion* (Heidelberg: Winter, 2000), 106–7. On "Cartesianism" as an "*ism*" gaining traction in the 1950s, see Stefan L. Brandt, *The Culture of Corporeality: Aesthetic Experience and the Embodiment of America, 1945–1960* (Heidelberg: Winter, 2007), 92–122.
4. The cliché of a rationalist and falsely universalist Enlightenment in today's cultural theory is in part the long-term result of one-sided retrospection through the lens of German Idealism. On the tendency to privilege Continental European over British and American intellectual traditions that

has accompanied the critical reception history of "the" Enlightenment in its migration from the political right to the left in the twentieth century, see also Porter, *Enlightenment*, xvii–xxi, chap. 1; and Jonathan Israel, *Democratic Enlightenment*, 2–4.

5. William Hamilton, "An Oration Delivered in the African Zion Church, on the Fourth of July, 1827, in Commemoration of the Abolition of Slavery in this State," in *Early Negro Writing, 1760–1837*, ed. Dorothy Porter, 96–104 (1971; Baltimore, MD: Black Classic P, 1995), 101 ("ambidexter philosopher, who can reason contrarywise").
6. E.g., TJ to Sheldon Clark, 5 December 1825; TJ to John Adams, 15 August 1820 ("useless"); TJ, *Notes*, 64 ("wretched philosophy").
7. TJ to John Adams, 11 January 1816.
8. On the eighteenth-century terminology of emotion, see Nicole Eustace, *Passion Is the Gale: Emotion, Power, and the Coming of the American Revolution* (Chapel Hill: U of North Carolina P, 2008), 481–86 (Appendix); and Sarah Knott, *Sensibility and the American Revolution* (Chapel Hill: U of North Carolina P, 2009), 4–15.
9. For a concise discussion of the problems of enlightened antirationalism, see Kelleter, *Amerikanische Aufklärung*, 32–37; see also Kondylis, *Rationalismus*.
10. On the idea of a "republican millennium" in Jefferson's thought, see Peter S. Onuf, *Jefferson's Empire: The Language of American Nationhood* (Charlottesville: U of Virginia P, 2000), esp. 107–8; and Peter S. Onuf and Nicholas G. Onuf, *Nations, Markets and War: Modern History and the American Civil War* (Charlottesville: U of Virginia P, 2006), esp. 221–25. On the fusion of millennial thought and enlightened theories of political history and scientific progress, see also Ruth H. Bloch, *Visionary Republic: Millennial Themes in American Thought, 1756–1800* (Cambridge: Cambridge UP, 1985), esp. 103–5.
11. Today, the most detailed intellectual histories of eighteenth-century concepts of prejudice are in German, perhaps reflecting the relatively great importance attributed to conceptual discussions of prejudice in the German-language Enlightenment itself. See Werner Schneiders, *Aufklärung und Vorurteilskritik: Studien zur Geschichte der Vorurteilstheorie* (Stuttgart-Bad Cannstatt: frommann-holzboog, 1983), esp. chap. 1, 13–36; K. Reisinger and O. R. Scholz, "Vorurteil," in *Historisches Wörterbuch der Philosophie*, ed. Joachim Ritter, Karlfried Gründer, and Gottfried Gabriel, 12 vols., 11:1249–63 (Darmstadt: Wissenschaftliche Buchgesellschaft, 2001); and Rainer Godel, *Vorurteil—Anthropologie—Literatur: Der Vorurteilsdiskurs als Modus der Selbstaufklärung im 18. Jahrhundert* (Tübingen:

Niemeyer, 2007). For two recent studies that stress the importance of prejudice in the American context, including in Jefferson's case, see Nicholas Guyatt, *Bind Us Apart: How Enlightened Americans Invented Racial Segregation* (New York: Basic, 2016); and Robert G. Parkinson, *The Common Cause: Creating Race and Nation in the American Revolution* (Chapel Hill: U of North Carolina P, 2016).

12. On contemporaneous uses of the term *prejudice* in the context of social "condition" (slavery and its aftermath) rather than physical characteristics, see Melish, "'Condition' Debate."

1. I FEEL: THEREFORE I EXIST

1. John Locke, *An Essay Concerning Human Understanding*, ed. and abr. John W. Yolton (London: Dent, 2000), 78 (2.9.1).
2. Ibid., 119, 368 (2.20.1; 4.11.3).
3. David Hume, *A Treatise of Human Nature*, ed. L. A. Selby-Bigge, 2nd ed., with text revised and variant readings by P. H. Nidditch (1888; Oxford: Clarendon, 1978), 1–2 (1.1.1).
4. Henry Home, Lord Kames, *Elements of Criticism* (1840; repr., Honolulu: UP of the Pacific, 2002), 458.
5. On this point, see Stephen Bending and Stephen Bygrave, introduction to *The Man of Feeling*, by Henry Mackenzie, ed. Brian Vickers, vii–xxiv (Oxford: Oxford UP, 2001), xvi. On the prehistory of Jefferson's Enlightenment of Feeling in colonial America, see Eustace, *Passion*; on the culture of sensibility in revolutionary American in contradistinction to British culture, see Knott, *Sensibility*; and in early national culture, see Andrew Burstein, *Sentimental Democracy: The Evolution of America's Romantic Self-Image* (New York: Hill and Wang, 1999), which opens with the discovery of an 1803 pamphlet that brought together excerpts from *The Man of Feeling* and Jefferson's *Notes on the State of Virginia* (preface, xi–xiii). For arguments that stress the oppositional potential of *feeling*, see Julia A. Stern, *The Plight of Feeling: Sympathy and Dissent in the Early American Novel* (Chicago: U of Chicago P, 1997); and Christine Levecq, *Slavery and Sentiment: The Politics of Feeling in Black Atlantic Antislavery Writing, 1770–1850* (Durham: U of New Hampshire P, 2008).
6. Kames's *Elements of Criticism* was on the early reading list that accompanied his letter to Robert Skipwith, 3 August 1771.
7. Kames, *Elements of Criticism*, ix–x.
8. Locke, *Essay*, 356 (4.9.3).
9. Ibid. (4.13.18).

10. This stress on the self-conscious, artfully crafted nature of Jefferson's simplicity departs from earlier interpretations as innocence or actual simplicity in Jefferson's Enlightenment, as in, e.g., Henry Steele Commager, *Jefferson, Nationalism, and the Enlightenment* (New York: George Braziller, 1975), xi.
11. Locke, *Essay*, 356 (4.9.3).
12. Ibid., 291 (4.1.2).
13. On the long-term trajectory from Locke's account of feeling via Jonathan Edwards and Ralph Waldo Emerson (but not Jefferson) to Pragmatism as the quintessentially American philosophy, see Joan Richardson, *A Natural History of Pragmatism: The Fact of Feeling from Jonathan Edwards to Gertrude Stein* (Cambridge: Cambridge UP, 2006).
14. TJ to John Adams, 14 March 1820: "Mr. Locke, you know, and other materialists have charged with blasphemy the Spiritualists who have denied to the Creator the power of endowing certain forms of matter with the faculty of thought."
15. The tradition's major early proponent, Etienne Bonnot de Condillac, seems to be exempt from this tendency, likely because Jefferson disapproved of Condillac's immaterial concept of the soul.
16. TJ to Francis Wayles Eppes, 27 June 1821.
17. TJ to John Adams, 14 October 1814. For a similar attitude in Jefferson's reaction to Cabanis's *Rapports du physique et du moral de l'homme*, see TJ to Cabanis, 12 July 1803. In this context, Charles A. Miller describes Jefferson's "skepticism, in a way an unconcern, about the likelihood of actually proving the connections between a finding about nature itself (that the mind is matter) and our experience of nature (how the mind senses the external world)" (Miller, *Jefferson and Nature: An Interpretation* [Baltimore, MD: Johns Hopkins UP, 1988], 28–29).
18. TJ to John Adams, 15 August 1820. For a different interpretation of this exchange, see Ari Helo, *Thomas Jefferson's Ethics and the Politics of Human Progress: The Morality of a Slaveholder* (Cambridge: Cambridge UP, 2014), 46–50. Helo reads Jefferson's rejection of "hyperphysical and antiphysical" speculations as an even-handed rejection of "philosophical claims" about "either material or immaterial" views of the universe. However, as will be discussed further below, "hyperphysical" for Jefferson meant "supernatural" rather than the intensified physicality ("hyper" in today's understanding) that Helo seems to attribute to the term (49). Thus, like the phrase "once we quit the basis of sensation, all is in the wind," which Helo reads as begging the question of materialism or spiritualism,

it expressed Jefferson's decided preference for what he described as his strongly materialist belief or "creed."
19. TJ to John Adams, 15 August 1820; compare TJ to John Cartwright, 5 June 1824.
20. TJ to William Short, 13 April 1820.
21. Locke, *Essay*, 303–7 (4.3.6).
22. TJ, *Jefferson's Literary Commonplace Book*, ed. Douglas L. Wilson (Princeton, NJ: Princeton UP, 1989), 26–27 (§ 11). Late in life, Jefferson still showed himself fascinated by the possibility that even plants may be endowed with the faculty of thinking. See the postscript of TJ to Francis Adrian Van der Kemp, 9 February 1818.
23. TJ to John Adams, 14 March 1820. Compare Adams to TJ, 12 May 1820; TJ to Edmund Randolph, 3 February 1794; TJ to Isaac Story, 5 December 1801; TJ to Hugh White, 28 April 1812. Jefferson's best-known reference to a pillow in another context that is not completely unrelated to the theme of ignorance, as the following chapters will show, concerned Jefferson's earliest childhood memory, of being carried on a pillow by an enslaved person riding on horseback (see Roger Wilkins, *Jefferson's Pillow: The Founding Fathers and the Dilemma of Black Patriotism* [Boston: Beacon, 2002], 4).
24. John Adams to TJ, 12 May 1820.
25. TJ, *Notes*, 33: "Ignorance is preferable to error; and he is less remote from the truth who believes nothing, than he who believes what is wrong."
26. Peter Thompson, "'I Have Known': Thomas Jefferson, Experience, and Notes on the State of Virginia," in *A Companion to Thomas Jefferson*, ed. Francis D. Cogliano, 60–74 (Malden, MA: Blackwell, 2012), 61.
27. Locke, *Essay*, 15 (1.1.5). On the broader history of philosophical modesty, see Steven Shapin, *A Social History of Truth: Civility and Science in Seventeenth-Century England* (Chicago: U of Chicago P, 1994).
28. Locke, *Essay*, 7 ("The Epistle to the Reader").
29. Ibid., 15 (1.1.5).
30. On the conceptual tensions within *useful knowledge* since Bacon, see Wolfgang Krohn, *Francis Bacon* (Munich: Beck, 1987), 83–85, 181.
31. TJ to Sheldon Clark, 5 December 1825 (emphasis underlined in the original). For a similar evaluation of what Jefferson called metaphysics compare, e.g., TJ to Francis Eppes, 27 June 1821.
32. In the twentieth century, an unsuspected parallel to Jefferson's combination of professing a love of books while voicing an anti-intellectualist disdain for the "useless" philosophy of elite European and African American thinkers may be found in the work of another famous American rebel,

who also shared with Jefferson the penchant for making a political point of wearing his red hair *au naturel*. As Malcolm X put it in the prison library chapter of his autobiography: "Schopenhauer, Kant, Nietzsche, naturally, I read all of those. I don't respect them [. . .] because it seems to me that most of their time was spent arguing about things that are not really important. They remind me of so many of the Negro 'intellectuals,' so-called, with whom I have come in contact—they are always arguing about something useless" (*The Autobiography of Malcolm X*, with the assistance of Alex Haley, introd. Paul Gilroy [1965; London: Penguin, 2001], 275).

33. On Jefferson's "uncritical" habit of asserting a benevolent framing of the universe, see Saillant, "American Enlightenment," 264.
34. TJ, *Jefferson's Memorandum Books: Accounts, with Legal Records and Miscellany, 1767–1826*, ed. James A. Bear Jr. and Lucia C. Stanton, 2 vols. (Princeton, NJ: Princeton UP, 1997), 338 (May 5, 1773: "Pd. Treasurer of Philosoph. Society 18/").
35. For a concise discussion of the key conceptual innovations of Bacon's *Instauratio Magna*, see Krohn, *Bacon*, esp. 60–74, 81–89. For a compelling Baconian reading of *Notes*, see Dustin Gish and Daniel Klinghard, *Thomas Jefferson and the Science of Republican Government: A Political Biography of Notes on the State of Virginia* (Cambridge: Cambridge UP, 2017), esp. 87–93.
36. TJ, *Notes*, 277n104.
37. TJ to John Trumbull, 15 February 1789.
38. See Miller, *Jefferson and Nature*, 35–38.
39. TJ to Sheldon Clark, 5 December 1825. There is a vast literature on Jefferson's active interests in science and his scientific experiments, including Silvio A. Bedini, *Thomas Jefferson: Statesman of Science* (New York: Macmillan, 1990); I. Bernard Cohen, *Science and the Founding Fathers: Science in the Political Thought of Jefferson, Franklin, Adams, and Madison* (New York: Norton, 1995); Timothy Sweet, "Jefferson, Science, and the Enlightenment," in *The Cambridge Companion to Thomas Jefferson*, ed. Frank Shuffleton, 101–13 (Cambridge: Cambridge UP, 2009); and Keith S. Thomson, *Jefferson's Shadow: The Story of His Science* (New Haven, CT: Yale UP, 2012).
40. TJ, *Notes*, 64.
41. Jonathan Lyons, *The Society for Useful Knowledge: How Benjamin Franklin and Friends Brought the Enlightenment to America* (New York: Bloomsbury, 2013), chaps. 1–3.
42. Ibid., 11.
43. On the national(ist) dimension of this empiricism, see Cohen, *Science*, 56–58; and Gish and Klinghard, *Political Biography*, 77–81. On the

democratizing and (proto-)nationalist tendencies in American natural history in particular, see also Pamela Regis, *Describing Early America: Bartram, Jefferson, Crèvecoeur, and the Influence of Natural History* (Philadelphia: U of Pennsylvania P, 1999); Susan Scott Parrish, *American Curiosity: Cultures of Natural History in the Colonial British Atlantic World* (Chapel Hill: U of North Carolina P, 2006); and Andrew Lewis, *A Democracy of Facts: Natural History in the Early Republic* (Philadelphia: U of Pennsylvania P, 2011).

44. TJ to Peter Carr, 22 June 1792: "Your objection to Ld. Kaims that he is too metaphysical is just, and it is the chief objection to which his writings are liable."
45. Knott, *Sensibility*, 106–263, 262 ("postcolonial").
46. See Gish and Klinghard, *Political Biography*, 77, for a characterization of Jefferson's subjectivist empiricism (which they label as "skepticist") by today's theoretical term *lived experience*.
47. This use of *postcolonial* obviously differs from today's dominant uses of the term, with their main points of reference among the postcolonial movements of the latter half of the twentieth century. However, there are a number of interesting parallels between Jefferson's displacement of the Cartesian *cogito* in his Enlightenment of Feeling and today's calls for reconstructing "postcolonial Enlightenments" that were opposed to "Eurocentrism" and "European rationalism." Compare, for instance, Anke Bartels, Lars Eckstein, Nicole Waller, and Dirk Wiemann, "Postcolonial Enlightenments," in *Postcolonial Literatures in English: An Introduction*, 61–78 (Stuttgart: Metzler, 2019), 64: "This interrogation of European Enlightenment claims to the monopoly on representation and to universal validity motivates and energizes many postcolonial interventions. These include, among others, the critique of conceptual universalism; the deconstruction of the linear teleology of history as progress; the questioning of an abstract and disembodied notion of the subject as *cogito;* and the exposure of the concomitant epistemic violence with which all alternative world views and forms of knowledge production were systematically degraded as immaturity, superstition and benightedness." According to this definition, Jefferson's draft of the Declaration of Independence or his *Notes on the State of Virginia*, for example, have to be classified as "postcolonial interventions." On the United States as the first among several postcolonial nations in the early nineteenth century, and their founding logic of "postcolonial inversion," see Eliga Gould, "Independence and Interdependence: The American Revolution and the Problem of Postcolonial Nationhood, ca. 1802," *William and Mary Quarterly* 74.4 (October

2017): 734–35; on Jefferson as a postcolonial, see Kariann A. Yokota, *Unbecoming British: How Revolutionary America Became a Postcolonial Nation* (Oxford: Oxford UP, 2010), 3–9, 62–63, 187–89.
48. TJ to Maria Cosway, 24 April 1788. On the letter in the context of Hemings, see Gordon-Reed, *Hemingses*, 281–83.
49. TJ, *Notes*, 73.
50. See TJ, *Jefferson's Legal Commonplace Book*, ed. David T. Konig, Michael P. Zuckert, Les Harris, and W. Bland Whitley (Princeton, NJ: Princeton UP, 2019), 426–89 (§ 775–801).
51. Peter S. Onuf uses the term in "Antiquarian America: Isaiah Thomas and the New Nation's Future," in *Revolutionary Prophecies*, ed. Robert M. S. McDonald and Onuf (Charlottesville: U of Virginia P, 2020), 19 (term); and in Onuf, *Mind of Jefferson*, 8–12, 169–78; Peter S. Onuf, *Jefferson and the Virginians: Democracy, Constitutions, and Empire* (Baton Rouge: Louisiana State UP, 2018), 20–25, 50–51. Compare Matthew Crow's concept of "civic identity" constituted through Virginia's legal history in *Thomas Jefferson, Legal History, and the Art of Recollection* (Cambridge: Cambridge UP, 2017).
52. TJ, *Notes*, 146; TJ to David Rittenhouse, 19 July 1778; TJ to George Wythe, 13 August 1786; TJ to Thomas Griffin, 3 January 1822.
53. Quoted in Porter, *Enlightenment*, xxiv.
54. Chad Wellmon, *Organizing Enlightenment: Information Overload and the Invention of the Modern Research University* (Baltimore, MD: Johns Hopkins UP, 2015), 10 ("history of a cultural anxiety").
55. Johann Neem, "'From Ancients to Axioms' to 'Every Branch of Science': Thomas Jefferson's Philosophy of Liberal Education," in *The Founding of Thomas Jefferson's University*, 306–24 (Charlottesville: U of Virginia P, 2019). On the lifelong development of Jefferson's educational ideas culminating in the founding of the University of Virginia, see O'Shaughnessy, *Illimitable Freedom*.
56. TJ to Roger C. Weightman, 24 June 1826.
57. On TJ's project of politically leveling (up) Virginia citizens, see Onuf, *Virginians*, esp. 10–11, 17–46.
58. Linda K. Kerber, *Federalists in Dissent: Imagery and Ideology in Jeffersonian America* (Ithaca, NY: Cornell UP, 1980), xiv, 67. An intriguing neo-Federalist critique of Jefferson can be found in Wilson J. Moses, *Thomas Jefferson: A Modern Prometheus* (Cambridge: Cambridge UP, 2019).
59. Kerber, *Federalists in Dissent*, 74.
60. Henry Adams, *History*, 144.
61. Washington Irving, *A History of New York*, with an introduction and notes by Elizabeth L. Bradley (New York: Penguin, 2008), 137–39.

62. Carla L. Peterson, *Black Gotham: A Family History of African Americans in Nineteenth-Century New York City* (New Haven, CT: Yale UP, 2011), 219–20. McCune Smith's work will be discussed in chapters 6 and 7.
63. Irving, *History*, 138.
64. TJ to John Adams, 15 August 1820.
65. For an analysis of Jefferson's Lucrecian empiricism, see Miller, *Jefferson and Nature*, chap. 2, esp. 23–27.
66. TJ to William Short, 31 October 1819, containing a "Syllabus of the doctrines of Epicurus."
67. TJ to Maria Cosway, 22 October 1786.
68. Ibid.
69. Locke, *Essay*, 17 (1.1.8).
70. For a brief critical account of twentieth-century suppositions of a "veil of perception problem" in Locke's *Essay*, see John W. Yolton, introduction to Locke, *Essay*, xl–xlii.
71. TJ to William Short, 31 October 1819. Compare TJ to Charles Thomson, 9 January 1816, in which he praised the Epicurus he found in "Gosindi's" (Gassendi's) *Syntagma* as offering "the most rational system remaining of the philosophy of the ancients, as frugal of vicious indulgence, and fruitful of virtue as the hyperbolical extravagances of his rival sects."
72. Miller, *Jefferson and Nature*, 29 ("scientific naiveté"); Bruce Dain, *A Hideous Monster of the Mind: American Race Theory in the Early Republic* (Cambridge, MA: Harvard UP, 2003), 14 ("naïve empiricism").

2. UNCRITICAL REASON

1. See, e.g., Allen Jayne, *Jefferson's Declaration of Independence: Origins, Philosophy, and Theology* (Lexington: UP of Kentucky, 1998), 168.
2. Paul K. Conkin, "The Religious Pilgrimage of Thomas Jefferson," in *Jeffersonian Legacies*, ed. Peter S. Onuf, 19–45 (Charlottesville: UP of Virginia, 1993), 25. Thanks to Andrew O'Shaughnessy for alerting me to this interpretation.
3. TJ to John Adams, 15 August 1820 (my emphasis).
4. Compare Rush's "Thoughts on Common Sense" (1791), in *Essays, Literary, Moral & Philosophical*, 249–56 (Philadelphia, 1798), 255.
5. Locke, *Essay*, 395–96 (4.12.2).
6. TJ to John Adams, 15 August 1820; compare TJ to Francis Adrian Van der Kemp, 30 July 1816: Jefferson's argument against the Trinity did not rely on reason itself, but claimed that reason depended entirely on the material provided by experience ("ideas must be distinct before reason can act upon them; and no man ever had a distinct idea of the trinity").
7. Miller, *Jefferson and Nature*, 27.

8. TJ to Thomas Law, 13 June 1814 (my emphasis); compare TJ to John Adams, 5 May 1817. Jefferson also reflected on the moral sense in TJ to Martha Jefferson, 11 December 1783; TJ to Peter Carr, 19 August 1785, and 10 August 1787.
9. TJ to Peter Carr, 10 August 1787.
10. TJ to Law, 13 June 1814. Compare TJ to Carr, 10 August 1787: "It is given to all human beings in a stronger or weaker degree, as force of members is given them in a greater or less degree. It may be strengthened by exercise, as may any particular limb of the body. This sense is submitted indeed to the guidance of reason; but it is a small stock which is required for this: even a less one than what we call common sense."
11. Peter S. Onuf and Ari Helo, "Jefferson, Morality, and the Problem of Slavery," in Onuf, *Mind of Jefferson*, 236–70, esp. 243–48.
12. Locke, *Essay*, 407–14 (4.18).
13. TJ, *Literary Commonplace Book*, esp. 30–38 (§18–32).
14. TJ to Robert Skipwith, 3 August 1771.
15. TJ to Samuel Miller, 23 January 1808 (my emphasis).
16. Compare TJ to Miles King, 26 September 1814: "Your reason, not mine, is to judge of this: and if it shall be his pleasure to favor me with a like admonition, I shall obey it with the same fidelity with which I would obey his known will in all cases. Hitherto I have been under the guidance of that portion of reason which he has thought proper to deal out to me."
17. TJ, *Notes*, 159.
18. TJ, *Literary Commonplace Book*, 35 (§ 28); compare 36 (§30).
19. Eugene R. Sheridan, introduction to TJ, *Jefferson's Extracts from the Gospels*, ed. Dickinson W. Adams and Ruth W. Lester, 3–42 (Princeton, NJ: Princeton UP, 1983), 3.
20. TJ to Adrian Van der Kemp, 30 July 1816.
21. Sheridan, introduction to TJ, *Jefferson's Extracts from the Gospels*, 9.
22. TJ to Adrian Van der Kemp, 30 July 1816 ("until some rational creed can occupy the void which the obliteration of their [i.e., of 'the mountebanks calling themselves the priests of Jesus'] duperies would leave in the minds of our honest and unsuspecting brethren").
23. TJ, *Notes*, 159.
24. TJ to Joseph Priestley, 19 June 1802 (my emphasis).
25. Conkin, "Religious Pilgrimage," 25.
26. Compare TJ to Peter Carr, 10 August 1787; and TJ to John Adams, 22 August 1813.
27. Compare TJ to James Madison, 14 February 1783; TJ to William Short, 13 April 1820; TJ to John Adams, 20 December 1786; TJ to Ezra Stiles,

24 December 1786; TJ to Alexander von Humboldt, 13 June 1813; TJ to Caesar A. Rodney, 7 October 1818; TJ to Joseph Priestley, 29 November 1802; and TJ to James Monroe, 10 July 1796.
28. Compare TJ to Comte Diodati, 3 August 1789; TJ to Roger C. Weightman, 24 June 1826; TJ to Ogilvie, 4 August 1811, TJ to James Madison, 16 December 1786, TJ to A. L. C. Destutt de Tracy; TJ to Marc Auguste Pictet, 26 December 1820; and TJ to William Roscoe, 27 December 1820.
29. TJ, *Notes*, 159.
30. TJ to James Sullivan, 9 February 1797.
31. TJ to John Tyler, 28 June 1804.
32. TJ to David Harding, 20 April 1824.
33. TJ to William G. Munford, 18 June 1799.
34. On the eighteenth-century evolution of *critique* and *critical* reason, see Reinhart Koselleck, *Kritik und Krise* (1959; Frankfurt/M.: Suhrkamp, 1973), chap. 2, esp. 85–103; Kelleter, *Amerikanische Aufklärung*, esp. 25–29; and Jürgen Habermas, *Auch eine Geschichte der Philosophie*, 2 vols., vol. 2: *Vernünftige Freiheit: Spuren des Diskurses über Glauben und Wissen* (Frankfurt/M.: Suhrkamp, 2019), 314–17.
35. For example, see TJ to John Adams, 28 October, 1813: "but we differ as rational friends, using the free exercise of our own reason, and mutually indulging it's errors." On the expectation of different results of personal uses of reason including in religion, compare TJ to Miles King, 26 September 1814.
36. TJ to Peter Carr, 10 August 1787; TJ to Miles King, 26 September 1814; TJ to John F. Watson, 17 May 1814.
37. On this problem in the history of differentiating between belief and knowledge, see, e.g., Habermas's *Vernünftige Freiheit*, which sees the central problem of modern philosophy in finding the normative foundation of natural rights in subjective human reason alone (i.e., subjective human reason without providential support [137, 201]).
38. TJ to Sheldon Clark, 5 December 1825, discussed above.
39. I have discussed Jefferson's concepts of time in *Thomas Jefferson, Time, and History* (Charlottesville: U of Virginia P, 2011).

3. OPINION IS POWER

1. Robert M. S. McDonald, "Thomas Jefferson's Changing Reputation as Author of the 'Declaration of Independence': The First Fifty Years," *Journal of the Early Republic* 19 (1999): 169–95.
2. TJ to William Fleming, 1 July 1776.
3. TJ to Henry Lee, 8 May 1825.

4. For concise discussions of one of the key interpretative questions of the Declaration of Independence, of whether independence was conceived as a textual event or merely celebrated as de facto independence that had already been achieved, see Eric Slauter, "The Declaration of Independence and the New Nation," in *The Cambridge Companion to Thomas Jefferson*, ed. Frank Shuffleton, 12–34 (Cambridge: Cambridge UP, 2009), esp. 14–18, 23; and Robert G. Parkinson, "The Declaration of Independence," in *A Companion to Thomas Jefferson*, ed. Francis D. Cogliano, 44–59 (Malden, MA: Blackwell, 2012).
5. TJ to Edward Carrington, 16 January 1787.
6. TJ to Henry Lee, 8 May 1825. On this conceit in the context of national mobilization, see Peter S. Onuf, "The Declaration of Independence for a New Millennium," in *The Cambridge Companion to the Declaration of Independence* (Cambridge: Cambridge UP, forthcoming): "Nationhood thus was both the product of their precocious consciousness of 'self-evident' truths, already present in the 'American mind,' that Jefferson merely reduced to writing, and of an ongoing process of mobilization that forced colonists to make up their minds."
7. TJ to James Madison, 30 August 1823.
8. This and the following quotations are from "Jefferson's Original Rough Draught of the Declaration of Independence," 11 June–4 July 1776.
9. For a helpful overview of recent critical studies of the "emotional hegemony" of positive affects such as happiness, especially in the context of slavery, see Nicole Eustace, "Emotional Pursuits and the American Revolution," *Emotion Review* 12.3 (July 2020): 146–55.
10. "Jefferson's Original Rough Draught of the Declaration of Independence," 11 June–4 July 1776.
11. Hannah Arendt, *On Revolution* (New York: Viking, 1963), 193.
12. E.g., in Jill Lepore, *These Truths: A History of the United States* (New York: Norton, 2019).
13. Kelleter, *Amerikanische Aufklärung*, 70. On the relationship between self-evidence and reason, see ibid., 70–71, 116–18.
14. Michael P. Zuckert, *The Natural Rights Republic: Studies in the Foundation of the American Political Tradition* (Notre Dame, IN: U of Notre Dame P, 1996), chap. 3, 45–46.
15. On the debates surrounding the Declaration's speaking subject, see Slauter, "Declaration," 25–27.
16. Zuckert, *Natural Rights Republic*, 45. Zuckert distinguishes between epistemological and "functional and political" self-evidence (48). For a different interpretation focusing on the list of truths as self-evident if

understood as "a three-part truth" rather than separate truths, see Danielle Allen, *Our Declaration: A Reading of the Declaration of Independence in Defense of Equality* (New York: Liveright, 2014), 163–66, 161 (quote). From the perspective of Jefferson's radicalized Lockeanism, however, it is likely that Jefferson tended to harbor considerable skepticism against syllogistic reasoning as a guide to truth, perhaps also on this account leaving the "incongruously" subjective "We hold" in the sentence after "self-evident" was introduced.

17. See Peterson, *Jefferson Image*, 164–71.
18. TJ, *Notes*, 160.
19. Jefferson subscribed to Locke's mode of conceiving of opinion and belief in terms of assent. See TJ to John Adams, 22 August 1813. For an influential interpretation of the role of *assent* in American culture from the perspective, not of Enlightenment epistemology, but of the "set of rituals" and "the system of sacred-secular symbols" bequeathed by American Puritanism, see Sacvan Bercovitch, *Rites of Assent: Transformations in the Symbolic Construction of America* (New York: Routledge, 1993), chap. 2, 35.
20. Brian Steele, "Getting 'the Hang of the Declaration': The Declaration in American Nationalism," in *The Cambridge Companion to the Declaration of Independence* (Cambridge: Cambridge UP, forthcoming).
21. Allen, *Our Declaration*, 137.
22. Onuf, *Virginians*, 28.
23. For this English translation of the 1789 Declaration by the French National Assembly, see https://www.elysee.fr/en/french-presidency/the-declaration-of-the-rights-of-man-and-of-the-citizen.
24. TJ to Edward Carrington, 16 January 1787.
25. Steele, "Getting 'the Hang of the Declaration'" (forthcoming).
26. For Jefferson's characteristic blend of uncertainty and conviction in *Notes on Virginia*, see Thompson, "I Have Known," 61, discussed above.
27. TJ to John Adams, 11 January 1816.
28. John Adams to TJ, 2 February 1816.
29. According to Wolfgang Krohn, Bacon himself did not actually identify knowledge and power as crudely as the maxim attributed to him suggests (see Krohn, *Bacon*, 81–89).
30. TJ to George Ticknor, 25 November 1817.
31. TJ to William Short, 13 April 1820.
32. TJ to John Page, 25 December 1762.
33. TJ, *Literary Commonplace Book*, 24 (§4). On the difference between popular and public opinion, see Kirk Wetters, *The Opinion System: Impasses of the Public Sphere from Hobbes to Habermas* (New York: Fordham UP,

2008), 8–9; Colleen A. Sheehan, *James Madison and the Spirit of Republican Government* (New York: Cambridge UP, 2009), 67–69.
34. On Montesquieu's "psychologization" of liberty, see Mark G. Schmeller, *Invisible Sovereign: Imagining Public Opinion from the Revolution to Reconstruction* (Baltimore, MD: Johns Hopkins UP, 2016), 18–19.
35. Keegan Callanan, "Liberal Constitutionalism and Political Particularism in Montesquieu's *The Spirit of the Laws*," *Political Research Quarterly* 67.3 (2014): 590.
36. On modern opinion as "privative" concept ("mere opinion"), see Wetters, *Opinion System*, 127–28.
37. TJ, *Legal Commonplace Book*, 448, 451 (translation) (§ 768).
38. On this motto see Wetters, *Opinion System*, 1–3.
39. Schmeller, *Invisible Sovereign*, 17.
40. TJ, *Notes*, 163.
41. On different concepts of *l'opinion publique* in their relevance for Madison's concept, see Sheehan, *Spirit of Republican Government*, chap. 3, esp. 64–79.
42. See "Jefferson's Notes from Condorcet on Slavery" for his apparent difficulties translating this sentence.
43. TJ to Edward Carrington, 16 January 1787.
44. Onuf, *Virginians*, 102–3.
45. Schmeller, *Invisible Sovereign*, 7–10; TJ, *Notes*, 93.
46. Montesquieu, Book XV of *De l'esprit des lois* from *Oeuvres de Monsieur Montesquieu* (London, 1767), in TJ, *Legal Commonplace Book*, 459, 461 (§789).
47. Thanks to my father, ancient historian and closeted classical philologist Peter Spahn, for one of his favorite illustrations of the importance of historical semantics.
48. On *manners* as precursor concept of *opinion*, see Wetters, *Opinion System*, 14, 61–69.
49. TJ to Samuel Kercheval, 12 July 1816.
50. Although this argument runs parallel to Locke's concept of a "law of opinion or reputation" in some respects, Jefferson seems not to have been particularly interested in Locke's "philosophical law" or "law of private censure." For summaries of the problems of Locke's concept, see Koselleck, *Kritik*, esp. 42–48, 138–39; Wetters, *Opinion System*, esp. 138–44; and Schmeller, *Invisible Sovereign*, 14–15.
51. TJ, *Notes*, 163.
52. TJ, Second Inaugural Address, 4 March 1805.
53. TJ to Adams, 30 August 1787; TJ to Jay, 22 September 1787; TJ to George Washington, 2 May 1788; TJ to William Short, 24 January 1791.

54. TJ to Henry Lee, 8 May 1825.
55. TJ to Joseph Priestley, 21 March 1801.
56. James Madison, "Federalist # 10," in *The Federalist Papers*, ed. Isaac Kramnick (London: Penguin, 1987), 126.
57. Onuf, *Virginians*, 104; for comparisons to Hume and Madison, see Colleen A. Sheehan, "Public Opinion and the Formation of Civic Character in Madison's Republican Theory," *Review of Politics* 67.1 (Winter 2005): 37–48; and Colleen A. Sheehan, *Spirit of Republican Government*, chap. 6, 124–55, esp. 138–42.
58. Martin Luther King, "I Have a Dream," in *A Testament of Hope: The Essential Writings of Martin Luther King, Jr.*, ed. James Melvin Washington, 217–20 (San Francisco: Harper & Row, 1986).
59. Locke, *Essay*, 386–94 (4.16); John Stuart Mill, "On Liberty," in *On Liberty, Utilitarianism, and Other Essays*, ed. with introduction and notes by Mark Philp and Frederick Rosen, 1–112 (1991; Oxford: Oxford UP, 2015), 9.
60. Locke, *Essay*, 387 (4.16.3).
61. Wetters, *Opinion System*, 140.
62. Schmeller, *Invisible Sovereign*, 90–98.
63. See Jefferson's commonplace entry of Montesquieu's definition, *Literary Commonplace Book*, 24 (§4).
64. See Schmeller, *Invisible Sovereign*, 92, on Madison's "Property" essay (1792). There may be a conceptual overlap between Madison's emphasis on property and Jefferson's emphasis on involuntary opinion, if the concept of *involuntary possession*, relevant for Jefferson in the context of slavery, inheritance, and debt, is taken into account. Thanks to Sean Harvey for this interesting suggestion that would merit further study.
65. Wetters, *Opinion System*, 142.
66. TJ, *Notes*, 160. For a prominent reference to the Procrustes myth in African American literature, see Charles Chesnutt's short story "Baxter's Procrustes," in *The Portable Charles W. Chesnutt*, ed. William L. Andrews, 194–206 (London: Penguin, 2008).
67. Locke, *Essay*, 388 (4.16.4). As Kirk Wetters argues, Locke risked severely undermining his discourse of rational persuasion by variously emphasizing the intractability of opinions (Wetters, *Opinion System*, 140).
68. TJ, *Notes*, 160.
69. On the dating of the Montesquieu entries in this period, see the introduction to TJ, *Legal Commonplace Book*, 21–22.
70. TJ, *Legal Commonplace Book*, 488–89 (§801).
71. See Appendix, "Letter 1. Letter of Helvetius to President Montesquieu." Jefferson had made sure that the two letters attributed to Helvetius were

included in the American edition of the *Commentaries* (TJ to William Duane, 16 September 1810).
72. See Callanan, "Political Particularism," 590.
73. "Observations on the Twenty-Ninth Book of The Spirit of Laws by the late M. de Condorcet," in the Appendix of Destutt de Tracy, *A Commentary and Review of Montesquieu's Spirit of Laws* (Clark, NJ: Lawbook Exchange, 2006), chap. 18, 273–74. For a discussion in the context of the "spirit of moderation" in chap. 2, see Aurelian Craiutu, *A Virtue for Courageous Minds: Moderation in French Political Thought, 1748–1830* (Princeton, NJ: Princeton UP, 2012), 56–57.
74. "Observations by the late M. de Condorcet," chap. 2.
75. TJ to William Duane, 12 August 1810; compare TJ to William Duane, 16 September 1810.
76. TJ to William Duane, 16 September 1810.
77. On Jefferson's concept of manners in the context of slavery and his insight that "[a]s society progressed, he and his kind would eventually disappear," see Gordon-Reed and Onuf, *Patriarchs*, 90–94, 93 (quote).
78. TJ, *Notes*, 87.
79. Henry Home, Lord Kames, *Historical Law-Tracts*, 2d ed. (Edinburgh, 1761), in TJ, *Legal Commonplace Book*, 236 (§ 558).
80. John Dalrymple, *An Essay towards a General History of Feudal Property in Great Britain* (London, 1757), in TJ, *Legal Commonplace Book*, 288 (§ 579).
81. Ibid., in TJ, *Legal Commonplace Book*, 269 (§ 570).
82. Jefferson spoke of the *public mind* extensively in his correspondence, even before he began to use the term *public opinion* in the mid-1780s (see, e.g., TJ to George Washington, 17 July 1779).
83. TJ to Joseph Priestley, 19 June 1802 (my emphasis).
84. TJ, First Inaugural Address (4 March 1801), in TJ, *Writings*, ed. Peterson, 493. For a discussion of this phrase in the context of Jefferson's concept of a "right to untruth" within an idealized concept of public communication, see Kelleter, *Amerikanische Aufklärung*, 591–92. Frederick Douglass referenced and adjusted the passage in "The Proclamation and a Negro Army," as will be discussed in chapter 7.
85. TJ, *Notes*, 163.
86. Ibid.
87. Minutes of the Board of Visitors of the University of Virginia, 4 October 1819.
88. Onuf, *Virginians*, 102–3 (discussed above).

4. DEEP-ROOTED PREJUDICES

1. See Wetters, *Opinion System*, 140.
2. On the reception of *Notes*, see Gish and Klinghard, *Political Biography*, 8–9, 74–77; and Robert Pierce Forbes, introduction to *Notes on the State of Virginia: An Annotated Edition*, by TJ, ed. and with an introduction and notes by Forbes, xix–lx (New Haven, CT: Yale UP, 2022), l–lvi. Forbes's valuable new edition, based on comparing the first 1785 edition and the printer's manuscript, came to my attention after finishing the manuscript, which still refers to the conventional Peden edition. However, I have tried to incorporate into the following discussion some of the new findings from Forbes's important comparison.
3. TJ, *Notes*, 138.
4. Since Jefferson specifically used the term "black" to indicate that African Americans were *no* Americans, it is difficult to repeat his terms *black* and *race* uncritically. In order to distinguish the book's argument from Jefferson's perspective, his terms will be italicized or placed in quotation marks whenever possible.
5. TJ, *Notes*, 138.
6. Although it has turned out to be among the statements most damaging to Jefferson's reputation, a consensus on the details of his argument still seems difficult to reach. For instance, interpreters differ on the question of whether the Jefferson of Query XIV has to be seen as the founding father of nineteenth-century "scientific" racism or, to the contrary, as an example of the failure or refusal to move beyond a worldview closely tethered to an "increasingly obsolescent" eighteenth-century natural history (see, e.g., Jordan, *White over Black*, 429–81; Dain, *Hideous Monster*, 1–39, 38 [quote]; and Thomson, *Jefferson's Shadow*, 118–42). Another major point of divergence among readers of this query has been the evaluation of the relative weight Jefferson gave to physical, moral, and mental attributes, in particular the faculties of reason and imagination, in their supposed relevance as requirements for citizenship (see Onuf and Helo, "Jefferson and Slavery"; Gates, *Trials*; and Jarrett, *Representing*, chap. 1).
7. Schneiders, *Vorurteilskritik*, Godel, *Vorurteilsdiskurs*; Reisinger and Scholz, "Vorurteil," in *Historisches Wörterbuch*, 11:1249–63. Perhaps as a result of eighteenth- and nineteenth-century debates on the status of African Americans, *prejudice* may be more closely tied to meanings surrounding "race" in English than in German.
8. Godel, *Vorurteilsdiskurs*, chap. 2, esp. 78–81.
9. John H. Zammito's illuminating English-language review of Godel's *Vorurteilsdiskurs* is in *Monatshefte* 101.3 (Fall 2009): 416–18.

10. It is possible that Jefferson took the metaphor of "deep roots" directly from Francis Bacon's aphorisms on the idols in the first book of the *Novum Organum*. Compare Bacon, "Aphorisms of the Interpretation of Nature and Kingdome of Man": "Idols, mistakes, and mis-apprehensions [. . .] are deeply rooted in Mans understanding." *The Novum Organum of Sir Francis Bacon, Baron of Verulam, Viscount St. Albans. Epitomized for a clearer understanding of his natural history. Trans. and taken out of the Latine by M.D.* (London, 1676), 3. On the idols, see Krohn, *Bacon*, 93–107.
11. Hans-Georg Gadamer, *Wahrheit und Methode: Grundzüge einer philosophischen Hermeneutik* (Tübingen: Mohr, 1960). Gadamer took the inspiration for his broader view of prejudice (and likely for his strawman of a supposed Enlightenment "prejudice against prejudice") from Martin Heidegger's early work (see G. Kühne-Bertram, "Vorverständnis," in *Historisches Wörterbuch*, 11:1267–71).
12. John Locke, *The Conduct of the Understanding* (Dublin, 1782), 31.
13. Edmund Burke, *Reflections on the Revolution in France*, ed. Frank M. Turner (New Haven, CT: Yale UP, 2003), 74–75.
14. The "Apologie de Raimond Sebond" is discussed in Godel, *Vorurteilsdiskurs*, 17n78.
15. Rush, "Common Sense," 256.
16. Madison, "Federalist #49," in *Federalist Papers*, 314.
17. Jefferson owned several works by d'Holbach, including *Le bon sens* and several editions of *Système de la nature* (see TJ, *Legal Commonplace Book*, 600n). On Jefferson's use of d'Holbach in the context of "The Life and Morals of Jesus of Nazareth," see Kevin J. Haynes, *The Road to Monticello: The Life and Mind of Thomas Jefferson* (New York: Oxford UP, 2008), chap. 9.
18. Quoted in Reisinger and Scholz, "Vorurteil," in *Historisches Wörterbuch*, 11:1254–55.
19. On Jefferson's project of politically leveling (up) Virginia citizens, see Onuf, *Virginians*, esp. 10–11, 17–46. See also Jack P. Greene, "The Intellectual Reconstruction of Virginia in the Age of Jefferson," in *Jeffersonian Legacies*, 225–53, for a long-standing tradition of criticizing Virginians. However, Jefferson's remarks on Virginian national character combined negative with positive aspects. Compare TJ to Madison, 1 September 1785.
20. TJ to Chastellux, 16 January 1784. By the late eighteenth century, admitting one's own prejudice had become such a common form of enlightened self-criticism that it was often difficult to separate it from forms of politeness and civility, as Jefferson's case illustrates. Compare what may have

been Thomas Paine's somewhat more sincere engagement with prejudice as a "spider of the mind," quoted and discussed in Guyatt, *Bind Us Apart*, 27–28.

21. TJ, *Notes*, 64.
22. Compare Jefferson's draft of the Declaration of Independence as included in his "Autobiography," which capitalized the word MEN when referring to the men, women, and children who were the victims of the Atlantic slave trade (TJ, *Writings*, ed. Peterson, 22).
23. Locke, *Essay*, 180 (2.27.9). Locke defined *person* here as "a thinking intelligent being that has reason and reflection and can consider itself as itself, the same thinking thing in different times and places."
24. Ibid.
25. A similarly nonchalant attitude to rational quantification can be found in TJ to Chastellux, 7 June 1785. Almost in the manner of the Western tall tale, he claimed that some of the anthropological information presented in *Notes* was based on his having personally seen and "conversed much" with "some thousands" of Native Americans (see Thompson, "I Have Known," 68).
26. This ambiguity is continued later under Query XIV, which oscillates between Jefferson's recognition that in the faculty of memory "blacks" were "equal to the whites," and his opposite claim that their "griefs" were "transient" and the "numberless afflictions" of human existence "sooner forgotten with them" (TJ, *Notes*, 139).
27. Wetters, *Opinion System*, 140, discussed above. The following paragraphs under Query XIV leave little doubt on the systematically prejudgmental structure of Jefferson's observations, in which the viewpoints of "blacks" were excluded from a "white" perspective first and disqualified for their supposed physical and intellectual attributes second.
28. Parkinson, *Common Cause*, 22, 583.
29. TJ, *Notes*, 163.
30. Ibid., 138.
31. TJ to Henry Lee, 8 May 1825.
32. On African Americans as a "captive nation" and potentially "internal enemy" due to the latent state of war that was slavery, see Onuf, *Jefferson's Empire*, 147–88; and Onuf, *Mind of Jefferson*, 205–35.
33. Forbes shows that Jefferson manipulated the dating of the manuscript twice to make it appear that it was completed in 1782 rather than 1783 or 1785, possibly to create the illusion that it was solely a product of the American Revolution and the revolutionary war (Forbes, introduction to *Notes on the State of Virginia*, xxiii–xxv; Susan Manning, "Naming of Parts;

or, The Comforts of Classification: Thomas Jefferson's Construction of America as Fact and Myth," *Journal of American Studies* 30.3 [December 1996]: 345–64, 348 ["war book"]).
34. On this change from active to passive voice in 1788, see Lucia Stanton, *"Those Who Labor for My Happiness": Slavery at Thomas Jefferson's Monticello* (Charlottesville: U of Virginia P, 2012), 132–33.
35. TJ, *Notes*, "Advertisement," 2.
36. Gordon-Reed and Onuf, *Patriarchs*, 86.
37. Charles Thomson to TJ, 6 March 1785.
38. Robert A. Ferguson, *Law and Letters in American Culture* (Cambridge, MA: Harvard UP, 1984), 41.
39. TJ to Stockdale, 27 February 1785.
40. Thomas Nagel, *The View from Nowhere* (New York: Oxford UP, 1989).
41. TJ, *Notes*, 76, Query VII: "This position (Monticello) being nearly central between our northern and southern boundaries, and between the bay and Alleghaney, may be considered as furnishing the best average of the temperature of our climate." On Jefferson's view of the piedmont of Virginia as the center of the state in various contexts, see Gordon-Reed and Onuf, *Patriarchs*, 87.
42. For instance, as will be discussed further below, from what would become known as Harpers Ferry or the Natural Bridge. TJ, *Notes*, 19–20, 24–25.
43. Ibid., 25.
44. For situating the latter, see David Simpson, *Situatedness, or, Why We Keep Saying Where We're Coming From* (Durham, NC: Duke UP, 2002). Jefferson's rhetoric may have anticipated the ambivalence of what Simpson analyzes as today's "at once modest and aggressive" rhetoric of situatedness (1).
45. Ibid., 2. To be sure, this phrase by itself was not so much the intentional expression of cultural nationalism as part of the ostensible effort to prevent a pirated edition of *Notes* (see TJ to John Stockdale, 27 February 1785).
46. TJ, *Notes*, 55. There had been even more subjective qualifications of knowledge in the printer's manuscript of the 1785 edition. E.g., Forbes, ed., *Annotated Edition*, 211n52: Jefferson's rhetorical question of whether skin color was "of no importance" originally contained the openly subjectivist "to us."
47. On Jefferson's rearrangement of what was originally Marbois's third query as the first query of *Notes* and additional implications of the first line, "Virginia is bounded on the East by the Atlantic," in the context of literary originality, see Ezra Tawil, *Literature, American Style: The Originality of*

Imitation in the Early Republic (Philadelphia: U of Pennsylvania P, 2018), 94–95.

48. On Jefferson's insight into the improved methods of land measurement in the 1780s, see Gish and Klinghard, *Political Biography*, 62–63.
49. TJ, *Notes*, 138. In this paragraph under Query XIV, he used the term *real* twice within a few lines referring to his subjective experience, rather than knowledge, of "racial" difference: "the real distinctions which nature has made" and "the difference is fixed in nature, and is as real as if its seat and cause were better known to us."
50. This was the central theme of Sterne's *A Sentimental Journey through France and Italy by Mr. Yorick*, as condensed in its opening phrase, "—They order, said I, this matter better in France—" (Laurence Sterne, *A Sentimental Journey and Other Writings*, ed. Ian Jack and Tim Parnell [Oxford: Oxford UP, 2003], 3).
51. TJ to Horatio G. Spafford, 11 May 1819.
52. TJ, *Notes*, 55. In this context, Jefferson's idiosyncratic choice of paintings for Monticello opens an intriguing window on his empiricism, as explored by Oliver C. O'Donnell in chapter 4 of *Portraits of Empiricism: Art Histories from an Intellectual Tradition* (University Park: Pennsylvania State UP, forthcoming).
53. Stein, *Worlds*, 352–60. On Jefferson's interest in (Newtonian) optics, see TJ to David Rittenhouse, 11 November 1784; and TJ to Bishop James Madison, 19 July 1788.
54. These include Joshua Shaw, *View from the Arch of the Bridge Looking down the Creek, Rockbridge County, VA* (ca. 1820); and possibly Caleb Boyle, *Jefferson at the Natural Bridge* (ca. 1801).
55. Queries XVIII, "Manners," and XIX, "Manufactures," move on to discuss the people whose perspective shifts in this manner, offering reasons for the subjective boundaries of their point of view as well as possible means to "level up" their perspective and widen their horizon.
56. TJ, *Notes*, 19, 24, 20. On the move from war to peace, see Manning, "Naming of Parts," 352–57.
57. Ibid., 19, 25.
58. Gordon-Reed and Onuf, *Patriarchs*, 27.
59. TJ, *Notes*, 80 (my emphasis).
60. Antonello Gerbi, *The Dispute of the New World: The History of a Polemic, 1750–1900* (1973; Pittsburgh: U of Pittsburgh P, 2010).
61. Jefferson's idiosyncratic literary optics would be targeted by the Federalist Fisher Ames in 1801: "He strains his optics to look beyond its circumference, and contemplates invisibility, till he thinks nothing else is real."

Quoted in the context of accusations of Francophilia in Sophia Rosenfeld, *Common Sense: A Political History* (Harvard: Harvard UP, 2011), 218.
62. TJ, *Notes*, 138.
63. James Weldon Johnson, *The Autobiography of an Ex-Coloured Man*, "Preface to the Original Edition of 1912," in *The Essential Writings of James Weldon Johnson*, ed. Rudolph P. Byrd (New York: Modern Library, 2008), 27.
64. TJ, *Notes*, 143.
65. Ibid., 138.
66. Ibid., 143 (my emphasis).
67. James McCune Smith, "On the Fourteenth Query of Thomas Jefferson's Notes on Virginia," in *The Works of James McCune Smith: Black Intellectual and Abolitionist*, ed. John Stauffer, 264–81 (Oxford: Oxford UP, 2006), 266–67. Smith's work will be discussed in chapters 6 and 7.
68. On contemporary criticism by David Ramsay, Gilbert Imlay, Noah Webster, William Short, Marquis de Chastellux, and Samuel Stanhope Smith, among others, see Guyatt, *Bind Us Apart*, esp. 26–27, 34–35, 61–62, 115–17, 129–30.
69. Thompson, "I Have Known," 61.
70. TJ to Maria Cosway, 14 January 1789. See O'Shaughnessy, *Illimitable Freedom*, chap. 8.
71. Maurizio Valsania, *Jefferson's Body: A Corporeal Biography* (Charlottesville: U of Virginia P, 2017), 201n26.
72. Compare TJ to Henri Grégoire, 25 February 1809: "whatever be their degree of talent it is no measure of their rights. Because Sir Isaac Newton was superior to others in understanding, he was not therefore lord of the person or property of others."
73. In the above letter to Abbé Grégoire, Jefferson himself helped initiate the logic of "refutation" that would later be taken up by abolitionists such as David Walker. As Jefferson wrote to Grégoire, whose *De la littérature des nègres* (1808) had made a case for black moral and intellectual equality while explicitly criticizing Jefferson, "no person living wishes more sincerely than I do, to see a complete refutation of the doubts I have myself entertained and expressed on the grade of understanding allotted to them by nature, and to find that in this respect they are on a par with ourselves." That Jefferson may have been somewhat disingenuous in these hopes for a "complete refutation" of Query XIV is suggested by his later admission that he had given Grégoire a "soft answer" (TJ to Joel Barlow, 8 October 1809). On this point, see especially Kelleter, *Amerikanische Aufklärung*, 675–77, 694–95.
74. Walker's arguments will be discussed in chapters 5 through 7. On the problem of uncritically continuing abolitionist arguments of "dehumanization" in

today's historiography of slavery, see Walter Johnson, "To Remake the World: Slavery, Racial Capitalism, and Justice," in Walter Johnson and Robin D. G. Kelley, *Boston Review, Forum 1: Race Capitalism Justice*, ed. Deborah Chasman and Joshua Cohen (Boston: Boston Critic, 2017), 13–31; and Nicholas Trinehart, "The Man That Was a Thing: Reconsidering Human Commodification in Slavery," *Journal of Social History* 50.1 (Fall 2016): 28–50.

75. Onuf, *Mind of Jefferson*, 208: "Jefferson's commitment to racial separation was fundamental, not provisional."
76. TJ, *Notes*, 139.
77. Ibid., 139–40.
78. Ibid., 140.
79. Ibid. On this point, see William H. Robinson, *Phillis Wheatley: A Bio-Bibliography* (Boston: Hall, 1981), 39; and John C. Shields, *Phillis Wheatley's Poetics of Liberation: Backgrounds and Contexts* (Knoxville: U of Tennessee P, 2008), 1–2. Jefferson may have felt corroborated in his radical exclusion of Wheatley from his judgment also by her portrait on the frontispiece of her *Poems*. As Jennifer Chuong shows, its line engraving creates the effect of an impenetrable veil, unlike the softer surfaces created by the stipple engravings in contemporaneous portraits of Sancho or Olaudah Equiano. At the same time, line engraving could also be associated with rationality, stability, and uniformity (see Chuong, "Engraving's 'Immoveable Veil': Phillis Wheatley's Portrait and the Politics of Technique," *Art Bulletin* 104.2 [June 2022]: 63–88).
80. Gates, *Trials*, 74–84; see also Shields, *Poetics*, 1–13, 43–69. For a recent assessment of Wheatley as an assimilationist racist and mere "black exhibit," see Ibram Kendi, *Stamped from the Beginning: The Definitive History of Racist Ideas in America* (New York: Bold Type, 2016), chap. 8.
81. TJ, *Notes*, 146.
82. TJ to John Holmes, 22 April 1820; compare TJ to Albert Gallatin, 26 December 1820, which extended the metaphor of *diffusion* to "*spreading* them over a larger surface."
83. See Onuf, *Virginians*; and Alan Taylor, *The Internal Enemy: Slavery and War in Virginia, 1772–1832* (New York: Norton, 2013).
84. TJ, *Notes*, 163. African American uses of Query XVIII will be discussed in chapter 7.
85. For a sophisticated example, see Karen E. Fields and Barbara J. Fields, *Racecraft: The Soul of Inequality in American Life* (New York: Verso, 2014).
86. In his manuscript, Jefferson had included himself even more explicitly in the "we" of Virginia slaveholders than in the printed version (see TJ, *Annotated Edition*, ed. Forbes, 248–49n2).

87. TJ, *Notes*, 162: "Our children see this, and learn to imitate it"; "[f]rom his cradle to his grave he is learning to do what he sees others do"; "the child looks on, catches the lineaments of wrath."
88. TJ, *Notes*, 58–65. Martin Delany would later reinterpret the meaning of this passage, as will be discussed in chapter 6.
89. For Jefferson as "race maker," see Onuf, *Mind of Jefferson*, 211.
90. TJ, "Report of the Commissioners for the University of Virginia" (4 August 1818), in TJ, *Writings*, 457–73. On the interconnectedness of intellect and manners, see esp. 460: "To develop the reasoning faculties of our youth, enlarge their minds, cultivate their morals, and instill into them the precepts of virtue and order; [. . .] and generally, to form them to habits of reflection and correct action, rendering them examples of virtue to others, and of happiness within themselves"; on the formation of "American character," 469. On the Report, see esp. O'Shaughnessy, *Illimitable Freedom*, 60–64.
91. Compare Jarrett, *Representing*, chap. 1, for a sophisticated reading that sees David Walker "ideologically overlapping" with Jefferson on this point (47). As discussed above, I see Jefferson's antirationalist Enlightenment going in a different direction. The sources coming closest to letting Jefferson appear a proponent of *black uplift* are his polite but formulaic replies to Benjamin Banneker, 30 August 1791, and the Abbé Grégoire, 25 February 1809. Compare TJ to Joel Barlow, 8 October 1809. On the ethical ambiguity of empathy and resentment in Jefferson's concept of civility, see Kelleter, "A Literature of Civic Indignation."
92. Benjamin Banneker to TJ, 19 August 1791; Charles W. Chesnutt, "Journal Entry: May 29, 1880," in *The Journals of Charles W. Chesnutt*, ed. Richard H. Brodhead (Durham, NC: Duke UP, 1993), 139–40. On *white uplift*, see Richard Newman, "Good Communications Corrects Bad Manners: The Banneker-Jefferson Dialogue and the Project of White Uplift," in *Contesting Slavery: The Politics of Bondage and Freedom in the New American Nation*, ed. John Craig Hammond and Matthew Mason, 69–93 (Charlottesville: U of Virginia P, 2012). This concept will be further discussed in chapters 6 and 7.

II. WHEATLEY'S ENLIGHTENMENT OF PRINCIPLE

1. PW to Samson Occom, 11 February 1774, in PW, *Complete Writings*, 152–53. On this famous letter, see, e.g., Charles Akers, "'Our Modern Egyptians': Phillis Wheatley and the Whig Campaign against Slavery in Revolutionary Boston," *Journal of Negro History* 60 (July 1975): 297–310; Zafar, *We Wear the Mask*, chap. 1, esp. 20–24; Kelleter, *Amerikanische*

Aufklärung, chap. 11, 693–94; David Waldstreicher, "Ancients, Moderns, and Africans: Phillis Wheatley and the Politics of Empire and Slavery in the American Revolution," *Journal of the Early Republic* 37.4 (Winter 2017): 701–33; Waldstreicher, "Women's Politics, Antislavery Politics, and Phillis Wheatley's American Revolution," in *Revolutions and Reconstructions: Black Politics in the Long Nineteenth Century*, ed. Van Gosse and David Waldstreicher, 24–40 (Philadelphia: U of Pennsylvania P, 2020), 24–40; and Michael Monescalchi, "Phillis Wheatley, Samuel Hopkins, and the Rise of Disinterested Benevolence," *Early American Literature* 54.2 (Spring 2019): 413–44.

2. On PW's "politically savvy" interactions with major political figures in America and Britain, see especially Waldstreicher, "Phillis Wheatley: The Poet Who Challenged the American Revolutionaries," in *Revolutionary Founders: Rebels, Radicals, and Reformers in the Making of the Nation*, ed. Alfred F. Young, Gary B. Nash, and Ray Raphael, 97–113 (New York: Vintage, 2011), 98, 105–16.

3. Vincent Carretta, *Phillis Wheatley: Biography of a Genius in Bondage* (Athens: U of Georgia P, 2011), 159–61.

4. PW to Samson Occom, 11 February 1774, in PW, *Complete Writings*, 152–53.

5. Contemporaneous African Americans in Boston used similar terms. On the phrase "civil and religious liberty" and the metaphor of the "breast" fired by "the spirit of freedom," compare the printed broadside of a letter by Peter Bestes, Sambo Freeman, Felix Holbrook, and Chester Joie to local representatives in Boston (20 April 1773), in *Black Americans in the Revolutionary Era: A Brief History with Documents*, ed. Woody Holton (New York: Bedford/St. Martin's, 2009), document 8, 46–47.

6. PW, "To the Right Honourable WILLIAM, Earl of DARTMOUTH, His Majesty's Principle Secretary of State for North-America, &c." On the political context and meanings of the poem, see especially Carretta, *Genius*, 130–33; Waldstreicher, "Challenged," 97–100; and Woody Holton, *Liberty Is Sweet: The Hidden History of the American Revolution* (New York: Simon & Schuster, 2021), 122–24. For her concept of liberty, see also the two variants of the poem reprinted in this edition and her late "LIBERTY and PEACE, A POEM" (1784), in PW, *Complete Writings*, 39–40, 128–31, 101–2.

7. James Sidbury, *Becoming African in America: Race and Nation in the Early Black Atlantic, 1760–1830* (New York: Oxford UP, 2007), chap. 1.

8. On this displacement in the terms of her emergent evangelical ethics of disinterestedness, see Montescalchi, "Disinterested Benevolence."

9. On the sense of "African dignity and self-worth" as well as the connection between "familial terms" of her language of natural rights in this poem

preceding Thomas Paine's *Common Sense*, see Zafar, *We Wear the Mask*, 21–22.
10. Ralph Ellison, *Invisible Man* (1952; London: Penguin, 1965), 462–63.
11. PW to Occom, in *Complete Writings*, 153.
12. Ellison, *Invisible Man*, 467.
13. Albert Murray, *The Omni-Americans: Some Alternatives to the Folklore of White Supremacy* (New York: Da Capo, 1970), 43–44; compare 37, 39. On Ellison and Murray's friendship and shared views, see Henry Louis Gates Jr., "King of Cats: Albert Murray," in *The Henry Louis Gates, Jr. Reader*, ed. Abby Wolf, 313–31 (New York: Basic Civitas, 2012) (originally published in the *New Yorker*, 8 April 1996, 70–81).
14. W. E. B. Du Bois, *The Souls of Black Folk* (Oxford: Oxford UP, 2007), 13–14; compare 44.
15. This comparative European perspective is not meant to suggest, of course, that the historical result of harvesting great works of philosophy and literature made a situation worthwhile in which children were sold away from their parents. For a succinct discussion of the "compensatory" dangers of "culturalist" readings that one-sidedly celebrate African American agency without properly appreciating the heavy obstacles and material dangers early African Americans had to face, often causing their hopes and projects to fail, see Rael, *Black Identity*, 8–11. My account of Wheatley's Enlightenment tries to do justice to this point within intellectual and literary history. It hopes to convey the autonomy and creativity of African American intellectuals, but it understands them as partly tragic in nature. For a long time various factors combined, for example, to deny African American accounts of rationality their originality and transhistorical impact, following the conceit that they were by necessity derivative of, or complicit with, supposedly preexistent, hegemonic "white" standards.
16. For this dialectical argument on paradoxical creativity in Jefferson's involuntary "midwifing" function for African American literature, see Gates, *Trials*.
17. Shields, *Poetics*, 43–69; Shields, *Phillis Wheatley and the Romantics* (Knoxville: U of Tennessee P, 2010). *De la littérature des nègres* (1808) by the Abbé Grégoire places a great emphasis on translating and discussing Wheatley's poetry, while repeatedly criticizing Jefferson. However, his work likely exerted a far greater influence on Haitian than on African American authors. I am indebted to Marie-Jeanne Rossignol's lecture "Revisiting 'An Enquiry Concerning the Literature of Negroes' by the Abbé Grégoire, 1808: New Research on the First Anthology of African American Literature," at the Kennedy-Institute for North American Studies, Freie Universität Berlin, 18 May 2022.

18. Carretta, *Genius*, 188–91.
19. Gates, *Trials*, 74–84.
20. Ibid., 82–83.
21. See, e.g., Christina Sharpe, *In the Wake: On Blackness and Being* (Durham, NC: Duke UP, 2016), 41–45, 52–53; and Kendi, *Stamped*, chap. 8.
22. Gates, *Figures*, 67–79; Gates, "In Her Own Write," series introduction to *The Schomburg Library of Nineteenth-Century Black Women Writers* (New York: Oxford UP, 1988); Gates, *Trials*, 68–74; 81; Jacqueline Bacon, *Freedom's Journal: The First African-American Newspaper* (Lanham, MD: Lexington, 2007), 85; Shields, *Romantics*; Caretta, *Genius*, 197–202; Kabria Baumgartner, *In Pursuit of Knowledge: Black Women and Educational Activism in Antebellum America* (New York: New York UP, 2019), 201; Lurana D. O'Malley, "'Why I Wrote the Phyllis Wheatley-Pageant Play': Mary Church Terrell's Bicentennial Activism," *Theatre History Studies*, 27 (2018): 225–55. Especially as part of the African American women's club movement, clubs and educational institutions were named in Wheatley's honor.
23. Gates, *Trials*, 50–51.
24. Lemuel Haynes, "Liberty Further Extended," in *The Literatures of Colonial America: An Anthology*, ed. Susan Castillo and Ivy Schweitzer, 573–80 (Malden, MA: Blackwell, 2001), 573.
25. Frederick Douglass, "What to the Slave Is the Fourth of July?," a speech delivered in Rochester, New York, on 5 July 1852 and published as a pamphlet (Rochester, 1852), in *The Essential Douglass: Selected Writings & Speeches*, ed. and introd. Nicholas Buccola, 50–71 (Indianapolis: Hackett, 2016), 53.
26. Frederick Douglass, "The American Colonization Society. Speech in Faneuil Hall, June 8, 1849," *Liberator*, 8 June 1849, reprinted in *The Life and Writings of Frederick Douglass*, ed. Philip S. Foner (New York: International Publishers), 1:387–99.

5. THE LESSONS OF REASON

1. That *principle* was a heavily contested term especially in the context of slavery is suggested, for instance, by Noah Webster's gradualist warning against "the danger of taking too deep hold of *principles*" concerning abolition. Quoted from the *American Minerva* (8 February 1796) in Sean Wilentz, *No Property in Man: Slavery and Antislavery at the Nation's Founding. With a New Preface* (Cambridge, MA: Harvard UP, 2021), 34. In her pamphlet *Religion and the Pure Principles of Morality* (1831), the Boston educator Maria Stewart claimed the term for her anthropology, illustrating what

made the universalism of *principle* potentially dangerous for gradualists: "Then why should one worm say to another, 'Keep you down there while I sit up yonder; for I am better than thou?' 'Tis not the color of the skin that makes the man, but it is the principles formed within the soul" (Porter, ed., *Early Negro Writing*, 461). By the end of the century, the concept had become so conventional that Charles Chesnutt could satirize it in his short story "A Matter of Principle" (1899), in *Portable Chesnutt*, 89–108.
2. TJ to Spencer Roane, 6 September 1819.
3. Quoted from Martin Delany's *Mystery* (16 September 1843) in Robert S. Levine, "Part I. Pittsburgh, the *Mystery*, Freemasonry," in *Martin R. Delany: A Documentary Reader*, ed. Levine, 25–29 (Chapel Hill: U of North Carolina P, 2003), 27. For an interpretation of Delany as a "rationalist," see Paul Gilroy's discussion of the serialized novel *Blake; or, the Huts of America*. However, Gilroy understands Delany's rationalism as part of the "politics of fulfilment [. . .] mostly content to play occidental rationality at its own game." The word *mostly* may be the most interesting one in this context (Gilroy, *Black Atlantic*, 19–29, 38 [quote]).
4. The "principles" of the Declaration were considered to be so timeless that, in a Fourth of July speech at the Banneker Institute in 1859, it could even make sense for the Philadelphia teacher Jacob White to make the anachronistic claim that Crispus Attucks had died for them in the Boston Massacre of 1770 (see Christopher J. Bonner, *Remaking the Republic: Black Politics and the Creation of American Citizenship* [Philadelphia: U of Pennsylvania P, 2020], 137–40).
5. On concepts from the American Revolution in early republican and antebellum antislavery and abolitionist arguments on both sides of the "color-line," see especially Quarles, "Antebellum Free Blacks and the 'Spirit of '76'"; Jacqueline Bacon, "'Do You Understand Your Own Language?' Revolutionary 'Topoi' in the Rhetoric of African-American Abolitionists," *Rhetoric Society Quarterly* 28.2 (Spring 1998): 55–57; Rael, *Black Identity*, esp. chap. 7, 255–61; Richard S. Newman, *The Transformation of American Abolitionism: Fighting Slavery in the Early Republic* (Chapel Hill: U of North Carolina P, 2002); John Stauffer, *The Black Hearts of Men: Radical Abolitionists and the Transformation of Race* (Cambridge, MA: Harvard UP, 2002); Jacqueline Bacon and Glen McGish, "Descendents of Africa, Sons of '76: Exploring African American Rhetoric," *Rhetoric Society Quarterly* 36 (2006): 1–29; Mia Bay, "See Your Declaration Americans!!! Abolitionism, Americanism, and the Revolutionary Tradition in Free Black Politics," in *Americanism: New Perspectives on the History of an Ideal*, ed. Michael Kazin and Joseph A. McCartin, 25–52 (Chapel Hill: U of North

Carolina P, 2006); Timothy P. McCarthy and John Stauffer, eds., *Prophets of Protest: Reconsidering the History of American Abolitionism* (New York: New Press, 2006); Richard S. Newman and Roy E. Finkenbine, eds., "Forum: Black Founders and the New Republic," *William and Mary Quarterly* 64.1 (January 2007); Drexler and White, eds., *Beyond Douglass*; Douglas R. Egerton, *Death or Liberty: African Americans and Revolutionary America* (New York: Oxford UP, 2009); Richard S. Newman, "Prince Hall, Richard Allen, and Daniel Coker: Revolutionary Black Founders, Revolutionary Black Communities," in *Revolutionary Founders: Rebels, Radicals, and Reformers in the Making of the Nation*, ed. Alfred S. Young, Gary B. Nash, and Ray Raphael, 305–21 (New York: Vintage, 2011); Edward Countryman, *Enjoy the Same Liberty: Black Americans in the Revolutionary Era* (Lanham, MD: Rowman & Littlefield, 2012); Manisha Sinha, *The Slave's Cause: A History of Abolition* (New Haven, CT: Yale UP, 2016), esp. chap. 2, 41–47; Christina Proenza-Coles, *American Founders: How People of African Descent Established Freedom in the New World*, with a foreword by Edward L. Ayers (Sydney: New South, 2019); Holton, *Liberty*; Paul J. Polgar, *Standard-Bearers of Equality: America's First Abolition Movement* (Chapel Hill: U of North Carolina P, 2019); Bonner, *Remaking*; Kate Masur, *Until Justice Be Done: America's First Civil Rights Movement, from the Revolution to Reconstruction* (New York: Norton, 2021); and David H. Fisher, *African Founders: How Enslaved People Expanded American Ideas* (New York: Simon & Schuster, 2022).

6. Martin Luther King Jr., "Letter from Birmingham City Jail," in *A Testament of Hope: The Essential Writings of Martin Luther King, Jr.*, ed. James Melvin Washington, 289–302 (San Francisco, CA: Harper & Row, 1986), 298.

7. James Forten, "Series of Letters by a Man of Colour," in *Pamphlets of Protest: An Anthology of Early African American Protest Literature, 1790–1860*, ed. Richard Newman, Patrick Rael, and Philip Lapsansky, 61–72 (New York: Routledge, 2001) (discussed below); Habermas, *Vernünftige Freiheit*. Although Habermas does not discuss Forten, Jefferson, or the African American tradition, his history of modern philosophy as the search to find purely secular criteria for the distinction between knowledge and belief, grounding natural right in "subjective human reason *alone*" (137), may offer an interesting perspective on the American context. Since Jefferson's Enlightenment of Feeling never arrived at a fully secular grounding, as has been shown, it may to a large extent have been the secular dimension of African Americans' rational transformations of Jefferson's Enlightenment—i.e., their rights claims in the secular present, as when referring to the man-made document of the Declaration of Independence

rather than directly to God—that contributed most decisively to this process in the early United States. White abolitionists would later also refer to the concept of *rational liberty* in the Declaration, as in Thaddeus Stevens's 1850 argument that "there can be no fanaticism, however high the enthusiasm, in the cause of rational, universal liberty—the liberty of the Declaration of Independence" (Stevens, "The California Question" [10 June 1850], in *The Selected Papers of Thaddeus Stevens*, ed. Beverly W. Palmer and Holly B. Ochoa, 2 vols. [Pittsburgh: Pittsburgh UP, 1997], 1:120).

8. See Kelleter, *Amerikanische Aufklärung*, chap. 11, 705–6 ("normative potential").
9. Charles Chesnutt, "The Disfranchisement of the Negro," in *Portable Chesnutt*, 478.
10. Lincoln's use of the metaphor from Proverbs 25:11 is in "Fragment on the Constitution and the Union" (ca. January 1861), in *The Collected Works of Abraham Lincoln*, ed. Roy P. Basler, 8 vols. (New Brunswick, NJ: Rutgers UP, 1953), 4:168–69.
11. Nero Brewster and other New Hampshire Slaves, "Petition to the New Hampshire Legislature (12 November 1779)," *Black Americans*, ed. Holton, 73 (document 20; my emphasis).
12. John Cuffee and other free blacks from Dartmouth, "Petition to the Massachusetts Legislature (10 February 1780)," *Black Americans*, ed. Holton 76 (document 21). On the activity involved in "apprehending" knowledge in the Dartmouth petition, see Bacon, "Descendents," 9–10.
13. On revolutionary language as a "lingua franca" for early African American abolitionists, see Bay, "See Your Declaration," 27.
14. See Eric Slauter, *The State as a Work of Art: The Cultural Origins of the Constitution* (Chicago: Chicago UP, 2009), chap. 4, 173–75 (on Haynes); 174 (on slavery as a "buried referent" in the late eighteenth-century language of rights); and Holton, *Liberty Is Sweet*, chap. 19, 248–49.
15. The phrase has become famous through Pauline Maier, *American Scripture: Making the Declaration of Independence* (New York: Knopf, 1997).
16. Saillant, *Black Puritan*, 15–46. On Haynes's place in nineteenth-century accounts of an "African" tradition of intellectuals, see Sinha, *Slave's Cause*, 44–45.
17. Ruth Bogin, "'Liberty Further Extended': A 1776 Antislavery Manuscript by Lemuel Haynes," *William and Mary Quarterly* 40.1 (January 1983): 85–105.
18. Compare Jefferson, "A Summary View of the Rights of British America": "a right which nature has given to all men, of [. . .] establishing new societies, under such laws and regulations as to them shall seem most likely to promote public happiness" (Jefferson, *Writings*, ed. Peterson, 105–6).

19. For the argument that in the original phrase *self-evidence* is grounded in syllogism, see Allen, *Our Declaration*, 160–70.
20. Saillant, *Black Puritan*, chap. 1, 15ff.; chap. 3, 87–90. For an analysis of Edwards's important role in shaping the American Enlightenment, see Kelleter, *Amerikanische Aufklärung*, chaps. 4–6, 189–377.
21. Haynes, "Liberty," 575.
22. Ibid., 574–75, 579.
23. On the importance of the sense of sight for Haynes's abolitionism, see Saillant, *Black Puritan*, 43–45.
24. Haynes, "Liberty," 574.
25. Ibid.
26. Ibid., 576. I have analyzed Haynes's position in African American discourses of blood at greater length in "Blood and Character in Early African American Literature," in *The Cultural Politics of Blood, 1500–1900*, ed. Kimberly Anne Coles, Ralph Bauer, Zita Nunes, and Carla L. Peterson, 146–67 (Basingstoke, UK: Palgrave, 2015).
27. Haynes, "Liberty," 576.
28. Ibid., 574.
29. Benjamin Banneker to TJ, 19 August 1791; TJ to Banneker, 30 August 1791.
30. McDonald, "Jefferson's Changing Reputation." I thank Andrew O'Shaughnessy for this observation, which highlights Banneker's prescience as well as the crucial role African American intellectuals have played from the start in the hermeneutics of the Declaration of Independence.
31. Gordon-Reed, "Engaging Jefferson," 173. On enslaved African Americans' manifold personal engagements with Jefferson, see Gordon-Reed, *Hemingses of Monticello*; and Gordon-Reed and Onuf, *Patriarchs*.
32. On Banneker's life and the historical impact of the letter, see Silvio A. Bedini, *The Life of Benjamin Banneker* (New York: Scribner, 1972); Angela G. Ray, "'In My Own Handwriting': Benjamin Banneker Addresses the Slaveholder at Monticello," *Rhetoric and Public Affairs* 1.3 (Fall 1998): 387–405; William Andrews, "Benjamin Banneker's Revision of Thomas Jefferson: Conscience vs. Science in the Early American Antislavery Debate," in *Genius in Bondage: Literature of the Early Black Atlantic*, ed. Vincent Carretta and Philip Gould, 218–41 (Lexington: UP of Kentucky, 2001); Newman, "White Uplift"; and Britt Rusert, *Fugitive Science: Empiricism and Freedom in Early African American Culture* (New York: New York UP, 2017), chap. 1:33–64.
33. Haynes, "Liberty," 574.
34. See Rusert, *Fugitive Science*, 39; and Herschthal, *Science of Abolition*, 57–58.

35. Forten, "Letters," Letter I, in *Pamphlets of Protest*, ed. Newman, Rael, and Lapsansky, 67.
36. See Julie Winch, *A Gentleman of Color: The Life of James Forten* (Oxford: Oxford UP, 2002), chap. 2, 30–31.
37. Forten, "Letters," Letter I, in *Pamphlets of Protest*, ed. Newman, Rael, and Lapsansky, 67.
38. Ibid., Letter IV, in *Pamphlets of Protest*, ed. Newman, Rael, and Lapsansky, 71.
39. Ibid.
40. George Lawrence, "Oration on the Abolition of the Slave Trade, Delivered on the First Day of January, 1813, in the African Methodist Episcopal Church," in Porter, ed., *Early Negro Writing*, 379.
41. Ibid.
42. Lawrence, "Oration," 381.
43. Alexander Crummell, "'The Assassination of President Garfield,' Preached Sunday, July 10, 1881," in *Destiny and Race. Selected Writings, 1840–1898*, ed. and introd. Wilson J. Moses (Amherst: U of Massachusetts P, 1992), 231.
44. Moses, "Introduction," *Destiny*, 5.
45. Crummell, "Assassination," *Destiny*, 229–30.
46. William Hamilton, "An Oration Delivered in the American Zion Church, on the Fourth of July, 1827, in Commemoration of the Abolition of Slavery in this State," in Porter, ed., *Early Negro Writing*, 96–104.
47. Gates, *Trials*, 62–63.
48. Bacon, *Freedom's Journal*, 89–91.
49. William Hamilton, "An Address to the New York African Society, for Mutual Relief, Delivered in the Universalist Church, January 2, 1809," in *Early Negro Writing*, 36. Irving's caricature is discussed in chapter 1.
50. Hamilton, "Oration," 97.
51. Ibid., 98–99. This part of Hamilton's speech was reprinted in *Freedom's Journal* on 12 October 1827.
52. Ibid., 101.
53. Ibid., 101–2 (my emphasis).
54. On Jefferson's role in *Walker's Appeal*, see especially Peter P. Hinks, *To Awaken My Afflicted Brethren: David Walker and the Problem of Antebellum Slave Resistance* (University Park: Pennsylvania State UP, 1997), 178–79, 206–9; Carla L. Peterson, *"Doers of the Word": African-American Women Speakers and Writers in the North (1830–1880)* (1995; New Brunswick, NJ: Rutgers UP, 1998), 64–65; Gates, *Trials*, 57–62; Ian F. Finseth, *Shades of Green: Visions of Nature in the Literature of American Slavery,*

1770–1860 (Athens: U of Georgia P, 2009), 171; John Saillant, "Aspirant Citizenship," in *Beyond Douglass*, ed. Drexler and White, 123–40; Jarrett, *Representing*, chap 1; and Peter Thompson, "David Walker's Nationalism—and Thomas Jefferson's," *Journal of the Early Republic* 37.1 (Spring 2017): 47–80.

55. David Walker, *David Walker's Appeal to the Coloured Citizens of the World*, ed. and introd. Peter P. Hinks (University Park: Pennsylvania State UP, 2000), 6–7.
56. I have discussed the question of Walker's audience at greater length in "Cosmopolitanism, Character, and the Theories of Early African American Literature," in *African American Literature in Transition, 1830–1850*, ed. Benjamin Fagan, 177–201 (Cambridge: Cambridge UP, 2021).
57. Walker, *Walker's Appeal*, 2.
58. E.g., Walker, *Walker's Appeal*, 6: "I will not here speak of the destructions which the Lord brought upon Egypt. [. . .] I say, I shall not take up time to speak of the causes which produced so much wretchedness and massacre among the heathen nations, for I am aware that you know too well, that God is just [. . .]. I shall leave almost unnoticed, that avaricious and cruel people, the Portuguese [. . .] I shall occupy but a little time, leaving a plenty of room for the candid and unprejudiced to reflect."
59. TJ, *Notes*, 64.
60. Walker, *Walker's Appeal*, 4.
61. Ibid., 5.
62. Ibid., 30. The concept of "enlightening" the enslaved was also strong, for instance, in the work of an author of the following generation who might seem quite far removed from Walker in terms of profession, gender, region, religion, and politics: the successful Cincinnati hairdresser Eliza Potter. As she put it in her 1859 autobiography, "Some will say it is very queer and they can not understand how the slaves get so enlightened; it is very easily understood. Some of them are very easily learned, and if a family has a favorite servant they will treat them as one of the family, but for the slightest offense they will sell them, and if they can, to the farthest plantation possible, and they will of course teach others. When I commenced going down South, a widow and an overseer could, without difficulty manage a hundred slaves, now it takes three overseers and the master to rule the same number; times are fast, masters and mistresses are more enlightened, and so are the servants" (Eliza Potter, *A Hairdresser's Experience in High Life*, ed. Xiomara Santamarina [Chapel Hill: U of North Carolina P, 2009], 92).

63. Walker, *Walker's Appeal*, 22–27.
64. TJ to Isaac Story, 5 December 1801; compare TJ to John Adams, 14 March 1820; TJ to Edmund Randolph, 3 February 1794; TJ to Hugh White, 28 April 1812. The "pillow of ignorance" is discussed at greater length in chapter 1. On the biographical context of the pillow metaphor related to slavery, see also Wilkins, *Jefferson's Pillow*, 4.
65. TJ, *Notes*, 33.
66. Jefferson's own repertory included classical Enlightenment attacks on ignorance as well, especially on a national level. See, e.g., TJ to Charles Yancey, 6 January 1816: "if a nation expects to be ignorant & free, in a state of civilisation, it expects what never was & never will be."
67. Walker, *Walker's Appeal*, 33–35.
68. Ibid., 72.
69. On Walker's typographical radicalism, see Hinks, *To Awaken*, esp. 193–95; Robert S. Levine, *Dislocating Race and Nation: Episodes in Nineteenth-Century American Literary Nationalism* (Chapel Hill: U of North Carolina P, 2008), 98–99; Alex W. Black, "Abolitionism's Resonant Bodies: The Realization of African American Performance," *American Quarterly* 63.3 (September 2011): 619–20; and Marcy J. Dinius, "'Look!! Look!!! At This!!!!': The Radical Typography of David Walker's *Appeal*," *PMLA* 126.1 (2011): 55–57.
70. Walker, *Walker's Appeal*, 78–79.
71. Ibid., 79.
72. Ibid., 27.
73. TJ to Henry Lee, 8 May 1825.
74. Walker, *Walker's Appeal*, 73.
75. Maria W. Stewart, "Religion and the Pure Principles of Morality, the Sure Foundation on Which We Must Build, Productions from the Pen of Mrs Maria W. Stewart," in Porter, ed., *Early Negro Writing*, 471.
76. See Hinks, *To Awaken*, 113–15.
77. Maria W. Stewart, "An Address Delivered at the African Masonic Hall, Boston, February 27, 1833," in *Pamphlets of Protest*, ed. Newman, Rael, and Lapsansky, 123. Compare Stewart, "Religion and the Pure Principles of Morality," 460, 461, 466.
78. Maria W. Stewart, "Religion and the Pure Principles of Morality," 470.
79. Henry Highland Garnet, *Walker's Appeal, with a Brief Sketch of his Life, by Henry Highland Garnet, and Also Garnet's Address to the Slaves of the United States of America* (New York: Tobitt, 1848). The edition may have been sponsored by John Brown (see Levine, *Dislocating*, 116–17). On the context of Garnet's controversial "Address," see also Bonner, *Remaking*, 63–65.

80. Garnet, "Address to the Slaves of the United States," in *Pamphlets of Protest*, ed. Newman, Rael, and Lapsansky, 161.
81. William Wells Brown, "An Appeal to the People of Great Britain and the World" (August 1, 1851), in *Clotel and Other Writings*, ed. Ezra Greenspan (New York: Library of America, 2014), 878–80.
82. William Wells Brown, *Clotel; or, The President's Daughter: A Narrative of Slave Life in the United States*, ed. with an introduction and notes by M. Giulia Fabi (New York: Penguin, 2004), 1; William Craft, preface to *Running a Thousand Miles for Freedom*, by William and Ellen Craft (1860; New York: Arno and New York Times, 1969), iii; Solomon Northup, *Twelve Years a Slave: Narrative of Solomon Northup, a Citizen of New York, Kidnapped in Washington in 1841, and Rescued in 1853, from a Cotton Plantation near the Red River in Louisiana* (Auburn, Buffalo, and London, 1853), 56; 207; James Monroe Whitfield, "America," in *The Works of James M. Whitfield: America and Other Writings by a Nineteenth-Century African American Poet*, ed. Robert S. Levine and Ivy G. Wilson (Chapel Hill: U of North Carolina P, 2011), 4–46. The Crafts' sensational escape from slavery in 1848, with Ellen dressing up as a disabled white man accompanied by his ostensible slave William, served as the inspiration for Clotel's fictional cross-dressing in the novel.
83. In the second and third editions of *Walker's Appeal*, Walker described "the English" as "the greatest benefactors we have upon earth." On the changes Walker made between editions, which also concerned the spelling of the word *Coloured* in the title, see Hinks, "Editor's Notes," in *Walker's Appeal*, xlix–l. On African American forms of Anglophilia more broadly, see Elisa Tamarkin, *Anglophilia: Deference, Devotion, and Antebellum America* (Chicago: U of Chicago P, 2008), 178–246.
84. Brown, *Clotel and Other Writings*, 878n80. It is not included, for instance, in *We, the Other People: Alternative Declarations of Independence by Labor Groups, Farmers, Woman's Rights Advocates, Socialists, and Blacks, 1829–1975*, ed. with introduction and notes by Philip S. Foner (Urbana: U of Illinois P, 1976). This collection includes instead the "Negro Declaration of Independence by the National Independent Political Union, February, 1876" and the "Black Declaration of Independence, by the National Committee of Black Churchmen, July 4, 1970," which may be interpreted as following in the footsteps of Brown's *Appeal*. Compare *Other People*, 89–94, 163–69.
85. John Adams to Benjamin Rush, 21 June 1821.
86. Gates, *Trials*, 63–65.
87. Bacon, *Freedom's Journal*, 89–91. This threat continued to be relevant later. See, e.g., the account of the Fourth of July, 1834, in Samuel Ringgold

Ward, *Autobiography of a Fugitive Negro: His Antislavery Labours in the United States, Canada, & England* (1855; New York: Arno, 1968), 46–47: "It was Independence Day—a day, of all days, sacred to freedom. What Mr. Brown came to tell us was, that the principles, enunciated in a few words, in the Declaration of Independence—'We hold these truths to be self-evident truths, that all men are created equal, and are endowed by their Creator with certain inalienable rights, among which are life liberty, and the pursuit of happiness'—applied as well to black men as to white men. This the aristocracy of New York could not endure; and therefore, just fifty-eight years from the very hour that the Declaration of 1776 was made, the mob of the New York merchants broke up this assembly."

88. Douglass, "What to the Slave," 54; Ellison, "The Little Man at Chehaw Station: The American Artist and His Audience," in *The Collected Essays of Ralph Ellison*, ed. and introd. John F. Callahan, preface by Saul Bellow (New York: Modern Library, 1995), 501.
89. Douglass, "What to the Slave," 53.
90. Ibid., 54 ("eternal principles").
91. Ibid., 70.
92. Ibid., 55.
93. Ibid., 71.
94. Ibid., 70.
95. Ibid., 52.
96. In his near-contemporaneous novella *The Heroic Slave* (1853), Douglass identified its protagonist, the historical Madison Washington who led a successful slave uprising on the slaver *Creole* in 1841, with "the principles of 1776" (Douglass, *The Heroic Slave: A Cultural and Critical Edition*, ed. John R. McKivigan, John Stauffer, and Robert S. Levine [New Haven, CT: Yale UP, 2015], 50–51). See also Kelvin C. Black, "Bound by 'the Principles of 1776': Dilemmas in Anglo-American Romanticism and Douglass's *The Heroic Slave*," *Studies in Romanticism* 56.1 (Spring 2017): 93–112.
97. Douglass, "What to the Slave," 60.
98. The evolution of the veil metaphor from Wheatley and Jefferson to the twentieth century is the subject of chapter 8.

6. MALIGNANT PREJUDICE

1. William J. Wilson ("Ethiop"), "What Shall We Do with the White People?," *Anglo-African Magazine* 2.2 (February 1860): 41–45; reprinted in *Black on White: Black Writers on What It Means to Be White*, ed. and introd. David R. Roediger (New York: Schocken, 1998), 58–66; Wheatley, "To the University of CAMBRIDGE, in NEW ENGLAND," in PW, *Complete*

Writings, 11–12. Wilson had not been the first to invert the relation between subject and object in Jefferson's question: James McCune Smith's 1859 *Anglo-African* article on the subject quoted Jefferson's question verbatim; it will conclude this chapter. For instance, after Wilson, Robert Hamilton (brother to the *Anglo-African*'s editor, Thomas Hamilton) would again take up Jefferson's question, in an editorial in the *Weekly Anglo-African* on 23 November 1861 ("What Shall Be Done with the Slaves?") and so would Frederick Douglass, as in "The Black Man's Future in the Southern States" (1862), in *Douglass Papers*, 3:499 ("What shall be done with the four million slaves if emancipated?") or in his speech "The Mission of the War" (13 January 1864), in *Douglass Papers*, 4: 12. See also his speech at the Annual Meeting of the Massachusetts Anti-Slavery Society in Boston on 26 January 1865, "What the Black Man Wants," in *Essential Douglass*, ed. Buccola, 196. In this speech, which was published in the *Liberator* on 10 February 1865, Douglass repeated the question and answered, "Do nothing with us! Your doing with us has already played the mischief with us."

2. On Wilson's double discourse in this article, see Mia Bay, *The White Image in the Black Mind: African-American Ideas about White People, 1830–1925* (New York: Oxford UP, 2000), 75–77; and Derrick R. Spires, *The Practice of Citizenship: Black Politics and Print Culture in the Early United States* (Philadelphia: U of Pennsylvania P, 2019), 161–63. On the uniquely ambitious format of the *Anglo-African Magazine*, see Ivy G. Wilson, "THE BRIEF AND WONDROUS LIFE OF THE ANGLO-AFRICAN MAGAZINE Or, Antebellum African American Editorial Practice and Its Afterlives," in *Publishing Blackness: Textual Constructions of Race since 1850*, ed. George Hutchinson and John K. Young, 18–37 (Ann Arbor: U of Michigan P, 2012).

3. Robert Finley, *Thoughts on the Colonization of Free Blacks* (Washington, DC, 1816), 1. For a discussion of Finley and the founding of the American Colonization Society (ACS) in 1816, see Polgar, *Standard-Bearers of Equality*, 229–36. On colonization more broadly, see especially David Brion Davis, *The Problem of Slavery in the Age of Emancipation* (New York: Knopf, 2014), chaps. 3–7. On Jefferson's nineteenth-century views on colonization, see TJ to Jared Sparks, 4 February 1824.

4. TJ, *Notes*, 143.

5. Onuf, *Jefferson's Empire*, 147–88; Onuf, *Mind of Jefferson*, 205–35. The exception is a letter to the double agent Edward Bancroft, 26 January 1789, in which Jefferson claimed he was planning to import Germans and "intermingle" them with the formerly enslaved as tenants on small farms, so that their children could become "good citizens."

6. On African Americans as imagined "problem-people" located "*outside* the systems of order and rationality," see Lewis R. Gordon, "African-American Philosophy, Race, and the Geography of Reason," in *Not Only the Master's Tools*, ed. Gordon and Gordon, 7.
7. Wilson, "What Shall We Do," 65.
8. Bruce Dain reads *Notes* as a "home-grown interpretation of an increasingly obsolescent natural philosophy" in *Hideous Monster*, chap. 1, 37–38.
9. TJ, *Notes*, 143.
10. Wilson, "What Shall We Do," 60. "Glittering generalities" had become a catchphrase in the polarized debates on the Declaration in the years leading up to the Civil War, likely coined by an 1856 public letter by the Massachusetts Whig Rufus Choate announcing his support for the Democrats ("the glittering and sounding generalities of natural rights which make up the Declaration of Independence") (see Peterson, *Jefferson Image*, 201–2).
11. Wilson, "What Shall We Do," 59, 60, 62, 64, 62, 61.
12. Du Bois, *Souls*, 7.
13. For Douglass's discussion of who constituted "the problem" in American society, see, e.g., his pamphlet "The Nation's Problem: A Speech Delivered by Frederick Douglass, before the Bethel Literary and Historical Society (Washington, DC: Bethel Literary and Historical Society, 1889)," in *Essential Douglass*, ed. Buccola, 314–31; and "The Race Problem: Great Speech by Frederick Douglass, delivered before the Bethel Library and Historical Association, in the Metropolitan A.M.E. Church, Washington, D.C., 28 October, 1890," Daniel Murray Pamphlet Collection, African American Perspectives: Materials Selected from the Rare Books Collections, Rare Book and Special Collections Division, Library of Congress, https://www.loc.gov/resource/lcrbmrp.t0c13/. On this speech, see Andrew Hammann, *Freedom in Black and White: The Politics of Slavery and Black Expatriation in Nineteenth-Century America* (Charlottesville: U of Virginia P, forthcoming).
14. For excellent studies on African American ethnographic counterarguments to Query XIV, see Bay, *White Image*; Dain, *Hideous Monster*; Rusert, *Fugitive Science*; and Herschthal, *Science of Abolition*.
15. PW, *Complete Writings*, 13.
16. See Melish, "'Condition' Debate," 653; Rael, *Black Identity*, 180–83; and Bacon, *Freedom's Journal*, 101–8.
17. Finley, *Thoughts*, 5.
18. St. George Tucker, *Dissertation on Slavery: With a Proposal for the Gradual Abolition of It, in the State of Virginia* (Philadelphia, 1796). Like Jefferson, Tucker refrained from committing himself in the question of "natural" inferiority. As he explained in a footnote, "[e]arly prejudices, had we more

satisfactory information than we can possibly possess on the subject at present, would render an inhabitant of a country where Negroe slavery prevails, an improper umpire between them [i.e., David Hume and James Beattie]." Unlike later colonizationists, he still paid lip service to the possibility of the eventual disappearance of prejudice: "Under such an arrangement we might reasonably hope, that time would either remove from us a race of men, whom we wish not to incorporate with us, or obliterate those prejudices, which now form an obstacle to such incorporation." On Tucker's notion of prejudice in the Virginia context of Jefferson and George Wythe, see Melvin Patrick Ely, "Richard and Julia Randolph, St. George Tucker, George Wythe, Syphax Brown, and Hercules White: Racial Equality and the Snares of Prejudice," in *Revolutionary Founders*, ed. Young et al., 323–36; and in relation to the emergent ideology of the ACS, see Polgar, *Standard-Bearers*, 212–29.

19. On these arguments by colonizationists, see Fredrickson, *Black Image*, chap. 1; Rael, *Black Identity*, 163, 180–82; Bacon, *Freedom's Journal*, 62, 130, 187–88; and Polgar, *Standard-Bearers*, 250–60. On the theological background of admitting white prejudice without censoring it, see especially Davis's discussion of Leonard Bacon's 1823 "Report on Colonization," in *Age of Emancipation*, chap. 6, esp. 155–62.

20. Douglass, "American Colonization Society," *Liberator* (8 June 1849), in Douglass, *Life and Writings*, 1:387–99. In the beginning of the Civil War, Douglass also criticized "the arrogant and malignant nonsense about natural repellancy and the incompatibility of races" in Abraham Lincoln's rhetoric ("'The President and His Speeches,' and essay published in *Douglass' Monthly*, September 1862," in *Essential Douglass*, 181). On Douglass's nuanced concept of conventional rather than natural prejudice, see Peter C. Myers, *Frederick Douglass: Race and the Rebirth of American Liberalism* (Lawrence: UP of Kansas, 2008), 161–66.

21. To some extent, this nineteenth-century view may go back to Edmund Burke's positive concept of prejudice as "latent wisdom" (Burke, *Reflections*, 74–75).

22. On Allen's life, see R. J. M. Blackett, "William G. Allen: The Forgotten Professor," *Civil War History* 26.1 (1980): 39–52. Allen's love story would be fictionalized by Louisa May Alcott. See Sarah Elbert, "An Inter-Racial Love Story in Fact and Fiction: William and Mary King Allen's Marriage and Louisa May Alcott's Tale, 'M.L.,'" *History Workshop Journal* 53.1 (Spring 2002): 17–42.

23. William G. Allen, "Letter from William G. Allen," *Frederick Douglass' Paper* 5.19 (29 April 1852): 3.

24. I have taken the term *white uplift* from Richard Newman's illuminating discussion of Banneker's letter to Jefferson in "White Uplift."
25. On antebellum black uplift as a potentially empowering and unifying end in itself rather than an attempt to please white Americans, see Rael, *Black Identity*; Elizabeth McHenry, *Forgotten Readers: Recovering the Lost History of African American Literary Societies* (Durham, NC: Duke UP, 2002); Bacon, *Freedom's Journal*, chap. 4; and Erica L. Ball, *To Live an Antislavery Life: Personal Politics and the Making of the Black Middle Class* (Athens: U of Georgia P, 2015). For a more traditionally negative assessment of uplift as the flawed ideology of an insufficiently politicized African American middle class, going back to E. Franklin Frazier's polemic against the black bourgeoisie, see, e.g., Kevin R. Gaines, *Uplifting the Race: Black Leadership, Politics, and Culture in the Twentieth Century* (Chapel Hill: U of North Carolina P, 1996). In her recent memoir, Annette Gordon-Reed has analyzed an additional reason for the twentieth-century loss of cultural capital of black uplift. A rarely discussed fact of school integration in the South, she shows in the history of her family, was that often African American teachers no longer taught after the schools were integrated, whereas white teachers continued to teach. As a result, the functions of teaching and of role models in African American communities changed significantly, and the "explicit mission of race uplift" lost personal appeal and prestige (Gordon-Reed, *On Juneteenth* [New York: Liveright, 2021], 49–53, 50 [quote]).
26. Benjamin Banneker to TJ, 19 August 1791; Jefferson to Banneker, 30 August 1791. On the implications of the publication of the exchange as "the formal start of black Americans' conflicted political engagement" with Jefferson, see Gordon-Reed, *Hemingses of Monticello*, 474–79; see also Gordon-Reed, "Engaging Jefferson," 173–74.
27. Writers from William Wells Brown, Martin Delany, and William Still to George Washington Williams in his *History of the Negro Race in America, 1619–1880* (1882) reflected on the Banneker-Jefferson correspondence. The reproduction of Jefferson's polite answer sometimes had the effect, as in the work of Williams, of painting a relatively rosy picture of Jefferson. On the long-term significance of the Banneker-Jefferson exchange, see especially Andrews, "Banneker's Revision"; Newman, "White Uplift"; Rusert, *Fugitive Science*, 33–64; and Herschthal, *Science of Abolition*, 48–59.
28. William G. Allen, *Wheatley, Banneker, and Horton* (Boston, 1849).
29. TJ, *Notes*, 140.
30. Ibid., 138. As discussed in chapter 4, this analogy was not only widely criticized at the time but constituted a blatant, and likely intentional, anachronism also by Jefferson's own standards.

31. Ibid., 138–43.
32. Martin Delany, "Not Fair," *Mystery*, 16 December 1846, in *Martin R. Delany: A Documentary Reader*, ed. Robert S. Levine (Chapel Hill: U of North Carolina P, 2003), 32–33. On the evolution of Delany's reputation as "the" nineteenth-century personification of race pride, from his *Origin and Objects of Ancient Freemasonry* (1853) and *Principia of Ethnology: The Origin of Races and Color* (1879) to the 1960s, see Robert S. Levine, introduction to *Documentary Reader*, 1–22; 2–6. On the significance of the pseudonyms in *Frederick Douglass' Paper*—Wilson's "Ethiop" in conversation with James McCune Smith's "Communipaw" and Philip Bell's "Cosmopolite"—see Peterson, *Black Gotham*, 217–22.
33. For a sophisticated example, in recent historiography, of the tradition of reading XVIII against XIV, with a tendency to assume that XIV presented the more authentic version of Jefferson, see Fields and Fields, *Racecraft*. For a concise discussion of the antislavery content of Banneker's almanacs, see Sinha, *Slave's Cause*, 144–46.
34. William Still, "Self-Improvement," *Weekly Anglo-African*, 17 March 1860.
35. Banneker to Jefferson, 19 August 1791.
36. TJ, *Notes*, 162–63. African American readings of Query XVIII will be discussed in chapter 7.
37. TJ to Edward Coles, 25 August 1814. Compare *Freedom's Journal* 1.6–7 (20 and 27 April 1827), which reprinted on its front page an article from the *Christian Recorder* entitled "People of Colour" that heavily criticized Jefferson's gradualism in the Coles letter ("the facts are all the other way"). The article saw the root of the problem in the "feeling of the planters."
38. TJ, *Notes*, 138.
39. For the source and interpretation of this fascinating letter, which may or may not have been written by an enslaved African American, see Thomas N. Baker, "'A Slave' Writes to Thomas Jefferson," *William and Mary Quarterly* 68.1 (January 2011): 127–54. On page 127, "A Slave" repeats the term *pitiful* in the context of America's epistemological and moral confusion: "'Treason and Integrity, Religion and Superstition, Reason and Error, go hand in hand in the world, and the tyrant & the priest of every pitiful teritory arbitrarily decide by law, which is truth & which is error.' This is just the pitiful case in America."
40. PW, "A Hymn to Humanity," in PW, *Complete Writings*, 51.
41. TJ, *Notes*, 160, as discussed in chapter 3. Ironically, TJ's own undisguised performance of "deep rooted prejudices" under Query XIV may thus originally have been intended to illustrate that, contrary to today's estimate, he prided himself on not being a hypocrite.

42. The *Colored American*, 13 March 1841, is quoted and discussed in Patrick Rael's illuminating chapter on prejudice in relation to antebellum discourses of respectability (Rael, *Black Identity*, 157–208, esp. 173–79).
43. This conceptual ambiguity concerning the subject-object relation would later plague the uplift metaphor as well, as suggested by the specification in the motto of the National Association of Colored Women (NACW) in the 1890s, "Lifting As We Climb."
44. Robert Hamilton, *Weekly Anglo-African*, 23 November 1861.
45. Sinha, *Slave's Cause*, 150–52.
46. William Hamilton, "An Address to the New York African Society, for Mutual Relief, Delivered in the Universalist Church, January 2, 1809," in *Early Negro Writing*, ed. Porter, 36; compare TJ, *Notes*, 142.
47. PW, "To Maecenas," in PW, *Complete Writings*, 10; Ward, *Fugitive Negro*, 87; James McCune Smith, "The Destiny of the People of Color" (1843), in McCune Smith, *Works*, ed. Stauffer, 53.
48. Hamilton, "Address," 36.
49. Irving's caricature of Jefferson is discussed in chapter 1. On the inspiration James Mc Cune Smith took from Irving's *History of New York*, see Peterson, *Black Gotham*, 219–20.
50. On the self-consciously simple appearance of Jefferson's Enlightenment of Feeling, see chapter 1.
51. TJ, *Notes*, 162; Hamilton, "Address," 36.
52. Hamilton, "Address," 37; TJ, *Notes*, 138.
53. Joseph Sidney, "An Oration, Commemorative of the Abolition of the Atlantic Slave Trade in the United States; Delivered before the Wilberforce Philanthropic Association, in the City of New York on the Second of January, 1809," in *Early Negro Writing*, ed. Porter, 361–62. For further differences between the two speeches and a third speech in New York on this day, by Henry Sipkins at the African Zion Church, see Leslie Alexander, *African or American? Black Identity and Political Activism in New York City, 1784–1861* (Urbana: U of Illinois P, 2008), 19–22.
54. On the political and cultural relationship between Federalism and antislavery, see Rachel Hope Cleves, "'Hurtful to the State': The Political Morality of Federalist Antislavery," in *Contesting Slavery*, ed. Hammond and Mason, 207–26, 219–20 (on Sidney).
55. William Hamilton, "An Oration Delivered in the African Zion Church on the Fourth of July, 1827, in Commemoration of the Abolition of Domestic Slavery in this State," in *Early Negro Writing*, ed. Porter, 98–100. For the context of the speech and the ensuing debate on whether to celebrate abolition on July Fourth or Fifth, including in *Freedom's Journal*,

see Alexander, *African or American*, 54–65; and Peterson, *Black Gotham*, 71–74.
56. On the hierarchy implied in feelings of pity, compare, e.g., Samuel Ringgold Ward's refusal to ask for pity: "Wronged, outraged, 'scattered, peeled, killed all the day long,' as they are, I never so compromised my own self-respect, nor ever consented to so deep a degradation of my people, as to condescend to ask pity for them at the hands of their oppressors" (Ward, *Autobiography*, 86). As described by Leslie Alexander and Carla Peterson above, as young boys both Ward and McCune Smith partook in the New York July Fifth parade in 1827.
57. Hamilton, "Oration," 97.
58. William Hamilton, "Address to the National Convention of 1834," in *Pamphlets of Protest*, ed. Newman, Rael, and Lapsansky, 111–13.
59. Lawrence, "Oration on the Atlantic Slave Trade," in *Early Negro Writing*, ed. Porter, 380.
60. Ibid.
61. Walker, *Walker's Appeal*, 16.
62. Ibid., 17.
63. Ibid., 18.
64. Ibid., 12; compare 15.
65. Ibid., 25–27, 29.
66. Ibid., 35.
67. TJ to Condorcet, 30 August 1791. On 25 February 1809, he expressed similar sentiments in a letter to the Abbé Grégoire, who had sent him his *De la littérature des nègres*, but retracted some of them in an oft-discussed letter to Joel Barlow, 8 October 1809 ("I have a long letter from Banneker which shews him to have had a mind of very common stature indeed. as to Bishop Gregoire, I wrote him, as you have done, a very soft answer").
68. Parkinson, *Common Cause*; Onuf, *Virginians*, 8–9.
69. Walker, *Walker's Appeal*, 12, 14–18, 29; compare 30: "For my part, I am glad Mr. Jefferson has advanced his positions for our sake, for you will either have to contradict or confirm him by your own actions, and not by what our friends have said or done for us."
70. Ibid., 17, 30; compare 29.
71. Ibid., 17.
72. Ibid., e.g., 19–20, 22, 26.
73. Ibid., 6–7.
74. Ibid., 6, 77.
75. Ibid., 47.
76. Ibid., 45, 73.

77. Ibid., 58 (my emphasis).
78. Ibid., 73.
79. For a broad discussion of the impact of *Walker's Appeal*, see Hinks, *To Awaken My Afflicted Brethren*, chap. 5, 116–72.
80. William Hamilton, "An Oration, on the Abolition of the Slave Trade [. . .] By William Hamilton, a Descendant of Africa," in *Early Negro Writing*, ed. Porter, 399.
81. Quoted from Amos Beman's scrapbooks, 2:4 in Hinks, *To Awaken*, 114.
82. Maria W. Stewart, "Religion and the Pure Principles of Morality," in *Early Negro Writing*, ed. Porter, 470.
83. Henry Highland Garnet, *The Past and Present Condition and Destiny of the Colored Race: A Discourse Delivered at the Fifteenth Anniversary of the Female Benevolent Society of Troy, New York, February 14, 1848* (Miami, FL: Mnemosyne, 1969), 28.
84. Sinha, *Slave's Cause*, 418.
85. Henry Highland Garnet, "Address to the Slaves of the United States" (1848), in *Pamphlets of Protest*, ed. Newman, Rael, and Lapsansky, 164.
86. Levine, *Dislocating*, 116–17.
87. Hosea Easton, *A Treatise on the Intellectual Character, and Civil and Political Condition of the Colored People of the U. States; and the Prejudice Exercised toward Them* (1837), 54, republished in *To Heal the Scourge of Prejudice: The Life and Writings of Hosea Easton*, ed. George R. Price and James Brewer Stewart (Amherst: U of Massachusetts P, 1999). For this biographical explanation, see also Dain, *Hideous Monster*, 171–72.
88. Unlike Easton, Forten, who thought that "Knowledge is power," showed himself convinced of the feasibility of uplift: "we may gather [. . .] some conception of the destructiveness, and bitter malignity of prejudice, and see in the mean time the necessity of our strangling the monster; and we can do so, and that too by the agency of the giant power of Education; for I am satisfied, fully satisfied, sir, that this demon is not invincible, as the enemies to the rights of man would feign have us believe" (James Forten, Jr., "An Address Delivered before the American Moral Reform Society, Philadelphia, 17 August 1837," in *Early Negro Writing*, ed. Porter, 228; 231).
89. Easton, *Treatise*, 35.
90. Ibid., 45, 46.
91. Ibid., 38.
92. Ibid., 38–39, 46.
93. Ibid., 24, 23. This argument became quite prominent later, reappearing, for instance, in William Wells Brown's novel *Clotel*: "The prejudice that

94. Easton, *Treatise*, 35.
95. Ibid., 37.
96. See Baumgartner, *Knowledge*, chap. 6, esp. 192–95.
97. Easton, *Treatise*, 40–41.
98. Ibid., 40.
99. Ibid., 42.
100. Ibid., 44.
101. See Herman E. Thomas, *James W. C. Pennington: African-American Churchman and Abolitionist* (New York: Garland, 1995).
102. Mischa Honneck, *We Are the Revolutionists: German-Speaking Immigrants and American Abolitionists after 1848* (Athens: U of Georgia P, 2011), 1–2.
103. James W. C. Pennington, *A Text Book of the Origin and History, etc. etc. of the Colored People* (Hartford, 1841), 3.
104. Ibid., 6–7.
105. Ibid., 89–90.
106. Ibid., 74.
107. Ibid., 74–77.
108. Ibid., 77–78.
109. Ibid., 84–85, 78–86.
110. Ibid., 86–87.
111. Ibid., 87–89.
112. Ibid., 87.
113. For this argument, see Rusert, *Fugitive Science*, 45–46. On Morton's antislavery background as a Philadelphia Quaker, see Herschthal, *Science of Abolition*, 202–3.
114. Walker, *Walker's Appeal*, 14.
115. TJ, *Notes*, 143.
116. Pennington, *Text Book*, 52–54.
117. Henry Louis Gates, foreword to James McCune Smith, *The Works of James McCune Smith*, ed. John Stauffer (Oxford: Oxford UP, 2006), x. On McCune Smith's life, also see John Stauffer, introduction, ibid., xiii–l; on McCune Smith as "the fulfillment of David Walker's dreams," see Davis, *Age of Emancipation*, 216.
118. McCune Smith, "On the Fourteenth Query of Thomas Jefferson's Notes on Virginia," in McCune Smith, *Works*, ed. Stauffer, 264–65.
119. Ibid., 265.

(continued from previous page)

exists in the Free States against coloured persons, on account of their colour, is attributable solely to the influence of slavery, and is but another form of slavery itself" (Brown, *Clotel*, 146).

120. McCune Smith, "Book Buying at Baillière's," in McCune Smith, *Works*, ed. Stauffer, 103–7. McCune Smith's use of Mill will be discussed below.
121. McCune Smith, "Fourteenth Query," 281.
122. Ibid., 266–67.
123. Ibid., 274.
124. Ibid., 271.
125. Ibid., 273.
126. Ibid., 266.
127. This topic is treated in chapter 7.
128. McCune Smith, "Fourteenth Query," 274.
129. TJ to John Adams, 8 April 1816 ("my temperament is sanguine"); Irving, *History of New York*, 137, book 4, chap. 1: "The corners of his mouth were curiously modeled into a kind of fret work, not a little resembling the wrinkled proboscis of an irritable pug dog—in a word he was one of the most positive, restless, ugly little men, that ever put himself in a passion about nothing."
130. McCune Smith, "Fourteenth Query," 277–78. McCune Smith likely derived this three-part classification from James Cowles Prichard, who was also important for Douglass, e.g., in *My Bondage and My Freedom* and "On the Claims of the Negro Ethnologically Considered" (see Dain, *Hideous Monster*, 261–62).
131. James McCune Smith, "The Destiny of the People of Color" (1843), in McCune Smith, *Works*, ed. Stauffer, 53.
132. On McCune Smith's genius for "playing the game of literary and cultural criticism according to its prevailing rules" while "not only playing the game, but playing with the game," see Daniel Hack, *Reaping Something New: African American Transformations of Victorian Literature* (Princeton, NJ: Princeton UP, 2017), 54.
133. McCune Smith, "Fourteenth Query," 277. In her essay "Our Greatest Want," Frances Watkins Harper discussed a similarly voluntarist concept of public opinion in the *Anglo-African Magazine* in 1859. See *A Brighter Coming Day: A Frances Ellen Watkins Harper Reader* (New York: Feminist Press at the City University of New York, 1990), 102–3.
134. McCune Smith, "Fourteenth Query," 280; compare Mill, "On Liberty," 70–71.
135. Mill, "On Liberty," 8.
136. Ibid., 9.
137. McCune Smith, "Fourteenth Query," 266. Compare Alexis de Tocqueville, *De la démocratie en Amérique* (Paris: Gallimard, 1961), 1.2.10, esp. 498–530. Wilson likewise appears to have been interested in Tocqueville,

as his repeated references to white Americans' "restlessness" may suggest (Wilson, "What Shall We Do," 59, 66). See also Alvin B. Tillery Jr., "Reading Tocqueville behind the Veil: Receptions of Democracy in America, 1835–1900," *American Political Thought* 7 (Winter 2018): 1–25. Tillery does not discuss McCune Smith or Wilson but focuses on the beginnings of African American criticism of the "Three Races" chapter in the *Colored American* in 1841, which, like the critique of Query XIV discussed in this chapter, concerned the concept of prejudice as well as the comparison between ancient and modern slavery (7–15).

138. Tocqueville, *Démocratie*, 1.2.7, 369–89. This chapter concludes by Tocqueville citing Jefferson as "le plus puissant apôtre qu'ait jamais eu la démocratie" (389); compare McCune Smith, "On the Fourteenth Query," 274 ("apostle of democracy").
139. On McCune Smith's questioning of identity, see Carla Peterson, "Untangling Genealogy's Tangled Skeins: Alexander Crummell, James McCune Smith, and Nineteenth-Century Black Literary Traditions," in *A Companion to American Literary Studies*, ed. Caroline Levander and Robert S. Levine (Malden, MA: Blackwell, 2011), 500–516, esp. 511–15.
140. James McCune Smith, "The German Invasion," *Anglo-African Magazine* 1.2 (February 1859): 44–52.
141. McCune Smith, "Fourteenth Query," 280.
142. On this dialectical approach to Wheatley and Jefferson, see Gates, *Trials*.
143. Compare Albert Murray, "The Dynamics of Heroic Action," in *The Hero and the Blues*, 35–63 (New York: Vintage, 1973).

7. PEDAGOGIES OF CHARACTER

1. "Hannah" to TJ, 15 November 1818; "Life among the Lowly, No. 1," *Pike County (Ohio) Republican*, 13 March 1873 (Appendix A: Madison Hemings, "The Memoirs of Madison Hemings"), in Annette Gordon-Reed, *Thomas Jefferson and Sally Hemings: An American Controversy* (Charlottesville: UP of Virginia, 1997), 247.
2. Such fears would turn out to have been justified less than eight years later: Jefferson would emancipate only seven enslaved people in his will, and nothing is known about Hannah's fate after his death in 1826.
3. "Hannah" to TJ, 15 November 1818. On Hannah's literacy and that of others in the enslaved communities of Monticello and Poplar Forest, see Stanton, *Those Who Labor*, 23, 164–65; and O'Shaughnessy, *Illimitable Freedom*, 205–7.
4. The proslavery interpretation of Paul had already been attacked by Lemuel Haynes in 1776 (see Saillant, *Black Puritan*, 34–35). For contemporaneous

antislavery hermeneutics of Ephesians 6:5 and Colossians 3:22, see Daniel Coker, "A Dialogue between a Virginian and an African Minister," in *Pamphlets of Protest*, ed. Newman, Rael, and Lapsansky, 59. The "Dialogue" will be discussed below.

5. Andrew Burstein, *Jefferson's Secrets: Death and Desire at Monticello* (New York: Basic, 2005), 30–32.
6. TJ, *Notes*, 163. The significance of "a conviction in the minds of the people" in the context of Jefferson's concept of opinion is discussed in chapter 3. Compare Forbes, introduction to *Annotated Edition*, xxxix–xlii, liii; 250nn8–9: Forbes has found that this passage was added in a tiny hand to the manuscript, possibly after Jefferson read Richard Price's pamphlet *Observations on the Importance of the American Revolution, and the Means of Making it a Benefit to the World* (1784), which contains a similar passage. The transatlantic origins of a phrase that became so important in the nineteenth century are an intriguing possibility. Forbes has found that the exclamation mark after "interference" was merely a full stop in the manuscript. This might support the reading that Jefferson introduced the passage as a rhetorical effort to redirect Price's criticism. The phrase was omitted in the 1786 French translation by the Abbé Morellet.
7. Hamilton, "Slave Trade," 399 (discussed in chapter 6); Peterson, *Jefferson Image*, 181–82.
8. TJ, *Notes*, 162–63. The terms *passion* and *(in)temperate* are used repeatedly in this passage.
9. Ibid.
10. On Jefferson Davis's use of the metaphor in a speech on 12 April 1860, opposing African American education, see Ibram Kendi, "An Intellectual History of a Book Title: Stamped from the Beginning," *Black Perspectives: Blog of the African American Intellectual History Society* (AAIHS), 8 April 2016, https://www.aaihs.org/an-intellectual-history-of-a-book-title/. The intellectual history is of Kendi's own book title, *Stamped from the Beginning: The Definitive History of Racist Ideas in America* (2016). Ironically, this title has made the malevolent but also rather lame and obscure use of the metaphor in Davis's speech much better-known in contemporary society than it ever was in its own day.
11. A classic example for a depiction of the dehumanizing influence of slavery on the enslavers is the transformation of Mrs. Auld in chapter 6 of the 1845 *Narrative of the Life of Frederick Douglass, an American Slave, Written by Himself*, ed. William L. Andrews and William S. McFreely (New York: Norton, 1997), 29–30. Well-known antebellum depictions of southern "white trash" can be found, e.g., in William Wells Brown's *Clotel* and

William Wilson's "Afric-American Picture Gallery" (discussed below) or in Harriet Jacobs's *Incidents in the Life of a Slave Girl* (1861), and of northern white mobs, in Frank J. Webb's *The Garies and Their Friends* (1857). On the genre of *white life novels*, see especially John C. Charles, *Abandoning the Black Hero: Sympathy and Privacy in the Postwar African American White-Life Novel* (New Brunswick, NJ: Rutgers UP, 2012); Veronica T. Watson, *The Souls of White Folk: African American Writers Theorize Whiteness* (Jackson: UP of Mississippi, 2013); and Stephanie Li, *Playing in the White: Black Writers, White Subjects* (New York: Oxford UP, 2015).

12. Elisa Tamarkin, *Anglophilia: Deference, Devotion, and Antebellum America* (Chicago: U of Chicago P, 2008), chap. 3.

13. Such positive depictions of Canadian and European society can be found, for instance, in Samuel Ringgold Ward's *Autobiography of a Fugitive Negro* (1855) or in Eliza Potter's *A Hairdresser's Experience in High Life* (1859). On African Americans "co-fabricating" concepts of character in interaction with white American society, see Rael, *Black Identity*, chapters 4 and 5 (150); Ball, *Antislavery Life*; and Baumgartner, *Knowledge*. In the context of Frances Harper's work, Michael Stancliff interprets "character as a powerful set of egalitarian precepts" (see Stancliff, *Frances Ellen Watkins Harper: African American Reform Rhetoric and the Rise of the Modern Nation State* [New York: Routledge, 2012], 17). On nineteenth-century conceptions of character more broadly, see Warren I. Susman, "'Personality' and the Making of Twentieth-Century Culture," in *New Directions in American Intellectual History*, ed. John Higham and Paul K. Conkin (Baltimore, MD: Johns Hopkins UP, 1979), 212–26; Stefan Collini, "The Idea of 'Character' in Victorian Political Thought," *Transactions of the Royal Historical Society*, 3rd ser., 35 (1985): 29–51; Deidre S. Lynch, *The Economy of Character: Novels, Market Culture, and the Business of Inner Meaning* (Chicago: U of Chicago P, 1998); Nancy Ruttenburg, *Democratic Personality: Popular Voice and the Trial of American Authorship* (Stanford, CA: Stanford UP, 1998), chap. 5; Cathy Boeckmann, *A Question of Character: Scientific Racism and the Genres of American Fiction, 1892–1912* (Tuscaloosa: U of Alabama P, 2000); Thomas Winter, *Making Men, Making Class: The YMCA and Workingmen, 1877–1920* (Chicago: U of Chicago P, 2002); Thomas Augst, *The Clerk's Tale: Young Men and Moral Life in Nineteenth-Century America* (Chicago: U of Chicago P, 2003); James Salazar, *Bodies of Reform: The Rhetoric of Character in Gilded Age America* (New York: New York UP, 2010); Jonathan Lamb, *The Things Things Say* (Princeton, NJ: Princeton UP, 2011); Christopher J. Lukasik, *Discerning Characters: The Culture of Appearance in Early America* (Philadelphia: U of Pennsylvania P,

2011); Brian D. Steele, *Thomas Jefferson and American Nationhood* (Cambridge: Cambridge UP, 2012), chap. 3; Susan Manning, *Poetics of Character: Transatlantic Encounters, 1700–1900* (Cambridge: Cambridge UP, 2013); and Michael J. Drexler and Ed White, *The Traumatic Colonel: The Founding Fathers, Slavery, and the Phantasmatic Aaron Burr* (New York: New York UP, 2014).

14. TJ, *Notes*, 163.
15. TJ to Edward Coles, 25 August 1814; compare *Freedom's Journal*, 1.6–7 (20 and 27 April 1827).
16. TJ to Edward Coles, 25 August 1814; compare *Aeneid*, trans. Michael Oakley, Everyman's Library (London: Dent, 1964), 2.509–11.
17. On *character* as an "analogical" concept premised on likeness and thus, unlike the polarization of sameness and difference inherent in the concept of *identity*, able to contain a degree of difference, see Manning, *Poetics of Character*, 3–53.
18. Ariela J. Gross, *Double Character: Slavery and Mastery in the Antebellum Southern Courtroom* (Princeton, NJ: Princeton UP, 2000).
19. Coker, "Dialogue," 53–65.
20. On Coker's life and possible motivation for his change of interests, see Rhondda R. Thomas, "Exodus and Colonization: Charting the Journey in the Journals of Daniel Coker, a Descendant of Africa," *African American Review* 41.3 (Fall, 2007): 507–19.
21. Newman, "White Uplift." The correspondence is discussed in chapters 5 and 6. For a recent interpretation that stresses the differences between Banneker and Coker's long *Dialogue*, see William L. Andrews, "Daniel Coker, David Walker, and the Politics of Dialogue in Early Nineteenth-Century African American Literature," in *African American Literature in Transition, 1830–1850*, ed. Benjamin Fagan, 44–70 (Cambridge: Cambridge UP, 2021). Andrews points out the possible influence of Samuel Hopkins's "Dialogue Concerning the Slavery of the Africans" (1776) on Coker, a text reprinted in *The Columbian Orator* (1797) that likewise became important for the young Frederick Douglass.
22. Benjamin Banneker to TJ, 19 August 1791.
23. Coker, "Dialogue," 55–56.
24. Ibid. 63.
25. Ibid., 56.
26. Ibid., 57–59. Col. 3.22, 2 Cor. 6.3, and 1 Cor. 7:21 are among the different parts of the Bible directly referenced in the text.
27. Coker, "Dialogue," 59.
28. TJ to Edward Coles, 25 August 1814.

29. Coker, "Dialogue," 61. Samuel Ringgold Ward, who likewise administered to white congregations, described a similar inversion of roles in his own household. He concluded: "Thus it will be, in my opinion, as between the blacks and the whites in America. They are now in the relation of teacher and taught, in the matter of liberty and progress, they will reverse positions ere the struggle be over, unless some sudden unforeseen changes occur" (Ward, *Autobiography*, 100).
30. William Wells Brown, *The Black Man: His Antecedents, His Genius, and His Achievements* (Boston, 1863), 51–58.
31. On the problems of understanding Brown as a "trickster narrator" and a historian, see John Ernest, *Liberation Historiography: African American Writers and the Challenge of History, 1794–1861* (Chapel Hill: U of North Carolina P, 2004), 334–39.
32. The tradition of depicting Jefferson's dinners included, for instance, Jabez Hammond's *faux* African American memoir, *Life and Opinions of Julius Melbourn* (1847), the authentic memoirs of Israel Jefferson (discussed below), and John F. Kennedy's famous quip.
33. Brown, *Black Man*, 58.
34. William G. Allen, "Letter to the Editor," *Frederick Douglass' Paper*, 29 April 1852. Allen's intervention is discussed in chapter 6.
35. Brown, *Black Man*, 56.
36. Ibid., 58.
37. Jefferson's materialist outlook, as expressed most succinctly in his letter to John Adams on 15 August 1820, is discussed in chapters 1 and 2.
38. Frederick Douglass, "Inhumanity of Slavery: Extract from a Lecture on Slavery at Rochester, December 8, 1850," in *My Bondage and My Freedom*, 440 (appendix).
39. Frederick Douglass, "The Proclamation and a Negro Army" (speech at the Cooper Institute, New York, 6 February 1863), reprinted in *The Frederick Douglass Papers. Series One: Speeches, Debates, and Interviews*, ed. John W. Blassingame (New Haven, CT: Yale UP, 1985–92), 3:549–69. On Douglass's recuperation of Jefferson during the Civil War, see Gates, *Trials*, 86–87.
40. "The Clock-Maker," *Frederick Douglass' Paper*, 20 October 1848.
41. For a discussion of the "Great Clock" in the context of TJ's philosophy, see my *Time and History*, 31–36.
42. TJ to Joseph Priestley, 21 March 1801.
43. John Ware Willard, *A History of Simon Willard, Inventor and Clockmaker. Together with Some Account of His Sons—His Apprentices—and the Workmen Associated with Him, with Brief Notices of Other Clockmakers of the Family

Name (Boston: Printed by E. O. Cockayne, 1911), 20. See also Silvio A. Bedini, "Thomas Jefferson, Clock Designer," *Proceedings of the American Philosophical Society* 108, no. 3 (June 1964): 163–80.

44. Compare Willard, *A History of Simon Willard, Inventor and Clockmaker*, 24–26.
45. Joseph Coolidge to TJ, 5 August 1825; Benjamin Waterhouse to TJ, 22 October 1825; Ellen Wayles Randolph Coolidge to TJ, 26 December 1825; Joseph Coolidge to TJ, 27 February 1826; TJ to Coolidge, 4 June 1826; Coolidge to TJ, 15 June 1826; Joseph Coolidge to Nicholas P. Trist, 15 March 1827.
46. Benjamin Banneker, "Epitaph on a Watch-Maker," in *Bannaker's Virginia, Pennsylvania, Delaware, Maryland and Kentucky Almanack and Ephemeris, for the year of our Lord 1797* (Baltimore, 1796), 14. On the antislavery content of the epitaph and its inspiration by Benjamin Franklin's print analogy, see Newman, "White Uplift," 80–81.
47. William J. Wilson ("Ethiop"), "Afric-American Picture Gallery," *Anglo-African Magazine*, February–October, 1859, Text prepared by Leif Eckstrom and Britt Rusert, 1. Just Teach One: Early African American Print: https://jtoaa.americanantiquarian.org/welcome-to-just-teach-one-african-american/afric-american-picture-gallery/.
48. Wilson, "Picture Gallery," 8–9.
49. Ibid., 13.
50. Ibid., 4. On the significance of eighteenth-century philosophical history for Jefferson, including its relation to the visual arts, see my *Time and History*, chap. 4.
51. Wilson, "Picture Gallery," 4–5.
52. Ibid., 5.
53. On the manifold interconnections between individual and national character in the nineteenth century, see especially Manning, *Poetics of Character*; and Anna Brickhouse, *Transamerican Literary Relations and the Nineteenth-Century Public Sphere* (Cambridge: Cambridge UP, 2004).
54. Wilson, "Picture Gallery," 2–3. Benjamin Fagan and Derrick Spires suggest the younger editor may be Wilson himself (Spires, *Practice of Citizenship*, 179).
55. Wilson, "Picture Gallery," 3.
56. Ibid., 5.
57. Ibid., 5, 26.
58. Ibid., 20.
59. Ibid., 21.
60. Brown, *Black Man*, 240, 230, 233.

61. See Ivy G. Wilson, *Spectres of Democracy: Blackness and the Aesthetics of Politics in the Antebellum U.S.* (Oxford: Oxford UP, 2011), 145.
62. "From our Brooklyn Correspondent," *Frederick Douglass' Paper* 6.12 (11 March 1853): 3, republished as document 28 in *The Black Abolitionist Papers*, ed. Peter C. Ripley, vol. 4 (Chapel Hill: U of North Carolina P, 1991), 140–45.
63. Wilson, "Picture Gallery," 8.
64. Ibid.
65. On the theme of pity in the African American tradition, see also chapter 6 and this book's conclusion.
66. Wilson, "Picture Gallery," 8–9.
67. Murray, *Hero and the Blues*, 37–38.
68. On divergent views on the "great thing" of *character* in the writings of Douglass and Alexander Crummell, see Wilson J. Moses, *Creative Conflict in African American Thought* (Cambridge: Cambridge UP, 2004), 1–4.
69. Douglass, "What Are the Colored People Doing for Themselves?," *North Star*, 14 July 1848, republished in *The Life and Writings of Frederick Douglass*, ed. Philip S. Foner (New York International, 1950), 1:314–20.
70. Compare the notion of character possession in Mill's liberalism which, as discussed in chapter 6, intrigued James McCune Smith: "A person whose desires and impulses are his own—are the expression of his own nature, as it has been developed and modified by his own culture—is said to have a character. One whose desires and impulses are not his own, has no character, no more than a steam-engine has a character" (Mill, *On Liberty*, 59). On Mill's ethology, see especially Terence Ball, "The Formation of Character: Mill's 'Ethology' Reconsidered," *Polity* 33.1 (Autumn 2000): 25–48; Jerrold Seigel, "Necessity, Freedom, and Character Formation from the Eighteenth Century to the Nineteenth," in *Character, Self, and Sociability in the Scottish Enlightenment*, ed. Thomas Ahnert and Susan Manning, 249–65 (New York: Palgrave, 2011).
71. Frances Watkins Harper, *Anti-Slavery Bugle*, 29 September 1860, quoted and discussed in Peterson, *Doers of the Word*, 119–45, 134 (quote). On the concept of character in Harper's work, see also Stancliff, *Harper*; and in the work of the Boston educator Susan Paul, see Baumgartner, *Knowledge*, chap. 6.
72. King, "I Have a Dream," 219.
73. Wilson, "Picture Gallery," 25.
74. "From our Brooklyn Correspondent," *Frederick Douglass' Paper*, 11 March 1853.
75. TJ, *Notes*, 163.

76. Wilson, "Picture Gallery," 9, 11.
77. Ibid., 13.
78. Ibid., 14.
79. Ibid.
80. Ibid.
81. Ibid., 16.
82. Ibid., 17. See Wilson, *Spectres*, 155.
83. Wilson, "Picture Gallery," 17.
84. "From Our Brooklyn Correspondent," *Frederick Douglass' Paper*, 11 March 1853.
85. Lynch, *Economy of Character*, 1–20.
86. James W. C. Pennington, *The Fugitive Blacksmith; or, Events in the History of James W. C. Pennington, Pastor of a Presbyterian Church, New York, Formerly a Slave in the State of Maryland, United States* (London, 1849), xii.
87. Gordon Wood has captured a sense of Monticello's eeriness in his comparison to Faulkner's "Dark House" in "The Ghosts of Monticello," in *Sally Hemings and Thomas Jefferson: History, Memory, and Civic Culture*, ed. Jan E. Lewis and Peter S. Onuf (Charlottesville: UP of Virginia, 1999), 19–34. See also Carmen Gillespie's poetry collection with the same title, *The Ghosts of Monticello: A Recitatif* (Fairfax, VA: Stillhouse, 2017). Chet'la Sebree has continued the theme in her collection *Mistress* (Kalamazoo, MI: New Issues, 2019).
88. Walker, *Walker's Appeal*, 16.
89. On Ruggles's bookstore, Stewart, and *Walker's Appeal*, see Graham R. G. Hodges, *David Ruggles: A Radical Black Abolitionist and the Underground Railroad in New York City* (Chapel Hill: U of North Carolina P, 2019), 60–61, 40–41.
90. David Ruggles, *The 'Extinguisher' Extinguished, or David M. Reese, M.D. 'Used Up'* (New York, 1834), 44. For more information on this pamphlet, see Hodges, *Ruggles*, 70–76.
91. Allen, "Letter from William G. Allen," *Frederick Douglass' Paper*, 5.19 (29 April, 1852): 3.
92. "Thomas Jefferson (N.Y. Tribune)," *Frederick Douglass' Paper*, 12.10 (18 February, 1859): 1.
93. James McCune Smith, "The Black News-Vender," in *Works of James McCune Smith*, ed. John Stauffer, 192. Signed by "Communipaw," this sketch appeared as "'Heads of the Colored People,' Done with a Whitewash Brush: The Black News-Vendor," in *Frederick Douglass' Paper*, 25 March 1852.
94. Ibid., 191.

95. Ibid. As a complex reflection on literary and visual representation, McCune Smith's African American Jefferson likeness may also have alluded to the question of political representation condensed in the epithet "Negro president," pointing to Jefferson's narrow victory in the electoral college due the three-fifths clause, discussed in Garry Wills, *Negro President: Jefferson and the Slave Power* (Boston: Houghton Mifflin, 2003).
96. Black Jeffersons would also appear in twentieth-century African American literature, often, accidentally or not, as important but lower-class, initially uneducated characters. See, e.g., the Jefferson in Ralph Ellison's short story "Flying Home," or the protagonist and innocent victim of a death sentence in Ernest J. Gaines's novel *A Lesson before Dying*. The family name *Jefferson* became prominent in popular culture, of course, in the CBS sitcom *The Jeffersons* (1975–85). Most recently, McCune Smith's African American Jefferson has found a glamorous descendent in Daveed Diggs's performance of Jefferson in the Broadway musical *Hamilton*.
97. McCune Smith, "News-Vender," 191–92. On the fates of Jefferson's children in the white world, compare Gordon-Reed, *Hemingses*, esp. 285, 592–695.
98. McCune Smith, "News-Vender," 192.
99. TJ, *Notes*, 162.
100. McCune Smith, "News-Vender," 192.
101. Ibid.
102. Ibid., 193.
103. For a comparison from the perspective of disability studies between McCune Smith's repeated accounts of shipwreck with Douglass's near-contemporaneous account of weathering the storm in *The Heroic Slave*, see Jacob Crane, "'Razed to the Knees': The Anti-Heroic Body in James McCune Smith's 'The Heads of the Colored People,'" *African American Review* 51.1 (Spring 2018): 7–21.
104. Claude McKay, *Romance in Marseille*, ed. and introd. Gary Edward Holcomb and William J. Maxwell (New York: Penguin, 2020).
105. McCune Smith, "News-Vender," 194.
106. William Wells Brown, "Narrative of the Life and Escape of William Wells Brown," in *Clotel; or, The President's Daughter: A Narrative of Slave Life in the United States*, ed. with an introduction and notes by M. Giulia Fabi (New York: Penguin, 2004), 31.
107. Clotel's oft-discussed cross-dressing not only aligns her with her fictional father, as discussed here, but also alludes to historical exigencies of escape and resistance, as made famous by Ellen Craft's spectacular flight from slavery disguised as a man or Harriet Tubman's request of a bloomer

costume for her expeditions. See Craft and Craft, *Running a Thousand Miles*; and Tubman, "Dictated Letter to Franklin B. Sanborn about the Combahee River Raid" (30 June 1863), document 6 in Jean M. Humez, *Harriet Tubman: The Life and the Life Stories* (Madison: U of Wisconsin P, 2003), 283–84.

108. Brown, *Clotel*, 181.
109. Ibid.
110. Ibid., 184–85.
111. Ibid., 186.
112. The Haynes abridgment is discussed in chapter 5.
113. Brown, *Clotel*, 47.
114. Ibid., 43, 50.
115. Ibid., 47.
116. Ibid., 51.
117. Ibid., 209.
118. Ibid., 129.
119. Ibid., 130.
120. Ibid., 130–31. Compare TJ, *Notes*, 162–63; TJ, "Answers and Observations for Démeunier's Article on the United States in the *Encyclopédie Methodique*"; TJ to Démeunier, 22 June 1786, in TJ, *Writings*, ed. Peterson, 592.
121. Most famously (but not exclusively) outlined in TJ to James Madison, 6 September 1789.
122. Brown, *Clotel*, 131.
123. Laura Soderberg, "One More Time with Feeling: Repetition, Reparation, and the Sentimental Subject in William Wells Brown's Rewritings of *Clotel*," *American Literature* 88.2 (June 2016): 241–67; Christopher Stampone, "Are We Reading the Right Clotel(le)? Revolutions in Early African American Literature," *Studies in American Fiction* 45.2 (Fall 2018): 191–211.
124. Madison Hemings, "The Memoirs of Madison Hemings," in Annette Gordon-Reed, *Thomas Jefferson and Sally Hemings: An American Controversy* (Charlottesville: UP of Virginia, 1997), 245–48 (Appendix B). On Madison Hemings, see Gordon-Reed, *American Controversy*, chap. 1; and Gordon-Reed, *Hemingses of Monticello*, esp. chap. 28.
125. Hemings, "The Memoirs of Madison Hemings," 246, 248. For the perspective of the descendants today, see Lanier, *Children*; and White, *Reclamation*.
126. Hemings, "The Memoirs of Madison Hemings," 245.
127. Ibid., 247.
128. Ibid. McCune Smith's recourse to Irving's language is discussed in chapter 6.

129. Ibid., 246. On this treaty and Jefferson as a man who kept his promises (unlike Dolley Madison, who, according to Hemings, had promised a gift to his mother if she named him after her husband, but never lived up to the promise), see Stanton, *Those Who Labor*, 95–96. On Hemings's childhood perspective in comparing himself to Jefferson's white grandchildren rather than children, see Gordon-Reed, *American Controversy*, 44–45.

130. To be sure, TJ's aversion to conflict has also been noted by biographers in other contexts (see, e.g., Gordon-Reed and Onuf, *Patriarchs*, 245–47, 253–59). However, there are also reports of moments when he let his guard down and became "frantic and upset," as during the illness of his valet Burwell Colbert (see Gordon-Reed, *Hemingses*, 621–26).

131. Israel Jefferson, "The Memoirs of Israel Jefferson," in Gordon-Reed, *American Controversy*, 249–53 (Appendix C), published as "Life among the Lowly, No. 3," *Pike County (Ohio) Republican*, 25 December 1873.

132. Ibid., 252.

133. Ibid.

134. Ibid.

135. Ibid., 250. On the comparison to Lafayette, see Stanton, *Those Who Labor*, 97.

136. Peter F. Fossett, "Once the Slave of Thomas Jefferson," *New York Sunday World*, 30 January 1898, in Kevin J. Hayes, *Jefferson in His Own Time: A Biographical Chronicle of His Life, Drawn from Recollections, Interviews, and Memoirs, by Family, Friends, and Associates* (Iowa City: U of Iowa P, 2012), 187–93.

137. Ibid., 188.

138. Ibid., 189, 191; compare TJ, "Memoirs," 252.

139. Fossett, "Once the Slave," 191.

140. Gordon-Reed, *Hemingses*, 626–28.

141. Fossett, "Once the Slave," 193.

8. ABOVE JEFFERSON'S VEIL

1. TJ, *Notes*, 138.

2. Ibid.

3. PW, "Thoughts on the WORKS of PROVIDENCE"; "To the Rev. Dr. THOMAS ARMORY on reading his Sermons on DAILY DEVOTION, in which that Duty is recommended and assisted" ("sable veil"), in *Poems on Various Subjects*, 26–29, 48–49. Following Gates's argument about Wheatley as the "mother" of African American literature and Jefferson as its paradoxical "midwife," her earlier use of the "veil," of course, hardly seems surprising (see Gates, *Trials*, 50–51 ["mother"; "midwife"]).

4. Immanuel Kant, *Kritik der reinen Vernunft*, 2nd ed. (1787; Hamburg: Felix Meiner Verlag, 1956), 95 (B 75): "Gedanken ohne Inhalt sind leer, Anschauungen ohne Begriffe sind blind."
5. TJ, *Notes*, 138.
6. For a prominent example that includes the metaphor of the veil (as discussed in chapter 5), see, e.g., Douglass, "What to the Slave," 60, 52, 58 ("thin veil," "blinded by prejudice"). The association between prejudgment and a breakdown of subjective vision was made by many other authors as well, including Lemuel Haynes, William Hamilton, and David Walker, discussed above.
7. TJ, *Notes*, 162.
8. Ellison, *Invisible Man*, 7.
9. James Baldwin, "The White Man's Guilt," in *Collected Essays*, ed. Toni Morrison (New York: Library of America, 1998), 725.
10. TJ to Henry Lee, 8 May 1825.
11. Harper, *Iola Leroy, or, Shadows Uplifted*, ed. Hollis Robbins (London: Penguin, 2010), 145; Chesnutt, *The Marrow of Tradition*, ed. Werner Sollors (New York: Norton, 2012), 190. On African American women's "doubled veil" as a literary convention, see Zafar, *We Wear the Mask*, chaps. 5 and 6, esp. 152–55. On the resonances of George Eliot in Harper's work, see Hack, *Reaping*, chap. 3. Hack tends to argue against the relevance of "The Lifted Veil" in particular, while the shared character of Dr. Latimer may suggest otherwise.
12. See Gould, "Postcolonial Nationhood," 734–35 ("postcolonial inversion").
13. Jerold J. Savory, "The Rending of the Veil in W. E. B. Du Bois's *The Souls of Black Folk*," *CLA Journal* 15.3 (March 1973): 335.
14. PW, "Amory," in PW, *Complete Writings*, 48.
15. Amory's sermons are quoted and discussed in Ann Beebe, "Phillis Wheatley's TO THE REV. DR. THOMAS AMORY ON READING HIS SERMONS ON DAILY DEVOTION, IN WHICH THAT DUTY IS RECOMMENDED AND ASSISTED," *The Eplicator* 73.3 (2015): 231.
16. PW, "Providence," in PW, *Complete Writings*, 28.
17. Ibid., 27. For her gratification with being "presented with a Folio Edition of Milton's Paradise Lost, printed on a Silver Type" while in London, see PW to Col. David Worcester, 18 October 1773, in PW, *Complete Writings*, 146.
18. See PW, "To Maecenas"; "On Being Brought from AFRICA to AMERICA," in PW, *Complete Writings*, 10, 13.
19. TJ, *Notes*, 140: "Religion indeed has produced a Phyllis Whately, but it could not produce a poet."

20. PW to Samson Occom, 11 February 1774. Compare the political and social dimension of freedom, e.g., in "To the Right Honourable WILLIAM, Earl of DARTMOUTH, His Majesty's Principle Secretary of State for North-America, &c.," or in her later poem, "LIBERTY and PEACE, A POEM" (1784), in PW, *Complete Writings*, 152–53, 39–40, 101–12.
21. PW to John Thornton, 30 October, 1774, in PW, *Complete Writings*, 159. On the context of this letter and Thornton's suggestion as the possible result of a prior misunderstanding between him and PW, see Carretta, *Genius in Bondage*, 160–64.
22. See Kelleter, *Amerikanische Aufklärung* 704–5. Apart from Wheatley's subscription to the secular Enlightenment goal of freedom of movement, Kelleter describes her universalism in this letter as a universalism that was national as well as oppositional and conscious of difference (705 ["differenzbewusster Universalismus"]).
23. Du Bois, *Souls*, 178.
24. Ibid., 3; compare 123, 136.
25. Du Bois, *Souls*, 8. On concepts of *double consciousness* prior to Du Bois, see especially Joel Porte, "Emerson, Thoreau, and the Double Consciousness," *New England Quarterly* 41.1 (March 1968): 40–50; and Anita Paterson, *From Emerson to King: Democracy, Race, and the Politics of Progress* (Cary: Oxford UP, 1997), chap. 7.
26. Du Bois, *Souls*, 47, 65, 141–44, 176.
27. Ibid., 152, 5.
28. Ibid., 3, 144, 146, 176.
29. Ibid., 176, 178 ("The Afterthought").
30. Ibid., 76. Du Bois added additional layers to his concept of the Veil later, sometimes going in a more universalist, sometimes in a more particularist direction. Compare, e.g., his various uses of the concept in *Darkwater: Voices from within the Veil* (1920; New York: AMS, 1969).
31. Ibid., 8.
32. James Weldon Johnson, *The Autobiography of an Ex-Coloured Man*, "Preface to the Original Edition of 1912," in *The Essential Writings of James Weldon Johnson*, ed. Rudolph P. Byrd (New York: Modern Library, 2008), 27.
33. Ibid., 29–30.
34. Robert B. Stepto, *From behind the Veil: A Study of Afro-American Narrative* (Urbana: U of Illinois P, 1979), 100–101.
35. Hume, *Treatise*, 259.
36. Jefferson's favorite novel had already referred to the problem of identity as a "puzzle." The term prominently appears again in Ellison's *Invisible Man*, discussed below. Compare Laurence Sterne, *The Life and Opinions*

of *Tristram Shandy, Gentleman*, ed. Melvyn New and Joan New (London: Penguin, 1997), 434 (vol. 7, chap. 23).
37. Johnson, *Ex-Coloured Man*, 29.
38. Joseph J. Ellis, *American Sphinx: The Character of Thomas Jefferson* (New York: Knopf, 1997).
39. Johnson, *Ex-Coloured Man*, 140.
40. See Ellen Daugherty, "Negotiating the Veil: Tuskegee's Booker T. Washington Monument," *American Art* 24.3 (Fall 2019): 52–77.
41. On the Emancipation Monument and the comparison, see Daugherty, "Negotiating," 63ff.; David W. Blight, *Frederick Douglass: Prophet of Freedom* (New York: Simon & Schuster, 2018), 1–9; and Gabrielle Everett, "Reading the 'Veil of Black' in Frederick Douglass and Thomas Jefferson: Affective Legibility and National Belonging," *African American Review* 53.3 (Fall 2020): 175.
42. Douglass, "'Oration of Frederick Douglass Delivered on the Occasion of the Unveiling of the Freedmen's Monument in Memory of Abraham Lincoln,' a speech delivered in Washington, DC, on April 14, 1876 and published as a pamphlet," in Douglass, *Selected Writings*, 242. The classic text on African Americans' relationship with Lincoln that emphasizes intimacy and sympathy is John E. Washington's *They Knew Lincoln* (1942), recently republished with a new introduction by Kate Masur (Oxford: Oxford UP, 2018).
43. Douglass, "Freedmen's Monument," 242. Douglass here referred to Jefferson's letter to Jean Nicolas Démeunier, 26 June 1786.
44. Ibid., 243.
45. Ibid., 241.
46. Ibid., 245.
47. Ibid., 241.
48. Johnson, *Ex-Coloured Man*, 29.
49. Ellison, *Invisible Man*, 33–34.
50. Compare Sterne, *Tristram Shandy*, 434.
51. Ellison, *Invisible Man*, 7.
52. Ibid., 464.
53. PW, e.g., "Providence," and PW to Samson Occom, 11 February 1774, in PW, *Complete Writings*, 28, 153; Du Bois, *Souls*, 176; Ellison, *Invisible Man*, 462, 464.
54. Johnson, *Ex-Coloured Man*, 30.
55. Ellison, *Invisible Man*, 9–10.
56. Ibid., 466.
57. Ibid., 468; compare 15–16.

58. Ellison, "Change the Joke and Slip the Yoke," in Ellison, *Collected Essays*, 111.
59. Ellison, *Invisible Man*, 9–10.
60. Ibid., 34.
61. Ibid., 18.
62. Ellison, "Slip the Yoke," 110.
63. Ellison, *Invisible Man*, 17, 463.
64. Ibid., 17–18. On Jefferson's continuation of the ancient concept of slavery as a latent state of war, see Onuf, *Jefferson's Empire*, 147–88; Onuf, *Mind of Jefferson*, 205–70; and Taylor, *Internal Enemy*.
65. Ellison, "Slip the Yoke," 110.
66. Ellison, *Invisible Man*, 462–63.
67. Ellison, "Chehaw Station," in Ellison, *Collected Essays*, 501. As Amanda Anderson has observed, the concern with "democratic principle in the epilogue" of *Invisible Man* is "somewhat marginal relative to the general sweep of serial disillusionment" in the novel and has therefore been "underexplored in the criticism." However, read against the historical backdrop of Wheatley's Enlightenment of Principle, the affirmation of "transpersonal principles that cannot be fully safeguarded by individual acts and actors" emerges as a key element in Ellison's political outlook (Anderson, *Bleak Liberalism* [Chicago: U of Chicago P, 2016], 121, 128).
68. Ellison, *Invisible Man*, 8–9.
69. Ibid., 462–63.
70. Ibid., 461.
71. Gates, *Trials*, 50–51.
72. Amanda Gorman, *The Hill We Climb: An Inaugural Poem for the Country*, with a foreword by Oprah Winfrey (New York: Viking, 2021), 14.
73. PW to Occom, 11 February 1774, in PW, *Complete Writings*, 152–53.

CONCLUSION

1. Hamilton, "Oration," 101.
2. Du Bois, *Souls*, 8. On concepts of *double consciousness* prior to Du Bois, see Porte, "Double Consciousness"; and Paterson, *Emerson to King*, chap. 7.
3. TJ, *Notes*, 165.
4. Abraham Lincoln, "Speech on the Dred Scott Decision" (26 June 1857), in *Political Writings and Speeches*, ed. Terence Ball (Cambridge: Cambridge UP, 2013), 50.

❖ WORKS CITED ❖

PRIMARY WORKS AND ANTHOLOGIES

Adams, Henry. *The History of the United States during the Administration of Thomas Jefferson*. 2 vols. New York: Library of America, 1986.

Allen, William G. "Letter from William G. Allen," *Frederick Douglass' Paper* 5.19 (29 April 1852): 3.

———. *Wheatley, Banneker, and Horton; with Selections from the Poetical Works of Wheatley and Horton, and the Letter of Washington to Wheatley, and of Jefferson to Banneker*. Boston, 1849.

Anon. "The Clock-Maker." *Frederick Douglass' Paper* 43.1 (20 October 1848): 4.

Anon. [Destutt de Tracy, Antoine Louis Claude.] *A Commentary and Review of Montesquieu's Spirit of Laws. Prepared for Press from the Original Manuscript in the Hands of the Publisher. To Which Are Annexed, Observations on the Thirty-First Book, by the Late M. Condorcet: And Two Letters of Helveticus, on the Merits of the Same Work*. Philadelphia: Duane, 1811. Reprint, Clark, NJ: Lawbook Exchange, 2006.

Aristotle. *The Politics*. Translated by Harris Rackham. Loeb Classical Library. Cambridge, MA: Harvard UP; London: Heinemann, 1932.

Bacon, Francis. *The Novum Organum of Sir Francis Bacon, Baron of Verulam, Viscount St. Albans. Epitomized for a clearer understanding of his natural history. Trans. and taken out of the Latine by M.D.* London, 1676.

Baker, Thomas N. "'A Slave' Writes to Thomas Jefferson." *William and Mary Quarterly* 68.1 (January 2011): 127–54.

Baldwin, James. *Collected Essays*. Edited by Toni Morrison. New York: Library of America, 1998.

Banneker, Benjamin. "Epitaph on a Watch-Maker." In *Bannaker's Virginia, Pennsylvania, Delaware, Maryland and Kentucky Almanack and Ephemeris, for the year of our Lord 1797*, 14. Baltimore, 1796.

———. "To Thomas Jefferson, 19 August, 1791." In *The Papers of Thomas Jefferson*, vol. 22, edited by Charles T. Cullen, 49–54. Princeton, NJ: Princeton UP, 1986.

Brown, William W. *The Black Man: His Antecedents, His Genius, and His Achievements*. Boston, 1863.

———. *Clotel; or, The President's Daughter: A Narrative of Slave Life in the United States*. Edited with an introduction and notes by M. Giulia Fabi. New York: Penguin, 2004.

———. *Clotel and Other Writings*. Edited by Ezra Greenspan. New York: Library of America, 2014.

Burke, Edmund. *Reflections on the Revolution in France*. Edited by Frank M. Turner. New Haven, CT: Yale UP, 2003.

Chesnutt, Charles W. *The Journals of Charles W. Chesnutt*. Edited by Richard H. Brodhead. Durham, NC: Duke UP, 1993.

———. *The Marrow of Tradition*. Edited by Werner Sollors. New York: Norton, 2012.

———. *The Portable Charles W. Chesnutt*. Edited by William L. Andrews. London: Penguin, 2008.

Craft, William and Ellen. *Running a Thousand Miles for Freedom*. 1860. New York: Arno and New York Times, 1969.

Crummell, Alexander. *Destiny and Race. Selected Writings, 1840–1898*. Edited and with an introduction by Wilson J. Moses. Amherst: U of Massachusetts P, 1992.

Delany, Martin R. *Martin R. Delany: A Documentary Reader*. Edited by Robert S. Levine. Chapel Hill: U of North Carolina P, 2003.

Douglass, Frederick. *The Essential Douglass: Selected Writings & Speeches*. Edited and with an introduction by Nicholas Buccola. Indianapolis, IN: Hackett, 2016.

———. *The Frederick Douglass Papers. Series One: Speeches, Debates, and Interviews*. Edited by John W. Blassingame. New Haven, CT: Yale UP, 1985–92.

———. *The Heroic Slave: A Cultural and Critical Edition*. Edited by John R. McKivigan, John Stauffer, and Robert S. Levine. New Haven, CT: Yale UP, 2015.

———. *The Life and Writings of Frederick Douglass*. 4 vols. Edited by Philip S. Foner. New York: International, 1950–52.

———. *My Bondage and My Freedom*. 1855. New York: Arno and New York Times, 1968.

———. *Narrative of the Life of Frederick Douglass, an American Slave, Written by Himself*. Norton Critical Edition. Edited by William L. Andrews and William S. McFreely. New York: Norton, 1997.

———. "The Race Problem: Great Speech by Frederick Douglass, Delivered before the Bethel Library and Historical Association, in the Metropolitan A.M.E. Church, Washington, D.C., 28 October, 1890." Daniel Murray Pamphlet Collection, African American Perspectives: Materials Selected from the Rare Books Collections, Rare Book and Special Collections Division. Library of Congress. https://www.loc.gov/resource/lcrbmrp.t0c13/.

Du Bois, W. E. B. *Darkwater: Voices from within the Veil*. 1920. New York: AMS, 1969.

———. *The Souls of Black Folk*. Oxford: Oxford UP, 2007.

Easton, Hosea. *A Treatise on the Intellectual Character, and Civil and Political Condition of the Colored People of the U. States; and the Prejudice Exercised toward Them* (1837). Republished in *To Heal the Scourge of Prejudice: The Life and Writings of Hosea Easton*, edited by George R. Price and James Brewer Stewart. Amherst: U of Massachusetts P, 1999.

Ellison, Ralph. *The Collected Essays of Ralph Ellison*. Edited and with an introduction by John F. Callahan. Preface by Saul Bellow. New York: Modern Library, 1995.

———. *Flying Home and Other Stories*. Edited by John F. Callahan. 1996. London: Penguin Classics, 2016.

———. *Invisible Man*. 1952; London: Penguin, 1965.

Finley, Robert. *Thoughts on the Colonization of Free Blacks*. Washington, DC, 1816.

Foner, Philip S., ed. *We, the Other People: Alternative Declarations of Independence by Labor Groups, Farmers, Woman's Rights Advocates, Socialists, and Blacks, 1829–1975*. Urbana: U of Illinois P, 1976.

Fossett, Peter F. "Once the Slave of Thomas Jefferson." In *Jefferson in His Own Time: A Biographical Chronicle of His Life, Drawn from Recollections, Interviews, and Memoirs, by Family, Friends, and Associates*, edited by Kevin J. Hayes, 187–93. Iowa City: U of Iowa P, 2012.

Garnet, Henry H. *The Past and Present Condition and Destiny of the Colored Race: A Discourse Delivered at the Fifteenth Anniversary of the Female Benevolent Society of Troy, New York, February 14, 1848*. Miami, FL: Mnemosyne, 1969.

———. *Walker's Appeal, with a Brief Sketch of his Life, by Henry Highland Garnet, and Also Garnet's Address to the Slaves of the United States of America*. New York, 1848.

Gillespie, Carmen. *The Ghosts of Monticello: A Recitatif*. Fairfax, VA: Stillhouse, 2017.

Gorman, Amanda. *The Hill We Climb: An Inaugural Poem for the Country*. Foreword by Oprah Winfrey. New York: Viking, 2021.

Harper, Frances Ellen W. *A Brighter Coming Day: A Frances Ellen Watkins Harper Reader.* Edited and introduced by Frances Smith Foster. New York: Feminist Press at the City University of New York, 1990.

———. *Iola Leroy, or, Shadows Uplifted.* Edited by Hollis Robbins. London: Penguin, 2010.

Haynes, Lemuel. "Liberty Further Extended." In *The Literatures of Colonial America: An Anthology,* edited by Susan Castillo and Ivy Schweitzer, 573–80. Malden, MA: Blackwell, 2001.

Hemings, Madison. "The Memoirs of Madison Hemings." Appendix B in Annette Gordon-Reed, *Thomas Jefferson and Sally Hemings: An American Controversy,* 245–48. Charlottesville: UP of Virginia, 1997.

Holton, Woody, ed. *Black Americans in the Revolutionary Era: A Brief History with Documents.* New York: Bedford/St. Martin's, 2009.

The Holy Bible. An Exact Reprint in Roman Type, Page for Page, of the Authorized Version Published in the Year 1611. 1833. Oxford: Oxford UP, 1985.

Home, Henry, Lord Kames. *Elements of Criticism.* 1840. Reprint, Honolulu: UP of the Pacific, 2002.

Hume, David. *A Treatise of Human Nature.* Edited by L. A. Selby-Bigge. 2nd ed., with text revised and variant readings by P. H. Nidditch. 1888. Oxford: Clarendon, 1978.

Irving, Washington. *A History of New York.* With an introduction and notes by Elizabeth L. Bradley. New York: Penguin, 2008.

Jefferson, Israel. "The Memoirs of Israel Jefferson." Appendix C in Annette Gordon-Reed, *Thomas Jefferson and Sally Hemings: An American Controversy,* 249–53. Charlottesville: UP of Virginia, 1997.

Jefferson, Thomas. *Founders Online,* National Archives. Correspondence and Other Writings of Seven Major Shapers of the United States: George Washington, Benjamin Franklin, John Adams (and family), Thomas Jefferson, Alexander Hamilton, John Jay, and James Madison. Fully annotated, from the authoritative Founding Fathers Papers projects. https://founders.archives.gov/.

———. *Jefferson's Extracts from the Gospels. "The Philosophy of Jesus" and "The Life and Morals of Jesus."* Edited by Dickinson W. Adams. Princeton, NJ: Princeton UP, 1983.

———. *Jefferson's Legal Commonplace Book.* Edited by David T. Konig, Michael P. Zuckert, Les Harris, and W. Bland Whitley. Princeton, NJ: Princeton UP, 2019.

———. *Jefferson's Literary Commonplace Book.* Edited by Douglas L. Wilson. Princeton, NJ: Princeton UP, 1989.

———. *Jefferson's Memorandum Books: Accounts, with Legal Records and Miscellany, 1767–1826.* Edited by James A. Bear Jr. and Lucia C. Stanton. 2 vols. Princeton, NJ: Princeton UP, 1997.

———. *Notes on the State of Virginia*. Edited by William Peden. 1954. Chapel Hill: U of North Carolina P, 1982.

———. *Notes on the State of Virginia: An Annotated Edition*. Edited by Robert P. Forbes. New Haven, CT: Yale UP, 2022.

———. *The Papers of Thomas Jefferson*. Edited by Julian P. Boyd, Charles Cullen, John Catanzariti, Barbara Oberg, and James P. McClure. 46 vols. to date. Princeton, NJ: Princeton UP, 1950–.

———. *The Papers of Thomas Jefferson: Retirement Series*. Edited by J. Jefferson Looney. 19 vols. to date. Princeton, NJ: Princeton UP, 2004–.

———. *Thomas Jefferson: Writings*. Edited by Merrill D. Peterson. New York: Library of America, 1984.

Johnson, James W. *The Essential Writings of James Weldon Johnson*. Edited by Rudolph P. Byrd. New York: Modern Library, 2008.

Kant, Immanuel. *Kritik der reinen Vernunft*. 2nd ed. 1787. Hamburg: Felix Meiner Verlag, 1956.

———. "What Is Enlightenment?" In *The Portable Enlightenment Reader*, edited and with an introduction by Isaac Kramnick, 1–7. New York: Penguin, 1995.

King, Martin Luther, Jr. *A Testament of Hope: The Essential Writings of Martin Luther King, Jr.* Edited by James Melvin Washington. San Francisco: Harper & Row, 1986.

Locke, John. *The Conduct of the Understanding*. Dublin, 1782.

———. *An Essay Concerning Human Understanding*. Edited and abridged by John W. Yolton. London: Dent, 2000.

Lincoln, Abraham. *The Collected Works of Abraham Lincoln*. Edited by Roy P. Basler. 8 vols. New Brunswick, NJ: Rutgers UP, 1953.

———. *Political Writings and Speeches*. Edited by Terence Ball. Cambridge: Cambridge UP, 2013.

Madison, James, Alexander Hamilton, and John Jay. *The Federalist Papers*. Edited by Isaac Kramnick. London: Penguin, 1987.

McCune Smith, James. "The German Invasion." *Anglo-African Magazine* 1.2 (February 1859): 44–52.

———. Introduction to *My Bondage and My Freedom*, by Frederick Douglass. 1855. New York: Arno and New York Times, 1968.

———. *The Works of James McCune Smith: Black Intellectual and Abolitionist*. Edited by John Stauffer. Oxford: Oxford UP, 2006.

McKay, Claude. *Romance in Marseille*. Edited and with an introduction by Gary Edward Holcomb and William J. Maxwell. New York: Penguin, 2020.

Mill, John Stuart. *On Liberty, Utilitarianism, and Other Essays*. Edited and with an introduction and notes by Mark Philp and Frederick Rosen. 1991. Oxford: Oxford UP, 2015.

Murray, Albert. *The Omni-Americans: Some Alternatives to the Folklore of White Supremacy*. New York: Da Capo, 1970.

Newman, Richard, Patrick Rael, and Philip Lapsansky, eds. *Pamphlets of Protest: An Anthology of Early African American Protest Literature, 1790–1860*. New York: Routledge, 2001.

Northup, Solomon. *Twelve Years a Slave: Narrative of Solomon Northup, a Citizen of New York, Kidnapped in Washington in 1841, and Rescued in 1853, from a Cotton Plantation near the Red River in Louisiana*. Auburn, Buffalo, and London, 1853.

Pennington, James W. C. *Fugitive Blacksmith; or, Events in the History of James W. C. Pennington, Pastor of a Presbyterian Church, New York, Formerly a Slave in the State of Maryland, United States*. London, 1849.

———. *A Text Book of the Origin and History, etc. etc. of the Colored People*. Hartford, CT, 1841.

Porter, Dorothy, ed. *Early Negro Writing, 1760–1837*. 1971. Baltimore, MD: Black Classic P, 1995.

Potter, Eliza. *A Hairdresser's Experience in High Life*. Edited by Xiomara Santamarina. Chapel Hill: U of North Carolina P, 2009.

Ripley, C. Peter, ed. *The Black Abolitionist Papers*. 5 vols. Chapel Hill: U of North Carolina P, 1985–92.

Roediger, David R., ed. *Black on White: Black Writers on What It Means to Be White*. New York: Schocken, 1998.

Ruggles, David. *The 'Extinguisher' Extinguished, or David M. Reese, M.D. 'Used Up.'* New York, 1834.

Rush, Benjamin. "Thoughts on Common Sense." In *Essays, Literary, Moral & Philosophical*, 249–56. Philadelphia, 1798.

Sebree, Chet'la. *Mistress*. Kalamazoo, MI: New Issues, 2019.

Sterne, Laurence. *The Life and Opinions of Tristram Shandy, Gentleman*. Edited by Melvyn New and Joan New. London: Penguin, 1997.

———. *A Sentimental Journey and Other Writings*. Edited by Ian Jack and Tim Parnell. Oxford: Oxford UP, 2003.

Stevens, Thaddeus. *The Selected Papers of Thaddeus Stevens*. 2 vols. Edited by Beverly W. Palmer and Holly B. Ochoa. Pittsburgh: Pittsburgh UP, 1997.

Tocqueville, Alexis de. *De la démocratie en Amérique*. 2 vols. Paris: Gallimard, 1961.

Tubman, Harriet. "Dictated Letter to Franklin B. Sanborn about the Combahee River Raid" (30 June 1863). Document 6 in Jean M. Humez, *Harriet Tubman: The Life and the Life Stories*, 283–84. Madison: U of Wisconsin P, 2003.

Tucker, St. George *Dissertation on Slavery: With a Proposal for the Gradual Abolition of It, in the State of Virginia*. Philadelphia, 1796.

[Virgil] Publius Virgilius Maro. *Aeneid.* Translated by Michael Oakley. 1954. London: Dent, 1964.

Walker, David. *David Walker's Appeal to the Coloured Citizens of the World.* Edited and with an introduction by Peter P. Hinks. University Park: Pennsylvania State UP, 2000.

Ward, Samuel R. *Autobiography of a Fugitive Negro: His Antislavery Labours in the United States, Canada, & England.* 1855. New York: Arno, 1968.

Washington, John E. *They Knew Lincoln.* With a new introduction by Kate Masur. 1942. Oxford: Oxford UP, 2018.

Wheatley, Phillis. *Complete Writings.* Edited by Vincent Carretta. London: Penguin, 2001.

Whitfield, James M. *The Works of James M. Whitfield: America and Other Writings by a Nineteenth-Century African American Poet.* Edited by Robert S. Levine and Ivy G. Wilson. Chapel Hill: U of North Carolina P, 2011.

Willard, John W. *A History of Simon Willard, Inventor and Clockmaker. Together with Some Account of His Sons—His Apprentices—and the Workmen Associated with Him, with Brief Notices of Other Clockmakers of the Family Name.* Boston: Printed by E. O. Cockayne, 1911.

Wilson, William J. "From Our Brooklyn Correspondent." *Frederick Douglass' Paper* 6.12 (11 March 1853): 3.

———. "Afric-American Picture Gallery." *Anglo-African Magazine*, February–October, 1859. Text prepared by Leif Eckstrom and Britt Rusert. *Just Teach One: Early African American Print.* https://jtoaa.americanantiquarian.org/welcome-to-just-teach-one-african-american/afric-american-picture-gallery/.

———. "What Shall We Do with the White People?" *Anglo-African Magazine* 2.2 (February 1860): 41–45.

X, Malcolm. *The Autobiography of Malcolm X.* With the assistance of Alex Haley. Introduction by Paul Gilroy. 1965. London: Penguin, 2001.

SECONDARY WORKS

Akers, Charles. "'Our Modern Egyptians': Phillis Wheatley and the Whig Campaign against Slavery in Revolutionary Boston." *Journal of Negro History* 60 (July 1975): 297–310.

Alexander, Leslie. *African or American? Black Identity and Political Activism in New York City, 1784–1861.* Urbana: U of Illinois P, 2008.

Allen, Danielle. *Our Declaration: A Reading of the Declaration of Independence in Defense of Equality.* New York: Liveright, 2014.

Anderson, Amanda. *Bleak Liberalism.* Chicago: U of Chicago P, 2016.

Anderson, Benedict. *Imagined Communities: Reflections on the Origins and Spread of Nationalism.* 1983. New York: Verso, 2016.
Andrews, William L. "Benjamin Banneker's Revision of Thomas Jefferson: Conscience vs. Science in the Early American Antislavery Debate." In *Genius in Bondage: Literature of the Early Black Atlantic,* edited by Vincent Carretta and Philip Gould, 218–41. Lexington: UP of Kentucky, 2001.
———. "Daniel Coker, David Walker, and the Politics of Dialogue in Early Nineteenth-Century African American Literature." In *African American Literature in Transition, 1800–1830,* edited by Benjamin Fagan, 44–70. Cambridge: Cambridge UP, 2021.
Arendt, Hannah. *On Revolution.* New York: Viking, 1963.
Augst, Thomas. *The Clerk's Tale: Young Men and Moral Life in Nineteenth-Century America.* Chicago: UP of Chicago, 2003.
Bacon, Jacqueline. "'Do You Understand Your Own Language?': Revolutionary 'Topoi' in the Rhetoric of African-American Abolitionists." *Rhetoric Society Quarterly* 28.2 (Spring 1998): 55–57.
———. *Freedom's Journal: The First African-American Newspaper.* Lanham, MD: Lexington, 2007.
Bacon, Jacqueline, and Glen McGish. "Descendents of Africa, Sons of '76: Exploring African American Rhetoric." *Rhetoric Society Quarterly* 36 (2006): 1–29.
Bailyn, Bernard. *The Ideological Origins of the American Revolution.* 1967. Cambridge, MA: Harvard UP, 2017.
Ball, Erica L. *To Live an Antislavery Life: Personal Politics and the Making of the Black Middle Class.* Athens: U of Georgia P, 2015.
Ball, Terence. "The Formation of Character: Mill's 'Ethology' Reconsidered." *Polity* 33.1 (Autumn 2000): 25–48.
Bartels, Anke, Lars Eckstein, Nicole Waller, and Dirk Wiemann. "Postcolonial Enlightenments." In *Postcolonial Literatures in English: An Introduction,* 61–78. Stuttgart: Metzler, 2019.
Baumgartner, Kabria. *In Pursuit of Knowledge: Black Women and Educational Activism in Antebellum America.* New York: New York UP, 2019.
Bay, Mia. *The White Image in the Black Mind: African-American Ideas about White People, 1830–1925.* New York: Oxford UP, 2000.
———. "See Your Declaration Americans!!! Abolitionism, Americanism, and the Revolutionary Tradition in Free Black Politics." In *Americanism: New Perspectives on the History of an Ideal,* edited by Michael Kazin and Joseph A. McCartin, 25–52. Chapel Hill: U of North Carolina P, 2006.
Bedini, Silvio A. *The Life of Benjamin Banneker.* New York: Scribner, 1972.
———. "Thomas Jefferson, Clock Designer." *Proceedings of the American Philosophical Society* 108.3 (June 1964): 163–80.

———. *Thomas Jefferson: Statesman of Science*. New York: Macmillan, 1990.

Beebe, Ann. "Phillis Wheatley's TO THE REV. DR. THOMAS AMORY ON READING HIS SERMONS ON DAILY DEVOTION, IN WHICH THAT DUTY IS RECOMMENDED AND ASSISTED." *The Eplicator* 73.3 (2015): 229–34.

Bending, Stephen, and Stephen Bygrave. Introduction to *The Man of Feeling*, by Henry Mackenzie. Edited by Brian Vickers, vii–xxiv. Oxford: Oxford UP, 2001.

Bercovitch, Sacvan. *Rites of Assent: Transformations in the Symbolic Construction of America*. New York: Routledge, 1993.

Black, Alex W. "Abolitionism's Resonant Bodies: The Realization of African American Performance." *American Quarterly* 63.3 (September 2011): 619–39.

Black, Kelvin C. "Bound by 'the Principles of 1776': Dilemmas in Anglo-American Romanticism and Douglass's *The Heroic Slave*." *Studies in Romanticism* 56.1 (Spring 2017): 93–112.

Blackett, R. J. M. "William G. Allen: The Forgotten Professor." *Civil War History* 26.1 (1980): 39–52.

Blight, David W. *Frederick Douglass: Prophet of Freedom*. New York: Simon & Schuster, 2018.

Bloch, Ruth H. *Visionary Republic: Millennial Themes in American Thought, 1756–1800*. Cambridge: Cambridge UP, 1985.

Boeckmann, Cathy. *A Question of Character: Scientific Racism and the Genres of American Fiction, 1892–1912*. Tuscaloosa: U of Alabama P, 2000.

Bogin, Ruth. "'Liberty Further Extended': A 1776 Antislavery Manuscript by Lemuel Haynes." *William and Mary Quarterly* 40.1 (January 1983): 85–105.

Bonner, Christopher J. *Remaking the Republic: Black Politics and the Creation of American Citizenship*. Philadelphia: U of Pennsylvania P, 2020.

Brandt, Stefan L. *The Culture of Corporeality: Aesthetic Experience and the Embodiment of America, 1945–1960*. Heidelberg: Universitätsverlag Winter, 2007.

Brickhouse, Anna. *Transamerican Literary Relations and the Nineteenth-Century Public Sphere*. Cambridge: Cambridge UP, 2004.

Burstein, Andrew. *Democracy's Muse: How Thomas Jefferson Became an FDR Liberal, a Reagan Republican, and a Tea Party Fanatic, All the While Being Dead*. Charlottesville: U of Virginia P, 2015.

———. *Jefferson's Secrets: Death and Desire at Monticello*. New York: Basic, 2005.

———. *Sentimental Democracy: The Evolution of America's Romantic Self-Image*. New York: Hill and Wang, 1999.

Callanan, Keegan. "Liberal Constitutionalism and Political Particularism in Montesquieu's *The Spirit of the Laws*." *Political Research Quarterly* 67.3 (2014): 589–692.

Carpio, Glenda R., Gene A. Jarrett, R. Baxter Miller, Sonnet Retman, Marlon B. Ross, Xiomara Santamarina, Rafia Zafar, and Kenneth W. Warren. "What Was African American Literature?" *PMLA* 218.2 (2013): 386–408.

Carretta, Vincent. *Phillis Wheatley: Biography of a Genius in Bondage*. Athens: U of Georgia P, 2011.

Cassirer, Ernst. *The Philosophy of the Enlightenment*. With a new foreword by Peter Gay. Princeton, NJ: Princeton UP, 2009.

Charles, John C. *Abandoning the Black Hero: Sympathy and Privacy in the Postwar African American White-Life Novel*. New Brunswick, NJ: Rutgers UP, 2012.

Chuong, Jennifer Y. "Engraving's 'Immoveable Veil': Phillis Wheatley's Portrait and the Politics of Technique." *Art Bulletin* 104.2 (June 2022): 63–88.

Cleves, Rachel H. "'Hurtful to the State': The Political Morality of Federalist Antislavery." In *Contesting Slavery: The Politics of Bondage and Freedom in the New American Nation*, edited John Craig Hammond and Matthew Mason, 207–26. Charlottesville: U of Virginia P, 2012.

Cogliano, Francis D. *Thomas Jefferson: Reputation and Legacy*. Edinburgh: Edinburgh UP, 2006.

Cohen, Bernard. *Science and the Founding Fathers: Science in the Political Thought of Jefferson, Franklin, Adams, and Madison*. New York: Norton, 1995.

Collini, Stefan. "The Idea of 'Character' in Victorian Political Thought." *Transactions of the Royal Historical Society* 35 (1985): 29–51.

Commager, Henry S. *The Empire of Reason: How Europe Imagined and America Realized the Enlightenment*. Garden City, NY: Doubleday, 1977.

———. *Jefferson, Nationalism, and the Enlightenment*. New York: George Braziller, 1975.

Conkin, Paul K. "The Religious Pilgrimage of Thomas Jefferson." In *Jeffersonian Legacies*, edited by Peter S. Onuf, 19–49. Charlottesville: UP of Virginia, 1993.

Countryman, Edward. *Enjoy the Same Liberty: Black Americans in the Revolutionary Era*. Lanham, MD: Rowman & Littlefield, 2012.

Craiutu, Aurelian. *A Virtue for Courageous Minds: Moderation in French Political Thought, 1748–1830*. Princeton, NJ: Princeton UP, 2012.

Crane, Jacob. "'Razed to the Knees': The Anti-Heroic Body in James McCune Smith's 'The Heads of the Colored People.'" *African American Review* 51.1 (Spring 2018): 7–21.

Crow, Matthew. *Thomas Jefferson, Legal History, and the Art of Recollection*. Cambridge: Cambridge UP, 2017.

Dain, Bruce. *A Hideous Monster of the Mind: American Race Theory in the Early Republic*. Cambridge, MA: Harvard UP, 2003.

Darnton, Robert. *George Washington's False Teeth: An Unconventional Guide to the Eighteenth Century*. New York: Norton, 2003.

Daugherty, Ellen. "Negotiating the Veil: Tuskegee's Booker T. Washington Monument." *American Art* 24.3 (Fall 2019): 52–77.

Davis, David B. *The Problem of Slavery in the Age of Emancipation*. New York: Knopf, 2014.

Delgado, Richard, and Jean Stefancic. *Critical Race Theory: An Introduction*. 3rd ed. New York: New York UP, 2017.

Dinius, Marcy J. "'Look!! Look!!! At This!!!!': The Radical Typography of David Walker's *Appeal*." *PMLA* 126.1 (2011): 55–72.

Drexler, Michael J., and Ed White, eds. *Beyond Douglass: New Perspectives on Early African-American Literature*. Lewisburg, PA: Bucknell UP, 2008.

———. *The Traumatic Colonel: The Founding Fathers, Slavery, and the Phantasmatic Aaron Burr*. New York: New York UP, 2014.

Egerton, Douglas R. *Death or Liberty: African Americans and Revolutionary America*. New York: Oxford UP, 2009.

Elbert, Sarah. "An Inter-Racial Love Story in Fact and Fiction: William and Mary King Allen's Marriage and Louisa May Alcott's Tale, 'M.L.'" *History Workshop Journal* 53.1 (Spring 2002): 17–42.

Eliot, T. S. "Tradition and the Individual Talent." Reprinted in *The Sacred Wood*, by Eliot, 42–53. London: Methuen, 1920.

Ellis, Joseph J. *American Sphinx: The Character of Thomas Jefferson*. New York: Knopf, 1997.

Ely, Melvin P. "Richard and Julia Randolph, St. George Tucker, George Wythe, Syphax Brown, and Hercules White: Racial Equality and the Snares of Prejudice." In *Revolutionary Founders: Rebels, Radicals, and Reformers in the Making of the Nation*, edited by Alfred F. Young, Gary B. Nash, and Ray Raphael, 323–36. New York: Vintage, 2011.

Ernest, John. *Liberation Historiography: African American Writers and the Challenge of History, 1794–1861*. Chapel Hill: U of North Carolina P, 2004.

Eustace, Nicole. "Emotional Pursuits and the American Revolution." *Emotion Review* 12.3 (July 2020): 146–55.

———. *Passion Is the Gale: Emotion, Power, and the Coming of the American Revolution*. Chapel Hill: U of North Carolina P, 2008.

Everett, Gabrielle. "Reading the 'Veil of Black' in Frederick Douglass and Thomas Jefferson: Affective Legibility and National Belonging." *African American Review* 53.3 (Fall 2020): 163–80.

Eze, Emmanuel Chukwudi. *On Reason: Rationality in a World of Cultural Conflict and Racism*. Durham, NC: Duke UP, 2008.

Ferguson, Robert A. *The American Enlightenment*. Cambridge, MA: Harvard UP, 1997.

———. *Law and Letters in American Culture*. Cambridge, MA: Harvard UP, 1984.

Fields, Karen E., and Barbara J. Fields. *Racecraft: The Soul of Inequality in American Life*. New York: Verso, 2014.

Finseth, Ian F. *Shades of Green: Visions of Nature in the Literature of American Slavery, 1770–1860*. Athens: U of Georgia P, 2009.

Fisher, David H. *African Founders: How Enslaved People Expanded American Ideas*. New York: Simon & Schuster, 2022.

Forbes, Robert P. Introduction to *Notes on the State of Virginia: An Annotated Edition*, by Thomas Jefferson. Edited and with an introduction and notes by Forbes, xix–lx. New Haven, CT: Yale UP, 2022.

Fredrickson, George M. *The Black Image in the White Mind: The Debate on Afro-American Character and Destiny, 1817–1914*. New York: Harper & Row, 1971.

Gadamer, Hans-Georg. *Wahrheit und Methode: Grundzüge einer philosophischen Hermeneutik*. Tübingen: Mohr, 1960.

Gaines, Kevin R. *Uplifting the Race: Black Leadership, Politics, and Culture in the Twentieth Century*. Chapel Hill: U of North Carolina P, 1996.

Gates, Henry L., Jr. "Editor's Introduction: Writing 'Race' and the Difference It Makes." *Critical Inquiry* 12.1 (Autumn 1985): 1–20.

———. *Figures in Black: Words, Signs, and the "Racial" Self*. Oxford: Oxford UP, 1989.

———. *The Henry Louis Gates, Jr. Reader*. Edited by Abby Wolf. New York: Basic Civitas, 2012.

———. "In Her Own Write." Series introduction to *The Schomburg Library of Nineteenth-Century Black Women Writers*. New York: Oxford UP, 1988.

———. Foreword to *The Works of James McCune Smith*. Edited by John Stauffer, viii–xii. Oxford: Oxford UP, 2006.

———. *The Signifying Monkey: A Theory of Afro-American Literary Criticism*. New York: Oxford UP, 1988.

———. *The Trials of Phillis Wheatley: America's First Black Poet and Her Encounters with the Founding Fathers*. New York: Basic, 2003.

Gates, Henry L., Jr., and Andrew S. Curran. *Who's Black and Why? A Hidden Chapter from the Eighteenth-Century Invention of Race*. Cambridge, MA: Harvard UP, 2022.

Gates, Henry L., Jr., and Nellie Y. McKay. "Introduction: Talking Books." In *Norton Anthology of African American Literature*. 2nd ed. New York: Norton, 2004.

Gay, Peter. *The Enlightenment: An Interpretation*. 2 vols. Vol. 2, *The Science of Freedom*. New York: Knopf, 1969.

Gerbi, Antonello. *The Dispute of the New World: The History of a Polemic, 1750–1900*. 1973. Pittsburgh: U of Pittsburgh P, 2010.
Gilroy, Paul. *The Black Atlantic: Modernity and Double Consciousness*. Cambridge, MA: Harvard UP, 1993.
Gish, Dustin, and Daniel Klinghard. *Thomas Jefferson and the Science of Republican Government: A Political Biography of Notes on the State of Virginia*. Cambridge: Cambridge UP, 2017.
Godel, Rainer. *Vorurteil—Anthropologie—Literatur: Der Vorurteilsdiskurs als Modus der Selbstaufklärung im 18. Jahrhundert*. Tübingen: Niemeyer, 2007.
Gordon, Lewis R., and Jane Anna Gordon, eds. *Not Only the Master's Tools: African-American Studies in Theory and Practice*. London: Routledge, 2006.
Gordon-Reed, Annette. "Engaging Jefferson: Blacks and the Founding Father." *William and Mary Quarterly* 57.1 (January 2000): 171–82.
———. *The Hemingses of Monticello: An American Family*. New York: Norton, 2008.
———. *On Juneteenth*. New York: Liveright, 2021.
———. *Thomas Jefferson and Sally Hemings: An American Controversy*. Charlottesville: U of Virginia P, 1997.
Gordon-Reed, Annette, and Peter S. Onuf. *"Most Blessed of the Patriarchs": Thomas Jefferson and the Empire of the Imagination*. New York: Liveright, 2016.
Gould, Eliga. "Independence and Interdependence: The American Revolution and the Problem of Postcolonial Nationhood, ca. 1802." *William and Mary Quarterly* 74.4 (October 2017): 729–52.
Greene, Jack P. "The Intellectual Reconstruction of Virginia in the Age of Jefferson." In *Jefferson Legacies*, edited by Peter S. Onuf, 225–53. Charlottesville: UP of Virginia, 1993.
Gross, Ariela J. *Double Character: Slavery and Mastery in the Antebellum Southern Courtroom*. Princeton, NJ: Princeton UP, 2000.
Gutzman, Kevin R. C. *Thomas Jefferson—Revolutionary: A Radical's Struggle to Remake America*. New York: St. Martin's, 2017.
Guyatt, Nicholas. *Bind Us Apart: How Enlightened Americans Invented Racial Segregation*. New York: Basic, 2016.
Habermas, Jürgen. *Auch eine Geschichte der Philosophie*. 2 vols. Vol. 2, *Vernünftige Freiheit: Spuren des Diskurses über Glauben und Wissen*. Frankfurt/M.: Suhrkamp, 2019.
Hack, Daniel. *Reaping Something New: African American Transformations of Victorian Literature*. Princeton, NJ: Princeton UP, 2017.
Hammann, Andrew F. *Freedom in Black and White: The Politics of Slavery and Black Expatriation in Nineteenth-Century America*. Charlottesville: U of Virginia P, forthcoming.

Haynes, Kevin J. *The Road to Monticello: The Life and Mind of Thomas Jefferson.* New York: Oxford UP, 2008.
Helo, Ari. *Thomas Jefferson's Ethics and the Politics of Human Progress: The Morality of a Slaveholder.* Cambridge: Cambridge UP, 2014.
Herschthal, Eric. *The Science of Abolition: How Slaveholders Became the Enemies of Progress.* New Haven, CT: Yale UP, 2021.
Himmelfarb, Gertrude. *The Roads to Modernity: The British, French and American Enlightenments.* 1994. London: Vintage, 2008.
Hinks, Peter P. *To Awaken My Afflicted Brethren: David Walker and the Problem of Antebellum Slave Resistance.* University Park: Pennsylvania State UP, 1997.
Hodges, Graham R. G. *David Ruggles: A Radical Black Abolitionist and the Underground Railroad in New York City.* Chapel Hill: U of North Carolina P, 2019.
Holton, Woody. *Liberty Is Sweet: The Hidden History of the American Revolution.* New York: Simon & Schuster, 2021.
Honneck, Mischa. *We Are the Revolutionists: German-Speaking Immigrants and American Abolitionists after 1848.* Athens: U of Georgia P, 2011.
Horkheimer, Max, and Theodor Adorno. *Dialektik der Aufklärung: Philosophische Fragmente.* 1944. Amsterdam: de Munter, 1968.
Israel, Jonathan, *Democratic Enlightenment: Philosophy, Revolution, and Human Rights, 1750–1790.* New York: Oxford UP, 2011.
———. *The Expanding Blaze: How the American Revolution Ignited the World.* Princeton, NJ: Princeton UP, 2017.
Jarrett, Gene A. *Representing the Race: A New Political History of African American Literature.* New York: New York UP, 2011.
Jayne, Allen. *Jefferson's Declaration of Independence: Origins, Philosophy, and Theology.* Lexington: UP of Kentucky, 1998.
Johnson, Walter. "To Remake the World: Slavery, Racial Capitalism, and Justice." In Walter Johnson and Robin D. G. Kelley, *Forum 1: Race Capitalism Justice.* Boston Review, 13–31. Boston: Boston Critic, 2017.
Jordan, Winthrop D. *White over Black: American Attitudes toward the Negro, 1550–1812.* Chapel Hill: U of North Carolina P, 1968.
Kelleter, Frank. *Amerikanische Aufklärung: Sprachen der Rationalität im Zeitalter der Revolution.* Paderborn: Schöningh, 2002.
———. *Con/Tradition: Louis Farrakhan's Nation of Islam, the Million Man March, and American Civil Religion.* Heidelberg: Universitätsverlag Winter, 2000.
———. "A Literature of Civic Indignation: The Empathies and Resentments of American Liberalism, 1767–1826." Unpublished manuscript.
Kendi, Ibram X. "An Intellectual History of a Book Title: Stamped from the Beginning." *Black Perspectives: Blog of the African American Intellectual History Society*

(AAIHS), 8 April 2016. https://www.aaihs.org/an-intellectual-history-of-a-book-title/.

———. *Stamped from the Beginning: The Definitive History of Racist Ideas in America*. New York: Bold Type, 2016.

Kerber, Linda K. *Federalists in Dissent: Imagery and Ideology in Jeffersonian America*. Ithaca, NY: Cornell UP, 1980.

Kindermann, Wolf. *Man Unknown to Himself: Kritische Reflexion der amerikanischen Aufklärung: Crèvecoeur—Benjamin Rush—Charles Brockden Brown*. Tübingen: Narr, 1993.

Knott, Sarah. *Sensibility and the American Revolution*. Chapel Hill: U of North Carolina P, 2009.

Kondylis, Panajotis. *Die Aufklärung im Rahmen des neuzeitlichen Rationalismus*. Stuttgart: Klett-Cotta, 1981.

Koselleck, Reinhart. *Kritik und Krise*. 1959. Frankfurt/M.: Suhrkamp, 1973.

Krohn, Wolfgang. *Francis Bacon*. Munich: Beck, 1987.

Kühne-Bertram, G. "Vorverständnis." In *Historisches Wörterbuch der Philosophie*, 12 vols., edited by Joachim Ritter, Karlfried Gründer, and Gottfried Gabriel, 11:1267–71. Darmstadt: Wissenschaftliche Buchgesellschaft, 2001.

Lamb, Jonathan. *The Things Things Say*. Princeton, NJ: Princeton UP, 2011.

Lanier, Shannon, and Jane Feldman. *Jefferson's Children: The Story of One American Family*. New York: Random House, 2000.

Lepore, Jill. *These Truths: A History of the United States*. New York: Norton, 2019.

Levecq, Christine. *Slavery and Sentiment: The Politics of Feeling in Black Atlantic Antislavery Writing*. Durham: U of New Hampshire P, 2008.

Levine, Robert S. *Dislocating Race and Nation: Episodes in Nineteenth-Century American Literary Nationalism*. Chapel Hill: U of North Carolina P, 2008.

———. Introduction to *Martin R. Delany: A Documentary Reader*. Edited by Robert S. Levine, 1–22. Chapel Hill: U of North Carolina P, 2003.

Lewis, Andrew. *A Democracy of Facts: Natural History in the Early Republic*. Philadelphia: U of Pennsylvania P, 2011.

Lewis, Jan E., and Peter S. Onuf, eds. *Sally Hemings and Thomas Jefferson: History, Memory, and Civic Culture*. Charlottesville: U of Virginia P, 1999.

Li, Stephanie. *Playing in the White: Black Writers, White Subjects*. New York: Oxford UP, 2015.

Lorde, Audre. "The Master's Tools Will Never Dismantle the Master's House." In *Sister Outsider: Essays and Speeches*, 110–14. 1984. Berkeley, CA: Crossing P, 2007.

Lukasik, Christopher J. *Discerning Characters: The Culture of Appearance in Early America*. Philadelphia: U of Pennsylvania P, 2011.

Lynch, Deidre S. *The Economy of Character: Novels, Market Culture, and the Business of Inner Meaning.* Chicago: U of Chicago P, 1998.

Lyons, Jonathan. *The Society for Useful Knowledge: How Benjamin Franklin and Friends Brought the Enlightenment to America.* New York: Bloomsbury, 2013.

Maier, Pauline. *American Scripture: Making the Declaration of Independence.* New York: Knopf, 1997.

Manning, Susan. "Naming of Parts; or, The Comforts of Classification: Thomas Jefferson's Construction of America as Fact and Myth." *Journal of American Studies* 30.3 (December 1996): 345–64.

——. *Poetics of Character: Transatlantic Encounters, 1700–1900.* Cambridge: Cambridge UP, 2013.

Manning, Susan, and Francis D. Cogliano, eds. *The Atlantic Enlightenment.* Aldershot, UK: Ashgate, 2008.

Masur, Kate. *Until Justice Be Done: America's First Civil Rights Movement, from the Revolution to Reconstruction.* New York: Norton, 2021.

May, Henry F. *The Enlightenment in America.* Oxford: Oxford UP, 1976.

Mbembe, Achille. *Critique of Black Reason.* Durham, NC: Duke UP, 2017.

McCarthy, Timothy P., and John Stauffer, eds. *Prophets of Protest: Reconsidering the History of American Abolitionism.* New York: New Press, 2006.

McDonald, Robert M. S., ed. *Light and Liberty: Thomas Jefferson and the Power of Knowledge.* Charlottesville: U of Virginia P, 2012.

——. "Thomas Jefferson's Changing Reputation as Author of the 'Declaration of Independence': The First Fifty Years." *Journal of the Early Republic* 19 (1999): 169–95.

——, ed. *Thomas Jefferson's Lives: Biographers and the Battle for History.* Charlottesville: U of Virginia P, 2019.

McHenry, Elizabeth. *Forgotten Readers: Recovering the Lost History of African American Literary Societies.* Durham, NC: Duke UP, 2002.

Melish, Joanne P. "The 'Condition' Debate and Racial Discourse in the Antebellum North." *Journal of the Early Republic* 19.4 (Winter 1999): 651–72.

Miller, Charles A. *Jefferson and Nature: An Interpretation.* Baltimore, MD: Johns Hopkins UP, 1988.

Mills, Charles W. *Blackness Visible: Essays on Philosophy and Race.* Ithaca, NY: Cornell UP, 1998.

Monescalchi, Michael. "Phillis Wheatley, Samuel Hopkins, and the Rise of Disinterested Benevolence." *Early American Literature* 54.2 (Spring 2019): 413–44.

Moses, Wilson J. *Creative Conflict in African American Thought.* Cambridge: Cambridge UP, 2004.

———. Introduction to *Destiny and Race. Selected Writings, 1840–1898*, by Alexander Crummell. Edited and introduced by Moses. Amherst: U of Massachusetts P, 1992.

———. *Thomas Jefferson: A Modern Prometheus*. Cambridge: Cambridge UP, 2019.

Murray, Albert. "The Dynamics of Heroic Action." In *The Hero and the Blues*, 35–63. New York: Vintage, 1973.

Myers, Peter C. *Frederick Douglass: Race and the Rebirth of American Liberalism*. Lawrence: UP of Kansas, 2008.

Nagel, Thomas. *The View from Nowhere*. New York: Oxford UP, 1989.

Neem, Johann. "'From Ancients to Axioms' to 'Every Branch of Science': Thomas Jefferson's Philosophy of Liberal Education." In *The Founding of Thomas Jefferson's University*, edited by John A. Ragosta, Peter S. Onuf, and Andrew J. O'Shaughnessy, 306–24. Charlottesville: U of Virginia P, 2019.

Newman, Richard S. "Good Communications Corrects Bad Manners: The Banneker-Jefferson Dialogue and the Project of White Uplift." In *Contesting Slavery: The Politics of Bondage and Freedom in the New American Nation*, edited by John Craig Hammond and Matthew Mason, 69–93. Charlottesville: U of Virginia P, 2012.

———. "Prince Hall, Richard Allen, and Daniel Coker: Revolutionary Black Founders, Revolutionary Black Communities." In *Revolutionary Founders: Rebels, Radicals, and Reformers in the Making of the Nation*, edited by Alfred S. Young, Gary B. Nash, and Ray Raphael, 305–21. New York: Vintage, 2011.

———. *The Transformation of American Abolitionism: Fighting Slavery in the Early Republic*. Chapel Hill: U of North Carolina P, 2002.

Newman, Richard S., and Roy E. Finkenbine, eds. "Forum: Black Founders and the New Republic." *William and Mary Quarterly* 64.1 (January 2007): 83–182.

O'Donnell, Oliver C. *Portraits of Empiricism: Art Histories from an Intellectual Tradition*. University Park: Pennsylvania State UP, forthcoming.

O'Malley, Lurana D. "'Why I Wrote the Phyllis Wheatley-Pageant Play': Mary Church Terrell's Bicentennial Activism." *Theatre History Studies*, 27 (2018): 225–55.

O'Shaughnessy, Andrew J. *"The Illimitable Freedom of the Human Mind": Thomas Jefferson's Idea of a University*. Charlottesville: U of Virginia P, 2021.

Onuf, Peter S. "Antiquarian America: Isaiah Thomas and the New Nation's Future." In *Revolutionary Prophecies: The Founders and America's Future*, edited by Robert M. S. McDonald and Peter S. Onuf, 129–47. Charlottesville: U of Virginia P, 2020.

———. "The Declaration of Independence for a New Millennium." In *The Cambridge Companion to the Declaration of Independence*. Cambridge: Cambridge UP, forthcoming.
———. *Jefferson and the Virginians: Democracy, Constitutions, and Empire*. Charlottesville: U of Virginia P, 2018.
———. *Jefferson's Empire: The Language of American Nationhood*. Charlottesville: U of Virginia P, 2000.
———. *The Mind of Thomas Jefferson*. Charlottesville: U of Virginia P, 2007.
———. "The Scholars' Jefferson." *William and Mary Quarterly* 50.4 (1993): 671–99.
Onuf, Peter S., and Nicholas G. Onuf. *Nations, Markets and War: Modern History and the American Civil War*. Charlottesville: U of Virginia P, 2006.
Parkinson, Robert G. *The Common Cause: Creating Race and Nation in the American Revolution*. Chapel Hill: U of North Carolina P, 2016.
———. "The Declaration of Independence." In *A Companion to Thomas Jefferson*, edited by Francis D. Cogliano, 44–59. Malden, MA: Blackwell, 2012.
Parrish, Susan Scott. *American Curiosity: Cultures of Natural History in the Colonial British Atlantic World*. Chapel Hill: U of North Carolina P, 2006.
Paterson, Anita. *From Emerson to King: Democracy, Race, and the Politics of Progress*. Cary: Oxford UP, 1997.
Peterson, Carla L. *Black Gotham: A Family History of African Americans in Nineteenth-Century New York City*. New Haven, CT: Yale UP, 2011.
———. *"Doers of the Word": African-American Women Speakers and Writers in the North (1830–1880)*. 1995. New Brunswick, NJ: Rutgers UP, 1998.
———. "Untangling Genealogy's Tangled Skeins: Alexander Crummell, James McCune Smith, and Nineteenth-Century Black Literary Traditions." In *A Companion to American Literary Studies*, edited by Caroline Levander and Robert S. Levine, 500–516. Malden, MA: Blackwell, 2011.
Peterson, Merrill D. *The Jefferson Image in the American Mind*. New York: Oxford UP, 1960.
Polgar, Paul J. *Standard-Bearers of Equality: America's First Abolition Movement*. Chapel Hill: U of North Carolina P, 2019.
Porte, Joel. "Emerson, Thoreau, and the Double Consciousness." *New England Quarterly* 41.1 (March 1968): 40–50.
Porter, Roy. *Enlightenment: Britain and the Creation of the Modern World*. New York: Allen Layne/Penguin, 2000.
Proenza-Coles, Christina. *American Founders: How People of African Descent Established Freedom in the New World*. With a foreword by Edward L. Ayers. Sydney: New South, 2019.

Quarles, Benjamin. "Antebellum Free Blacks and the 'Spirit of '76.'" In *Black Mosaic: Essays in Afro-American History and Historiography*, 92–108. Amherst: U of Massachusetts P, 1988.

Rael, Patrick. *Black Identity and Black Protest in the Antebellum North*. Chapel Hill: U of North Carolina P, 2002.

Ragosta, John. *Religious Freedom: Jefferson's Legacy, America's Creed*. Charlottesville: U of Virginia P, 2013.

Ray, Angela G. "'In My Own Handwriting': Benjamin Banneker Addresses the Slaveholder at Monticello." *Rhetoric and Public Affairs* 1.3 (Fall 1998): 387–405.

Reed, Adolph, Jr., and Kenneth W. Warren. *Renewing Black Intellectual History: The Ideological and Material Foundations of African American Thought*. Boulder, CO: Paradigm, 2010.

Regis, Pamela. *Describing Early America: Bartram, Jefferson, Crèvecoeur, and the Influence of Natural History*. Philadelphia: U of Pennsylvania P, 1999.

Reisinger, K., and O. R. Scholz. "Vorurteil." In *Historisches Wörterbuch der Philosophie*, edited by Joachim Ritter, Karlfried Gründer, and Gottfried Gabriel, 12 vols, 11:1249–63. Darmstadt: Wissenschaftliche Buchgesellschaft, 2001.

Richardson, Joan. *A Natural History of Pragmatism: The Fact of Feeling from Jonathan Edwards to Gertrude Stein*. Cambridge: Cambridge UP, 2006.

Robinson, William H. *Phillis Wheatley: A Bio-Bibliography*. Boston: Hall, 1981.

Rosenfeld, Sophia. *Common Sense: A Political History*. Cambridge, MA: Harvard UP, 2011.

Rossignol, Marie-Jeanne. "Revisiting 'An Enquiry Concerning the Literature of Negroes' by the Abbé Grégoire, 1808: New Research on the First Anthology of African American Literature." Lecture at the Kennedy-Institute for North American Studies, Freie Universität Berlin, 18 May 2022.

Rusert, Britt. *Fugitive Science: Empiricism and Freedom in Early African American Culture*. New York: New York UP, 2017.

Ruttenburg, Nancy. *Democratic Personality: Popular Voice and the Trial of American Authorship*. Stanford, CA: Stanford UP, 1998.

Saillant, John. "The American Enlightenment in Africa: Jefferson's Colonizationism and Black Virginians' Migration to Liberia, 1776–1840." *Eighteenth-Century Studies* 31.3 (Spring 1998): 261–82.

———. "Aspirant Citizenship." In *Beyond Douglass: New Perspectives on Early African-American Literature*, edited by Michael J. Drexler and Ed White, 123–40. Lewisburg, PA: Bucknell UP, 2008.

———. *Black Puritan, Black Republican: The Life and Thought of Lemuel Haynes, 1753–1833*. Oxford: Oxford UP, 2003.

Salazar, James. *Bodies of Reform: The Rhetoric of Character in Gilded Age America.* New York: New York UP, 2010.
Savory, Jerold J. "The Rending of the Veil in W. E. B. Du Bois's *The Souls of Black Folk.*" *CLA Journal* 15.3 (March 1973): 334–37.
Schmeller, Mark G. *Invisible Sovereign: Imagining Public Opinion from the Revolution to Reconstruction.* Baltimore, MD: Johns Hopkins UP, 2016.
Schmidt, Leigh E. *Hearing Things: Religion, Illusion, and the American Enlightenment.* Cambridge, MA: Harvard UP, 2000.
Schneiders, Werner. *Aufklärung und Vorurteilskritik: Studien zur Geschichte der Vorurteilstheorie.* Stuttgart–Bad Cannstatt: frommann-holzboog, 1983.
Seigel, Jerrold. *The Idea of the Self: Thought and Experience in Western Europe since the Seventeenth Century.* Cambridge: Cambridge UP, 2005.
———. "Necessity, Freedom, and Character Formation from the Eighteenth Century to the Nineteenth." In *Character, Self, and Sociability in the Scottish Enlightenment,* edited by Thomas Ahnert and Susan Manning, 249–65. New York: Palgrave, 201.
Shapin, Steven. *A Social History of Truth: Civility and Science in Seventeenth-Century England.* Chicago: U of Chicago P, 1994.
Sharpe, Christina. *In the Wake: On Blackness and Being.* Durham, NC: Duke UP, 2016.
Sheehan, Colleen A. *James Madison and the Spirit of Republican Government.* New York: Cambridge UP, 2009.
———. "Public Opinion and the Formation of Civic Character in Madison's Republican Theory." *Review of Politics* 67.1 (Winter 2005): 37–48.
Sheridan, Eugene R. Introduction to *Jefferson's Extracts from the Gospels,* by Thomas Jefferson. Edited by Dickinson W. Adams and Ruth W. Lester, 3–42. Princeton, NJ: Princeton UP, 1983.
Shields, David S. *Civil Tongues and Polite Letters in British America.* Chapel Hill: U of North Carolina P, 1997.
Shields, John C. *Phillis Wheatley and the Romantics.* Knoxville: U of Tennessee P, 2010.
———. *Phillis Wheatley's Poetics of Liberation: Backgrounds and Contexts.* Knoxville: U of Tennessee P, 2008.
Sidbury, James. *Becoming African in America: Race and Nation in the Early Black Atlantic, 1760–1830.* New York: Oxford UP, 2007.
Simpson, David. *Situatedness, or, Why We Keep Saying Where We're Coming From.* Durham, NC: Duke UP, 2002.
Sinha, Manisha. *The Slave's Cause: A History of Abolition.* New Haven, CT: Yale UP, 2016.

Slauter, Eric. "The Declaration of Independence and the New Nation." In *The Cambridge Companion to Thomas Jefferson*, edited by Frank Shuffleton, 12–34. Cambridge: Cambridge UP, 2009.

———. *The State as a Work of Art: The Cultural Origins of the Constitution*. Chicago: Chicago UP, 2009.

Sluga, Hans. "Heidegger and the Critique of Reason." In *What's Left of Enlightenment?: A Postmodern Question*, edited by Keith M. Baker and Peter H. Reill, 50–70. Stanford, CA: Stanford UP, 2001.

Soderberg, Laura. "One More Time with Feeling: Repetition, Reparation, and the Sentimental Subject in William Wells Brown's Rewritings of *Clotel*." *American Literature* 88.2 (June 2016): 241–67.

Spahn, Hannah. "Blood and Character in Early African American Literature." In *The Cultural Politics of Blood, 1500–1900*, edited by Kimberly Anne Coles, Ralph Bauer, Zita Nunes, and Carla L. Peterson, 146–67. Basingstoke, UK: Palgrave, 2015.

———. "Cosmopolitanism, Character, and the Theories of Early African American Literature." In *African American Literature in Transition, 1830–1850*, edited by Benjamin Fagan, 177–201. Cambridge: Cambridge UP, 2021.

———. *Thomas Jefferson, Time, and History*. Charlottesville: U of Virginia P, 2011.

Spencer, Mark G., ed. *The Bloomsbury Encyclopedia of the American Enlightenment*. New York: Bloomsbury Academic, 2015.

Spires, Derrick R. *The Practice of Citizenship: Black Politics and Print Culture in the Early United States*. Philadelphia: U of Pennsylvania P, 2019.

Spivak, Gayatri Chakravorty. *An Aesthetic Education in the Era of Globalization*. Cambridge, MA: Harvard UP, 2013.

———. *A Critique of Postcolonial Reason: Toward a History of the Vanishing Present*. Cambridge, MA: Harvard UP, 1999.

Stampone, Christopher. "Are We Reading the Right Clotel(le)? Revolutions in Early African American Literature." *Studies in American Fiction* 45.2 (Fall 2018): 191–211.

Stancliff, Michael. *Frances Ellen Watkins Harper: African American Reform Rhetoric and the Rise of the Modern Nation State*. New York: Routledge, 2012.

Stanton, Lucia. *"Those Who Labor for My Happiness": Slavery at Thomas Jefferson's Monticello*. Charlottesville: U of Virginia P, 2012.

Stauffer, John. *The Black Hearts of Men: Radical Abolitionists and the Transformation of Race*. Cambridge, MA: Harvard UP, 2002.

———. Introduction to *The Works of James McCune Smith*, edited by Stauffer, xiii–xl. Oxford: Oxford UP, 2006.

Steele, Brian D. "Getting 'the Hang of the Declaration': The Declaration. in American Nationalism." In *The Cambridge Companion to the Declaration of Independence*. Cambridge: Cambridge UP, forthcoming.

———. *Thomas Jefferson and American Nationhood*. Cambridge: Cambridge UP, 2012.

Stepto, Robert B. *From behind the Veil: A Study of Afro-American Narrative*. Urbana: U of Illinois P, 1979.

Stewart, Matthew. *An Emancipation of the Mind: Radical Philosophy, the War over Slavery, and the Refounding of America*. New York: Norton, forthcoming.

Stern, Julia A. *The Plight of Feeling: Sympathy and Dissent in the Early American Novel*. Chicago: Chicago UP, 1997.

Stovall, Tyler. *White Freedom: The Racial History of an Idea*. Princeton, NJ: Princeton UP, 2021.

Susman, Warren I. "'Personality' and the Making of Twentieth-Century Culture." In *New Directions in American Intellectual History*, edited by John Higham and Paul K. Conkin, 212–26. Baltimore, MD: Johns Hopkins UP, 1979.

Sweet, Timothy. "Jefferson, Science, and the Enlightenment." In *The Cambridge Companion to Thomas Jefferson*, edited by Frank Shuffleton, 110–13. Cambridge: Cambridge UP, 2009.

Tamarkin, Elisa. *Anglophilia: Deference, Devotion, and Antebellum America*. Chicago: U of Chicago P, 2008.

Tawil, Ezra. *Literature, American Style: The Originality of Imitation in the Early Republic*. Philadelphia: U of Pennsylvania P, 2018.

Taylor, Alan. *The Internal Enemy: Slavery and War in Virginia, 1772–1832*. New York: Norton, 2013.

Thomas, Herman E. *James W. C. Pennington: African-American Churchman and Abolitionist*. New York: Garland, 1995.

Thomas, Rhondda R. "Exodus and Colonization: Charting the Journey in the Journals of Daniel Coker, a Descendant of Africa." *African American Review* 41.3 (Fall 2007): 507–19.

Thompson, Peter. "David Walker's Nationalism—and Thomas Jefferson's." *Journal of the Early Republic* 37.1 (Spring 2017): 47–80.

———. "'I Have Known': Thomas Jefferson, Experience, and Notes on the State of Virginia." In *A Companion to Thomas Jefferson*, edited by Francis D. Cogliano, 60–74. Malden, MA: Blackwell, 2012.

Thomson, Keith S. *Jefferson's Shadow: The Story of His Science*. New Haven, CT: Yale UP, 2012.

Tillery, Alvin B., Jr. "Reading Tocqueville behind the Veil: Receptions of Democracy in America, 1835–1900." *American Political Thought* 7 (Winter 2018): 1–25.

Trinehart, Nicholas. "The Man That Was a Thing: Reconsidering Human Commodification in Slavery." *Journal of Social History* 50.1 (Fall 2016): 28–50.
Valsania, Maurizio. *Jefferson's Body: A Corporeal Biography*. Charlottesville: U of Virginia P, 2017.
Waldstreicher, David. "Ancients, Moderns, and Africans: Phillis Wheatley and the Politics of Empire and Slavery in the American Revolution." *Journal of the Early Republic* 37.4 (Winter 2017): 701-33.
———. "Phillis Wheatley: The Poet Who Challenged the American Revolutionaries." In *Revolutionary Founders: Rebels, Radicals, and Reformers in the Making of the Nation*, edited by Alfred F. Young, Gary B. Nash, and Ray Raphael, 97–113. New York: Vintage, 2011.
———. "Women's Politics, Antislavery Politics, and Phillis Wheatley's American Revolution." In *Revolutions and Reconstructions: Black Politics in the Long Nineteenth Century*, edited by Van Gosse and David Waldstreicher, 24–40. Philadelphia: U of Pennsylvania P, 2020.
Warren, Kenneth W. *What Was African American Literature?* Cambridge, MA: Harvard UP, 2011.
Watson, Veronica T. *The Souls of White Folk: African American Writers Theorize Whiteness*. Jackson: UP of Mississippi, 2013.
Wellmon, Chad. *Organizing Enlightenment: Information Overload and the Invention of the Modern Research University*. Baltimore, MD: Johns Hopkins UP, 2015.
Wetters, Kirk. *The Opinion System: Impasses of the Public Sphere from Hobbes to Habermas*. New York: Fordham UP, 2008.
White, Gayle J. *Reclamation: Sally Hemings, Thomas Jefferson, and a Descendant's Search for Her Family's Lasting Legacy*. New York: Amistad, 2021.
Wilentz, Sean. *No Property in Man: Slavery and Antislavery at the Nation's Founding. With a New Preface*. Cambridge, MA: Harvard UP, 2021.
Wilkins, Roger. *Jefferson's Pillow: The Founding Fathers and the Dilemma of Black Patriotism*. Boston: Beacon, 2002.
Wills, Garry. *Negro President: Jefferson and the Slave Power*. Boston: Houghton Mifflin, 2003.
Wilson, Ivy G. *Spectres of Democracy: Blackness and the Aesthetics of Politics in the Antebellum U.S.* Oxford: Oxford UP, 2011.
———. "THE BRIEF AND WONDROUS LIFE OF THE ANGLO-AFRICAN MAGAZINE Or, Antebellum African American Editorial Practice and Its Afterlives." In *Publishing Blackness: Textual Constructions of Race since 1850*, edited by George Hutchinson and John K. Young, 18–37. Ann Arbor: U of Michigan P, 2012.

Winch, Julie. *A Gentleman of Color: The Life of James Forten*. Oxford: Oxford UP, 2002.

Winter, Thomas. *Making Men, Making Class: The YMCA and Workingmen, 1877–1920*. Chicago: Chicago UP, 2002.

Winterer, Caroline. *American Enlightenments: Pursuing Happiness in the Age of Reason*. New Haven, CT: Yale UP, 2016.

Wood, Gordon S. *The Creation of the American Republic*. Chapel Hill: U of North Carolina P, 1969.

———. "The Ghosts of Monticello." In *Sally Hemings and Thomas Jefferson: History, Memory, and Civic Culture*, edited by Jan E. Lewis and Peter S. Onuf, 19–34. Charlottesville: UP of Virginia, 1999.

Wright, Johnson K. "'A Bright Clear Mirror': Cassirer's *The Philosophy of the Enlightenment*." In *What's Left of Enlightenment?: A Postmodern Question*, edited by Keith M. Baker and Peter H. Reill, 71–101. Stanford, CA: Stanford UP, 2001.

Yokota, Kariann A. *Unbecoming British: How Revolutionary America Became a Postcolonial Nation*. Oxford: Oxford UP, 2010.

Yolton, John W. Introduction to *An Essay Concerning Human Understanding*, by John Locke. Edited and abridged by Yolton, xix–xlii. London: Dent, 2000.

Zafar, Rafia. *We Wear the Mask: African Americans Write American Literature, 1760–1870*. New York: Columbia UP, 1997.

Zammito John H. "Review of *Vorurteil—Anthropologie—Literatur: Der Vorurteilsdiskurs als Modus der Selbstaufklärung im 18. Jahrhundert*. By Rainer Godel." *Monatshefte* 101.3 (Fall 2009): 416–18.

Zuckert, Michael P. *The Natural Rights Republic: Studies in the Foundation of the American Political Tradition*. Notre Dame, IN: U of Notre Dame P, 1996.

❖ INDEX ❖

Italicized page numbers refer to illustrations.

abolitionism. *See* antislavery and abolitionism
Adams, Henry, 33, 38
Adams, John, 13, *14*, 22, 24–25, 34–38, 50, 213n14
Adorno, Theodor, 208n20
Aeneid (Virgil), 151
African American intellectuals: in American Enlightenment, 2, 4, 9, 10, 82, 85, 145, 183, 187, 193–94, 197, 201; Anglophilia among, 109, 150, 244n83; Black Arts Movement, 87; historical neglect of, 7, 208n21, 232n80, 235n15; Jefferson image shaped by, 4, 6; on Lincoln, 190–91, 269n42; prejudice against, 75–77, 79, 85–86, 121, 215n32; "principles" of Declaration of Independence and, 4, 5, 91–93, 99, 108, 112, 198; visual art discussed by, 162, 166–67, 189–91; women's club movement, 236n22. *See also* Convention Movement; Enlightenment; intellectual, use of term; Jeffersonian Enlightenment; Wheatley's Enlightenment of Principle; *specific authors*
African American literature: creativity of, 160, 235nn15–16; double character in, 152–54, 159, 166–67, 173; double consciousness in, 6, 78, 186, 198–99, 201, 268n25, 270n2; gothic elements in, 165–67; Jefferson as literary trope in, 4, 6, 15, 152–55, 169, 173–75, 201, 205n8, 264n96, 266n3; *Notes on the State of Virginia* in, 97–98, 120–23, 126, 130, 149–50, 171–75; Procrustes myth in, 224n66; as tradition, 4, 85, 88, 93, 161, 205n10; veil metaphor in, 72, 112, 181–89, 191–94; Wheatley as founding mother of, 87–88, 195, 266n3; white-life novels in, 150. *See also* appropriation; irony; paralipsis; signifying; *specific authors*
Allen, Richard, 103, 161
Allen, William G., 87, 118–20, 168, 248n22
American Academy of Arts and Sciences, 33
American Anti-Slavery Society, 167–68
American Colonization Society, 5, 118, 129, 153, 197, 246n3
American Philosophical Society, 26–28, 31–33
American Revolution: in antislavery and abolitionist arguments, 91, 237n5, 239n13; Banneker on, 123–24; Douglass on, 110–12; Ellison on, 194–95;

American Revolution (*continued*)
Jefferson on, 45, 91; Lafayette on, 178; principles of, 84, 91, 98; public opinion and, 54; slavery during, 66; useful knowledge and, 28, 31; Wheatley on, 83–84
Ames, Fisher, 230n61
Amory, Thomas, 183–84, 267n15
Anderson, Amanda, 270n67
Andrews, William L., 259n21
Anglo-African Magazine, 113, 125, 140, 144, 159, 161, 246n2
Anglophilia, 109, 150, 244n83
antagonistic cooperation, 145, 163
antirationalism, 207n18; of Jefferson's Enlightenment of Feeling, 8, 16, 20–21, 111, 197, 233n91; of Jefferson's trivialization of Wheatley, 87; "postcolonial inversions" and, 183
antislavery and abolitionism: American Revolution and, 91, 237n5, 239n13; Declaration of Independence and, 47, 94–95, 100, 102, 107, 112, 168; "dehumanization" arguments and, 74, 150, 231–32n74; Enlightenment and, 9, 209n23; Federalism and, 127–28, 251n54; gradualist, 154, 236–37n1, 250n37; immediatist, 103, 133, 141; logic of "refutation" and, 130–32, 231n73; *Notes on the State of Virginia* and, 149–50; "principles" and, 98, 236n1; rational liberty and, 239n7; rhetoric of, 112, 130, 170; slave trade and, 99, 126, 154, 208n21
appropriation, 3, 114, 152, 168, 186, 198–99
Arendt, Hannah, 47, 49
Aristotle, 27, 209n27
assent, 8, 26, 49, 94–95, 200; in Puritan culture, 222n19
Attucks, Crispus, 161, 237n4

Bacon, Francis, 27–28, 50, 62, 123, 215n35, 222n29, 227n10
Bailey, Harriet, 2

Baldwin, James, 182
Bancroft, Edward, 246n5
Banneker, Benjamin: almanacs by, 122, 158, 159, 250n33; on American Revolution, 123–24; on black uplift, 120; correspondence with Jefferson, 97–98, 120–23, 153, 155, 249n27; "Epitaph on a Watch-Maker," 158–59, 261n46; on humanity, 98; on knowledge vs. opinion, 98; paralipsis used by, 97, 198; on prejudice, 116, 132; on skin color, 121–22; weaning metaphor and, 80, 122–23, 125, 153; on white uplift, 80, 120, 122–24, 139
Baraka, Amiri, 87
Bartram, John, 28
Bayle, Pierre, 62
belief: assent and, 49, 222n19; coercion of, 124; "conversion economy" of, 55–56; involuntary, 55; knowledge vs., 25, 220n37, 238n7; national, 49; religious, 42, 59; secular, 14, 16; subjectivity of, 23, 44, 100; understood as "creed," 16, 23–25, 38–39, 41–44, 45–46, 49, 51, 54, 77. *See also* opinion; public opinion
Beman, Amos, 134
Berkeley, George, 13, 22–24
bias. *See* prejudice; racism
Bible: Coker's use of, 153; critical reading of, 40; depictions from, 29; Jefferson's compilations on, 41; popular opinion and, 51; on slavery, 93–94, 147–48, 154, 256–57n4, 259n26; truths in, 138; veil metaphor in, 183. *See also* religion; secularization
Black Arts Movement, 87
blackness: fictionality of, 187–88; as Jefferson's subjective experience, 5, 64–66, 74–75, 169, 180–82, 197; in monarchies, 150; nationhood and, 7, 131, 169, 181; nonhumanness equated with, 208n21; as optical rather than visual, 71–73, 181–82; use of term, 6,

206n12, 226n4; veil metaphor and, 71–78, 95, 112, 123, 170, 180–89, 192; Wilson on, 114. *See also* identity; race
black uplift: Banneker on, 120; cultural capital and, 249n25; Jefferson and, 80, 233n91; negative assessment of, 249n25; as pedagogical project, 6; Query XIV and, 141; rhetoric of, 119–20, 130; *Walker's Appeal* and, 105, 130, 134, 198. *See also* white uplift
blindness, 69–71, 72–73, 78, 101, 103, 112, 123, 127, 138, 181–82, 185–86, 191, 267n6. *See also* panopticon; sight; veil metaphor
Bolingbroke, Lord (St. John, Henry), 24, 40–42, 51, 160
Booker T. Washington Monument (Tuskegee Institute), 182, 189–94, *190*
Boston Massacre (1770), 161, 237n4
Brown, John, 135, 243n79
Brown, Mather, *14*
Brown, William Wells: *An Appeal to the People of Great Britain and the World*, 107–9; *The Black Man: His Antecedents, His Genius, and His Achievements*, 155, 162, 175; *Clotel*, 108–9, 170–75, *172*, 253–54n93, 264–65n107; on Declaration of Independence, 108, 245n87; on Wheatley's legacy, 87
Burke, Edmund, 62, 248n21

Cabanis, Pierre Jean George, 20, 23, 213n17
"captive nation" argument, 66, 228n32, 270n64. *See also* nationhood; race war
Caritat, Jean-Antoine-Nicolas (Marquis de Condorcet), 52, 56–57, 60, 131
Carr, Peter, 38, 40–41
Carrington, Edward, 52, 53, 59
Cartesianism, 7, 14, 19, 35, 206–7n12, 210n3, 216n47
Cassirer, Ernst, 203n2
chaos: Du Bois on, 186; Ellison on, 193; Wheatley on, 81–84

character: double, 152–54, 159, 166–67, 173; Douglass on, 164, 262n68; egalitarianism of, 258n13; formation of, 163–64; identity vs., 151, 198, 259n17; of Jefferson, 150–60, 167–70, 173–79, 201, 266n130; language of, 6, 89, 136; as likeness, 152, 161–63, 169, 259n17; malleability of, 151, 152; Mill on, 164, 262n70; moral instinct and, 39; national, 79, 149–50, 161, 164, 227n19, 233n90, 261n53; pedagogies of, 161, 165, 177–78, 199; public opinion and, 59; science of, 164, 262n70; stamp metaphor and, 149, 152
Chesnutt, Charles, 80, 183, 224n66, 237n1, 239n9
Choate, Rufus, 247n10
citizenship, 63, 73, 79, 118, 125, 131–32, 140–41, 198
Clay, Henry, 103, 132
climate, 30–31, 70–71, 229n41
Coker, Daniel, 152–55, 178, 259nn20–21
Colbert, Burwell, 266n130
Coles, Edward, 151, 154
colonization movement: Coker and, 152–53; Douglass on, 118; Jefferson on, 61, 114, 246n3; *Notes on the State of Virginia* and, 17, 113, 118–20; opposition to, 89, 99, 113, 118, 167–68; public opinion and, 114, 129; self-criticism instrumentalized for, 5, 8, 17, 61, 116–19, 132–33, 197, 209n25; Walker's critique of, 105–6, 132. *See also* American Colonization Society; prejudice; racism
Communipaw. *See* McCune Smith, James
communities of feeling: civic subjectivity of, 93; Declaration of Independence and, 47, 94, 100; dystopian vision of, 88–89; epistemological nationalism and, 86, 180–82; imagined boundaries of, 72, 78, 107, 181–82; Jefferson's family and, 176–77; long-term developments within, 79;

communities of feeling (*continued*)
    rifts between, 65–66, 77, 200; self-constrained, 201; subjectivity and, 184, 193, 197
Condillac, Etienne Bonnot de, 20, 213n15
Condorcet, Marquis de, 52, 56–57, 60, 131
conjectural history, 52–53, 59, 111
Constitution, Pennsylvania, 99
Constitution, US, 85, 92, 194
Convention Movement, 107, 129, 135, 161
Coolidge, Joseph, 157
Cooper, Anna Julia, 88
Cornish, Samuel, 161
Cosway, Maria, 29, 35
Craft, Ellen, 109, 244n82, 264n107
Craft, William, 109, 244n82
creed. *See* belief; opinion; public opinion
critical race theory, 207–8n19
Crummell, Alexander, 100–101, 262n68
Cuffe, Paul, 152

d'Alembert, Jean le Rond, 27
Dalrymple, John, 58
Dartmouth, Lord (William Legge), 81–84
Davis, Jefferson, 149–50, 257n10
Declaration of Independence: abolition of slavery and, 47, 94–95, 100, 102, 107, 112, 168; African American hermeneutics of, 4, 5, 91, 97, 108, 112, 198; communities of feeling and, 47, 94, 100; concept of humanity in, 47, 208n21; Douglass on, 88, 110–12; draft versions, 21–22, 45–49, 87, 92, 98, 208n21, 216n47, 228n22; Du Bois on, 85; Ellison on, 194–95; "Haynes abridgment," 88, 93–95, 100, 106–8, 115, 120, 173, 198; in historical debates, 47, 50, 54, 221n4; Jefferson's "political creed" and, 45, 46; King on promise of, 54; knowledge vs. opinion in, 46–49, 92–93; on "life, liberty, and the pursuit of happiness," 46–47, 88, 94–95, 102, 106, 108; Lincoln on "future use" of, 200; Murray on, 85; "principles" of, 4, 5, 91–95, 99–100, 108, 110–12, 128–29, 160, 194, 198, 237n4; in proslavery arguments, 47, 115; public opinion and, 45–49; rational liberty and, 92, 93, 99–102, 239n7; self-evident truth in, 47–48, 92, 94, 99, 221n6, 221–22n16; speaking subject of, 48, 221n15; subjectivity of, 46–48; universalism of, 17, 46–47, 91–102, 106–7, 110–11, 239n7; *Walker's Appeal* on, 105–7, 109, 130. *See also* Enlightenment; principle, use of term
Declaration of Sentiments (American Anti-Slavery Society), 167–68
Declaration of the Rights of Man and of the Citizen (France), 49
Delany, Martin, 87, 91, 121–22, 207n19, 237n3, 250n32
Démeunier, Jean-Nicolas, 174
democracy: knowledge and, 5, 31–33, 44, 49, 66, 77–78, 85, 93, 111, 115, 181, 183, 197–98, 201; public opinion and, 44, 49, 144, 197; racial homogeneity and, 141–42, 144–45; slavery and, 6, 85, 127–28, 150, 173, 200; universalist principles of, 11, 194, 199, 201
Descartes, René, 13–14, 19–22, 35, 210nn2–3, 216n47
Destutt de Tracy, Antoine Louis Claude, 20, 23, 56, 57, 60
d'Holbach, Baron, 63, 227n17
Dickens, Charles, 183
Diderot, Denis, 27
discrimination. *See* prejudice; racism
double character, 152–54, 159, 166–67, 173
double consciousness, 6, 78, 186, 198–99, 201, 268n25, 270n2. *See also* appropriation; Jeffersonian Enlightenment
Douglass, Frederick: on American Colonization Society, 118; on American Revolution, 110–12; on character, 164,

262n68; on Declaration of Independence, 88, 110–12; Freedmen's Memorial Address (1876), 190–91; *The Heroic Slave*, 245n96; love of knowledge, 2, 3, 203n4; McCune Smith on, 2–3, 204n6; "The Mission of the War," 246n1; *My Bondage and My Freedom*, 1–3, 156; *Narrative of the Life of Frederick Douglass*, 257n11; paralipsis radicalized by, 110; on prejudice, 119, 209n25, 248n20; on "problem-people," 115, 247n13; "The Proclamation and a Negro Army," 156, 225n84; veil metaphor used by, 112; on Walker, 107; "What Are the Colored People Doing for Themselves?," 164; "What to the Slave Is the Fourth of July?," 109–12

Dred Scott v. Sanford (1857), 166

Duane, William, 56, 57

Du Bois, W. E. B.: on chaos, 186; on Declaration of Independence, 85; double consciousness used by, 186, 199; *The Souls of Black Folk*, 115, 182, 185–87, 189; veil metaphor used by, 185–87, 268n30; on Walker, 107; on Wheatley's legacy, 88

Du Marsais, César Chesnau, 63

Dunmore, Lord (John Murray), 66

Duval, Alexander, 108

Easton, Hosea, 116, 135–38, 161

education, 79, 83, 133, 138; enslaved persons and, 148, 179, 242n62, 256n3; industrial, 189, 190; integration of, 249n25; moral sense and, 39; power of, 253n88; public, 31, 32, 79; in slave society, 78, 120, 149, 150, 233n87. *See also* black uplift; Enlightenment; white uplift; *specific institutions*

Edwards, Jonathan, 213n13, 240n20

ekphrasis, 69–70, 159, 193

Eliot, George, 183, 267n11

Ellison, Ralph: on American founding principles, 194–95; "Change the Joke and Slip the Yoke," 194; on chaos, 193; on Declaration of Independence, 194–95; "Flying Home," 264n96; *Invisible Man*, 79, 84–85, 89, 182, 191–95, 268n36, 270n67; "The Little Man at Chehaw Station," 110, 194; Murray's friendship with, 235n13; on revolutionary feeling, 110; and underground Enlightenment, 193–94

Emancipation Monument (Freedmen's Memorial), 182, 190–92

Emerson, Ralph Waldo, 199, 213n13

emotion. *See* feeling

empiricism: climate theory and, 30–31; as "lived experience," 216n46; Lucrecian, 218n65; materialism and, 22–25, 35–36, 38, 42, 51, 213n14, 213–14n18; metaphysics and, 7, 8, 15–16, 26, 27–29, 34, 44, 48, 59, 111, 181; Monticello paintings and, 230n52; naïve, 36, 218n72; nationalist dimension of, 28–29, 180–81, 215n43; racist dimension of, 5, 15–16, 71, 75, 180–81; radical, 13, 22–23, 34–35, 38, 121, 181; subjectivity of, 5, 8, 10, 26, 30, 50, 57, 68, 73, 78, 116, 120; useful knowledge and, 27–28. *See also* antirationalism; Jefferson's Enlightenment of Feeling; *specific authors*

Encyclopédie méthodique, 174

Encyclopédie ou dictionnaire raisonné des sciences, des arts et des métiers, 27

Encyclopedists, 27–28, 63

Enlightenment: abolitionism and, 9, 209n23; American, 3, 7, 10–11, 204n7, 208n20, 240n20; anti-Eurocentric, 6, 7, 14–16, 28–29, 111, 181; "complicity" with, 10, 109, 235n15; courage necessary for, 1–2, 9, 21, 201, 203n2; definition of, 1–3; Foucauldian interpretations of, 16, 21, 68–71; in the humanities, 7–9, 13–16, 199–200, 208nn20–22, 210–11nn3–4; misunderstood as "white," 2, 6–10, 208n21,

300 INDEX

Enlightenment (*continued*)
208–9n23; modernizations of, 4, 6, 15, 116, 199; prejudice in, 62–63, 227n11; progressive, 140, 145, 163; secular, 82, 209n23, 268n22; sense of sight and, 16–17, 21, 68–69; underground, 193–94; universalism of, 9–10, 85, 107, 111–12, 160, 187, 193, 208n21; Walker's hierarchical conception of, 104. *See also* Jeffersonian Enlightenment; Jefferson's Enlightenment of Feeling; secularization; Wheatley's Enlightenment of Principle
Epicurus and Epicureanism, 34–36, 42, 218n71
epistemological nationalism, 28, 66, 68, 69, 75, 77, 86, 180–82, 197. *See also* Jefferson's Enlightenment of Feeling
equality: character and, 167; in founding narratives, 200; intellectual, 75, 131, 200, 231n73; of republican citizens, 5, 32, 49, 79, 93, 99, 100, 108, 141, 181; universal, 8, 10, 47, 52, 83, 88, 95, 102, 148, 194
Equiano, Olaudah, 232n79
Ethiop. *See* Wilson, William J.
ethology, 164, 262n70

Federalists: abolitionism and, 127–28, 251n54; caricature of Jefferson, 15, 33, 101, 126; on "diffusion" of knowledge, 32–34; exclusion from community of feeling, 86; neo-Federalists, 217n58; slave trade orations by, 127–28
feeling: conceptualizations of, 19–22; of guilt, 5, 8, 89, 98, 175, 182; liberty and, 98, 120; Locke on, 20–22, 36; materialist "creed" and, 42; moral "creed" and, 42; oppositional potential of, 65, 212n5; "organic," 16, 17, 21–22, 36, 51, 55; pragmatism and, 213n13; revolutionary, 110; as sense of touch, 14, 16, 20–21, 36, 213n15; subjectivity of, 5, 8, 10, 26, 30, 50, 57, 68, 73, 78, 116, 120; terminology related to, 20, 211n8; thinking compared to, 13–14, 20; useful knowledge and, 36. *See also* communities of feeling; empiricism; Jefferson's Enlightenment of Feeling
Finley, Robert, 113, 117
Fleming, William, 45
Forten, Charlotte, 87
Forten, James, 92, 99, 135, 161, 253n88
Forten, James, Jr., 253n88
Fossett, Peter, 179
Fourth of July celebrations, 101, 109–12, 126, 128–29, 244–45n87
Franklin, Benjamin, 28, 81, 261n46
Frazier, E. Franklin, 249n25
Frederick II (Prussia), 63
Freedmen's Memorial (Emancipation Monument), 182, 190–92
freedom: of human mind, 42–44; love of, 5, 81, 83–84, 106, 196, 234n6; negatively construed, 11; of opinion, 5, 55, 60, 153, 156; from pain, 34, 36; of religion, 55, 60, 82, 184; social and political, 268n20. *See also* liberty
Freedom's Journal, 101, 109, 161, 241n51, 250n37, 251n55, 259n15
French Declaration of the Rights of Man and of the Citizen (1789), 49
Fry-Jefferson map of Virginia (1753), 69
fugitives from slavery, 85, 107–9, 172

Gadamer, Hans-Georg, 227n11
Gaines, Ernest J., 264n96
Gardner, Drew, 177
Garnet, Henry Highland, 107, 134, 134–35, 243n79
Garnet, Julia Ward Williams, 135
Garrison, William Lloyd, 110
Gassendi, Pierre, 35, 218n71
Gates, Henry Louis, Jr., 87, 205n8, 205–6n10, 235n16, 266n3
George III (England), 77, 81, 92, 108
Gillespie, Carmen, 263n87
Gilroy, Paul, 207n19, 237n3

INDEX

Goethe, Johann Wolfgang von, 199
Gordon-Reed, Annette, 67, 97, 179, 249n25
Gorman, Amanda, 270n72
government: basis of, 49–55; clockwork imagery and, 158, 159; principles of, 43, 47, 91, 99–100; rationality of, 63, 100, 101; self-government, 95, 115, 141
Grégoire, Henri, 86, 231n73, 235n17, 252n67

Habermas, Jürgen, 92, 238n7
Hack, Daniel, 267n11
Hamilton, Robert, 125, 246n1
Hamilton, Thomas, 125, 161
Hamilton, William, 101–2, 116, 124–30, 132, 139, 161, 198
Hammond, Jabez, 260n32
Hannah (enslaved woman at Poplar Forest), 146–48, *147*, 154, 178, 256n3
happiness: knowledge and, 2, 50, 51; pursuit of, 36, 46–47, 88, 94–95, 102, 106, 108, 129; slavery in relation to, 47, 221n9
Harper, Frances Watkins, 164, 183, 255n133, 258n13, 262n71
Hawthorne, Nathaniel, 183
Haynes, Lemuel: abolitionism of, 240n23; depiction of, *96*; and groundbreaking secularization, 94; "Haynes abridgment" of Declaration of Independence, 88, 93–95, 100, 106–8, 115, 120, 173, 198; *Liberty Further Extended*, 93–97; paralipsis used by, 97
Heidegger, Martin, 165, 210nn2–3, 227n11
Helvétius, Claude-Adrien, 56–57, 60, 224–25n71
Hemings, Madison, 146, 176–77, 179, 266n129
Hemings, Sally, 4, 29, 176–78
Home, Henry (Lord Kames), 20–21, 28, 39, 58, 212n6, 216n44
Hopkins, Samuel, 259n21

Horkheimer, Max, 208n20, 210n3
humanity: Banneker on, 98; in Declaration of Independence, 47, 208n21; "dehumanization" vs., 74, 150, 166–67, 208n21, 231n74, 257n11; in *Invisible Man*, 85, 194; McCune Smith on, 143, 170–71; Wheatley on, 81–82, 183–84
Humboldt, Wilhelm von, 144
Hume, David, 20, 22, 54, 188

identity: character vs., 151, 198, 259n17; civic, 217n51; extension from personal to collective, 64, 65, 188; fictionality of, 188; Hume on, 188; literary, 209n28; Locke on, 64; McCune Smith on, 144, 256n139; memory and, 64; national, 64, 144, 169; as "puzzle," 188, 193–94, 268n36; "racial," 5, 7–8, 17, 64, 188
Idéologues, 20, 23
ignorance: comforts of, 15–16; historical, 117, 126; moral dimension of, 104–7; national, 243n66; personal, 24–25, 36; pillow of, 24, 105, 197, 214n23, 243n64; as preferable to error, 24, 105, 214n25; of "principles" in Declaration of Independence, 100; veil of, 182, 189–91, *190*; willful, 127, 129
instinct, 26, 39, 51, 55
intellectual, use of term, 203n5, 215n32. *See also* African American intellectuals
irony: historical, 3, 6, 7, 54–55, 69, 85, 87, 88, 109, 110, 117, 133, 171, 173, 181, 199, 200, 208n21, 250n41, 257n10; verbal, 72, 84–85, 97, 105, 106, 113, 126, 136, 139, 141, 182, 185, 187, 191. *See also* paralipsis; signifying
Irving, Washington, 15, 33–34, 101, 126–27, 141–42, 144, 176

Jacobs, Harriet, 258n11
James, William, 199
Jefferson, Israel, 178, 179
Jefferson, Peter, 69

Jefferson, Thomas: Adams's correspondence with, 22, 25, 34–38, 213n14; in African American literature, 4, 6, 15, 152–55, 169, 173–75, 201, 205n8, 264n96, 266n3; as ambassador to France, 52; on American Revolution, 45, 91; antimetaphysical rhetoric of, 7, 8, 15–16, 26, 27–29, 34, 44, 48, 59, 111, 181; "Autobiography," 228n22; Banneker's correspondence with, 97–98, 120–23, 153, 155, 249n27; biblical compilations by, 41; blackness described as subjective experience by, 5, 64–66, 74–75, 169, 180–82, 197; "black" personhood and, 64, 228n23; caricatures of, 15, 33–34, 101, 126, 141–42, 176; character of, 150–60, 167–70, 173–79, 201, 266n130; children and grandchildren, 68, 176–79, *177*, 264n97, 266n129; on colonization, 61, 114, 246n3; death of (1826), 178, 256n2; depicted as embodiment of American contradictions, 6, 15, 78, 86, 88, 198, 200; double consciousness of, 6, 78, 198–99, 201; health problems, 146, 148; inaugural address (1801), 58; *Legal Commonplace Book*, 51, 58; *Literary Commonplace Book*, 51; memory of, 139–40, 178–79, 214n23; as "midwife" of African American literature, 195, 235n16, 266n3; performance of prejudice, 5, 16, 64–65, 72–79, 121, 180–82; polygenetic insinuations, 121, 136, 139; Poplar Forest, 146–48, *147*, 154, 178, 256n3; portraits of, *14*, *177*; presidential elections involving, 54, 91; as "race maker," 72–79, 180–82, 201, 233n89; racism of, 5, 15, 72–78, 85–86, 123, 232n75, 246n5; on republican millennium, 16, 44, 211n10; reputation of, 39, 45, 87, 122, 131, 226n6; scientific interests of, 32, 69, 215n39, 230n53; self-criticism by, 5, 8, 17, 63–65, 116, 175, 197, 227n20; skepticism and, 13, 22–24, 36, 193, 213n17, 222n16; *Summary View of the Rights of British America*, 94, 239n18; "Syllabus of the Doctrines of Epicurus," 35, 36; "Thomas Jefferson problem," 78; in *Walker's Appeal*, 103, 167, 241–42n54; on Wheatley, 76–77, 85–87, 139, 205n8, 232n79; worldview of, 4, 15–16, 22–23, 64, 68, 79. *See also* Declaration of Independence; Monticello; *Notes on the State of Virginia*; University of Virginia

Jeffersonian Enlightenment: "cofabrication" of, 5, 11, 207n13, 258n13; dialectical nature of, 6, 74, 117, 140, 145, 235n16; double consciousness in, 6, 78, 186, 198–99, 201; as an "*ism*," 4, 6, 11, 198, 201; as modernized Enlightenment philosophy, 4, 6, 15, 116, 199; rational standards of, 6, 199; as synthesis of Jefferson's Enlightenment of Feeling and Wheatley's Enlightenment of Principle, 4–6, 11, 15, 85, 88, 183, 199, 201; universalism of, 4, 88, 183, 201

Jefferson's Enlightenment of Feeling: and American creed, 16, 45–46, 49, 54, 77, 100, 111, 181; anti-Eurocentrism of, 5, 7, 14–16, 28–29, 31–33, 44, 49, 66, 77–78, 85, 93, 111, 115, 181, 183, 197–98, 201; antimetaphysical rhetoric of, 7, 8, 15–16, 26, 27–29, 34, 44, 48, 59, 111, 181; antirationalism of, 8, 16, 20–21, 111, 197, 233n91; artificial simplicity of, 21, 36, 127, 213n10, 251n50; blend of modesty and arrogance in, 8, 25, 54, 64, 67, 93, 181, 229n44; creation of race as subjective experience in, 5, 8, 17, 66, 68, 72–73, 78, 88, 180–81, 197, 230n49; "creed" in, 16, 23, 25, 39–44, 51, 65, 219n22; democratization of knowledge in, 5, 31–33, 44, 49, 66, 77–78, 85, 93, 111, 115, 181, 183, 197–98, 201; diffusion metaphor in, 29–34, 42, 43, 44, 77, 79, 232n82; dystopian

vision of, 115; embodied experience in, 5, 10, 14, 16, 22, 31, 67, 75, 180, 216n47; emotional dichotomies of, 177; flexibility of, 32, 50, 55, 70, 114, 119, 151, 152; interaction with Wheatley's Enlightenment of Principle, 3–4, 9–11, 85–88, 117, 145, 183; materialist "creed" in, 23–25, 42, 51, 213–14n18; metaphors in, 14, 43–44, 72, 77, 84, 89, 105, 112, 118, 149–51, 180–81, 227n10, 232n82, 243n64; moral "creed" in, 38–39, 42, 51; "political creed" in, 45, 46, 52, 181; as postcolonial, 5, 7, 10, 15, 28–29, 31, 32, 37, 44, 64, 66, 78, 93, 104, 107, 111–12, 180–82, 183, 197, 200, 201, 210n2, 216n47; precursors of, 19–23, 212n5; primary aim of, 5; public opinion in, 16, 45–49, 52–59, 111, 124; qualified concepts of knowledge and, 25–29; "rational creed" in, 39–42, 219n22; reason in, 5, 37–38, 44, 180; religious creed and, 39–42, 51; sense of touch in, 14, 16, 20–21, 36, 213n15; standpoint theory and, 206n12; subjectivity of, 5, 10, 13–14, 16–17, 22, 25, 31, 46–48, 50, 57, 60, 66–69, 71, 149, 180–81; toleration of technological imperfection in, 157; weaknesses of, 5, 8, 16, 43–44, 59, 98, 102, 123; Wheatley's universalism as challenge to, 86. *See also* colonization movement; Enlightenment; epistemological nationalism
jeremiad, 106, 130, 132
Johnson, James Weldon, 72, 182, 187–89, 193
Johnson, Samuel, 31, 86

Kames, Lord (Home, Henry), 20–21, 28, 39, 58, 212n6, 216n44
Kant, Immanuel, 1, 22, 38, 43–44, 181, 203n1, 215n32; and historical absence from American Enlightenment, 22, 199, 238n7; "resolution and courage" in Enlightenment definition of, 1, 203n2

Keck, Charles, 189
Kelleter, Frank, 48, 268n22
Kennedy, John F., 260n32
King, Martin Luther, Jr., 54, 91–92, 164
knowledge: access to, 42, 67, 71; American culture of, 63, 77; authoritative, 25, 92–93, 98, 101, 103–4, 106; Bacon's tree of, 27; barriers to, 181; Cartesian concept of, 19, 20; certainty in, 25–29; communal, 67, 69; and courage, 1–2, 9, 201; democratization of, 5, 31–33, 44, 49, 66, 77–78, 85, 93, 111, 115, 181, 183, 197–98, 201; "diffusion" of, 29–34, 42, 44, 77, 79, 111, 124, 181, 232n82; happiness and, 2, 50, 51; imperial economy of, 28; Locke on, 19–21, 24–26, 28, 35; love of, 2, 3, 102, 104, 203n4; objective, 25, 46, 51, 60, 131; opinion vs., 16, 25–26, 31, 38, 44, 98, 220n37, 238n7; "postcolonial inversions" and, 183; power of, 50, 107, 222n29, 253n88; production of, 62, 68, 216n47; theories of, 4–5, 23, 97, 185, 186, 198; truth and, 49, 98, 120; universal, 47, 49, 72, 79–80, 104, 111–12, 181, 185; useful, 26–36, 42, 44, 49, 50, 214n30. *See also* Enlightenment; epistemological nationalism; progress

Lafayette, Marquis de, 178
LaNier, Shannon, 177, 265n125
Law, Thomas, 38, 39
Lawrence, George, 99–100, 106, 129–30
laws: coercion of, 42; on education, 133; and etymological narrative of *nomos*, 53, 58, 223n47; moral progress and, 53, 58–59; of nature, 35, 40, 41, 71, 92, 97, 108; protection of, 99; public opinion and, 52, 53, 136; revisal of, 56, 61; on slavery, 58, 109, 136; uniformity of, 56–57; of vision, 71. *See also* manners; Query XIV, "Laws"
Legge, William (Lord Dartmouth), 81–84

liberty: civil, 82, 184; in Declaration of Independence, 46–47, 88, 94–95, 102, 106, 108; feeling and, 98, 120; in founding narratives, 200; paradox of, 59; philosophical, 51, 55; political, 51; psychologization of, 51, 223n34; public opinion and, 52, 53; rational, 92, 93, 99–102, 106, 239n7; republican, 131; universal, 8, 92, 106, 184, 239n7. *See also* freedom
Lifting the Veil of Ignorance (Tuskegee Institute), 182, 189–94, *190*
Lincoln, Abraham, 50, 92, 190–91, 200, 239n10, 248n20, 269n42
Locke, John: antimetaphysical tendencies in philosophy of, 28; on "conversion economy" of belief, 55–56; *Essay Concerning Human Understanding*, 19–21, 24–26; on feeling, 20–22, 36; on knowledge, 19–21, 24–26, 28, 35; materialism and, 23, 213n14; on opinion, 26, 55, 56, 223n50, 224n67; on personal identity, 64, 228n23; and philosophical modesty, 25, 214n27; on prejudice, 62; radicalization of, 20, 22–23, 34, 35, 222n16; on reason, 38–40; skepticism and, 22, 25; tabula rasa (blank slate), 22, 36, 105; veil of perception and, 35, 218n70
Longfellow, Henry Wadsworth, 111
Lorde, Audre, 9
L'Ouverture, Toussaint, 160–61
Lucretius, 35, 218n65

Mackenzie, Henry, 20
Madison, Dolley, 177, 266n129
Madison, James, 54, 55, 63, 224n64
Malcolm X, 215n32
manners: childhood experiences and, 123, 149; democratic vs. monarchical, 150; and etymological narrative of *nomos*, 53, 58, 223n47; intellect and, 79, 233n90, 233n92; in Native American societies, 52–53; as precursor to public opinion, 53, 223n48; preparing laws, 58, 79, 124; slavery and, 57–59, 79, 118, 123, 127, 138, 149, 225n77. *See also* laws; Query XVIII, "Manners"
Manning, Susan, 66, 259n17
Marbois, François de, 30, 67, 229n47
"master's tools," 9, 209n26
materialism, 22–25, 35–36, 38, 42, 51, 213n14, 213–14n18
McCune Smith, James ("Communipaw"): caricature of Jefferson, 34, 176; "Civilization," 141, 144; on Douglass, 2–3, 204n6; educational background, 140; "The German Invasion," 144; "Heads of the Colored People," 169–71; on humanity, 143, 170–71; on identity, 144, 256n139; literary and cultural criticism by, 255n132; on Mill, 141, 143–45, 262n70; paralipsis used by, 142, 169; on prejudice, 116; on public opinion, 140–44; on Query XIV, 73, 124–25, 140–43, 145, 169–70; on racial "mingling," 144, 204n6; on Tocqueville, 144, 255–56nn137–38; on whiteness, 140–41, 142–43, 169
McKay, Claude, 171
memory: identity and, 64; of Jefferson, 139–40, 178–79, 214n23; as mental faculty, 27, 64–65, 228n26; Wheatley on, 83
Middle Passage, 83, 84, 96, 185
Mill, John Stuart, 55, 141, 143–45, 164, 262n70
Milton, John, 184, 267n17
modernity, 111–12, 126, 149, 207n19
modesty, 8, 25, 54, 59–60, 67, 181, 214n27, 229n44
Montaigne, Michel de, 24, 62, 105
Montesquieu, 31, 51–53, 56–57, 185, 223n34
Monticello: as anti-panopticon, 16, 68–69; artwork at, 230n52; Great Clock at, 157, 260n40; in Jefferson's "sentimental geography," 70–71,

229n41; slavery at, 66, 68–69, 148, 178–79, 256n3
Moorhead, Scipio, 82
moral sense, 38–39, 219n8, 219n10, 226n6, 233n90
Morton, Samuel George, 139, 254n113
Murray, Albert, 85, 163, 235n13
Murray, John (Lord Dunmore), 66

National Association of Colored Women (NACW), 251n43
national character, 79, 149–50, 161, 164, 227n19, 233n90, 261n53
nationalism: American creed and, 16, 45–46, 49, 54, 77, 100, 111, 181; communities of feeling and, 47, 54, 66, 86, 100, 112, 182, 197; empiricism and, 28–29, 180–81, 215n43; epistemological, 28, 66, 69, 75, 77, 86, 182, 186, 197; natural history and, 216n43; public opinion and, 48–49, 59; relationship of race and, 30, 64, 74, 77–78, 114, 117, 119, 131–32, 144, 164, 180–81, 184, 186, 197; universalism and, 112, 123, 194, 268n22
nationhood, 4, 124, 138, 144, 148, 151, 164, 174, 181, 200, 216n47, 221n6, 228n32
natural history, 33, 114, 141, 216n43, 226n6
natural philosophy, 33, 247n8
natural rights: of conscience, 41; "Haynes abridgment" and, 95; human reason and, 238n7; intellect and, 74, 131, 231n72; normative foundation of, 220n37; universalism of, 8, 96; Wheatley on, 81–82, 234–35n9
Nell, William Cooper, 87, 162
Newman, Richard, 153, 249n24
Newton, Isaac, 27, 231n72
nomos, etymological narrative of, 53, 58, 223n47
Northup, Solomon, 109
Notes on the State of Virginia (Jefferson): abolitionism and, 148–50; "Advertisement" to, 66–68; in African American literature, 97–98, 120–23, 126, 130, 149–50, 171–75; colonization movement and, 17, 113, 118–20; contemporary criticism of, 73, 231n68; dating of manuscript, 228n33; embodied experience in, 67, 75, 180, 216n47; emphasis on subjective limitations in, 30, 66–69, 71, 72, 75, 77, 79, 180–82; epistemological nationalism as central project of, 66, 69, 75, 77, 180–82; performance of prejudice against "blacks" in, 5, 16, 64–65, 72–79, 121, 180–81; point of view technique in, 69–71, 74, 180–81, 230n61; as "postcolonial intervention," 216n47; Query I, "Boundaries of Virginia," 67–68; Query IV, "Mountains," 70, 71; Query V, "Cascades," 70, 71; Query VI, "Productions mineral, vegetable and animal," 79, 121–22; Query VII, "Climate," 30–31, 70, 229n41; Query VIII, "Population," 58; Query XVII, "Religion," 41–42, 55–57, 124; Query XIX, "Manufactures," 230n55; rational quantification in, 16, 64, 228n25; rhetoric of situatedness in, 67, 229n44; "view from nowhere" and, 67, 69; as "war book," 66, 228n33. *See also* Query XIV, "Laws"; Query XVIII, "Manners"

Occom, Samson, 81–82, 84–86, 89, 184–85
Onuf, Peter, 67, 217n51
opinion: assent and, 8, 26, 49, 222n19; coercion of, 56, 58, 124; false, 5, 8, 39, 42, 44, 48, 58, 61, 77, 98, 101, 122, 124, 138; freedom of, 5, 55, 60, 153, 156; involuntary, 55–56, 59, 78–79, 93, 105, 118, 131, 224n64; knowledge vs., 16, 25–26, 31, 38, 44, 98, 220n37, 238n7; law of, 223n50; Locke on, 26, 55, 56, 223n50, 224n67; power of, 16, 50, 52,

opinion (*continued*)
54, 107; and prejudice, 44, 55, 61; religious, 55–56; subjectivity of, 5, 10, 51, 55, 57, 60, 67–68, 78, 92, 95, 98, 103; uniformity of, 55–60. *See also* belief; public opinion
orangutan analogy, 73–74, 117, 121, 128, 131, 134, 136, 142

Paine, Thomas, 228n20, 235n9
panopticon, 16, 68–71. *See also* blindness; Monticello
paralipsis: Banneker and, 97, 198; Douglass and, 110; Hamilton and, 126–30; Haynes and, 97; Lawrence and, 129, 130; McCune Smith and, 142, 169; Pennington and, 138; Walker and, 104, 106, 130, 242n58; Wheatley and, 85–86
Paul, Susan, 137, 164, 262n71
Pennington, James W. C., 116, 124, 137–41, 167
pillow of ignorance, 24, 105, 197, 214n23, 243n64
pity, 102, 115, 124, 128, 138–39, 163, 170–71, 199, 250n39, 252n56
Plato, Ann, 164
polygenesis, 121, 136, 139
Poplar Forest, 146–48, 147, 154, 178, 256n3
Potter, Eliza, 242n62, 258n13
pragmatism, 213n13
prejudice: against African American intellectuals, 75–77, 79, 85–86, 121, 215n32; awareness of instrumentalized for colonization, 5, 8, 17, 61, 116–19, 132–33; Bacon's "idols" and, 62, 123, 227n10; of "color" or "condition," 17, 62, 117, 207n17, 212n12; conceptual transformation of, 116, 117, 124, 127; critiques of, 5–6, 62, 86, 116, 119, 209n25; depicted as inevitable group phenomenon, 5, 8, 10, 17, 77, 79, 113–14, 116, 119, 121, 132–33;

143–44, 209n25, 247–48nn18–20; Enlightenment and, 62–63, 227n11; intentionality of, 55, 124–25, 127, 136–38; Jefferson's performance of, 5, 16, 64–65, 72–79, 121, 180–81; latent wisdom of, 62, 248n21; and majority opinion, 44, 118, 144; malignant, 135–37, 248n20, 253n88; as moral problem, 89, 124, 138–39, 143; psychological mechanisms of, 132, 137; Query XIV on, 16–17, 61, 64–65, 72–74, 113–16, 228n27; rationalism and, 62, 64; self-criticism of, 5, 8, 17, 63–65, 116–19, 132–33, 175, 197, 209n25, 227n20; subjectivity of, 8, 68, 116, 117, 131; as supposed criterion of whiteness, 8, 63–65, 77, 79, 116–19, 132–33; toleration of, 57, 60, 62–63, 77, 116, 118, 248n19; voluntarist concept of, 117, 125, 127, 131–32, 135, 138, 143; weaning metaphor and, 80, 122–23, 125, 153. *See also* racism
Price, Richard, 257n6
Prichard, James Cowles, 255n130
Priestley, Joseph, 54, 157
principle, use of term: by Jefferson, 45, 47, 91, 95, 100; in Wheatley's Enlightenment of Principle, 4, 91–92, 94–95, 100, 236–37n1
print media, "diffusion" of knowledge through, 31–32
"problem-people," 114–16, 247n6
Procrustes myth, 56, 224n66
progress, 26, 27, 30–32, 44, 50, 53–54, 58–59, 101, 105, 111, 120, 123–24, 129, 136, 140, 143–45, 153, 163, 164, 197, 225n77, 260n29
Prussian Academy of Sciences, 63
public opinion: American Revolution and, 54; as basis of government, 49, 53, 54; colonization movement and, 114, 129; Declaration of Independence and, 45–49; democracy and, 44, 49, 144, 197; faith in, 54, 55; Jefferson's

Enlightenment of Feeling and, 16, 111, 124; laws and, 52, 53; liberty and, 52, 53; manners as precursor to, 53, 223n48; McCune Smith on, 140–44; nationalism and, 48–49, 59; vs. popular opinion, 51; power of, 52, 54, 107; on slavery, 57–59, 61; voluntarist concept of, 255n133. *See also* belief; conjectural history; opinion

Puritanism, 93–94, 95, 222n19

Query XIV, "Laws" (*Notes on the State of Virginia*): African American hermeneutics of, 130, 140; black uplift and, 141; conceptual frame of, 120–21; criticisms of, 73–75, 231n68; on "diffusion" of knowledge, 77; epistemological nationalism and, 75, 77; ethnographic content, 116, 247n14; identitarian views in, 6, 145; intellectual weaknesses of, 119, 126–28, 131, 139, 142; literary optics of, 70, 71; logic of "refutation" and, 130–32, 134, 141, 231n73; McCune Smith on, 73, 124–25, 140–43, 145, 169–70; on prejudice, 16–17, 61, 64–65, 72–74, 113–16, 228n27; on race, 72–75, 169, 230n49; reception history, 88, 120, 124, 133; as repertoire of rhetorical figures, 117; veil metaphor in, 71–78, 95, 112, 123, 170, 180–89, 192; on Wheatley, 76–77, 86, 87, 139, 205n8; white uplift and, 141

Query XVIII, "Manners" (*Notes on the State of Virginia*): doomsday vision in, 133, 135, 148–49; on involuntary opinion, 55, 59; language of character in, 6, 89; on liberty and public opinion, 52, 53; metaphor of "trembling" and, 89, 135, 149, 151, 166, 173–74, 177, 199; on perspective shifts, 230n55; on prejudice rooted in childhood experiences, 123, 137; on racial violence, 133, 165, 170, 172, 175, 180; reception history, 164; on slavery, 57–59, 78, 118, 123, 127, 148–51, 170, 174–75; stamp metaphor in, 89, 149–50, 164

race: as "color-line," 91, 114, 182, 185–88; critical race theory, 207–8n19; fictionality of, 187–88, 192–93; as identity, 5, 7–8, 17, 64, 188; "(inter)mingling" of races, 144, 204n6, 246n5; Jefferson as "race maker," 72–79, 180–82, 201, 233n89; McCune Smith on, 140–41, 143, 169; in monarchies, 150; nationalism and, 30, 64, 74, 77–78, 114, 117, 119, 131–32, 144, 164, 180–81, 184, 186, 197; and polarization of attitudes, 115, 133, 175, 201, 259n17; and polygenesis, 121, 136, 139; pride related to, 121–22, 250n32; Query XIV on, 72–75, 169, 230n49; self-criticism defining boundaries of, 63–65; as subjective experience, 5, 8, 17, 66, 78, 88, 169, 181–83, 197, 230n49; terminology of, 206n12, 226n4; veil metaphor and, 180–85; as zero-sum, 114, 170, 180. *See also* blackness; whiteness

race war, 133, 135, 165, 170, 172, 180, 194

racial uplift. *See* black uplift; white uplift

racism: democratic manners and, 150; in Enlightenment narratives, 7, 209n24; impressionistic, 72, 141; of Jefferson, 5, 15, 72–78, 85–86, 123, 232n75, 246n5; language and, 137; nationalism and, 5, 15–16, 71, 75, 180–81; orangutan analogy and, 73–74, 117, 121, 128, 131, 134, 136, 142; pseudo-scientific, 141, 226n6; segregation, 75, 116–17, 131, 180, 184, 189, 232n75; self-criticism and, 5, 8, 17, 61, 116–19, 132–33, 197, 209n25. *See also* colonization movement; prejudice

rationalism: Banneker and, 158–59; Cartesian, 19, 35; confused with rationality, 7, 207n19; in hermeneutics of Declaration of Independence, 5,

rationalism (*continued*)
91, 97, 101–2, 110, 112, 128; Jefferson's opposition to, 7, 22, 23, 77, 155, 197; misunderstood as "white," 7, 207n19, 208n21; "occidental," 7, 207n19, 237n3; prejudice and, 62, 64. *See also* antirationalism
rational liberty, 92, 93, 99–102, 106, 238–39n7
reason: "apostle of," 15, 37, 39; critical, 43, 220n34; in Declaration of Independence, 46–48, 91, 92, 95, 100, 102; divine, 44, 92, 100, 102, 103, 155; and Enlightenment, 5, 7, 8, 10, 13–14, 37, 44, 180, 197; human, 6, 40, 43, 44, 92, 102, 103, 129, 180, 184, 219n16, 220n35, 220n37, 238n7; "infinite," 185, 186, 188; Locke on, 38–40; monarchical, 63; and "principles," 91, 96, 98, 99, 100; religious creed and, 39–42; self-evidence and, 221n13; senses and, 34, 38, 219n10; subordinate role of, 37; supposed whiteness of, 6–7, 10, 208n21; uncritical, 38, 43–44, 215n33; understanding vs., 38, 43, 203n1; universal, 5, 10, 13–14, 79–80, 100, 102, 154–55, 197, 201, 210n28. *See also* antirationalism; rationalism; rational liberty
Reese, David, 167–68
religion: belief and, 42, 59; civil, 6; "civil and religious liberty," 82, 184, 234n5; diversity of opinion and, 55–56; evangelicalism, 77, 184, 234n8; faith and, 40–42; freedom of, 55, 60, 82, 184; Jefferson on, 39–42, 51; natural, 39; Puritanism, 95, 222n19; Query XVII on, 41–42, 55–57, 124; rational liberty and, 92; Roman Catholicism, 35; Unitarianism, 42, 218n6; Wheatley and, 76, 77, 82, 184, 234n8. *See also* Bible
reverse ekphrasis, 69–70
Revolutionary War. *See* American Revolution

Ruggles, David, 167–68
Rush, Benjamin, 38, 62, 86, 218n4

Sancho, Ignatius, 76, 86, 139, 232n79
sapere aude (dare to know), 1, 203n2
Scholasticism, 25, 34, 35
schooling. *See* education
secularization, 16, 27, 44, 52, 55, 59, 82, 92–95, 98, 100, 101, 104, 111, 145, 183, 184–85, 186–87, 193, 199, 200, 222n19, 238–39n7. *See also* Enlightenment; Jeffersonian Enlightenment; Jefferson's Enlightenment of Feeling; Wheatley's Enlightenment of Principle
segregation, 75, 116–17, 131, 180, 184, 189, 232n75. *See also* colonization movement; epistemological nationalism; racism
self-criticism: classified as antiracist, 117; defining subjective boundaries of race, 63–65; in Enlightenment, 63, 227n20; instrumentalized for colonization, 17, 116–19, 132–33, 197, 209n25; self-serving, 5, 8, 17, 116, 175, 181–82, 197. *See also* epistemological nationalism
self-evidence, 47–48, 55, 92, 94, 99, 221n6, 221n13, 221–22n16
Senghor, Léopold, 210n2
senses: moral, 38–39, 219n8, 219n10; reason and, 34, 38, 219n10; smell, 75; touch, 14, 16, 20–21, 36, 213n15. *See also* feeling; sight
Shakespeare, William, 110, 168
Short, William, 35, 36
Sidney, Joseph, 127–28
sight, 16–17, 21, 68–71, 75, 95–96, 117, 181–82, 240n23. *See also* blindness; veil metaphor
signifying, 113, 123, 127, 187
situatedness, 31, 67–68, 229n44
skepticism, 13, 22–25, 35–36, 193, 213n17, 216n46, 222n16
slavery and enslaved persons: during American Revolution, 66; Bible

on, 93–94, 147–48, 154, 256–57n4; compared to antiquity, 53, 76, 117, 126; Condorcet on injustice of, 52; "dehumanization" and, 47, 74, 150, 166–67, 231–32n74, 257n11, 280n21; democracy and, 6, 85, 127–28, 150, 173, 200; "diffusion" of, 77, 232n82; double character of, 152, 167; engagement with Jefferson, 97, 146–48, 240n31; enlightening of, 104, 242n62; fugitive, 85, 107–9, 172; happiness in relation to, 47, 221n9; intellectual property relations of, 9; as latent state of war, 66, 228n32, 270n64; literacy of, 148, 179, 256n3; malignant prejudice and, 136; manners and, 57–59, 79, 118, 123, 127, 138, 149, 225n77; at Monticello, 66, 68–69, 148, 178–79, 256n3; polarization of attitudes toward, 74, 133; at Poplar Forest, 146–48, *147*, 154, 256n3; public opinion on, 57–59, 61; Query XVIII on, 57–59, 78, 118, 123, 127, 148–51, 170, 174–75; resistance efforts, 109, 133; stamp metaphor and, 89, 149–50, 164; *Walker's Appeal* on, 103, 104, 107. *See also* antislavery and abolitionism

slave trade: abolition of, 99, 126, 154, 208n21; draft of Declaration of Independence on victims of, 47, 208n21, 228n22; Middle Passage, 83, 84, 96, 185; orations on, 126–29; Query VIII on laws for end to, 58

Smith, Adam, 20, 78

Soulouque, Faustin, 161

Sterne, Laurence, 20, 21, 51, 68, 188, 230n50, 268–69n36

Stevens, Thaddeus, 239n7

Stewart, Maria W., 107, 116, 134, 167, 236–37n1

Stewart, Matthew, 208–9n23

Still, William, 122, 249n27

St. John, Henry (Lord Bolingbroke), 24, 40–42, 51, 160

Stowe, Harriet Beecher, 152, 167

subjectivity: civic, 31, 92–93, 186; communities of feeling and, 184, 193, 197; in Declaration of Independence, 46–48, 92–93, 95, 100–101, 103, 222n16; of experience, 8, 17, 28–29, 31, 68, 72, 88, 197, 216n46, 230n49; of feeling, 5, 8, 10, 26, 30, 50, 57, 68, 73, 78, 116, 120; of Jefferson's Enlightenment of Feeling, 5, 8, 10, 14–17, 31, 39, 46–48, 50, 57, 60, 149, 199, 229n46; limitations of, 10, 16–17, 22, 69, 71–73, 95, 116, 117, 184, 230n55, 267n6; nationhood and, 5, 8, 66–68, 131, 181, 184, 201; and psychologization of liberty, 51–52, 55; race and, 5, 8, 17, 63–66, 72, 78, 86, 88, 119, 121, 169, 181, 188, 197, 229n46, 230n49; transcendence of, 95, 98, 119, 131, 176, 184, 193. *See also* epistemological nationalism

Taney, Roger B., 166

Terrell, Mary Church, 88

textile metaphors, *14*, 182. *See also* pillow of ignorance; veil metaphor

Thomson, Charles, 67

Thoreau, Henry David, 199

Thornton, John, 185, 268n21

Tocqueville, Alexis de, 144, 255–56nn137–38

touch, sense of, 14, 16, 20–21, 36, 213n15. *See also* feeling

tradition, 3–4, 85, 88, 205–6n10, 239n16

Trumbull, John, 27

truth: access to, 25, 97; biblical, 138; doctrinal, 42; "Haynes abridgment" and, 94–95; knowledge and, 49, 98, 120; self-evident, 47–48, 92, 94, 99, 221n6, 221–22n16; universal, 46, 97, 120

Tubman, Harriet, 264–65n107

Tucker, St. George, 118, 247–48n18

Turner, Nat, 109, 133, 172

Tuskegee Institute, 182, 189–94, *190*

Tyson, Edward, 73–74

universalism, 4, 7–9, 10–11, 57, 67–69, 71, 79, 82–89, 104, 112, 127, 129, 148, 155, 160, 165, 171, 180–85, 187–88, 195, 197–99, 201, 236–37n1, 268n22, 268n30; in Declaration of Independence, 17, 46–47, 91–102, 106–7, 110–11, 239n7; as "false," 7, 9–10, 14, 210n4, 216n47

University of Virginia: central clock of, 157; founding of, 31, 32, 217n55; library of, 27; progress of knowledge and, 31, 32, 50, 79, 197; public opinion and, 59, 124; "Rockfish Gap Report" for, 79

uplift discourse. *See* black uplift; white uplift

Van der Werff, Adriaen, *Sarah Presenting Hagar to Abraham*, 29

veil metaphor: biblical origins of, 183; Chesnutt's "veil of prejudice," 183; as "doubled veil," 267n11; Douglass's "thin veil," 112; Du Bois's "moveable veil of white," 185–87, 268n30; Jefferson's "immoveable veil of black," 71–78, 95, 112, 123, 170, 180–89, 192; Johnson's veil of fiction, 187–89; line engraving and, 232n79; Locke's "veil of perception," 35, 218n70; Tuskegee Veil, 182, 189–94, *190*; Wheatley's "sable veil," 112, 181, 183–84

Virginia: Bill for Establishing Religious Freedom (1786), 55; Bill for the More General Diffusion of Knowledge (1779), 31; Fry-Jefferson map of (1753), 69; landscape of, 67, 70–71; politics in, 32, 66, 77, 217n57; prejudice in, 61, 63–66, 113–16; slavery in, 58, 59, 61, 77; worldview from, 65–68, 69. *See also* Monticello; *Notes on the State of Virginia;* University of Virginia

Virginia Philosophical Society for the Advancement of Useful Knowledge, 27

Walker, David, and *Walker's Appeal*: Anglophilia and, 109, 244n83; on black uplift, 105, 130, 134, 198; colonization critiqued by, 105–6, 132; death of (1830), 103, 134; on Declaration of Independence, 105–7, 109, 130; "dehumanization" arguments of, 74; Garnet's edition of, *134*, 135; hierarchical conception of Enlightenment in, 104; on ignorance, 104–7; on Jefferson, 103, 167, 241–42n54; knowledge in, 103–4; paralipsis used by, 104, 106, 130, 242n58; on prejudice, 116, 131–33; on slavery, 103, 104, 107; typographical radicalism of, 106, 243n69; on whiteness, 130, 132; on white uplift, 132, 198

Ward, Samuel Ringgold, 244–45n87, 252n56, 258n13, 260n29

Washington, Booker T., 182, 188–94, *190*

Washington, George, 77, 86

Washington, John E., 269n42

Waterhouse, Benjamin, 157

Webb, Frank J., 258n11

Webster, Noah, 231n68, 236n1

Wedgwood, Josiah, 192

Wheatley, Phillis: admirers of, 77, 86; on African origins, 83–84, 185; on American Revolution, 83–84; on chaos, 81–84; continuing disdain for, 76–77, 87, 232n80; correspondence with Occom, 81–82, 84–86, 89, 184; death of (1784), 86; as "Ethiop," 113; as founding mother of African American literature, 87–88, 195, 266n3; on humanity, 81–82, 183–84; Jefferson on, 76–77, 85–87, 139, 205n8, 232n79; legacy of, 87–88, 161, 193; on love of freedom, 5, 81, 83–84, 106, 196, 234n6; on memory, 83; on natural rights, 81–82, 234–35n9; "On Being Brought from AFRICA to AMERICA," 117; paralipsis used by, 85–86; *Poems on Various Subjects, Religious and Moral*, 76, 81, 82, 181, 232n79; portrait of, *82*,

232n79; on rational principles, 81–85, 184; reception history of, 208n21; religion and, 76, 77, 82, 184, 234n8; on sense of sight, 117, 184; "Thoughts on the Work of Providence," 184; "To the Rev. Dr. Thomas Amory on reading his Sermons on Daily Devotion," 183; "To the Right Honorable William, Earl of Dartmouth," 82–84; universalism of, 82–87, 268n22; veil metaphor used by, 112, 181, 183–84; worldview of, 82. *See also* African American intellectuals; African American literature; tradition

Wheatley's Enlightenment of Principle: on citizenship, 118, 125, 131–32, 140–41, 198; "co-fabrication" of Jeffersonian Enlightenment, 5, 11; colonization movement critiqued by, 89, 99, 113, 118, 167–68; consolidation of universalist epistemology in, 4, 11, 107, 180, 182, 198; creation of democratic public sphere and, 10, 78, 151, 162; Enlightenment ideal of open debate and, 11, 78, 201; increased intellectual ambitions of, 11, 93, 103, 105, 156, 195, 197; interaction with Jefferson's Enlightenment of Feeling, 3–4, 9–11, 117, 145, 183; and Jeffersonian double consciousness, 6, 78, 198–99, 201; Jeffersonian Enlightenment shaped by, 85, 199, 201; on liberty and equality, 82–83, 88, 106, 184; metaphors in, 72, 122, 125, 138, 144, 164, 181–85, 187, 189, 191, 193, 234n5, 251n43, 267n6; pity in, 102, 115, 124, 128, 138–39, 163, 170–71, 199; prejudice critiqued by, 5–6, 86, 116, 119, 209n25; "principles" of Declaration of Independence and, 4, 5, 91–93, 99, 108, 112, 198, 236–37n1; secularization in, 82, 92, 94, 95, 98, 100, 101, 104, 111, 145, 183, 184–85, 186–87, 193, 199, 238n7, 268n22; unique historical position of, 116, 197; universalism of, 83–88, 129, 180, 182–85, 193, 197, 199, 238n7. *See also* black uplift; Enlightenment; white uplift; *specific authors*

White, Jacob, 237n4

white-life novels, 150

whiteness: as ahistorical monolith, 7–8, 87, 116–18, 132, 170, 180, 197; as alternative epistemology, 5, 66–68, 73–75, 77, 169, 180, 197; Enlightenment misunderstood in terms of, 2, 6–10, 142, 208–9n23; McCune Smith on, 140–41, 142–43, 169; in monarchies, 150; nationhood and, 7, 131, 169, 181; prejudice as supposed criterion of, 8, 17, 116–18, 132; use of term, 6; Walker on, 130, 132; Wilson on, 114, 165–66. *See also* identity; race; self-criticism

white uplift: origins of term, 249n24; as pedagogical project, 6, 80; Query XIV and, 141; rhetoric of, 120, 122–24, 128, 130, 134, 139; voluntarist concept of prejudice and, 131; *Walker's Appeal* and, 132, 198; weaning metaphor and, 80, 122–23. *See also* black uplift

Whitfield, James M., 109

Willard, Simon, 156–57, 159

Williams, George Washington, 249n27

Wilson, William J. ("Ethiop"): "Afric-American Picture Gallery," 159–67; on blackness, 114; on prejudice, 116; on "problem-people," 114–15; on Query XIV, 124, 125; "What Shall We Do with the White People?," 113–15, 140, 246n2; on Wheatley's legacy, 88, 161; on whiteness, 114, 165–66

Wood, Gordon, 263n87

Zuckert, Michael, 48, 221n16

Recent books in the series
JEFFERSONIAN AMERICA

Empire of Commerce: Western Expansion and the Mississippi River, 1775–1804
Susan Gaunt Stearns

Black Reason, White Feeling: The Jeffersonian Enlightenment in the African American Tradition
Hannah Spahn

Replanting a Slave Society: The Sugar and Cotton Revolutions in the Lower Mississippi Valley
Patrick Luck

The Celebrated Elizabeth Smith: Crafting Genius and Transatlantic Fame in the Romantic Era
Lucia McMahon

Rival Visions: How the Views of Jefferson and His Contemporaries Defined the Early American Republic
Dustin Gish and Andrew Bibby, editors

Revolutionary Prophecies: The Founders and America's Future
Robert M. S. McDonald and Peter S. Onuf, editors

The Founding of Thomas Jefferson's University
John A. Ragosta, Peter S. Onuf, and Andrew J. O'Shaughnessy, editors

Thomas Jefferson's Lives: Biographers and the Battle for History
Robert M. S. McDonald, editor

Jeffersonians in Power: The Rhetoric of Opposition Meets the Realities of Governing
Joanne B. Freeman and Johann N. Neem, editors

Jefferson on Display: Attire, Etiquette, and the Art of Presentation
G. S. Wilson

Jefferson's Body: A Corporeal Biography
Maurizio Valsania

Pulpit and Nation: Clergymen and the Politics of Revolutionary America
Spencer W. McBride

Blood from the Sky: Miracles and Politics in the Early American Republic
Adam Jortner

Confounding Father: Thomas Jefferson's Image in His Own Time
Robert M. S. McDonald

The Haitian Declaration of Independence: Creation, Context, and Legacy
Julia Gaffield, editor

Citizens of a Common Intellectual Homeland: The Transatlantic Origins of American Democracy and Nationhood
Armin Mattes

Between Sovereignty and Anarchy: The Politics of Violence in the American Revolutionary Era
Patrick Griffin, Robert G. Ingram, Peter S. Onuf, and Brian Schoen, editors

Patriotism and Piety: Federalist Politics and Religious Struggle in the New American Nation
Jonathan J. Den Hartog

Becoming Men of Some Consequence: Youth and Military Service in the Revolutionary War
John A. Ruddiman

Amelioration and Empire: Progress and Slavery in the Plantation Americas
Christa Dierksheide

Collegiate Republic: Cultivating an Ideal Society in Early America
Margaret Sumner

Era of Experimentation: American Political Practices in the Early Republic
Daniel Peart

Paine and Jefferson in the Age of Revolutions
Simon P. Newman and Peter S. Onuf, editors

Sons of the Father: George Washington and His Protégés
Robert M. S. McDonald, editor

www.ingramcontent.com/pod-product-compliance
Lightning Source LLC
Chambersburg PA
CBHW032056230426
43662CB00035B/433